Effective Instruction for Children with Autism

An Applied Behavior Analytic Approach

By Robert Gulick and Thomas Kitchen

Published by

The Dr. Gertrude A. Barber National Institute

This publication was supported by Grant and Cooperative Agreement No. Ehueeu324061-0 from the Department of Health and Human Services Center for Disease Control and Prevention. Its contents are solely the responsibility of the authors and do not necessarily represent the official views of the Department of Health and Human Services Center for Disease Control and Prevention.

Address all correspondence to:
The Dr. Gertrude A. Barber National Institute
100 Barber Place
Erie, PA 16507
814-453-7661
www.barberinstitute.com

Photo Credits
Tim Rohrbach

Disclaimer
This publication is not being sold for the purpose of rendering medical advice or other healthcare professional services. The information contained in this publication is general information and may or may not reflect current instructional developments regarding Autism Spectrum Disorders. The information in this publication is subject to change at any time without notice and should not be relied upon as a substitute for professional medical or healthcare advice. Neither the Dr. Gertrude A. Barber Educational Institute, Inc., publisher, distributor nor the authors make any guarantees or warranties concerning the information in this publication. If medical advice or other expert healthcare assistance is required, the services of a competent, experienced professional person should be sought.

Printed in U.S.A.
ISBN-13 978-1-890032-10-4
ISBN-10 1-890032-10-7

4 5 6 7 8 9 0

For Ryan, our best teacher.

Acknowledgements

This project would not have been possible without the support of our families and the administration of the Dr. Gertrude A. Barber National Institute, including CEO John Barber and Executive Vice President Dr. Maureen Barber-Carey. Further, we appreciate the professional support offered by our colleagues at the Institute and at the Elizabeth Lee Black School. Through our collaboration with these gifted professionals and paraprofessionals we have been able to advance our knowledge and understanding of effective instruction.

We also thank Dr. Phillip Belfiore at Mercyhurst College for his continued contributions to our scholarship and intellectual development. We offer special appreciation to our reviewers, Dr. Pamela Wolfe of Penn State University and Dr. James Carr of Western Michigan University, for their much-welcomed and, at times, humbling suggestions for our project. Their recommendations served to strengthen this text in innumerable ways.

Several notable members of the field of applied behavior analysis have provided us with critical mentoring, encouragement or inspiration both during our own professional development and during the writing of this text. They include Dr. Vincent Carbone, Dr. Sean Casey, Dr. Anthony Castrogiovanni, Stein Lund, Dr. Patrick McGreevey, Dr. Mark Sundberg and Dr. Bridget Taylor. Additionally, during the preparatory stages of our grant we received valuable input during our visits to the Carbone Clinic, the Princeton Child Development Institute and the Eden II School-Staten Island. We also are appreciative of the Center for Disease Control and Prevention's National Center on Birth Defects and Development Disabilities for their support of this project through a grant that made this work possible.

We also want to thank those who assisted us so much in the final preparation of this publication, including Jamie Williams, our developmental editor; Claire Barber, project specialist; and Douglas Vizzini, whose design talents helped bring order to our ideas.

We are especially grateful to our wives, Yvonne and Holly, for their steadfast support through this long process and their indulgence of our prolonged absences from home—particularly during the final crunch to complete this manuscript. Finally, and most importantly, we thank the individuals with autism and their families with whom we have worked. They have taught us so much more about the topic at hand than we could ever expect to teach anyone ourselves.

Robert Gulick & Thomas Kitchen
Erie, Pennsylvania

Message from the President

"Never doubt that a small group of thoughtful people could change the world. Indeed, it's the only thing that ever has."

– Margaret Mead

The year was 1952, a time when children and adults with disabilities throughout the United States were commonly sent to live in institutions, separated from the love and support of their families and communities. But in Erie, Pennsylvania, a courageous, pioneering educator and a group of dedicated parents were working to change that practice. They were committed to educating children with disabilities, not in some distant institution, but in a classroom in their own community.

The educator was Dr. Gertrude A. Barber, the daughter of Irish immigrants who recognized and celebrated the dignity and potential in all persons. With a classroom borrowed from the local Boys Club, Dr. Barber developed a curriculum and trained a handful of teachers to work with children with developmental challenges.

Word began to spread, and as a growing number of parents looked to Dr. Barber for help, more classrooms opened across the city. In 1958, the City of Erie donated a former hospital, and soon the Dr. Gertrude A. Barber Center had its first permanent home on Erie's bayfront.

The breadth of our services quickly grew to meet demands for early intervention for infants and toddlers, an approved private school, and other programs that would meet the gamut of emerging need. For adults, we began supported employment programs, a range of residential options and a senior center.

Geographically, we have spread throughout Northwestern Pennsylvania, as well as to Pittsburgh and Philadelphia. In a broader sense, we believe we are a "citizen of the world," having hosted visitors from nearly every continent who were also committed to developing the highest quality, most innovative programs.

The Barber Center was established with a mission of serving all children and adults with disabilities with the greatest dedication, expertise and best practices available. In the years to follow, many wonderful staff and families have worked with an unwavering commitment to meet this high standard.

As we approached the new millennium, we believed that we had to prepare for the evolving challenges and opportunities that advances in technology and research would afford us in the coming century. With the support of many generous donors who shared this view, we embarked on a major undertaking to expand and enhance our facilities for the delivery of education and services, as well as to promote professional development and an exchange of new ideas.

With our expanded focus, we became the Dr. Gertrude A. Barber National Institute, committed to carrying on the mission of our founder in the quickly changing environment of the 21st century. Key among those challenges is the growing number of children now being diagnosed with autism, and the development and funding of new services to meet the needs of these children as they become adults.

Those of us privileged to have worked with Dr. Gertrude Barber fondly remember her directing us to "export our knowledge to help others." It is in that spirit that we continue to work to offer greater hope and opportunity to individuals with disabilities, and remain devoted to the ideal that dreams can, in fact, come true.

John J. Barber
President & Chief Executive Officer
Dr. Gertrude A. Barber National Institute

Foreword

For most of my career, I have been privileged to be a part of the Barber National Institute, working along side dedicated professionals and families to offer state-of-the art services for children and adults with developmental disabilities. As an educator, it has been very fulfilling to be part of an organization that embraces new advances in diagnosis, training, and treatment. When we began to see a steadily increase in the number of children with autism, I remember meeting with Dr. Gertrude A. Barber (my aunt and founder of the Barber Center), and my brother, Dr. Joseph Barber, a pediatric neurologist. We sat at her dining room table discussing plans for the Barber Center to develop, design, and implement a comprehensive program for educating these children.

At that time, we felt that the Barber Center provided the highest quality of services for individuals with mental retardation and we wanted to offer the same quality of services for children living with autism.

Not long after our meeting, my own son was diagnosed with autism, spurring us to pursue this new focus even more passionately. Our goal was to not only develop exemplary services for my child, but also for all children with autism in need of support.

To accomplish this goal, we rigorously sought out organizations displaying best practices in the field of autism. Staff members spent months training with and learning from these leaders. Then, they returned to Erie to generate our own model programs for our students. Our autism program is dedicated to preparing children and adults with autism to live and work more effectively at home, at school, and in the community.

In 2004, we received a $140,000 grant from the Department of Health and Human Services, Centers for Disease Control and Prevention to develop a training program for practitioners working with children with autism. Over the next year, project co-coordinators Robert Gulick and Thomas Kitchen developed a pilot program that would help children learn through early intensive behavioral intervention. As part of the program we produced a training manual and an accompanying DVD to help parents and practitioners in teaching their children—regardless of geographic location.

Our charge from Dr. Gertrude Barber was to develop a high level of expertise in autism and at the same time, to "export" our knowledge nationally to parents and professionals. *Effective Instruction for Children with Autism*, an applied behavior analytic approach to education, is the result of these efforts.

I would like to thank the hundreds of families, Dr. Gertrude A. Barber National Institute administrators, faculty, and the late Dr. Barber for permitting us to dream and making these dreams come true.

Maureen Barber-Carey
Executive Vice President
Dr. Gertrude A. Barber National Institute

Table of Contents

Introduction

What Are We Doing Here?

Our Mission

Our purpose in undertaking this project is simple: to provide valid information that parents and professionals can use to help children with autism achieve the highest possible levels of independence and happiness.

This manual addresses what we believe are the core impairments related to autism spectrum disorders: communication, social/play interaction, cognitive development, and aberrant behavior. For each of these impairments, we provide a comprehensive description, as well as a strategic course of action for working through and around them. We include a framework that allows readers to assess impairments and understand the complexities of planning appropriate curricular activities. Finally, we provide a step-by-step guide designed to help parents and professionals implement effective teaching procedures for learners with autism.

As practitioners, we have had great success utilizing these approaches. At the same time, it is our strong assertion that not every available approach is equally effective. Further, we believe that providing ineffective treatment, even if it is in an effort to provide a "balance" of services, is unethical. Spending time and money to implement approaches that have not been validated ultimately diverts those resources from treatment that has been validated. Most importantly, a child who has not received effective services will not be provided with the same opportunities to enjoy all that life has to offer.

To that end, the development and implementation of effective procedures for children with autism is the goal of this manual. The reader does not have to be a formally trained teacher, behavior analyst, psychologist, etc., to be able to teach skills or reduce problem behaviors. Instead, they simply need to be proficient with the theory and techniques surrounding effective instructional principles.

We have seen parents develop skills that rival those of highly paid and trained autism professionals, and we have seen trained professionals deepen their skills. However, it is important to note that the level of proficiency in practicing behavior analysis is directly related to the nature, quantity, and quality of supervision provided. Professional supervision by a highly trained and qualified behavior analyst – particularly one who has worked with individuals with autism spectrum disorders – is an essential part of developing strong behavior analysis skills.

Practically speaking, this manual is intended to provide a text-based reference for a training program based on practical, hands-on experience and live instruction. However, as a stand-alone reference tool, it will serve as a terrific introduction to the identification and application of "what works" for children and adults with autism. The content is organized in units, chapters, and sections, with key terms and topics listed at the beginning of each chapter.

Applied Behavior Analysis and Autism

For children with autism and their families, treatment choices are often controversial and surrounded by hype. There are many approaches, each with articulate proponents, but only a select few offer years of peer-reviewed research and the data to prove their effectiveness.

Applied Behavior Analysis (ABA) provides a practical and theoretical framework for teaching skills to any type of learner, reducing problematic behaviors and measuring the effectiveness of specific approaches. Decades of research have shown that ABA-based methods are effective across learner and skill profiles. This includes instruction of academic content to typical children and adults, as well as instruction of life skills to children and adults with severe disabilities.

Most specifically, ABA is becoming accepted as the "gold standard" of evidence-based educational interventions for children with autism.

While a more technical definition of ABA is found in Chapter 4, the approach is based on a scientific understanding of how factors in the environment may explain why we do what we do (which allows us to influence this). It is heavily reliant upon data collection and analysis to guide the way. It differs from most other approaches to teaching children with autism primarily because of its focus on engineering conditions that exist *outside* of the individual to bring about change in behavior. Other approaches, in contrast, try to change things that exist within the learner that may be beyond our influence (if we can even observe or measure these things in the first place).

Applied Behavior Analysis is also concerned with teaching skills that allow the individual with autism to adapt and function as independently as possible within the environment. Unlike other approaches, which teach others to constantly adapt the environment to accommodate the behaviors of the person with autism, most ABA-based approaches provide skills that will allow the person with autism to accommodate the expectations of the environment.

In following chapters, the reader will become familiar with key concepts of ABA, particularly its application to teaching individuals with autism.

Giving Credit Where Credit is Due

It is important to note that we, as authors, are not presenting entirely new information. Thanks to the passionate work of numerous researchers in the field, there have been many advances made in the science of autism intervention. These advances are the result of countless hours spent developing and refining techniques, taking data, measuring outcomes, and determining what works and what does not. It is to these researchers that we all owe a debt of gratitude.

At the same time, we also recognize that any methodology is subject to evolution. Sometimes, this evolution follows a path to more effective, efficient instruction. At other times, the path becomes less clear, and varied interpretations of teaching methodologies have little or no effect. Unfortunately, there are also cases in which the beaten path should have been followed, where deviation has created a hindrance, rather than a help. It is our assertion that the data will lead the way: a learner's progress, or lack thereof, will indicate whether or not a method is sound.

Throughout the text, we intend to present information that may have its roots in the work of others, but has also come to us through our own learning and clinical experiences. We may utilize different ways to explain certain processes, and we may offer slightly different perspectives on curriculum development. We will certainly attempt to give credit where credit is due.

However, the reader should understand that we are applying a sound understanding of behavior analysis, and the principles and applications that follow from it. Because of this, we believe that many people well versed in the science would derive similar techniques to shape learning behaviors. This work is simply the product of the application of a natural-science approach to understanding human behavior and its application to learners with autism.

The Child with Autism—History, Prevalence, Diagnosis, and Characteristics

At a Glance

Chapter Points

- Individuals with autism exhibit deficits in communication and social interaction. They also demonstrate restricted interest in activities, as well as repetitive or other problematic behaviors.
- Early detection of autism's behavioral markers can lead to early diagnosis, early intensive intervention, and improved prognosis.
- Individuals with autism possess the same core behavioral symptoms as individuals with Asperger's Syndrome. The difference between the two disorders lies mainly in the degree of qualitative impairment exhibited by the individual.
- A sound diagnostic protocol involves indirect and direct evaluations conducted by a multidisciplinary team of professionals who possess clinical experience with autism.

Key Terms

Autism

Leo Kanner

Hans Asperger

Asperger's Syndrome

Psychoanalytical Theories

Bruno Bettelheim

Autism Spectrum Disorder (ASD)

Communicative Deficits

Social Impairment

Restrictive, Repetitive, and Stereotypic Patterns of Behavior

DSM-IV-TR

PDD

GARS

PIA

PDDST-II

ADI-R

STAT

CARS

ADOS-G

The Child with Autism

History, Prevalence, Diagnosis, and Characteristics

Scenario Number One

Jacob is a 13 year old who is enrolled in his local public middle school. He goes to classes on his own, can read 134 words per minute, and can do math computation at grade level. However, he is not able to answer many questions about the feelings, attitudes, or intentions of characters in stories he reads, and he is not able to complete story problems in math class.

Jacob desperately wants to have friends, but doesn't fit in. He cannot understand many jokes, and is often picked on by his peers because all he ever talks about are his computers. He has gotten into trouble because he has told teachers he doesn't like them, and he experiences difficulty when scheduled activities are changed or canceled. He has developed proficient computer skills, however, and likes nothing better than sitting at his computer for hours on end. He has ambitions of someday working as a software engineer, developing code for video game graphics.

Scenario Number Two

Allison is five years old. She does not talk, is not toilet trained, and can follow very few simple directions. She frequently has tantrums when she is directed to stop doing something that she enjoys, and she becomes aggressive if she sees something that she wants and cannot have. She engages in frequent self-injurious behaviors, such as hitting herself on the chin. Rather than play with peers or toys, she seems preoccupied with pieces of lint that she finds on the carpet, and repetitively picks them up and drops them in front of her eyes. Her parents and teachers are very concerned that they do not seem to be making much progress with her.

Scenario Number Three

Brian is eight years old. He is able to speak in three- to four-word sentences, usually to request things that he wants, or to answer simple questions. He will yell and scream if he doesn't get his way, but will usually settle down before too long. He is learning to play with a few age-appropriate toys, but he can't seem to play symbolically beyond the play scripts that he has been taught. Even though he is making quite a bit of progress behaviorally, he still begins to rock back and forth and flap his hands when excited or nervous. His parents and teachers are pleased that he is beginning to gain independence through a photographic activity schedule, and he is talking more every day.

All three of these children have **autism**. They represent the differences in both skills and impairments from one individual with autism to the next. There are some similarities in their behaviors, but the degree to which these behaviors manifest themselves is unique to each child. These brief glimpses demonstrate two very important things: first, the uniqueness of every person with autism; and second, the idea that autism is a "spectrum disorder," in which there are varying degrees of severity and manifestation of symptoms.

One of the purposes of this manual is to help develop effective intervention skills for individuals with autism. For this reason, readers should be familiar with the scope of challenges shared by these individuals and their families. It is also important to demystify the processes that lead to diagnosis and development of an instructional protocol for these children and adults. This chapter provides a basic understanding of the underlying characteristics of autism spectrum disorders, as well as current information regarding the prevalence of autism. It should serve as a foundation for the treatment suggestions presented in following chapters.

Section A - Historical Perspective

According to anecdotal and historical evidence, autism has probably been part of the human experience throughout the ages. It was not until 1943, however, that it was first characterized as a specific disorder with qualitative and clinical features distinguishing it from other known disorders. That year, an Austrian-born psychiatrist named **Leo Kanner** published the first account of a group of children, ". . . whose condition differs so markedly and uniquely from anything reported so far. . ." (Kanner, 1943).

Kanner was the first professional in the United States to carry the title "child psychiatrist," and had just established the Child Psychiatry Department at Johns Hopkins University School of Medicine. In his seminal report, he used case studies to describe 11 children who came under his care while at Johns Hopkins. The children, ranging from two-and-a-half to eleven years old, all displayed some common characteristics, but defied categorization according to known psychiatric and psychological disorders of the time.

The children in Kanner's case studies were marked by a general "self-sufficiency," accompanied by deficits in the use of language for communicative purposes (Kanner, 1943). Most of the children tended to have more of an affinity for inanimate objects than for people, and even their interactions with people seemed to resemble the types of manipulation one would use with objects.

Even though most of the children in Kanner's report eventually acquired at least some language, there was an almost universal lack of communicative intent in the way the language functioned. For many of the children, their words seemed to be used more for stereotypical routines than for declarative or inquisitive purposes. Even when a communicative attempt was made, there were usually significant problems with syntax, semantics, and pragmatics.

Even more significant in Kanner's report were his descriptions of the emotional expression displayed by his subjects, or the seeming lack thereof. Almost all of the children he described were frequently devoid of facial expressions that would typically correspond to the circumstances in which the children were involved. While most clinicians of his era would likely have tended to focus upon the cognitive and language anomalies associated with the disorder, Kanner made a remarkable decision to shift a large amount of his focus onto the lack of connectedness, or the affective dissociation, that the children in his report displayed. These children simply did not seem to be interested in others, and they appeared to be incapable of initiating or maintaining meaningful social contact with other people.

At the time of his report, the combined symptoms of this "new" disorder were quite similar to other known disorders. Primarily, Kanner's group displayed many symptoms similar to individuals afflicted by psychotic disorders such as schizophrenia, to the point where some of the children in his group had previously been diagnosed with them. Kanner, however, used several discrepancies to make the distinction between his subjects' disorder and other known psychotic disorders of the time.

The first discrepancy was that schizophrenia always indicated a change from one constant state of behavior or affect to another during times of psychosis. In addition, schizophrenia was seen as a "withdrawal" from relationships that had already been established. Based on the extensive developmental histories and anecdotal information he obtained from the families of the children he studied, Kanner determined that these children had shown signs of this disconnectedness throughout their entire lives.

The signs included "a failure to assume at any time an anticipatory posture preparatory to being picked up" (Kanner, 1943). Compared to typically developing children, who displayed behaviors such as facial tensioning and shoulder adjustment upon being lifted or held (even at a very early age), the children in his report made no bodily adjustments or posturing whatsoever.

Further, the families often reported that their children seemed "self sufficient" from their earliest days. In other words, these children did not necessarily seek out contact from others for social gratification. When they did seek to contact others, it was usually only seen as a means to an end, or as a way to obtain objects or activities that were meaningful to them.

In describing the children who were the subjects of his report, Kanner chose the word "autism." Derived from the Greek word "*autos*," meaning "self," the word was initially coined by pioneering Swiss psychoanalyst Eugen Bleuler to describe a withdrawal from the social world. From Bleuler's perspective, the term usually implied a willful removal of oneself from the social world and into a self-absorbed fantasy world. A student of Sigmund Freud and Wilhelm Max Wundt, Bleuler also coined the term "schizophrenia" and put forth many historically significant theories about the nature and treatment of various psychiatric disorders.

The introduction to Anne Donnellan's 1985 compilation, *Classic Readings in Autism*, notes that Kanner reluctantly chose the term due to the psychoanalytic connotations that may have been implied. Specifically, Kanner wanted to make the distinction between the children he observed, who never established connectedness to the social world, and those who (according to the classic definition of the term) had established relationships with the social world and withdrew these ties upon onset of symptoms (Donnellan, 1985).

However reluctantly adopted, Kanner's use of the term has become its accepted meaning, and Kanner's group of children has remained valid case studies in the nature of the disorder.

Hans Asperger

No history of autism is complete without touching upon the work of Austrian pediatrician **Hans Asperger**. During the same year Kanner's seminal article was published, Asperger was preparing a separate account of individuals under his study. In a moment of significant coincidence, Asperger also chose the word "autism" to describe the children he was studying (Asperger, 1944). By all accounts, the two had no familiarity or even knowledge of each other's work.

Asperger's subjects displayed some of the same lack of social connectedness or social understanding identified by Kanner. Also, like Kanner's children, Asperger's students were subject to preoccupation with objects, routines, or otherwise restricted interests. The difference between the two groups was the seemingly advanced language and writing abilities possessed by some of the children in Asperger's report.

Unfortunately, Asperger's work was predominantly published in German, and coincided with the Second World War. Because of this, and because he did not travel much, his work lay largely undiscovered and unstudied until 1981, when Lorna Wing published a paper that gave an account of it. Wing coined the term **"Asperger's Syndrome"** to describe children who shared the social impairments of Kanner's syndrome to varying degrees, yet possessed less obvious cognitive and language impairments. Today, it is also referred to as Asperger's Disorder.

Bruno Bettelheim and Psychoanalysis

During the medical and social climate of the 1940's, disorders like autism were often studied from the perspective of psychoanalysis. The field of neurology was in its infancy, and most behavioral or psychological abnormalities were viewed in terms of psychiatric theories. Their causes were placed upon relationships that went awry, failure to recognize unconscious motives, or other theoretical constructs. This is significant because many of the people who followed Kanner's initial report tended to focus upon the **psychoanalytical theories** of the day, placing blame for the disorder on the children's families or environments. Kanner himself, while proposing that genetic factors played a part, also suggested that the condition was caused by cold, rigid parenting (Kanner, 1949). The result was the theory of the "refrigerator mother."

Although this theory (and the term itself) is traditionally attributed to another Austrian, **Bruno Bettelheim**, it is more accurate to say that Bettelheim propagated the theory and further developed it. Bettelheim supported a notion in which blame was placed upon "maternal indifference" he felt was displayed by the mothers of children with autistic symptoms. The result of this psychodynamic influence – which was adopted by countless professionals working within the fields of psychology and psychiatry – was decades of shame, guilt, and embarrassment for families of children with autism.

The work of Bettelheim and his contemporaries also created a lingering social stigma surrounding the disorder, which many believe may have stunted exploration and discourse in the field for many years. It also led families to hide the disorder if possible, with many children with autism placed in institutions during the 1950's and 1960's.

Beyond his theories surrounding the causes of autism, Bettelheim also referred to individuals with autism as possessing repressed or hidden genius. In our opinion, this popular belief led to a cultural and social misunderstanding of the disorder that exists today.

For example, a common lay understanding of autism includes figures such as the character of "Raymond" in the movie *Rain Man*. As Raymond, actor Dustin Hoffman demonstrated an uncanny ability to memorize entire phone books and compute dizzying mathematic problems at first glance, while having little ability to relate to others. Part of this portrayal is somewhat accurate, including Raymond's limited interests and his desire to maintain routines. However, his "genius" skills are overemphasized and are not indicative of typical autistic traits.

What frequently *does* occur, though, is a preoccupation or fascination with an extremely narrow range of interests, which may lead to an unbalanced knowledge or understanding of one or more particular subjects. This, in turn, could give the impression to an occasional observer that the individual possesses extraordinary innate talents. Unfortunately, this is often the result of a limited repertoire of interests, combined with an equally bland imaginative repertoire.

Bernard Rimland and the Biological Component

Bettelheim's theories continued to gain and maintain acceptance until the publication of Bernard Rimland's chapter, "The Etiology of Infantile Autism: The Problem of Biological Versus Psychological Causation," in the book, *Infantile Autism*, published in 1964. In this chapter, Rimland (himself the father of a child with autism) questioned the theories surrounding the psychogenic causes of autism popularized by psychoanalysts of the day. Based on examples that supported the notion of a biological basis for autism, combined with a lack of evidence to support psychogenic theories, Rimland instead proposed that further investigation of autism's biological components was warranted.

Rimland's work became a catalyst for the trends in autism research that continue to this day. Additionally, his proposition removed the shroud of blame and secrecy that surrounded many families dealing with autism. Without fear of judgment, parents were more apt to seek help for their children, and in many cases were able to deal more effectively with each other and with their children.

Recent Research Efforts

All of the information about autism that has been produced in the past 60 years has, at its starting point, the initial paper by Kanner, and perhaps even the more recently discovered paper by Asperger. While (at first glance) the two papers may appear to describe two different types of individuals that share only a few common characteristics, current evidence places them even closer to each other than ever before. Today, it is believed that autism and Asperger's Syndrome describe individuals with very similar qualitative features, including social impairment (awkwardness at best), cognitive impairment that is similar in scope, if not in degree, and neurobiological features that are common across individual profiles.

Advances in medicine and technology have allowed researchers to study brain function via functional magnetic resonance imaging during specific cognitive tasks, and they are able to take a closer look at genetic factors that may play a role in autism. In addition, they continue to conduct epidemiological studies to determine familial or environmental risk factors in developing the disorder.

What does current research mean to us as practitioners, families, students, or members of the community at large? It means that we still have many questions to be answered, but we are on our way.

We have heard prominent autism researcher Nancy Minshew frequently point out in her lectures that the scientific community is well on its way to developing a "roadmap to a cure." First and foremost, this roadmap entails a complete understanding of the nature of the disorder across domains; once it is well understood, it will be easier to search for causal relationships. Subsequent to this is the ultimate objective: a treatment or cure.

Regardless of the suspected causes of autism, it has become very clear that *autism is a brain-based neurobiological disorder.* It is marked by a lack of synchrony between parts of the developing brain, which plays a role in how information is perceived and processed.

Today, most reputable experts agree that genetics play a significant role, and that there may be an environmental "X-factor," or unknown insult that results from an exposure to an environmentally produced toxin, or injury. According to this theory, genetics predispose an individual to be sensitive to certain toxins, or injuries, which are then encountered somewhere within the environment. The result of this combination of genetic predisposition and environmental insult is the development of autism. In any medical field, this type of causation theory is referred to as a "two-hit theory," in that two potential sources are implicated.

Autism – A Simple Definition

Autism is a brain-based disorder characterized by:

1. Communication impairment
2. Social impairment
3. Restrictive, repetitive or stereotypical patterns of behavior, interests, or activities

Other studies have been conducted to try to determine what, if any, particular environmental exposures could contribute to the development of autistic symptoms. This area is rife with controversy, riddled with pseudo-science and is under scrupulous investigation by some of the most brilliant minds of our time.

Although the autism community is in search of answers, we cannot forget the labor-intensive nature of true science, or its importance. The desire for a solution must be tempered by the fact that sound research simply cannot be rushed.

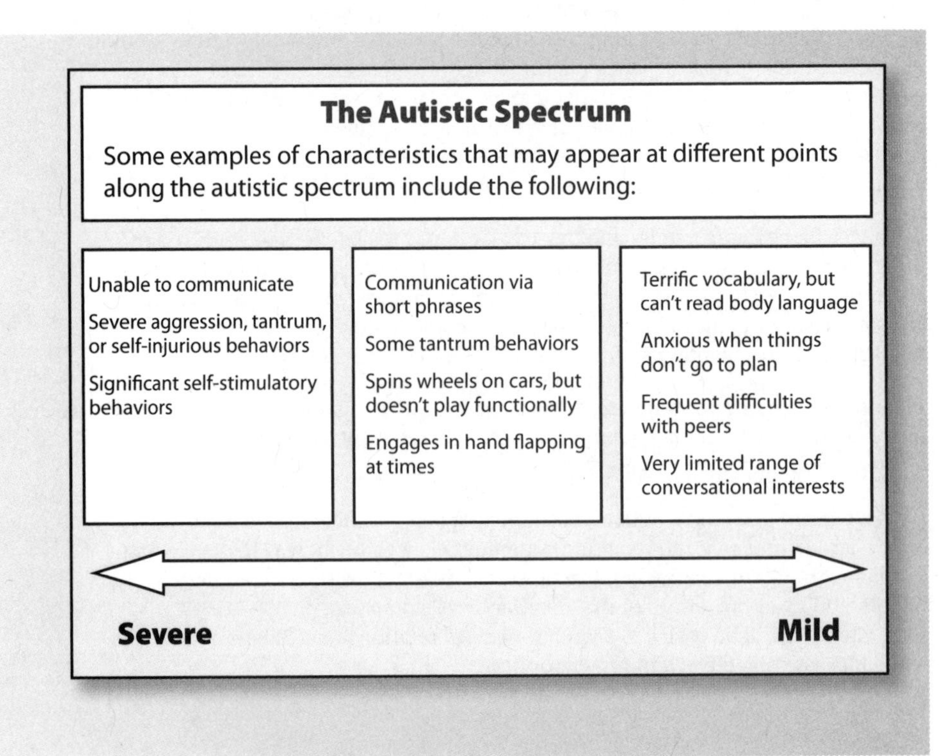

Autism's Dynamic Nature

The behavioral symptoms of autism, like any human behavior, are subject to influence (additional information on this topic will be discussed in following chapters). What should be understood is that autism is not necessarily a static condition. Instead, its symptoms and characteristics express themselves in different ways and to different degrees throughout the development of the individual with autism. Variables in intervention are also likely to affect the degree to which the individual with autism will exhibit symptoms throughout his or her life.

Section B – Symptoms

Autism is now referred to as a "spectrum disorder." In other words, our understanding of the disorder is that autism is expressed in many different forms. It helps to think of the "autistic spectrum" as a continuum, with one end considered "severe" and the other end considered "mild."

When an individual is diagnosed with an **autism spectrum disorder (ASD)**, most professionals place them somewhere along that spectrum. Regardless of where they are placed, autism's defining characteristics include **communicative deficits, social impairment,** and **restrictive, repetitive or stereotypic patterns of behavior.**

At the severe end of the spectrum are individuals who may represent the "classic" Kanner-esque description of autistic disorder. These individuals are likely to have significant deficits in, or even absence of, any type of social communication. Restricted interests can take the form of repetitive, non-functional behaviors (stereotypy). This could include self-stimulatory repetitive motions such as hand flapping, or the use of objects in similar ways (wheel spinning, for example). These individuals may never develop spoken language, and it may be extremely difficult to teach them new skills.

At the "mild" end of the spectrum are individuals who may have developed fairly refined language skills and may have less obvious cognitive deficits, but still demonstrate qualitative impairments in abstract reasoning, nonverbal communication, and concept formation[1]. Restricted interests within this group might include fascination with a very limited range of subjects (e.g. dinosaurs or 18th century French poetry) and a desire to obsessively acquire and regurgitate information about them. Individuals at this end of the spectrum also frequently demonstrate verbosity and one-sided communication styles. Formal language, or the demonstration of rule-governed components of language, is often quite intact. Language comprehension, on the other hand, is often impaired.

All along this continuum, individuals may exhibit different combinations of the core deficits associated with autism spectrum disorders, and to varying degrees. Subsequently, it is becoming increasingly difficult to define a "classic" case of autism. To further complicate matters, not only are there differences between people with autism, but there are also *intra-individual* differences (i.e. within each person) that occur with the disorder. A person subjected to any of numerous variables – including intervention, experience, or lack thereof and environmental/familial factors – may find themselves at different points along the continuum at different developmental periods in their life. In particular, effective intervention may enable certain individuals to acquire skills that could eventually place them at a different point on the spectrum.

---

[1] Concept formation: the ability to use known responses, in conjunction with executive function abilities, to formulate novel, generalized, or abstract responses.

Examples of Impairment Within Core Deficit Areas:

Communication

- A child is unable to speak
- A child cannot understand the language of others, or has a very limited understanding of others
- An adult may not understand metaphors or other figurative language
- A person has a difficult time interpreting implied communication, such as body language or inflection

Social Interactions

- A child does not make eye contact with others
- A teenager is unable to develop any friendships
- A child does not smile when others smile at her

Restrictive, Repetitive, and Stereotypic Patterns of Behavior

- Instead of playing with trains, a child just lines them up and counts them
- A child engages in frequent hand-flapping or toe-walking whenever he is excited or upset
- A child throws a tantrum when a different route is taken home from the grocery store

It is also helpful to understand that autism is considered a syndrome, or a disorder characterized by a constellation of common characteristics. One example of this is Down Syndrome, where characteristics include decreased muscle tone at birth, differences in skull shape, differences in facial features, and a detectable chromosomal abnormality. Almost all of these are recognizable physical features that are rather easy to detect and observe.

In the case of autism spectrum disorders, however, common characteristics include impairment in communication, impairment in social functioning and stereotypic or repetitive patterns of behavior. This makes the syndrome somewhat more challenging to diagnose, as there are no blood, chromosomal/genetic, or other physical tests available at this point in time. Instead, diagnosis of autism spectrum disorder is based on the presence or absence of symptoms, as opposed to purely medical evidence.

Because of this, it is increasingly important that diagnosticians become well versed in the characteristics of autism spectrum disorders, so that intervention can take place as soon as possible.

Section C - Detection

How does a family embark on the journey from giving birth to a child with autism, to suspicion of a problem, to diagnosis and then to intervention?

In retrospect, most parents of children diagnosed with autism would agree that they sensed something was wrong with their child at a very early stage in his or her development. While most children with autism do not receive a formal diagnosis until they are between two and three years old, behavioral symptoms are usually present at one year, and often earlier. Several studies have demonstrated this by reviewing home movies of children that were filmed years prior to their formal diagnosis (Adrien et al., 1992; Baranek, 1999; Osterling & Dawson, 1994). Close inspection of these early videotapes revealed subtle impairments in the child's ability to react to his or her name being called, eye contact, and joint attention – all skills that would later become diagnostic criteria for the child's disorder.

When parents of children with autism sit down and describe how their child came to be diagnosed, general patterns and similarities link their stories with those of hundreds of others.

Typically, the first sign that something is amiss with a child comes between the ages of 18 - 21 months. Parents routinely describe a total lack of language at this stage in development, when the child should be speaking at least in single words, if not already forming two-word utterances. The other common scenario involves the child who has developed single-word language, but now, for no apparent reason, has either begun to use his words less frequently or has abruptly stopped communicating altogether. For a brief overview of some common possible indicators of autism, please refer to Figure 2.1.

Figure 2.1

The following possible indicators of ASD were identified on the Public Health Training Network Webcast, *Autism Among Us*, and appear on the National Institute of Mental Health's website:

Possible Indicators of Autism Spectrum Disorders

- Does not babble, point, or make meaningful gestures by one year of age
- Does not speak one word by 16 months
- Does not combine two words by two years of age
- Does not respond to name
- Loses language or social skills

Some Other Indicators

- Poor eye contact
- Doesn't seem to know how to play with toys
- Excessively lines up toys or other objects
- Is attached to one particular toy or object
- Doesn't smile
- At times seems to be hearing impaired

Newschaffer CJ (Johns Hopkins Bloomberg School of Public Health). Autism Among Us: Rising Concerns and the Public Health Response [Video on the Internet]. Public Health Training Network, June 20, 2003. Available from:
http://www.publichealthgrandrounds.unc.edu/autism/webcast.htm.
http://www.nimh.nih.gov/publicat/autism.cfm#intro.

These symptoms often prompt a visit to the pediatrician who, given no evidence of limitations in other developmental milestones (i.e., the child's motor skills are within normal limits), might suggest a variety of commonly accepted reasons for the child's lack of expressive language. These often include shyness, gender differences ("girls talk earlier than boys"), individual developmental differences or the presence of older siblings who "talk for" the child. In general, however, the parents are left with the message that it is premature to be worrying about a language deficit and that the child will likely outgrow the problem.

An additional concern that surfaces during this same time period is a drawing inward, or loss of social connectedness on the part of the child. More time is spent in solitary or repetitive play. Physical contact with parents may be avoided, or may appear to cause great distress for the child. The parents note that when called by name, the child rarely looks or responds, and simple directives are seemingly ignored.

Social aloofness is also regularly attributed to shyness or explained away as a manifestation of the child's personality.

These symptoms of inattentiveness may lead many parents to suspect a hearing loss, and they respond by having their child scheduled for a complete audiological screening. If the results of the audiological exam rule out hearing loss, the parents are met with another dead end.

Finally, during the second and third years of development, a marked interest in repetitive or ritualistic activities will emerge – to the exclusion of age-appropriate play. Visual order may become paramount, with the child compelled to line up all toys, books, or stuffed animals, or place them in specific locations or in specific order. Play activities may lose all social significance and become solitary endeavors that involve a fascination with specific toys or parts of toys, the repetitive manipulation of objects, or the rhythmic movements of the child's own body. Interruption of these behaviors may cause the child to fly into a rage that does not stop until the disruption ceases and the ritual can be resumed.

Parental response to this third set of symptoms is typically one of tacit acceptance. The ritualistic play is explained as merely one of the child's odd little quirks, and not of any real consequence – a belief that is heavily reinforced following disastrous attempts at redirecting or interrupting these behaviors. Simply allowing the child to continue the repetitive behavior far outweighs dealing with the severity of tantrum, aggression, and self-injurious behavior that may result from directly trying to stop it. The family simply adapts and adjusts their lifestyle to accommodate the child's rituals or to ensure that those who come into contact with the child keep his or her "world" just the way he or she likes it.

Unfortunately, all three of the "red flags" described above – lack/loss of language, lack/loss of social connectedness, and repetitive/restricted play skills – taken in combination strongly suggest a diagnosis of autism. Moreover, the misguided search for answers from professionals, family, and friends may lead to a waste of valuable time.

This illustration of the plight of parents seeking a diagnosis is not intended to suggest that pediatricians, audiologists or the parents themselves are culpable for a misdiagnosis or delay in the correct diagnosis of autism. Until very recently, diagnostic criteria for autism were not widely disseminated among primary care professionals, let alone available to the general parent population. Normally, referral to an "autism expert" such as a developmental psychologist or pediatric neurologist did not occur until these early symptoms became seriously problematic and interfered with the child's or the family's functioning, often around age two or three.

What we hope will be understood from this illustration is that while autism may present itself in myriad individual manifestations, there does exist a core set of behavioral symptoms that most parents encounter within the first two years. Early detection of these markers can lead to early diagnosis, early intensive intervention and, as research has shown, a significantly improved prognosis (Dawson & Osterling, 1997; Rogers, 1996, 1998).

Autism Defined

The **Diagnostic and Statistical Manual of Mental Disorders — Fourth Edition, Text Revision** is perhaps the most widely used resource for classifying and diagnosing autism spectrum disorders, but there are others, including the 10th revision of the *International Classification of Diseases* (ICD-10), and Zero to Three's *Diagnostic Classification of Mental Health and Developmental Disorders of Infancy and Early Childhood, Revised.*

Additionally, U.S. Federal education law has a definition of autism, not necessarily for diagnostic purposes, but for eligibility for services that are provided to individuals meeting this definition. The Individuals with Disabilities Education Act defines autism as "A developmental disability significantly affecting verbal and nonverbal communication and social interaction, generally evident before age three that adversely affects a child's educational performance. Other characteristics often associated with autism are engagement in repetitive activities and stereotyped movement, resistance to environmental change or change in daily routine, and unusual responses to sensory experiences. The term Autism does not apply if a child's educational performance is adversely affected primarily because the child has an emotional disturbance" [IDEA 300.7 ©(1)(i)].

The core impairments of autism are categorized by the DSM-IV-TR within the general category of Pervasive Developmental Disorders **(PDD)**. These disorders are "characterized by severe and pervasive impairment in several areas of development; reciprocal social interaction skills, communication skills, or the presence of stereotyped behavior, interests, and activities" (the same three sets of symptoms earlier identified by our fictitious parents). See Figure 2.2.

This manual will focus primarily on autism spectrum disorders as they are defined by the DSM-IV-TR. In addition, we are limiting our review of the DSM-IV-TR to its descriptions of Autistic Disorder and Asperger's Disorder, and not the definitions of other PDDs.

Diagnostic Criteria for Autistic Disorder

Within the DSM-IV-TR, each of the domains listed in Figure 2.2 and Figure 2.3 is expanded upon with specific clinical features described in greater detail. For a diagnosis of autism to be made, a set number of these clinical features must be present in each of the three domains.

Domains Addressed in DSM-IV-TR, Definition of Autism

Qualitative Impairment in Communication

Manifested by at least one of the following:

a) delay in, or total lack of, the development of spoken language (not accompanied by an attempt to compensate through alternative modes of communication such as gesture or mime);

b) in individuals with adequate speech, marked impairment in the ability to initiate or sustain a conversation with others;

c) stereotyped and repetitive use of language, or idiosyncratic language; and

d) lack of varied, spontaneous make-believe, or social imitative play appropriate to developmental level

Qualitative Impairment in Social Interactions

Manifested by at least two of the following:

a) marked impairment in the use of multiple nonverbal behaviors, such as eye-to-eye gaze, facial expression, body postures, and gestures, to regulate social interaction;

b) failure to develop peer relationships appropriate to developmental level; and

c) lack of social or emotional reciprocity

Restrictive, Repetitive and Stereotypic Patterns of Behavior, Interests or Activities

Manifested by at least one of the following:

a) encompassing preoccupations with one or more stereotyped and restricted patterns of interest that is abnormal either in intensity or focus;

b) apparently inflexible adherence to specific nonfunctional routines or rituals;

c) stereotyped and repetitive motor mannerisms (e.g., hand or finger flapping or twisting, or complex whole-body movements); and

d) persistent preoccupation with parts of objects

A total of six of these clinical features spread across all three domains as indicated must be present for a diagnosis of autism to be made. In addition, the DSM-IV-TR stipulates that there must exist "delays or abnormal functioning in at least one of the following areas, with the onset prior to age three years: (1) social interaction, (2) language as used in social communication, or (3) symbolic or imaginative play" and that the "...disturbance is not better accounted for by Rett's Disorder or Childhood Disintegrative Disorder."

Figure 2.2

When reviewing the clinical features of Asperger Disorder's two domains, as listed in Figure 2.3, it quickly becomes apparent that they are also included in the diagnosis for Autistic Disorder, with one slight change. The one deviation between the two is within the "social domain" criteria for autism: *"a lack of spontaneous seeking to share enjoyment, interests, or achievements with other people (e.g., by a lack of showing, bringing, or pointing out objects of interest to other people)"* (p. 84). This feature could easily be included as part of the "lack of social or emotional reciprocity" listed in both diagnostic criteria.

What is most obviously missing in the diagnostic criteria for Asperger's Disorder is the Qualitative Impairment in Communication domain. With Asperger's Disorder there is "no clinically significant general delay in language" (p. 75). Additionally, there is "no clinically significant delay in cognitive development or in the development of age-appropriate self-help skills, adaptive behavior (other than in social interaction), and curiosity about the environment in childhood" (p. 75).

In other words, what we see in children with Asperger's Disorder is similar to what we see in individuals with autism, except for the early childhood language delays. Additionally, although it is not a diagnostic criterion, most children with autism have mental retardation, while most individuals with Asperger's Syndrome have average or above-average intelligence. For this reason and others, much controversy has surrounded the debate over whether Asperger's Disorder is nothing more than "high-functioning autism." It has also cast doubt on the claim of Asperger's Disorder as a separate diagnosis that requires alternative treatment methodologies.

Figure 2.3

Diagnostic criteria for 299.80 Asperger's Disorder is divided into two domains of core deficits. They include:

1. Qualitative Impairment in Social Interactions
2. Restrictive, Repetitive and Stereotypic Patterns of Behavior, Interests and Activities

What is important to remember from a behavioral intervention standpoint is that we are describing degrees of qualitative impairment between autism and Asperger's Disorder. A child with Asperger's Disorder is far different from a very low-functioning child with autism. Language, cognitive, and adaptive skills are at or above normal proficiency for the child with Asperger's Disorder *before* we intervene.

With autism, applied behavior analysis has been shown time and again to be the most effective means of teaching social skills and reducing reliance on repetitive or stereotypic behaviors in children displaying significantly higher levels of impairment. It stands to reason that a behavioral approach to teaching these same skills to a higher functioning child with Asperger's Disorder should be possible.

Section D – Diagnosis

As parents search for reasons or explanations for their child's atypical development, they are quite often led along a rather convoluted path from pediatrician to audiologist, to speech/language pathologist, to developmental specialist, to various psychologists, or eventually to a neurologist. Unfortunately, many of these professionals that the parents meet along the way may not have had any direct experience with autism, and the elusive diagnosis may not be made for months or even years. In the meantime, the undiagnosed child does not receive the therapy that he or she most desperately needs.

When a diagnosis is made, it usually comes from a child psychiatrist, neurologist or licensed psychologist. Although the criteria for assigning the diagnosis of autism typically falls within the parameters laid out in the DSM-IV-TR, the actual interview and assessment tools used by these professionals to evaluate children can vary substantially.

Both of these factors – the delays in detecting and diagnosing children with autism and the lack of a consistent or systematic protocol for conducting diagnostic activities – have led some professionals in the field to seek standards.

In 1999, a group of professionals with this task in mind was formed under the auspices of the Child Neurology Society and the American Academy of Neurology. It was comprised of 18 representatives from nine professional organizations and four parent organizations, with liaisons from the National Institutes of Health (Filipek, et al., 1999).

The composition of this multidisciplinary panel was a veritable "who's who" of autism experts drawn from the fields of neurology, psychiatry, pediatrics, psychology, occupational therapy and speech/language pathology. Following an extensive review of the scientific literature on autism screening and diagnosis, the panel formulated a standard, comprehensive protocol for the evaluation of children suspected of having autism. The systematic and cohesive quality of their finished product so impressed us that we have included a snapshot of their diagnostic protocol in this manual.

A few of the main points are as follows:

1) Well-child visits to the pediatrician should be enhanced to include developmental screenings for autism from infancy through the preschool years and "at any age thereafter if concerns are raised about social acceptance, learning, and behavior."

2) Once screened and identified as "at risk" for autism, children should be seen by professionals who specialize in the treatment of autism.

3) The diagnosis should be accurately made based on clinical and DSM-IV criteria, and should include the use of a diagnostic instrument with at least moderate sensitivity and good specificity for autism. Both standardized parent interview and direct structured observation of the child should be completed at this stage of evaluation.

Instruments for Standardized Parent Interviews

Standardized parent interview instruments include:

a) The *Gilliam Autism Rating Scale* ***(GARS)*** – a checklist used by parents, teachers and professionals to identify and estimate the severity of autistic symptoms. Designed for ages 3 to 22 years, the GARS is based on the three DSM-IV diagnostic domains: stereotypic behavior, communication and social interaction. An optional subtest is also included to review the child's developmental milestones over the first three years of life. The GARS provides a global rating of autistic symptoms.

b) The *Parent Interview for Autism* ***(PIA)*** – a structured interview conducted with parents of children suspected of having autism. The PIA consists of 118 items, organized into 11 dimensions, which assess social interaction, communication, and stereotypic behaviors. The PIA takes approximately 45 minutes to complete.

c) *The Pervasive Developmental Disorders Screening Test* – ***(PDDST-II)*** – a parent questionnaire that is divided into three stages. Questions probe for both positive and negative symptoms and inquire about regression. Stage 1 is designed for use in the primary care setting for children from birth to 36 months. Stage 2 is to be used in developmental disorders clinics, while Stage 3 has been developed for administration in autism or pervasive developmental disorder (PDD) clinics.

d) *The Autism Diagnostic Interview-Revised* ***(ADI-R)*** – the "gold standard" interviewing instrument in current research protocols. The ADI-R is a comprehensive structured parent interview that takes approximately one to two hours to administer and requires specific training and validation procedures. Due to these restrictions, the practicality of its use in primary care settings is questionable.

Instruments for Structured Observation

Direct, structured observation instruments include:

a) *Screening Tool for Autism in Two-year-olds* ***(STAT)*** – an interactive measure for children ages 24–35 months that can be administered by various early childhood professionals. It consists of a 20-minute play session with several activities that test for motor imitation, pretend and reciprocal play, and nonverbal communication. The STAT is designed to differentiate autism from other developmental disorders.

b) *Childhood Autism Rating Scale* ***(CARS)*** – a 15-item structured interview and observation instrument for children over 24 months of age. A seven-point rating scale for each item indicates severity of impairment, distinguishing mild-to-moderate from severe autism. The CARS takes 30-45 minutes to administer.

c) *Autism Diagnostic Observation Schedule-Generic* ***(ADOS-G)*** – a semi-structured observational assessment. Four modules include adult-directed activities that probe for deficits in social relatedness, communication and restricted interests or stereotypic behavior. The ADOS-G can be administered to nonverbal preschoolers as well as adults with autism who have some verbal skills. As with the ADI-R, the ADOS-G requires specific training and validation procedures.

The panel went on to make additional recommendations to develop this standard diagnostic protocol for use with all individuals suspected of having autism – including even those with mild symptoms. For physicians and neurologists, these include an expanded medical and neurological evaluation to rule out acquired brain injury or comorbid conditions, as well as investigating both nuclear and extended families for any history of autism or related disorders.

Other Diagnostic Tools

Additional assessments deemed critical in the diagnostic protocol were speech-language evaluations, cognitive and adaptive skills assessments, and sensorimotor skill assessments, as well as neuropsychological, behavioral, and academic assessments. In regard to these other disciplines, the panel was very clear in qualifying that evaluators or test administrators in these areas must have experience and expertise in treating children with autism. These include speech/language pathologists, psychologists, occupational therapists, teachers, and behavior analysts. Evaluating the family's functioning and ability to understand and/or deal with the diagnosis were also seen as critical pieces of the diagnostic puzzle.

Finally, laboratory evaluations may be required, depending on the symptoms presented at the primary care or neurological examinations. These can include metabolic testing, genetic testing, prolonged sleep-deprived EEG and neuroimaging. Furthermore, the panel stated that, "There is inadequate evidence to support routine clinical testing of individuals with autism for hair analysis for trace elements, celiac antibodies, allergy testing (in particular food allergies for gluten, casein, candida and other molds), immunological or neurochemical abnormalities, micronutrients such as vitamin levels, intestinal permeability studies, stool analysis, urinary peptides, mitochondrial disorders (including lactate and pyruvate), thyroid function tests, or erythrocyte glutathione peroxidase studies" (Filipek, et al., 1999).

A Word to Parents

No one can dispute that time is of the essence in diagnosing a child with autism. Over the past two decades, however, it has become clear that the diagnostic process takes time and is best accomplished by professionals who possess the skills and expertise that come from years of clinical experience with children with autism.

Right from the start, parents of children with autism are vulnerable to being led astray by misinformation, misguided professionals or unproven theories about the disorder. In addition, finding the right person to detect a potential developmental delay and then having access to a team of autism experts to conduct a comprehensive assessment can be an arduous and frustrating process. Even so, early diagnosis (prior to age three) is becoming easier and more commonplace.

These practice parameters give hope to parents who are faced with the daunting task of finding help for their children.

Section F - Prevalence

When autism first caught the eye of the scientific community, it was considered a rare, albeit severe, disorder. Noting two essential criteria, "a profound lack of affective contact" and "repetitive, ritualistic behavior, which must be of an elaborate kind," autism was considered to be a very remarkable disorder (Kanner & Eisenberg, 1956). While no major epidemiological studies were completed during this era, most professional estimates regarding the disorder placed prevalence near 1-2 children per 10,000. Using the same diagnostic criteria mentioned above, Lotter (1966) conducted an epidemiological study that placed prevalence at 0.45 per 1,000 individuals.

Several more studies conducted in the following years yielded similar low prevalence rates. However, when the third edition of the Diagnostic and Statistical Manual of Mental Disorders (DSM; American Psychiatric Association, 1980) was published, new diagnostic criteria were introduced, which were then refined in the 1987 version of the manual (DSM-III-R). Based on criteria from the DSM-III and the DSM-III-R, at least 12 notable epidemiological studies examining the prevalence of autistic disorders were conducted between 1983 and 1997.

Prevalence rates for these studies ranged from 0.25 cases per 1,000 (Ritvo, et al., 1989) to 1.60 per 1,000 (Ishii & Takahashii, 1983). Between 1996 and 1998, at least seven other widely read studies were conducted, using diagnostic criteria found in the International Classification of Diseases, 10th edition (ICD-10). Within these studies, prevalence rates ranged from 0.54 cases of autism per 1,000 (Fombonne, et al., 1997) to 6 cases per 1,000 (Kadesjo, Gillberg, & Hagberg, 1999).

Citing many of the above studies, the Centers for Disease Control and Prevention conducted a very large-scale epidemiological study of autism prevalence in Brick Township, New Jersey in 1998. The study utilized diagnostic criteria from the DSM-IV for autism spectrum disorders. The results of this study indicated a prevalence of autistic disorder at 4.0 cases per 1,000 for children aged 3-10 years (CDC, 2000). The overall rate for children of the same age who met the criteria for autistic disorder, as defined in DSM-IV, and other spectrum disorders (ASD) was 6.7 cases per 1,000 (CDC, 2000).

The Brick Township study was the first large-scale contemporary prevalence study in the United States that used very intensive identification methods. It yielded results similar to those found in studies conducted abroad during the same time period. Because of this, it has been considered for several years to be a hallmark study on autism prevalence, with its results frequently used in a wide variety of settings to support the notion that autism is indeed a disorder worthy of the public's close attention.

Perhaps the most significant prevalence figures yet are the most recent ones produced by the CDC. In February of 2007, the CDC announced the results of its first multi-community prevalence study, based on information collected during the reporting years of 2000 and 2002. This study reported the results of data collected across 14 different sites spanning the United States. The study examined the records of eight-year-old children (because most individuals with ASD have been identified by that time). It concluded that autism's prevalence was (on average) around 6.6 - 6.7 per 1,000 eight year olds, or that approximately 1 in 150 were on the autistic spectrum (CDC, 2007).

Today, autism is recognized in many circles as an "epidemic" or "crisis" that is directly impacting the lives of many millions of Americans. Thanks to devoted parents, committed researchers and nothing short of a media frenzy, autism has become the subject of close scrutiny, as well as a great deal of hype.

What is important to understand is this: while the rates found in the studies have increased as the years have passed, many believe they reflect an increase in *diagnoses* of ASD, as opposed to an increase in actual prevalence.

It can be argued that we have become much more skilled at identifying individuals who have autism spectrum disorders. With awareness of ASD increasing globally, deeper knowledge has undoubtedly made its way to physicians and other diagnosticians who may not have been as familiar with ASD 20 years ago. In addition, many individuals with ASD simply would not have been diagnosed with any disorder in the past – including the many adults receiving diagnoses of Asperger's Disorder who now account for a percentage of the ASD population. In other words, the perceived increase in prevalence could be attributed, in part, to better diagnostic tools and a greater sense of awareness.

The above arguments noted, many of the professionals conducting research on the neurobiological elements of autism, as well as many diagnosticians, continue to contend that they are simply seeing more children with autism than ever before. Science will eventually unravel the mysteries surrounding its causes and prevalence. Until then, it is safe to say that autism and related spectrum disorders are having quite a significant impact on a global scale.

Today, it is common for classroom teachers to have some experience with individuals with ASD. Likewise, it is common to encounter people with family members or friends who have been touched by the disorder in one way or another. Autism knows no ethnic, cultural, racial, economic, or gender boundaries. It is a global disorder – which is why it has become increasingly important for us to identify appropriate and effective interventions for children with ASD.

Terms and Labels That May Be Associated with Autism Spectrum Disorders:

Asperger's Disorder
Asperger's Syndrome
Autism
Autistic Disorder
Autistic Features
Autistic-like Symptoms
Childhood Disintegrative Disorder
High-functioning Autism
Mild Autism
Pervasive Developmental Disorder – Not Otherwise Specified (PDD-NOS)

References:

Adrien, J.L., Lenoir, P., Martineau, J., Perrot, A., Hameury, L., Larmande, C., & Sauvage, D. (1993). Blind ratings of early symptoms of autism based upon family home movies. *Journal of the American Academy of Child and Adolescent Psychiatry, 32*, 617-626.

American Psychiatric Association. (2000). *Diagnostic and Statistical Manual of Mental Disorders – Fourth Edition, Text Revision.* Washington, DC: American Psychiatric Association.

Text Box citations
Diagnostic criteria for 299.0 Autistic Disorder - page 75
Diagnostic criteria for 288.8 Asperger's Disorder – page 84

Asperger, H. (1944). Die "Autistischen Psychopathen" im Kindesalter. *Archiv für Psychiatrie und Nervenkrankheiten*, 117, 76-136.

Baranek, G. T. (1999). Autism during infancy: A retrospective video analysis of sensory-motor and social behaviors at 9-12 months of age. *Journal of Autism and Developmental Disorders*, *29*, 213-224.

Centers for Disease Control and Prevention (2000). "Prevalence of Autism in Brick Township, New Jersey, 1998" *Community Report.*

Centers for Disease Control and Prevention (2007). "Prevalence of the Autism Spectrum Disorders in Multiple Areas of the United States, Surveillance Years 2000 and 2002 A Report from the Autism and Developmental Disabilities Monitoring (ADDM) Network" Office of Enterprise Communication Press Release – February 8, 2007. http://www.cdc.gov/od/oc/media/pressrel/2007/f070208.htm.

Dawson, G., & Osterling, J. (1997). Early intervention in autism: Effectiveness and common elements of current approaches. In M. J. Guralnick (Ed.), *The effectiveness of early intervention: Second generation research* (pp. 307-326). Baltimore, MD: Paul H. Brookes.

DiLavore, P.C., Lord, C., & Rutter, M. (1995). The pre-linguistic autism diagnostic observation schedule. *Journal of Autism and Developmental Disorders*, *25*, 355-379.

Donnellan, A. (1985). *Classic readings in autism*. New York; Teachers College Press.

Eisenberg, L., & Kanner, L. (1956). Early infantile autism, 1943-1955. *American Journal of Orthopsychiatry*, *26*, 556-566.

Filipek, P.A., Pasquale, J.A., Baranek, G.T., Cook, E.H., Dawson, G., Gordon, B., Gravel, J., Johnson, C.P., Kallen, R.J., Levy, S.E., Minshew, N.J., Prizant, B.M., Rapin, I., Rogers, S.J., Stone, W.L., Teplin, S., Tuchman, R.F., & Volkmar, F.R. The screening and diagnosis of autistic spectrum disorders. *Journal of Autism and Developmental Disorders*, *29*, 439-484.

Fombonne E., Mazaubrun, C., Cans, C., & Grandjean, H. (1997). Autism and associated medical disorders in a French epidemiologic survey. *Journal of the American Academy of Child Adolescent Psychiatry*, 36, 1561-1569.

Gilliam, J.E. (1995). *Gilliam Autism Rating Scale (GARS)*. Austin, TX: Pro-Ed.

International Statistical Classification of Diseases and Related Health Problems (ICD), Tenth Revision. (1992). Geneva: World Health Organization.

Ishii, T. & Takahashi, I. (1983). The epidemiology of autistic children in Toyota, Japan: Prevalence. *Japanese Journal of Child and Adolescent Psychiatry*, *24*, 311-321.

Kanner, L. (1943). Autistic disturbances of affective contact. *Nervous Child*, *2*, 217-250.

Kadesjo, B., Gillberg, C., & Hagberg, B. (1999). Autism and Asperger Syndrome in seven-year-old children: A total population study. *Journal of Autism and Developmental Disorders*, *29*, 327-331.

Le Couteur, A., Rutter, M., Lord, C., Rios, P., Robertson, S., Holdgrafer, M., & McLennan, J. (1989). Autism diagnostic interview: A standardized investigator-based instrument. *Journal of Autism and Developmental Disorders*, *19*, 363-387.

Lord, C., Rutter, M., Goode, Sl, Heemsbergen, J., Jordan, H., Mawhood, L., & Schopler, E. (1989). Autism Diagnostic Observation Schedule: A standardized observation of communicative and social behaviour. *Journal of Autism and Developmental Disorders*, *19*, 185-212.

Lord, C., Rutter, M., DiLavore, P.C., & Risi, S. (1999). *Autism Diagnostic Observation Schedule-WPS (ADOS-WPS)*. Los Angeles: Western Psychological Services.

Lotter V. (1966). Epidemiology of autistic conditions in young children. *Social Psychiatry 1*, 124-137.

Osterling, J., & Dawson, G. (1994). Early recognition of children with autism: A study of first birthday home videotapes. *Journal of Autism and Developmental Disorders, 24*, 247-257.

Rimland, B. (1964). *Infantile autism.* New York: Appleton-Century-Crofts.

Ritvo, E.R., Freeman, B.J., Pingree, C., Mason-Brothers, A., Jorde, L., Jenson, W.R., McMahon, Petersen, P.B., Mo, A. & Ritvo, A. (1989). The UCLA-University of Utah epidemiologic survey of autism: Prevalence. *American Journal of Psychiatry, 146*, 194-199.

Rogers, S. J. (1996). Brief report: Early intervention in autism. *Journal of Autism and Developmental Disorders, 26*, 243-247.

Rogers, S.J. (1998). Empirically supported comprehensive treatments for young children with autism. *Journal of Clinical Child Psychology, 27*, 168-179.

Schopler, E., Reichler, R.J., & Rochen-Renner, B. (1988). *The Childhood Autism Rating Scale (CARS).* Los Angeles, CA: Western Psychological Services.

Siegel, B. (2004). *Pervasive Developmental Disorders Screening Test – II (PDDST).* San Antonio: Psychological Corporation/Harcourt Assessment

Stone, W.L., Coonrod., E.E., & Ousley, O.Y. (2000). Brief report: Screening Tool for Autism in Two-Year-Olds (STAT): Development and preliminary data. *Journal of Autism and Developmental Disorders, 23*, 639-652.

Stone, W.L. & Hogan, K.L. (1993). A structured parent interview for identifying young children with autism. *Journal of Autism and Developmental Disorders, 23*, 639-652.

Tuchman, R. (1996). Pervasive Developmental Disorder: Neurologic perspective. *Acta Neuropediatrica, 2*, 82-93.

Wing, L. (1981). Asperger's syndrome: A clinical account. *Psychological Medicine, 11*, 115-129.

Science, And Its Role in the Study of Behavior and Autism At a Glance

Chapter Points

- Factual understanding of events and processes can be attained as a result of scientific investigation.
- Applications of science have led to extraordinary improvements in the human condition.
- A scientific approach relies upon the application of specific principles or properties.
- Behavior, when viewed through a natural science approach and subject to the properties of science, is susceptible to external influence.

Key Terms

Science

Determinism

Empiricism

Parsimony

Manipulation

Philosophical Doubt

Systematic Manipulation

Pseudoscience

Science
And Its Role in the Study of Behavior and Autism

Information: Friend or Foe?

We live in an age of information, where words, images and sounds are only a mouse click away. Advances in **science**, medicine, and industry are disseminated to the public in a fraction of the time of past eras. In short, our modern world is one in which news travels quickly. *Very* quickly.

This new age of information access has shifted the paradigm by allowing people of varying educational and socioeconomic levels to access knowledge that was once reserved for highly-trained experts. As a result, people have become well-informed advocates for their own causes. They are learning the right questions to ask at the doctor's office, and are less likely to be taken advantage of by a mechanic. They are also learning how to better deal with problems they encounter in the education and care of their children – which brings us to the conditions that led us to develop this manual.

When a child is diagnosed with a disability (including autism), there is an added urgency for information. Families are often hurtled at full speed into a world of technical jargon, an army of professionals with many philosophical perspectives, a whirlwind of opinions from family and friends and an avalanche of paperwork. At the center of this firestorm is the child.

Parents find themselves desperate for answers to questions like: "What will their life be like?" "Will he or she at least be happy?" "Who can help us do the best we can for our child?" Caring and committed teachers and professionals feel a similar desire for answers, because they share in the responsibility of providing the child with the skills and experiences that will lead to the best quality of life possible. As a result, a furious search begins to gather as much information as possible, from as many sources as possible.

In the midst of this, there is a caveat: *while we live in an age of information, it includes both good* ***and bad*** *information.* There is an adage that one can possess too little information to be effective, but just enough to be dangerous. And, while there are devices that filter offensive material from entering a home or computer screen, there are none that block information that is bogus, or that could cause the investment of countless hours and endless dollars in ineffective treatments.

A consequence of unlimited information access is that many different paths of action can be presented, and to the untrained eye, all are equally valid. Science ultimately reveals the correct paths for effective treatment, but the Internet provides so many choices that parents and professionals are often too confused to look for the right markers.

Science and the Study of Human Behavior

Few areas share the breadth and scope of the study of human behavior. At every level, each of us has some experience with or opinion on the topic.

Perhaps it is because of the integral part behavior plays in the life of every human being that we have spent eons trying to understand what makes us do the things we do. At times, it seems like everyone is a self-proclaimed expert in human behavior, or at least has an opinion that they will argue.

As understandable as this may be, imagine if everyone held the same "lay expert" attitude in areas of medicine or physics. We would still hold faulty notions such as the flatness of the earth, or the idea that our health is determined and controlled by "humours" or even by the position of the stars and planets at our birth.

But because we have not ignored science, our world is a much better place. We now cure once-fatal diseases. We know how to replace organs. We are exploring the outer reaches of the solar system. Science has the power to continually point us toward a greater understanding about our world, and our place in it. Shouldn't we use the same principles of scientific inquiry to enhance our understanding of human behavior?

"If we are to use the methods of science in the field of human affairs, we must assume behavior is lawful and determined. We must expect to discover what a man does is the result of specifiable conditions and that once these conditions have been discovered, we can anticipate and to some extent determine his actions" (Skinner, p. 6).

This statement suggesting the application of scientific methods to the analysis and prediction of human behavior was made by B. F. Skinner over 50 years ago. And yet, the belief that human behavior is primarily a product of environmental conditions or contingencies and that these natural phenomena can be best understood through scientific investigation is not widely accepted. The psychological and educational communities continue to rely heavily on psychodynamic theories that place the origin of human action ultimately in the mind, the personality, or the will of the individual.

In the past century, the true science behind behavior has grown quite robust. There have been incredible advances in the understanding, measurement, prediction, and ability to change the behaviors of all sorts of living beings, including humans.

By approaching human behavior as a natural science – as a lawful, predictable, observable, measurable and malleable subject – we have been able to develop a great body of technology to shape and change people's lives for the better. Behavior has been largely demystified at the clinical level, and this has given rise to extremely effective interventions for problem behaviors, as well as a roadmap for teaching new behaviors quicker, and to higher levels of performance. Both of these applications are extremely relevant in our current quest to provide intervention services for individuals with autism.

In this chapter, we will explain the processes that have led us to this understanding. We will cover the principles of science, including how they can and should be used to understand the difference between proven, effective techniques for teaching children with autism and those that are ineffective or marginally effective at best.

We will also provide a scientific framework upon which the particulars of effective interventions can be evaluated and layered. Because the approaches presented in this manual rely upon the basic principles of science, progressing without this discussion might restrict the reader's perspective regarding effective autism intervention.

Section A – Properties of Science

Science is the organized body of knowledge about the natural world that is derived from a set of logical and observable methods. These methods provide for a systematic observation of natural phenomena so that we can better understand the world in which we live. Explanation of natural phenomena typically takes the form of a *theory* that tries to account for how things work, how natural events occur in predictable patterns or why phenomena appear to us as they do.

Our world has always been shaped by science, even when methods of inquiry were quite rudimentary. As inquisitive beings, it has always been important for us to understand how things work. In prehistoric times, science probably consisted of simple experimentation regarding which materials made the best tools, or which substances were worthy of eating. An idea came to mind, it was tested and the results were somehow passed along to others. Imagine being the first person to eat an egg! In many ways, science, at its very foundation, is a much more developed approach to these same early "experiments."

The state of science really did not experience vast growth before the classical era of Greece. There were certainly advances in lexicology, or the development of recorded language, and there were obvious advances in our ancestors' abilities to understand numbers, both of which play an integral part in the development of science. But there was no real method or systematic way to approach problems until sometime around the birth of the classical era.

Properties of Science

Parsimony –
Simpler is better. Given the option between two plausible explanations of a phenomenon, the simpler one should be chosen.

Determinism –
Things occur as the result of natural or mechanistic causes. In this way, almost all events are preceded and somewhat determined by other events.

Empiricism –
Information should be acquired through observation or experimentation. More weight is given to empirical information than that which exists in theory alone.

Systematic Manipulation –
Hypotheses are tested by systematically manipulating variables and measuring the results.

Philosophic Doubt –
All ideas are subject to provisional acceptance. If there is valid evidence to the contrary, one must be willing to relinquish those ideas and accept those with the preponderance of evidence.

The Greeks introduced the world to a new way of thinking. The age of rationalism dawned with the argument that the complexities of the universe could be explained through reason. Since then, the application of logic and reason to unraveling the mysteries of life has been highly refined. Using sophisticated tools for observation and measurement, along with rigorous methodological models, scientists are able to turn fiction into fact. Unexplained phenomena that have perplexed humans throughout history are being resolved, or at least accounted for.

Human behavior, including aberrant behavior (like that often associated with autism) is no exception. For this reason, the principles of science can and should be used to understand the difference between effective techniques for teaching children with autism and those that are not.

We can get a better sense of what science is by considering its properties. It is generally agreed that science possesses the qualities of **determinism**, **empiricism**, and **parsimony**. Additionally, science always involves the **manipulation** of natural phenomena and adopts an attitude of **philosophic doubt** or skepticism about its findings.

Determinism

Determinism is a philosophical belief that all events are determined by natural (or mechanistic) causes. In other words, all natural phenomena occur as a result of the interplay of other equally observable natural events or factors. Determinism also holds that this interplay of natural phenomena occurs in a lawful and orderly fashion. This position – that things don't happen in a haphazard manner – can't be proved or disproved. It is, however, central to scientific investigation.

In the casé of human behavior, determinism explains an individual's behavioral response to any given situation as the cumulative result of a myriad of environmental events or factors at that moment, and in his or her past. It does not, however, permit one to enter into a discussion of how an individual's free will governs how he or she acts, or how the individual simply "makes up his mind" to do something. Determinism does not allow for such unknowable or supernatural explanations for human behavior.

At times, this can be a difficult pill to swallow. Humans are very proud creatures, and the thought that we are not in complete control of our destiny can be very disconcerting. This sense of egocentrism has been one of the major stumbling blocks to the acceptance of a purely scientific investigation of human behavior.

Empiricism

According to the theory of empiricism, all knowledge is gained ultimately through the senses. While philosophical argument has long struggled with this notion, the natural sciences drew heavily on empiricism in the development of the scientific method and its dependence on objective observation, experimentation, and precise measurement.

When it comes to human behavior, science requires that its phenomena be observable, measurable and subject to manipulation. Most of what we do in our everyday lives, for example, can be easily accepted as behaviors that can be observed, measured, and changed.

Internal or private events, such as emotions, feelings, intuitions, thoughts, values and beliefs may seem at first glance to fall outside of the parameters of empirical phenomena. These, our most personal and private "possessions," somehow seem exempt from the cold eye of science. Granted, these behaviors are less obvious and do not always lend themselves well to the standard methods of measurement and manipulation.

They do, however, meet the requirements of empirical observation and measurement. They can be observed when one considers that this observation is simply limited to the person doing the thinking, feeling or believing. The observer can also quantify the rate and magnitude of thoughts or feelings. In addition, the notion that we can alter the thoughts, feelings and beliefs of others is a fundamental assumption without which the entire field of clinical psychology would find itself without purpose.

Parsimony

Parsimony has its origin in medieval philosophy. An English monk and philosopher, William of Ockham (ca. 1285-1349) coined the phrase *"Pluralitas non est ponenda sine neccisitate"* or "plurality should not be posited without necessity." Also known as *Ockham's Razor* (think of it as a tool for "cutting away' that which is not likely), parsimony requires that the pursuit of simpler explanations for natural phenomena occur before looking to more complex or abstract reasons.

As it developed, the academic community within the natural sciences embraced the principle of parsimony as another of science's defining attributes. Simply stated, science requires that all simple, logical explanations be ruled out experimentally before more complex or abstract explanations are considered.

Carl Sagan described a popular example of the need for parsimony in his book *The Demon-Haunted World: Science as a Candle in the Dark*. Sagan observed how the media and general public seized upon the phenomenon of "crop circles" as evidence of nocturnal visitation by creatures from outer space. A more "parsimonious" investigation, however, revealed that the vast majority (if not all) of these occurrences were the product of very human pranksters.

A science-based view of human behavior utilizes the principle of parsimony in its analytic processes. Rather than place the origin of human action in the unobservable, metaphysical province of the "mind," a scientific approach to behavior looks to simpler, more-observable environmental events around or within the individual.

Manipulation

The testing of scientific theories or hypotheses developed to describe the natural world eventually must involve **systematic manipulation** of the specific variable(s) involved.

Direct, empirical observation of a natural event allows us to begin to better understand the phenomenon, to describe it in more precise and systematic language and hopefully, to begin to see that the phenomenon can be linked to other natural phenomena according to some regular pattern.

Correlations between natural events (i.e., the fact that two separate phenomenon consistently occur in a regular temporal sequence) are what scientists love to discover, as they suggest the existence of a causal or functional relation that can be tested.

This leads scientists to formulate a hypothesis that a) postulates the existence of a functional relation between the two events, and b) predicts the future probability of that event occurring in the presence of the correlated event.

Proving the hypothesis, or the existence of a functional relation, requires scientific manipulation of the variables involved. Experiments are designed to systematically manipulate the occurrence of the two events in question while eliminating or controlling the effects of other naturally occurring variables. If it can be shown that one event can be reliably made to happen solely due to the presence of the other correlated event, then a *functional relation* between the two is said to exist.

Rigorous scientific pursuit does not cease at the single study, but requires replication to strengthen the case. Experiments are repeated to ensure that the natural phenomenon in question can again be caused to occur in the presence of the correlated event.

Experiments to test hypotheses concerning complex human behaviors are tricky to design – but not impossible. The wealth of research in the areas of functional analysis, skill instruction, behavior reduction, etc. conducted over the past several decades has made it abundantly clear we can effectively apply scientific methodology to human behavior. This is seen most obviously in the treatment of severe problem behavior. For example, the ability to analyze a child's behavior to accurately determine a functional relation between it and socially mediated variables such as attention or avoidance has resulted in the design of treatment programs of unparalleled efficacy.

Philosophic Doubt

While science attempts to explain how our world works, it does not view its knowledge as final or absolute. The attitude of philosophic doubt, or skepticism, requires that facts be viewed as tentative and subject to further questioning and experimentation.

Scientific knowledge undergoes continued development and refinement as the testing of theory progresses. The philosopher Karl Popper, in his book *The Logic of Scientific Discovery*, remarked that the unique characteristic of all scientific theories is that they are "capable of being tested by experience." Popper goes on to state that the more tests a theory undergoes, the greater its empirical content and the greater its general acceptance. Moreover, well-tested theories spawn new investigation, new theories, and the development of technologies that apply theoretical knowledge to improve our lives.

Science and Autism

Considering the realm of autism and the plethora of current theories and treatment options available to parents, it is interesting to note the relative poverty of well-tested theories. Theories about the causes of autism, for example, range from allergies to sensory integration deficits to early childhood vaccinations. But when held up to the standard of systematic manipulation of empirical phenomenon, these and many other "theories" are generally viewed by the scientific community as speculation or, at best, unproven.

The autism treatment technology that has emerged from the past 50 years of scientific inquiry and experimentation has been shown to be highly effective and replicable across a wide spectrum of children affected by autism. Unfortunately, these methods are labor intensive and require a certain level of expertise among their practitioners.

As a result, the more popular theories of autism and their respective therapeutic methodologies are attractive to the uninformed public because they guarantee success with relatively low effort and limited training requirements for their implementers. Some quickly pounce upon these "magic bullet" therapies.

The long-term costs of selecting the quick fix, however, are the loss of critical early intervention time pursuing unproven methods and their generally poor outcomes. How do such interventions gain esteem?

> *An interesting debate has gone on... between those who think that all doctrines that smell of pseudoscience should be combated and those who believe that each issue should be judged on its own merits, but that the burden of proof should fall squarely on those who make the proposals. I find myself very much in the latter camp. I believe that the extraordinary should be pursued. But extraordinary claims require extraordinary evidence.*
>
> *- Broca's Brain, by Carl Sagan*

Section B – Opponents of Science

Low effort and limited training requirements are the tip of the iceberg when it comes to reasons for choosing non-scientific approaches to autism intervention. Why would any person of sound reason turn their back on any approach that features the hallmarks of sound science, including built-in measures of effectiveness, replicability, procedural integrity, and the ability to concretely demonstrate the procedures responsible for the desired effect? We present several possibilities.

First, as stated, applying a scientifically sound approach typically involves both a significant amount of expertise and a high level of effort. Second, a scientific approach to learning, development, and disabilities (such as autism) places an emphasis on identifying and manipulating variables that are external to the person subject to intervention. This, in effect, removes the burden of the learning problem from the individual and places it upon those responsible for instruction and care.

Think of the potential ramifications of attributing a reading problem to an internal, unobservable state (dyslexia) that is the sole intellectual "baggage" of the person who fails to read. Because it is internal, educators could shirk their burden to teach the skill. Behavior analysts, on the other hand, use a scientific vantage point to look at the *external* variables surrounding the skill and its demonstration, or lack thereof. In this case, it is our burden to find a way to identify the contingencies that will allow the behavior to be shaped. This is why behavior analysts take the stance that "the learner is never wrong."

This example is only used as a way to explain the accountability that can be avoided by assuming an approach that is non-scientific. Attribution of problems to internal issues is one way to "explain away" problems so that we do not have to pursue an effortful intervention for which we may lack the necessary skills.

Another reason that people may steer away from scientific approaches is human pride. How can we be above laboratory animals if we are prone to follow the same rules of behavior? And what does a scientific view say about natural talents and gifts? People who excel in certain tasks tend to take pride in the notion that their success is the result of innate talent, something special and unique to them.

If such successes are reduced to behavioral terms such as reinforcement histories, prompting and opportunities for repetition, the uniqueness of their achievements seems to be lost. Unfortunately, people also fail to realize that a scientific account does not necessarily eliminate such phylogenic variables as genetics and natural characteristics.

A fourth reason has to do with the notion that our cultures have been shaped by mysticism and spirituality. While we make no attempt to challenge personal beliefs, there are inherent problems encountered when one tries to use a rational, empirical approach to explain phenomena that many prefer to view as rooted in supernatural or mystical constructs. Historically, we have also turned to non-scientific accounts of human affairs to make the realities of life more bearable. Let's face it – when one considers all of the variables that have a direct impact on the way we live our lives, reality can be a frightening proposition.

Science provides us with the ability to answer questions that have haunted us for years. At the same time, we also must perform a "gut check" to determine whether or not we really want to know the answers. Nineteenth century mathematician Henri Poincaire offered this supposition as he made the statement: "We also know how cruel the truth often is, and we wonder whether delusion is not more consoling."

Take for example, the notion of love. Who would ever want to reduce such a "magical" concept to quantifiable, observable, or manipulative terms? The same type of thinking pervades our perceptions of teaching and learning. In higher education, young teachers are often encouraged to place more emphasis on developing creative skills or the ability to entertain, rather than on developing scientific skills or the ability to design and evaluate teaching methods that are proven to be effective. Our mystical predispositions lead us to refer to the "art" of teaching, or to find teachers who will "unlock hearts and minds," rather than identify and teach discrete skills that will lead to advanced execution of complex skill repretoires.

A final challenge to scientists in the field of education or developmental disabilites is the proliferation of practitioners who capitalize on emotional vulnerability and even desperation embodied by many parents who care for their children and do not know where else to turn for help. Without science, it is relatively easy for an articulate person to sell his or her approach as a viable treatment option, regardless of any proven effect.

If we deny science, if we say that the symptoms of autism cannot be measured, or that there is no way (or need) to prove that an intervention is effective, then we open the door to accepting virtually any type of treatment. There are very intelligent people in the field who realize this, and who market their approaches on the basis of how they appeal to our emotions or value systems. Rather than rely upon hard evidence of treatment effects, they rely upon anecdotal information and market their services with an emphasis on value statements over fact.

There are also those who engage in "pseudoscience," or activities that are designed to appear scientific without meeting the rigor or basic qualities of true science. These professionals are much like the alchemists of old – using logic and terminology that is inventive and derivative of true science, but lacking in the application of its basic qualities, such as empiricism, systematic manipulation, philosophical doubt and parsimony. Their work may produce data, but the data cannot be achieved by others because there are no clearly defined or replicable parameters of the interventions themselves.

Section C – Suggestions

It is important for us to put forth some suggestions for identifying interventions that meet the requirements of science. These are the same guidelines that must be followed before a drug is brought to market, that govern medical treatment approaches and that have led to refinements in basically every technology. They are based on the idea that interventions resulting in what seem like far-fetched claims should be supported by rigorous evidence.

In his 1748 essay *Of Miracles*, the famous skeptic David Hume put forth the idea that "A wise man…proportions his belief to the evidence." This assertion was later revised by Carl Sagan to become perhaps the best-known rallying cry of skeptics everywhere: "Extraordinary claims require extraordinary evidence" (Sagan, 1979). This statement, from 1979's *Broca's Brain*, was part of a larger argument for actually studying what seem to be extraordinary claims, as opposed to merely dismissing them with a closed mind. When evaluating claims of treatment efficacy, or when trying to determine which course of action will yield the best results when dealing with a child with autism, our advice is to adopt a skepticism that will allow you to act objectively.

We strongly believe that skepticism is a healthy approach for anyone trying to decipher best practices from "flim-flam" – and we all know that the field of autism intervention is full of flim-flam. Skeptics are – by definition – required to maintain an open mind to new ideas, but simply cannot accept a claim as true without evidence. To quote Michael Shermer, a well known academician in scientific fields: *"Modern skepticism is embodied in the scientific method, which involves gathering data to test natural explanations for natural phenomena. A claim becomes factual when it is confirmed to such an extent that it would be reasonable to offer temporary agreement. But all facts in science are provisional and subject to challenge, and therefore skepticism is a method leading to provisional conclusions… The key to skepticism is to navigate the treacherous straits between 'know nothing' skepticism and 'anything goes' credulity by continuously and vigorously applying the methods of science"* (Shermer, 2002).

Science Versus Pseudoscience

We must attempt to look for a way to distinguish science from **pseudoscience**. Science shares several characteristics with history: they are both cumulative and progressive in that they continue to improve and refine knowledge of our world and our past, based on new observations and interpretations. "Pseudo history" and pseudoscience, if they change at all, change primarily for personal, political or ideological reasons (Shermer, 2002).

Our pursuit of real information in the face of pseudoscientific trends becomes a sort of wild goose chase for many who are not armed with the basic principles of scientific decision-making. Therefore, in an attempt to make the differences between pseudoscience and real science clear, we will show how both have shaped our lives. Science is both cumulative and progressive, because useful ideas, features and facts remain intact and relevant, while non-useful or faulty ideas, features, and fallacies are rejected. This takes place through the systematic confirmation or rejection of testable knowledge by those who apply scientific principles. As this process continues, our body of useable knowledge increases, while our paradigms shift to reflect this growth. Advances in physical and natural sciences, such as paleontology, astronomy, physics, chemistry, and medicine have occurred consistently and have instigated major changes in the way we understand our world.

Pseudoscience does not usually set into motion a paradigm shift. Advances in astrology, tarot reading, phrenology, pyramid power, or colonic administration have not really occurred, let alone triggered any kind of mass change within a discipline. Why, then, do we continue to fail to employ skepticism (and its offspring, scientific inquiry) in our evaluations of pseudoscience within the realm of social sciences, such as education?

Here, more than in almost any other discipline, we find ourselves regularly faced with outrageous and unsubstantiated claims that make their way into the general knowledge base of practitioners and consumers. In medicine, there are certainly proponents of homeopathic or alternative treatments, but these are seen as "the fringe," operating largely outside of conventional and evidence-based confines. In education and social disciplines, however, many untested approaches and ideas are accepted as status quo, and even become part of the dogma of the discipline.

Take, for example, the claims that one of the most effective ways to increase a child's achievement is to boost his or her self-esteem. As a result, a good portion of time that could be spent teaching skills is diverted to activities aimed at improving how children feel about themselves. However, there is little to no evidence to support such claims. To the contrary, as William Heward points out in his article, *Ten Faulty Notions That Hinder the Effectiveness of Special Education*, there is evidence to support the notion that boosting a child's achievement is positively correlated to improvements in self-esteem (Heward, 2003). This is but one example of the staggering number of faulty concepts that are propagated throughout the social sciences (or, more accurately, social pseudosciences), and accepted as fact.

How, then, should science be applied in the evaluation of treatment options?

First, be sure that the intervention in question has been shown to have an effect on the targeted problem. This is accomplished through controlled study and subsequent data collection and analysis. If proponents of any one approach cannot produce convincing data to demonstrate the effectiveness of the approach (anecdotes do not count – people can say anything did or did not happen), then it is not yet worth consideration.

Second, valid controlled investigations can, by nature, be replicated. If only one source has been able to produce favorable data, and others have failed to produce similar results, then the validity of the approach should be questioned. Applied behavior analytic approaches to teaching, learning, developmental disabilities, performance management, behavior problems, and other social issues continue to gain validity in this way.

In addition to empirical strengths, it is important to turn to other objective parties to determine the merits of a questionable approach. This is accomplished through publication in peer-reviewed journals, where standards of research protocol are upheld and results are challenged. If the components of a particular approach have not appeared in peer-reviewed literature, its selection is risky.

The following information on detecting pseudoscience is intended to prevent readers from investing time and effort in intervention approaches that lack scientific merit. Rory Coker, Ph.D., offers terrific advice for sorting real science from pseudoscience at the website www.quackwatch.org. This advice includes the following points:

First, pseudoscientific literature is generally aimed at the public, and is not subject to any kind of review, pre-publishing verification, or standards. Second, results can not be reproduced or verified. Third, failures are ignored, excused, hidden, lied about, discounted, explained away, rationalized, forgotten, and generally avoided at all costs. Fourth, no physical phenomena or processes are ever found or studied. No progress is made; nothing concrete is learned.

Fifth, practitioners of pseudoscience attempt to convince us by appealing to faith and belief. Pseudoscience has a strong quasi-religious element: it tries to convert, not to convince. You are to believe in spite of the facts, not because of them. The original idea is never abandoned, whatever the evidence. And finally, these practitioners, in general, earn some or all of their living by selling questionable products such as books, courses and dietary supplements, and/or pseudoscientific services (quackwatch.org - pseudoscience).

We also recommend Gina Green's chapter in *Behavioral Intervention for Young Children with Autism* (Maurice, et al., 1996) as an excellent resource for information on pseudoscience. In the same book, Tristram Smith devotes a chapter to evaluating autism treatments. We believe these chapters are particularly helpful for those who are interested in reviewing available intervention options for children with autism.

Finally, we offer the following suggestions:

- Be wary of approaches to intervention that employ testimonials as a prime source of information.

- Scrutinize provider-generated literature that is not referenced. The goal of such literature is often to advertise services or goods for sale, and it is possible that the provider has as much (or more) to gain from the sale as the consumer.

- There are published journals that are not devoted to experimental research. Pay close attention to the type of "research" that is being provided. Is it based upon surveys and other qualitative data (non-experimental), or is it based on the manipulation of events to test a hypothesis (experimental)?

- Look for peer-reviewed, experimental research. The process of peer review allows the research to be scrutinized to a high degree prior to publication.

- Understand both the usefulness and risks associated with the Internet. While it may be a terrific place to start your search for information on interventions, always proceed cautiously, and locate more solid evidence than what is posted on a web page.

In summary, maintain a healthy skepticism, and do so by remaining scientific and intelligent. This implies keeping an open mind, as scientific doubt requires one to change his or her stance when evidence requires it. In one of our favorite statements about the topic, Carl Sagan (1995) quotes a famed scientist and investigator of outrageous UFO claims: "Keeping an open mind is a virtue – but, as the space engineer James Oberg once said, not so open that your brains fall out" (p.177).

References:

Heward, W. L. (2003). Ten faulty notions that hinder the effectiveness of special education. *The Journal of Special Education, 36, 4,* 186-205.

Http://www.quackwatch.org/01QuackeryRelatedTopics/pseudo.html.

Maurice, C., Green, G., & Luce, S. (1996). *Behavioral Intervention for Young Children with Autism.* Austin: Pro-Ed.

Popper, K.R., (1959). *The Logic of Scientific Discovery.* New York: Harper Torchbooks.

Sagan, C. 1979. *Broca's Brain.* New York: Random House.

Sagan, C. (1995). *The Demon-Haunted World: Science as a Candle in the Dark.* New York: Random House.

Shermer, M. (2002). *Why People Believe Weird Things.* New York: Henry Holt and Company, LLC.

Skinner, B.F. (1953). *Science and Human Behavior.* New York: Macmillan.

Skinner, B.F. (1971). *Beyond Freedom and Dignity.* New York: Knopf.

Overview of Human Behavior Scope and Dimensions

At a Glance

Chapter Points

- Behavior refers to any interaction between an organism and the environment.
- The scope of human behavior includes almost everything we do.
- Behavior may be involuntary or voluntary.
- There are basic principles that account for how we learn behavior.
- Dimensions of behavior allow us to use empirical methods to observe and record them.

Key Terms

Behavior
Response

Environment

Stimulus

Antecedent Stimulus

Consequence Stimulus

Unconditioned Stimulus

Respondent Behavior

Elicit

Reflex

Neutral Stimulus

Respondent Conditioning

Pavlovian Conditioning

Conditioned Stimulus

Operant Conditioning

Applied Behavior Analysis

Dimensions

Temporal Locus

Movement Cycle

Frequency

Duration

Latency

Inter-response Time

Rate

Celeration

Overview of Human Behavior
Scope and Dimensions

When most people are asked to consider the term "behavior," they (including professionals in this field) tend to immediately think of challenging or socially inappropriate ones – i.e., those in need of reduction. Excessive behaviors are familiar, if only because of the great deal of media attention devoted to issues like obesity and overeating, sexual deviance, cigarette smoking, and alcoholism. But while the field of psychology and, more specifically, applied behavior analysis has devoted a great deal of time and research to these areas, they actually represent a mere fraction of all human behavior.

The view that "behavior" equals "bad" is extremely limiting, because it turns the primary focus of treatment to reducing negative behaviors. This approach often results in the use of punitive techniques to the exclusion of much preferred, positive reinforcement-based therapeutic options – which in turn has led to the commonly held view of behavior modification as cold and harsh. Consequently, many parents, agencies and school districts have been deterred from considering a behavioral approach to treating children with autism.

In this chapter and those that follow, we will introduce many terms that may be familiar to highly-trained clinicians, but new to parents and teachers. At times, the terminology will seem to be a bit confusing. However, we will be careful to also define these terms in "plain English" to help you understand them. It is important that you try to make sense of the technical explanations we offer, because the concepts introduced here will form the foundations for the techniques that are described in future chapters.

Section A – What is Behavior?

Simply stated, **behavior** is everything we do, including walking, talking, smiling, reading, cooking, bathing, thinking and breathing. More specifically, behavior is defined as any interaction between the muscles and glands of an organism and the environment. The classic definition of behavior coined by B.F. Skinner in 1938 states that behavior is "…the movement of an organism or of its parts in a frame of reference provided by the organism or by various external objects or fields" (Skinner, 1938, p.6).

Another way to define behavior is to consider what it is not. Ogden Lindsley, a student of Skinner, coined the term "Dead Man's Rule" to help determine if a specific phenomenon is or *is not* behavior. The rule states that if a dead man can do it, then it's not behavior. Figure 4.1 illustrates some examples of behavior vs. non-behavior according to the Dead Man's Rule.

The term **response** refers to an individual instance of behavior. This definition has been expanded upon and refined over the decades to account for public and private behavior. *Public behavior* can be observed and measured by others, while *private behavior*, such as thinking, can only be observed or measured by the person engaging in it. (The topic of private events will be discussed in more detail in Chapter 9, Verbal Behavior.)

Implicit in the definition of behavior is the complex relationship between behavior and environment. For our purposes, **environment** is defined as the entire spectrum of phenomena that can affect behavior. This includes everything that we come into contact with outside our bodies, as well as the various internal states our bodies experience.

When we speak of the environment, we tend to describe specific events instead of the environment in its entirety. In doing so, we usually refer to an individual aspect of the environment as a **stimulus**. According to the Merriam-Webster Online Dictionary, a stimulus is "an agent (as an environmental change) that directly influences the activity of a living organism or one of its parts (as by exciting a sensory organ or evoking muscular contraction or glandular secretion)" (Merriam-Webster, 2005). Replace the word "activity" with "behavior," and this definition serves us well – for our purposes, a stimulus would be an environmental change that affects behavior.

Stimuli occur in time and have an *onset*, or beginning, and an *offset*, or ending. We can also describe qualitative variations of stimuli when we speak of the *magnification* of a stimulus (increasing its intensity) or the *attenuation* of a stimulus (reducing its intensity).

In regard to time, stimuli can be thought of as belonging to two different types. A stimulus that precedes a behavioral response is said to be an **antecedent stimulus**, while one that follows a behavioral response is called a **consequence stimulus**. The role that antecedent and consequence stimuli play in learning will be discussed in more detail in the "conditioning" sections of this chapter.

Behavior	Not Behavior
Sleeping	Lying still
Eating	Not listening
Walking	Not following directions
Talking	Waiting
Reading	Being quiet
Crying	Not hitting
Thinking	
Dreaming	

External Versus Internal Stimuli

External environmental stimuli obviously include such things as our physical surroundings and fluctuations in light, heat and noise. On a more subtle level, however, external environmental stimuli include the presence and quality of social interaction with others, the availability of pleasant or unpleasant experiences and the level of demand placed on us at any given time.

Internal environmental stimuli include the presence (or absence) of pain, discomfort, hunger, thirst, fatigue or sexual arousal. These primary conditions typically have connections to the external environment – for example, hunger and thirst fluctuate along with the availability of food and drink, while fatigue is tied to rest or sleep. More complex internal environmental stimuli are found in the realm of thoughts and emotions, but these too are influenced by contact with external environmental stimuli.

Environment and Behavior

What we are beginning to see is the relationship between environment and behavior. External events give rise to thoughts, feelings, and physical or verbal actions – to the point where it is impossible to think about behavior without the environment in which it occurs. To make matters even more complicated, these environmentally influenced behaviors typically result in a change in the environment that created them. This sets into motion a new set of behavioral responses with the potential for making additional environmental changes that evoke yet more behavior. When you consider that this process is going on simultaneously with everyone on the planet, it's a dizzying prospect.

The relationship between environment and behavior comes about in two different ways. First, we are born with these behaviors already "hard-wired" into our genetic code. They are innate – like the swallow response that occurs when food is placed on the back of the tongue. Because these behaviors are present at birth, we say that they are unlearned or **unconditioned**.

Behaviors can also be shaped by an individual's experiences in the environment as he or she grows and develops. Behaviors acquired in this manner are not present at birth, but rather are a product of the person's day-to-day interactions with the world. Because they are linked to experiential history, they are learned, or conditioned behaviors.

Section B – Respondent Conditioning

Unconditioned behaviors, as mentioned, are present at birth in all healthy humans, even though some of them, like sexual reflexes, might not appear until later years. These evolutionary processes are the product of thousands of years of natural selection. Being concerned primarily with adaptation and survival, unconditioned behaviors permit individual members to function efficiently within sometimes-hostile environments and to survive long enough to propagate the species.

Another term for unconditioned behavior is **respondent behavior** (Cooper, Heron, & Heward, 1987). Respondent behavior comes about when an *antecedent stimulus* causes or **elicits** a response from the individual. This is a result of a process that pairs a neutral stimulus with an unlearned antecedent that elicits a reflex. For example, we all remember the childhood friend who would feign a blow to your face just so he could have the satisfaction of saying "made you blink!" No learning was involved in your eye-blink response.

This combination of an antecedent stimulus (feigned blow to face) and an elicited response (eye blink) is known more commonly as a **reflex**.

Because these reflexive behaviors are linked to species survival, they tend to be protective in nature or are concerned with physiological regulation. Protective reflexes include eye blinking, knee jerking, gagging, and infantile sucking. Regulatory reflexes include salivating, sweating, crying, and changes in heart rate or respiration.

Reflexes are highly stereotypic in that they do not vary in form, frequency, strength, and time of appearance during development. Given a healthy, intact individual and a consistent antecedent stimulus, the same reflex will be elicited in the same manner each time the stimulus is presented.

Through the work of Ivan Pavlov and others, it has been shown that respondent behavior can also come under the control of novel or neutral stimuli. Pavlov showed that a tone (a **neutral stimulus**), accompanied by the presentation of meat powder caused dogs to salivate (an **unconditioned stimulus**). Eventually, the tone alone was sufficient to elicit the salivation response (Pavlov, 1927/1960).

This type of learning, called **respondent conditioning, Pavlovian conditioning** or **classical conditioning**, typically involves the repeated pairing of an unconditioned stimulus with a neutral stimulus. Over time, the neutral stimulus becomes a **conditioned stimulus** that is equally effective in eliciting the respondent behavior. See Figures 4.1 and 4.2.

Since respondent conditioning is tied primarily to species survival, it plays a lesser role in the learning and development of children diagnosed with autism. To provide effective treatment for young children with autism, we must turn our attention to the type of behavior that is maintained by consequences.

Figure 4.1

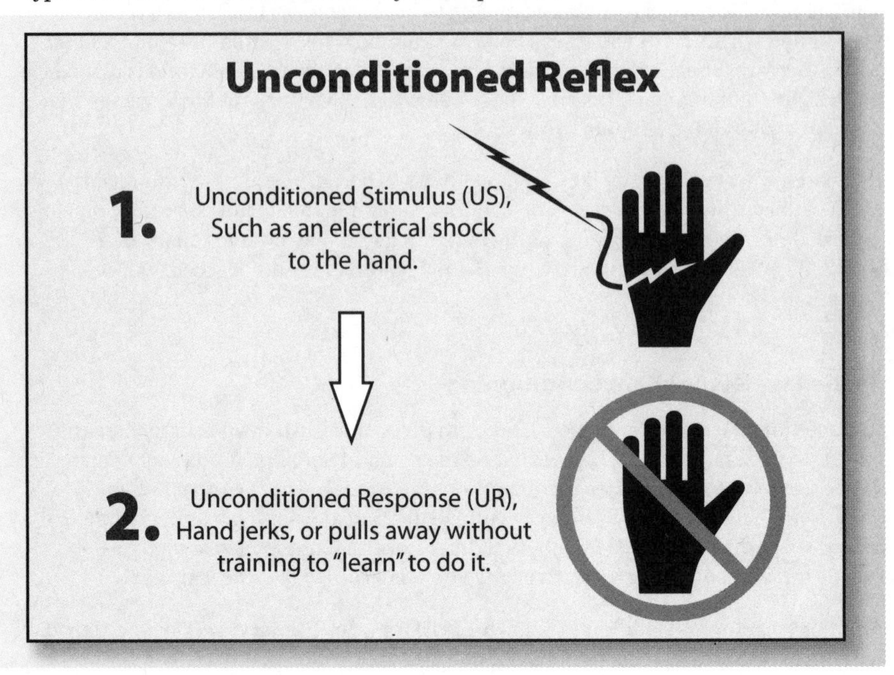

Section C – Operant Conditioning

When B.F. Skinner published *Behavior of Organisms*, he moved beyond the theoretical framework laid down by the behaviorists like Pavlov who preceded him. Skinner recognized that while the respondent conditioning model accurately defined many processes of basic human behavior, it simply didn't account for the vast behavioral repertoires we possess. His theory provided a conceptual framework that brought together the premise of external influence on behavior and the idea of choice or selection – even if choice is not necessarily overt.

From this sprung the principles of **operant conditioning**, Skinner's revolutionary contribution to the field of behavior analysis. This model of human behavior allows for a more complete understanding of why we do certain things under given conditions. It explains behaviors that previously were attributed to random manifestations of free will and other intangible factors. This model provides explanations for behaviors that are extremely simple, as well as for repertoires consisting of many complex behaviors linked together. Most importantly, Skinner provides a scientifically sound basis for developing behavior-changing interventions that can be applied to skill instruction, reduction of certain behaviors, and influence over motivational variables.

What, exactly, is operant conditioning, and how does it differ from respondent conditioning? Operant conditioning is concerned not only with the relationship between the antecedent stimulus and the response, but the consequence stimulus that follows the response. In operant conditioning, it is the consequence, or the stimulus that immediately follows a behavior, that has the most significant effect on the future reoccurrence of the behavior (Cooper et al., 1987).

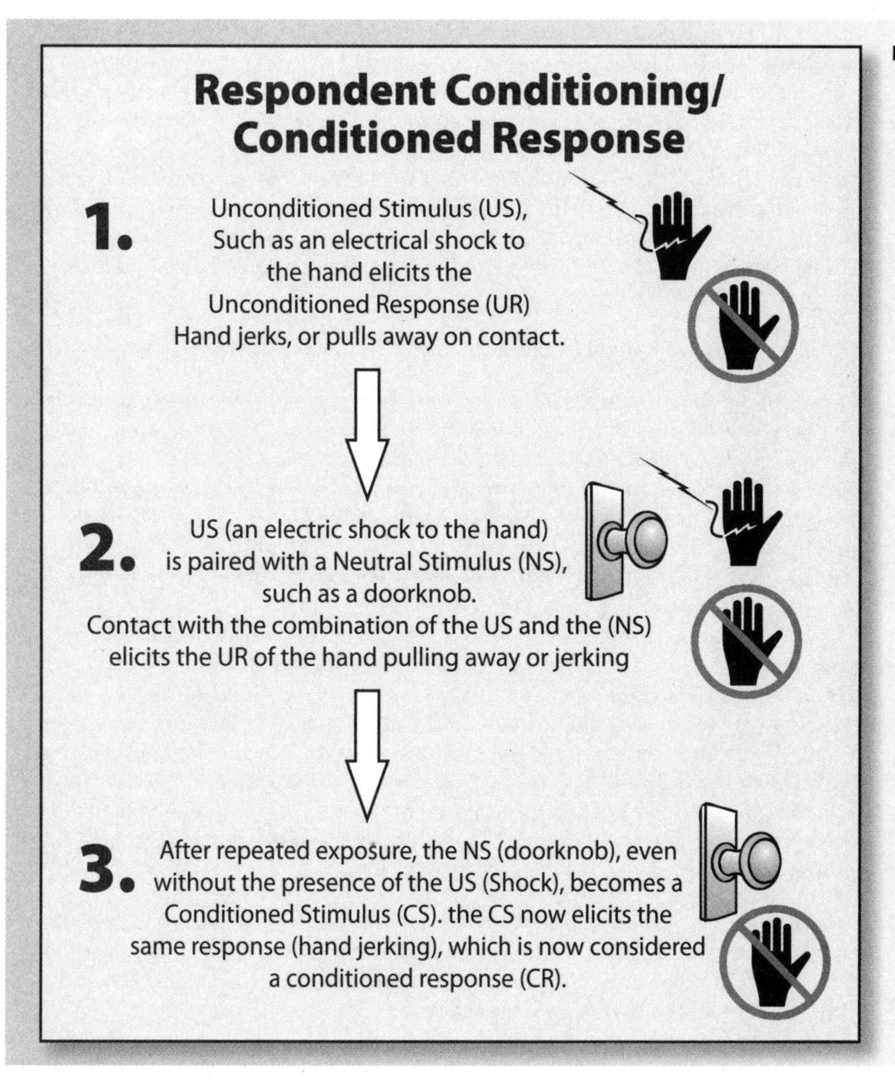

Figure 4.2

Given certain circumstances, once a behavior occurs, one of three things will happen:

- a consequence will occur that will make the behavior more likely in the future;
- a consequence will occur that will make the behavior less likely in the future; or
- no meaningful consequence will occur.

These types of consequences have names, which will be discussed shortly. First, however, it is necessary to point out the power of an antecedent/ response/ consequence contingency, and its ability to change behavior. Whether it happens by pure chance, or if someone designs the instruction intentionally, we all learn in this way.

In summary, operant conditioning is the process that is in effect any time a person's behavior changes due to a cause-and-effect relationship. It is safe to say that all operant behavior is learned behavior, with its future frequency influenced by consequences. The following scenario is a very common example of operant conditioning at work as a result of a somewhat accidental process:

Susan is learning to drive a car with a manual transmission. She gets into the car, turns the key and nothing happens. She puts her foot on the brake while turning the key, and nothing happens. While she is trying to start the car a third time, she inadvertently places her foot on the clutch, and the ignition begins to engage. Surprised, she takes her foot off of the clutch pedal and places it back on the brake. The ignition stops, and the car fails to start. She realizes that her foot on the clutch allowed the car to start, and she pushes in the clutch purposely while turning the key. The car starts, and she drives away. In all future instances, Susan pushes in the clutch pedal while turning the ignition key, and no longer has problems starting the car.

The following is a common example that pertains to many individuals with autism:

Christopher is a non-speaking two-year-old with autism. He is enjoying watching his favorite children's video when his mother turns it off. He is unhappy, but quietly stands by as the television screen goes blank. The next time he is watching the video and his mother is on her way to turn it off, and he accidentally falls off his chair and scrapes his knee. Startled and hurt, he begins to cry. His mother quickly diverts her attention from turning off the television and comes to his aid. He notices that the video remains on. Later that day, he is again watching the video. His mother approaches it to turn it off, and he purposely falls from his chair without crying. The video goes off. The next time the same scenario presents itself, Christopher stands up and cries. Fearing that he is again hurt, his mother abandons the television and comes to his aid – and again, the video remains on. On the very next occasion, Christopher cries in his chair as soon as his mother enters the room, and the video remains on. Through trial and error, Christopher has discovered that the video's termination may be postponed or avoided if he cries. In the future, he learns to cry every time he wants to avoid the termination of a preferred activity, and it becomes a problem for his family across environments.

In both of the above examples, there were several easily identifiable components of an operant conditioning process. Remember that operant conditioning is based on three categories of events: antecedent, response, and consequence. In both of these illustrations, all of the events were in place.

In Susan's case, the antecedent stimuli were the presence of the key, ignition and vehicle controls. The responses were her attempts to use the controls to start the car. The consequences were the non-starting, half-ignition and successful ignition of the car. Playing a large role in this process were the factors motivating her to drive the car. She would probably be more prone to shaping as it occurred if she were driving to cash a large check than if she were driving to the dentist for a root canal!

In Christopher's example, his mother's behavior of turning off the television (and later, her mere entrance into the room while the video was on), served as a stimulus. His falling and crying were the responses, in various combinations. The postponement of video termination was a consequence, and in one case the consequence was withheld.

The behavior in both examples was shaped through desired consequences for *successive approximations*. In other words, as the required behavior was approached (pushing the clutch or crying), Susan and Christopher were offered bits of what they were after, which led them to refine and repeat the behaviors.

Note that while operant conditioning includes consequential stimuli, it would not necessarily be accurate to claim that it is a consequence-based paradigm. While consequent stimuli are extremely important and hold a great deal of potential for behavior change, operant conditioning also relies on other components to account for the establishment of behaviors. There usually must be some form of motivation. There is also an antecedent stimulus for behavior. Additionally, we must look at the behavior itself, for it is very difficult to measure or classify behavior if we are not certain how it is performed. Finally, we pay close attention to the consequences that follow the behavior.

Now that we have a basic understanding of the contingencies involved in operant conditioning, we can begin to study each of the components more closely in following chapters. Please see Figure 4.3 for further illustration.

Figure 4.3

Operant Conditioning

1. Antecedent to behavior occurs
(Child is asked to walk to cafeteria)

2. Behavior occurs
(Child drops to the floor)

3. Consequence occurs

(a. Behavior is followed by verbal reprimand – told to "Stand up")

(b. Behavior is ignored – adult monitors child while casually talking to others)

(c. Behavior is followed by a physical assist to stand and walk to cafeteria)

Depending on the function of the behavior for the child and his/her particular learning history, each of these consequences could lead to one of the following:

- ❑ an increase in frequency of floor drop behavior
- ❑ a decrease in frequency of floor drop behavior
- ❑ no change in the frequency of floor drop behavior

Skinner's Legacy

Skinner's initial principles, the experimental work with laboratory animals that strengthened his assertions and the work of his predecessors all contributed to the foundation for an entire scientific field: behavior analysis. From this general field sprang two related but focally different disciplines: the experimental analysis of behavior (EAB), and **applied behavior analysis** (ABA).

The EAB field uses scientific principles to understand behavior as a measurable and somewhat predictable area of study. In EAB, scientists are concerned primarily with understanding and manipulating the external events surrounding behavior, for the sake of gaining understanding alone. In ABA, however, scientists are concerned primarily with the social implications associated with a scientific application of behavior analytic principles. Essentially, ABA is a social science that strives to improve the human condition through a natural science approach to human behavior. The generally accepted, "official" definition of ABA as derived from Baer, Wolf, and Risley (1968), and synthesized by Cooper et al. (1987) in the text *Applied Behavior Analysis* is as follows:

Applied behavior analysis is the science in which procedures derived from the principles of behavior are systematically applied to improve socially significant behavior to a meaningful degree and to demonstrate experimentally that the procedures employed were responsible for the improvement in behavior. (p. 14)

It is through ABA, namely the operant conditioning paradigm, that we can develop and measure replicable methodologies for producing meaningful change to important behavior. The impact of behavior analysis can be felt anywhere there is a need to increase behaviors (learning), and anywhere there is a need to reduce behaviors. It presents us with a tremendous opportunity to enhance the human condition. This opportunity, unfortunately, is seldom capitalized upon outside the fields of autism and other developmental disabilities. However, these fields have turned to ABA as a starting point for effective intervention, and the results that are encountered when such an approach is employed can be staggering.

Section D – Dimensions of Human Behavior

As a result of the information covered thus far, the reader should understand that children with autism exhibit many behaviors that are worth tracking and shaping, including desired behaviors and inappropriate behaviors. The next step of the journey is to delve into the **dimensions** of human behavior.

When building a structure, contractors are concerned with the precision of the building's dimensions, including length, width, height, etc. In the same way, bakers and chefs are concerned with the dimensional qualities of their products, using volume (cups, teaspoons) or weight (ounces). In fact, any field that requires precision or adherence to specific procedures requires the establishment of dimensional properties. The same holds true for any field concerned with measuring results or products.

Behavior analysis is definitely a field in which measurement is important. When we identify dimensions of behavior, it allows us to apply scientific principles that stem from observation. When we quantify behavior, it teaches us more about it before we intervene, shows us exactly how we should intervene and reveals what the effects of our intervention are. And when we clearly define parameters, we're able to eliminate some of the guesswork often associated with observing and recording behaviors.

Dimensional Qualities Identified

Now that we've described the need to establish dimensional qualities within a study of behavior, let's take a look at the dimensional qualities themselves. First, it is important to understand that behavior is most effectively quantified if we realize that it has what behavior analysts refer to as a **"temporal locus."** In other words, behavior is something that happens with regard to a particular point in time (temporal = pertaining to time; locus = center of concentration or focus). Many of the dimensional properties associated with behavior have to do with time.

Additionally, since we know that behavior is the interaction of an organism and the environment, we also know that behavior, by definition, involves movement of some sort. It is difficult, if not impossible to identify any interactive relationship between an organism and its environment that does not involve movement. For this reason, we often use the term **"movement cycle"** as a way to specifically identify a behavior.

When we define a behavior targeted for observation or measurement, we must identify the places where it begins and ends. The starting point, the end and everything in between comprise the movement cycle of the behavior. Take, for example, the behavior of blinking. We can say that the movement cycle begins with the downward motion of the eyelid, continues through the actual closure of the eyelid, and ends with the return of the eyelid to its starting position. By this definition, one movement cycle has been completed.

This understanding of behavior as having a basis in time and being comprised of movement cycles gives us a point from which we can look more closely at specific dimensions.

One of the most common dimensions used to quantify behavior is that of **frequency**, or the number of times a behavior occurs within a given period of time. Common applications of frequency tracking include development and monitoring of behavior plans, gathering baseline information, or almost any scenario in which extremely basic data are sufficient.

Another dimension of behavior directly related to temporal locus (position in time) is **duration**. The duration of a behavior refers to the amount of time that passes between the beginning and end of any movement cycle. This type of information is useful across many scenarios – think of all of the times that it is important to know how long a behavior lasts. Some applications indicate a desire for very short duration (length of "tantrum" behaviors, for example), while other applications are identified with a desire to increase duration (such as length of time engaged in academic tasks).

Latency is associated with the length of time that passes between an antecedent stimulus and the beginning of the behavior's movement cycle. For example, if someone asks a customer assistance representative at a local hardware store where they can find duct tape, and the representative thinks for 10 seconds before answering, the latency between question and response is 10 seconds. Latency is a useful dimension when looking at the functionality or fluency of a particular behavior. Typically, the more established a behavior is in someone's repertoire, the lower the latency between antecedent stimuli and display of the behavior. Conversely, behavioral repertoires that are not as well established tend to be marked by increased latency between stimulus and response.

Latency is a useful dimension to measure when ascertaining skill competency (such as how long it takes to answer a given math problem), or when looking at the strength of particular inappropriate behaviors (such as how quickly a problem behavior occurs following a demand).

Another dimension of behavior is that of **inter-response time**. This refers to the length of time between the end of one movement cycle and the beginning of another. An example of this dimension comes from watching and tracking sneezing behavior in an individual. The inter-response time, or **IRT**, is the length of time between one sneeze and the beginning of another. Obviously, this dimension can be applied to any behavior, especially those that occur often. Inter-response time can sometimes be correlated to the strength of a behavior, because behaviors that occur in succession with little time in between are often fairly well established.

Rate is another extremely significant dimension of behavior that has many applications – in fact, frequency and rate are perhaps the two most commonly measured and recorded dimensions of behavior within the field. Rate simply refers to the frequency of a behavior divided by a unit of time. The basic formula for determining rate is $R = F/T$, *where* R = *rate*, F = *frequency, and* T = *time.* For example, if a person stomps his or her feet 36 times in the course of 12 minutes, the rate of foot-stomping would be three times per minute. Keep in mind that "responses per minute" is only one way to express rate, which can actually be calculated based on any defined unit of time.

It is important to note that, while rate is derived using frequency, it differs from frequency alone. In the above example, the frequency of the behavior during the observation period was 36. The rate also took into account the unit of time that was chosen, and the response per minute figure was then generated.

A final, significant dimension that is less often a focus is **celeration**. This is concerned primarily with fluency, or the ability for a skill to be repeated with accuracy, speed, endurance and stability. In the simplest terms, celeration is the measurement of rate per session, against calendar days. This measurement allows us to determine if there is an increase (celeration) or a decrease (deceleration) in rate of responding. For simple rate derivation, the $R = F/T$ equation given above is applied. Behaviors with higher celeration (acquired more quickly) are usually said to be more fluent. Accordingly, behaviors with lower celeration are found to be less fluent. Later chapters will discuss fluency in much greater detail.

Celeration data can be extremely useful for making decisions regarding instructional methodologies. Because this data shows how quickly behaviors are acquired, they are an excellent source of information to determine the efficacy of a particular intervention.

"Everyday" Examples of the Dimensions of Behavior

Frequency	Duration	Latency	Rate	IRT
- The number of times you used profanity while driving to work this morning. - The number of cups of coffee you drank today.	- The time you spent at work today. - How long you stayed on the treadmill.	- The time it takes between the light turning green and your foot depressing the accelerator. - The time it takes for you to answer the telephone.	- The number of days per week that you go to the gym. - The number of sick days that you use each calendar year.	- The length of time between phone calls to your mother. - The length of time between snacks.

A Final Note

"Human behavior" encompasses almost all that we do. When working with children with autism, we must become experts on the topic of behavior. Our understanding of the mechanics of behavior helps us make better sense of the behaviors we see in others, and improves our ability to have an impact on those behaviors. This understanding also puts us in a better position to teach new skills (there are ***many*** skills to teach a learner with autism) and reduce problematic behaviors.

Know that the majority of our focus in autism intervention is on voluntary behaviors. Because of this, we will be discussing techniques related to operant conditioning throughout most of the book. If you can understand and apply the basic principles of operant conditioning, you will be an effective interactive partner for a learner with autism.

Pay great attention to the fact that we are encouraging a natural science approach to behavior. Like all natural sciences, behavior is ideal for observation, measurement, and quantification. Observing and discussing behavior with regard to the dimensions and qualities we described in this chapter will make you more sensitive to the roles that environmental factors play in a child's behavior. It will also make you more aware of the types of environmental conditions that might be at play.

The bottom line? We want to take some of the perceived mystery out of human behavior, so that you can be empowered to make minute-to-minute decisions that will ultimately help the children with whom you work.

References:

Baer, D.M., Wolf, M.M., & Risley, T.R. (1968). Some current dimensions of applied behavior analysis. *Journal of Applied Behavior Analysis*, 1, 91-97.

Cooper, J. O., Heron, T. E., & Heward, W.L. (1987). *Applied behavior analysis.* Upper Saddle River: Prentice-Hall.

Johnston, J.M., & Pennypacker, H.S. (1980). *Strategies and tactics of human behavioral research.* Hillsdale: Lawrence Erlbaum Associates.

Merriam Webster Online Dictionary – http://www.webster.com/cgi-bin/dictionary?book=Dictionary&va=stimulus.

Pavlov, I. P. (1960). *Conditioned reflexes* (G. V. Anrep, Trans.). New York: Dover. (Original work published 1927).

Pennypacker, H. S., Koenig, C. H., & Lindsley, O. R. (1972). *Handbook of the standard behavior chart.* Kansas City, KS: Precision Media.

Skinner, B.F. (1938). *The behavior of organisms: An experimental analysis.* New York: Appleton-Century-Crofts.

Measurement of Behavior At a Glance

Chapter Points

- Measurement of behavior allows us to know if we are being effective.
- Measurement of behavior depends on a precise operational definition of the target behavior.
- Data collection tools differ according to the dimension being measured.
- Data should be collected systematically.
- In order for data to be most effectively utilized, they must be considered in relation to time and the child's opportunity to respond.

Key Terms

Baseline

Operational Definition

Pinpoint

Response Topography

Event Recording

Whole Interval Recording

Partial Interval Recording

Probe

Line Graph

Rate

Free Operant

Restricted Operant

Percentage Correct

Probe Data

Measurement of Behavior

Thus far, we have developed the idea that both learning behaviors and maladaptive behaviors are subject to observation and analysis. Our next task is to understand how to analyze behavior so that we can become agents of change.

This chapter deals with measurement, which is the first step in developing a strategic plan for changing behavior. We know that behavior can be characterized by properties with measurable dimensions, such as duration, frequency, rate, celeration, inter-response time, and latency. We must learn how to determine the values of these properties, quantify them, record them, and analyze the resulting data – as efficiently as possible.

That is the purpose of this chapter. In it, the reader will learn methods for pinpointing behavior and ways to identify relevant dimensions for data collection. We also include a sampling of effective tools for data collection.

The Need for Measurement

Why is it important to apply systems of measurement to human behavior? Measurement allows us to identify needs, establish performance markers, and know whether or not interventions have been effective. Individuals with autism and other developmental disorders possess very complex behavioral repertoires, some of which we would like to increase (communicative, social, and cognitive skills), and some of which we would like to decrease (maladaptive or problematic behaviors that impede progress or inclusion).

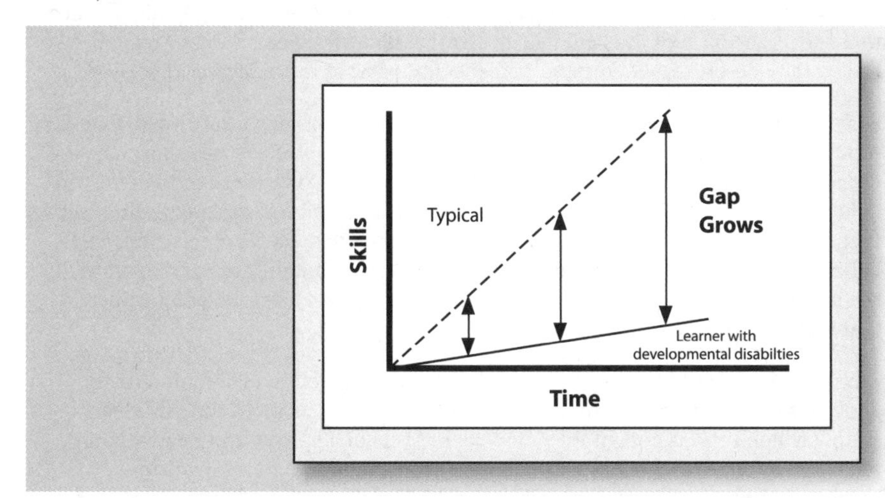

Figure 5.1

Because of the general nature of these individuals' learning differences, they frequently do not learn necessary skills without explicit instruction. To understand a typical individual's learning trajectory, imagine a moderate slope (Figure 5.1) consisting of a 45° line drawn between a horizontal (x) and vertical (y) axis. The horizontal axis represents passage of time, and the vertical axis represents the acquisition of skills.

An individual with a less efficient or slower learning history will have a learning trajectory that is more gradual. Both trajectories begin at the same point, but over time, the space between the steeper and gradual slopes grows larger until it is nearly impossible to bridge. The result – an enormous amount of skill building to accomplish, and a very limited timeframe in which it can be achieved – means that the methods we use *have* to be as efficient and effective as possible.

Measurement helps us know if we're succeeding. By knowing how often a behavior occurs (desired or not), we can decide whether intervention is necessary. Measurement also provides a clear picture of how often the behavior occurs before we select and implement an intervention.

Regardless of the type of data we collect, we must start with a **baseline**, or the overall trend or level of the behavior prior to any changes being made. After a change, the behavior will increase, decrease, or remain the same, which will be reflected in the next set of data. By comparing the new data with the baseline, we can know if the selected intervention is worth continuing or if it must be changed.

Pinpointing Behavior

Pinpointing behavior is also referred to as developing an **operational definition** that identifies and describes all of the components of a particular behavior's movement cycle. In other words, it gives the observer a very clear picture of what a behavior "looks like" as it is occurring.

This helps answer the critical question: "How will this behavior be counted?" Operational definitions or behavior **pinpoints** allow us to objectify the behavior so that everyone who observes it can agree or disagree on whether or not it occurred, how long it took to begin, how long it endured, etc. Once you have established a solid definition that is clear to everyone, you can begin to count the behavior for the purpose of establishing a baseline.

How a behavior is actually carried out by a person is known as the behavior's **response topography**. To make this clearer, think in terms of a topographical map that shows the form of the land in a given area. Likewise, behavioral or response topography describes the form of the behavior, or what the behavior looks like.

Developing a behavioral pinpoint is the first step in identifying a specific response topography, and using it to count or measure occurrences of the behavior. When doing so, it is important to avoid the trap of using nouns or adjectives to define the behavior. Instead, think in terms of verbs that best describe it, and focus upon action verbs, or verbs that involve some type of physical movement. There certainly are behaviors that do not meet the physical action verb definition, such as "thinking," but almost all behaviors we are concerned with involve some type of movement within the environment.

Using observable actions as descriptors within our operational definitions also allows us to identify the beginning of a behavior, as well as its ending. By clearly stating which actions constitute a movement cycle of a behavior, we can reliably tell whether or not it is occurring, according to its definition. This leads to measurements of frequency, duration, and the like.

Identifying Components of Behavior

Developing procedures for environment-based behavior changes requires a systematic approach, beginning with a solid operational definition of the behavior(s) of concern. When doing so, the following should be kept in mind:

Defining Behavior

Examples of behaviors that can be observed and measured:	**Examples of terms that do not lend themselves to measurement without further elaboration:**
Writing Speaking Hitting Pushing	Knowing Having a "bad attitude" Being upset Respecting

Example of a precise operational definition:

Hitting – striking another with a closed fist or open hand, with enough force to be audible.

- It is important to identify all components of a behavior, and to do this with relative precision.
- When some behaviors are defined, they must take dimensional properties into account.
- Some behaviors targeted for change may be much more complex than a simple, single response. In this case, the "behavior" that must be pinpointed is actually a constellation of behaviors, or a "response class" of behaviors that differ somewhat in topography but serve the same function.

In the latter case, the differences are sometimes slight enough, or occur within close enough proximity to one another, that they should be counted as a single event. In these instances, it is necessary to define all of the particular movement cycles that comprise the larger movement cycle.

Take, for example, the behavior known as a "tantrum." The noun "tantrum" represents a variety of topographies to observers – rarely can one be described as a simple event with only one movement cycle involved. To pinpoint the behavior, all components that are applicable to the individual case must be included in the definition.

The following *might* be an operational definition for tantrum behavior: "Vocal protests above conversational volume that endure beyond five consecutive seconds, accompanied by crying (tearing of the eyes), and possibly accompanied by banging of feet or hands at audible levels against stationary objects." Notice that several discrete behaviors are included in the above definition (vocal protests, crying, and feet/hand banging). Also note that the dimensions of duration (five consecutive seconds) and magnitude (above conversational volume, at audible levels) are necessary components in the definition.

People often encounter problems when they try to define a target behavior using ambiguous or subjective terms. When this type of mistake is made, we can often place the root of the problem at the failure to focus upon action words and physical descriptions of the behavior of concern.

Consider the following example: "I want Robert to be respectful to his teachers more often." In this case, the target behavior (being respectful) is very poorly defined. What exactly does "respectful" mean? Given cultural, familial, and individual differences, the term can mean many things to many people. This makes it next to impossible to come to agreement on what behaviors constitute respect without further explanation.

Additionally, no movement cycle has been identified, so there is no way to tell when such behaviors begin to occur. Is it a certain type of look from Robert toward his teachers? Does it begin with a verbal response that is viewed unfavorably? Clearly, this type of definition leaves much to the interpretation of the observer, and is next to useless for any kind of accurate measurement of behavior.

A more precise definition of the behaviors that indicate "respect" could include the specific types of physical or verbal behavior that Robert tends to engage in during these times. For example, "Robert will speak using a conversational volume (you could include a decibel measurement for magnitude if you want to be *very* specific!)," or "Robert will turn to face adults and make eye contact with them within two seconds of adult conversation initiation," or even "Robert will initiate compliance with instructional requests within five seconds of their delivery by a supervising adult."

Regardless of which definition is selected for behaviors previously defined in subjective terms, make sure that the definition is precise enough that anybody who reads it or anybody who might be responsible for tracking the behavior or analyzing the data knows exactly what they are looking for.

Section A – Measurement of Frequency

The **frequency** of a behavior, as previously defined, refers to its occurrence or non-occurrence in a given period of time. This can be a single observation session

Figure 5.2

*** Daily Behavioral Record ***

Name:_______________

Target Behavior(s) *Operational Definition*	Date_____ **Monday**	Date_____ **Tuesday**	Date_____ **Wednesday**	Date_____ **Thursday**	Date_____ **Friday**	
	Daily total:_____	Daily total:_____	Daily total:_____	Daily total:_____	Daily total:_____	weekly total:_____
	Daily total:_____	Daily total:_____	Daily total:_____	Daily total:_____	Daily total:_____	weekly total:_____
	Daily total:_____	Daily total:_____	Daily total:_____	Daily total:_____	Daily total:_____	weekly total:_____

consisting of only a few seconds, or it can be an ongoing period in which the behavior is continually tracked. Frequency is one of the most basic, yet most significant dimensions of any behavior, and it is the dimension that is measured most often in behavior analysis. If we know how many times the behavior occurs in given situations, we can determine baseline rates, effects of intervention, and progress/regression.

Figure 5.3

Behavior Frequency Data Collection Form

Name ______________________________

Date	/ /	/ /	/ /	/ /	/ /	
	Monday	**Tuesday**	**Wednesday**	**Thursday**	**Friday**	
43	O	O	O	O	O	43
42	O	O	O	O	O	42
41	O	O	O	O	O	41
40	O	O	O	O	O	40
39	O	O	O	O	O	39
38	O	O	O	O	O	38
37	O	O	O	O	O	37
36	O	O	O	O	O	36
35	O	O	O	O	O	35
34	O	O	O	O	O	34
33	O	O	O	O	O	33
32	O	O	O	O	O	32
31	O	O	O	O	O	31
30	O	O	O	O	O	30
29	O	O	O	O	O	29
28	O	O	O	O	O	28
27	O	O	O	O	O	27
26	O	O	O	O	O	26
25	O	O	O	O	O	25
24	O	O	O	O	O	24
23	O	O	O	O	O	23
22	O	O	O	O	O	22
21	O	O	O	O	O	21
20	O	O	O	O	O	20
19	O	O	O	O	O	19
18	O	O	O	O	O	18
17	O	O	O	O	O	17
16	O	O	O	O	O	16
15	O	O	O	O	O	15
14	O	O	O	O	O	14
13	O	O	O	O	O	13
12	O	O	O	O	O	12
11	O	O	O	O	O	11
10	O	O	O	O	O	10
9	O	O	O	O	O	9
8	O	O	O	O	O	8
7	O	O	O	O	O	7
6	O	O	O	O	O	6
5	O	O	O	O	O	5
4	O	O	O	O	O	4
3	O	O	O	O	O	3
2	O	O	O	O	O	2
1	O	O	O	O	O	1

Target behavior ______________________________

Recording the actual occurrence of a behavior is known as **event recording**, which allows us to tell in various ways how often or seldom a behavior occurs. The measurement of frequency is just one way in which event recording is utilized.

Figure 5.4

Frequency data are usually relatively easy to obtain, but there can be complications when the behavior in question occurs at extremely high rates. As a result, there must be flexibility in behavior measurement technology to allow for tracking the occurrence of behaviors that happen very frequently or very seldom.

Once a precise definition of a behavior is established, the simplest method to measure its frequency is a simple tally count. Any of a number of data collection forms can be used to help track the number of occurrences – from placing a simple tally mark to checking off or coloring in circles each time a behavior occurs (see Figures 5.2 and 5.3).

If the behavior happens so frequently there is no time to mark a sheet, several other options are available. One popular method is to employ tally counters, or mechanical devices that allow each occurrence of the behavior to be recorded with the simple push of a button (Figure 5.4).

It is important to note that these measurement tools are only effective if the target behavior's frequency and the environment in which it occurs allow each individual occurrence to be counted. Sometimes, behaviors occur with such high frequency that it is difficult to obtain accurate data. In these cases, it is still necessary to measure the occurrence of the behavior, and event recording is still a viable way to do this. Simple frequency counts will not work, however, so other forms of event recording must be utilized.

Section B – Interval Recording

Interval recording refers to recording a behavior during a pre-set time period. As opposed to counting the behavior itself, interval recording counts the number of intervals in which the behavior occurs. While less precise than frequency recording, it is a way to gather event data that can be used to infer information related to frequency.

When utilizing interval recording, a pre-set observation time, or interval, is established. During the interval, the observer looks for the target behavior, and records whether or not it occurred. Behavior analysts are concerned with two types of interval data: **whole interval data and partial interval data**. Each of these data collection systems has its advantages and disadvantages, as well as specific situations where they may or may not be useful.

To use whole interval measurement, the observer records the number of times the behavior occurred repeatedly throughout the entire interval. The following example demonstrates this concept.

For "tantrum" behaviors tracked via this method (with "tantrum" clearly and precisely defined prior to data collection), the observation intervals may be set up to consist of consecutive five-minute[1] periods. In other words, every five minutes, the

[1] Interval length may range from seconds to hours. Length depends on the purposes of the data collection (e.g. day-to-day tracking vs. clinical research), and the level of precision desired or feasible.

observer must record whether the target behavior occurs, or does not. In the whole interval scenario, the observer only scores an interval if the target behavior occurs for the *entire* interval. However, if the behavior occurs for only a portion of the interval, that interval is not scored.

There are several ways to collect data when utilizing interval recording. First, a simple chart can be developed in which there are cells for marking the target behaviors, and cells for identifying the interval (Figures 5.5 and 5.6). Additionally, a form can record intervals based on time of day (Figure 5.7). On this type of form, the same recording rules apply: only boxes in which the target behavior occurs continuously from beginning to end of the interval are recorded.

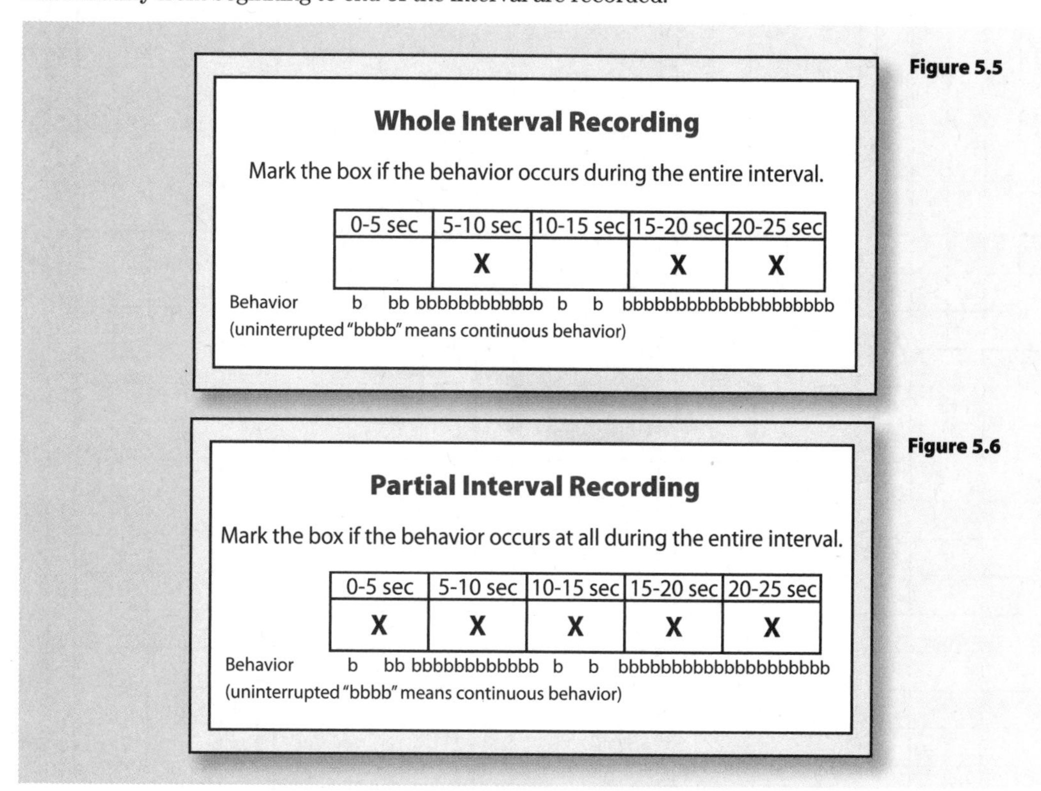

Whole Interval Recording

Mark the box if the behavior occurs during the entire interval.

0-5 sec	5-10 sec	10-15 sec	15-20 sec	20-25 sec
	X		X	X

Behavior b bb bbbbbbbbbbbb b b bbbbbbbbbbbbbbbbbbbb
(uninterrupted "bbbb" means continuous behavior)

Figure 5.5

Partial Interval Recording

Mark the box if the behavior occurs at all during the entire interval.

0-5 sec	5-10 sec	10-15 sec	15-20 sec	20-25 sec
X	X	X	X	X

Behavior b bb bbbbbbbbbbbb b b bbbbbbbbbbbbbbbbbbbb
(uninterrupted "bbbb" means continuous behavior)

Figure 5.6

Whole interval recording can be extremely useful when tracking behaviors you would like to see increase. This is primarily due to the fact that the behavior must occur at a greater frequency, rate, or duration in order to be recorded. If this type of measurement indicates an increase in behavior, the increase is likely to be significant. Whole interval recording is also recommended for behaviors for which duration is a significant dimension.

A potential drawback with whole interval recording is the possibility that significant behaviors may be "missed" because they do not continue throughout the entire interval, and are not recorded. As a result, whole interval recording tends to *underestimate* the occurrence of the behavior being measured.

Partial interval recording is very similar to whole interval recording, and the same data collection forms can be used. Where it differs is in the criteria for scoring. In partial interval recording, the behavior can occur at any point during the course of the interval for it to be scored as one in which the behavior occurred. Figure 5.6 shows an example scored according to partial interval data.

Name ____________________

Time Interval Data Form

Date:	Monday					Tuesday					Wednesday					Thursday					Friday				
Mark the box if the behavior occurs *Interval:*	*Aggression*					*Aggression*					*Aggression*					*Aggression*					*Aggression*				
8:30-8:45																									
8:45-9:00																									
9:00-9:15																									
9:15-9:30																									
9:30-9:45																									
9:45-10:00																									
10:00-10:15																									
10:15-10:30																									
10:30-10:45																									
10:45-11:00																									
11:00-11:15																									
11:15-11:30																									
11:30-11:45																									
11:45-12:00																									
12:00-12:15																									
12:15-12:30																									
12:30-12:45																									
12:45-1:00																									
1:00-1:15																									
1:15-1:30																									
1:30-1:45																									
1:45-2:00																									
2:00-2:15																									
2:15-2:30																									
2:30-2:45																									
2:45-3:00																									
3:00-3:15																									
3:15-3:30																									

Figure 5.7

Partial interval recording can be very useful in tracking behaviors that are targeted for reduction, because the interval is scored even if the behavior occurs only once within the interval. If partial interval data show a reduction in target behaviors, it is likely that the reduction is significant.

One of the obvious drawbacks of partial interval recording is the diminished precision that it shares with whole interval recording. Two intervals can be scored identically, even though the frequency of target behavior in one interval was much higher than that in another interval. Just as whole interval recording tends to underestimate the occurrence of behavior, partial interval recording tends to *overestimate* it. On a positive note, although partial and whole interval recording include error, they are often sensitive enough to detect change.

Section C – Measurement of Duration

When measuring duration, we are simply recording the length of time it takes for a movement cycle to be completed. Some behaviors, such as academic, "on-task" behaviors, lend themselves well to duration measurement, as do inappropriate behaviors (like tantrums). In the case of the tantrum behaviors, it is not uncommon to see either:

- a decrease in frequency but increase in the duration, or
- an increase in frequency but a decrease in the duration of the behaviors involved.

When the first occurs, it may appear as if the behavior is improving, when in fact its duration might actually indicate a regression. In the second example, increases in the frequency might lead an analyst to conclude that the behavior is getting worse, but the decrease in duration might actually represent an overall improvement. Please note that with complex chains of behavior like tantrums, the duration might include the time it takes for all of the behaviors within the chain to progress through their movement cycles.

Duration is recorded in several ways. The most common is a simple duration-per-occurrence collection. In this method, the duration of each individual occurrence of the behavior is documented by noting the time it began and stopped. Duration is then determined by calculating the time units between the two points.

There are also times when we are interested in total duration, or a sum of the times for each occurrence of the behavior within a specific period of time. Average or mean measures of duration are also sometimes helpful. These data can be tracked or recorded on any form that helps to organize the information in an efficient and easy-to-use format. A sample data sheet for recording simple duration appears in Figure 5.8. Figure 5.9 shows a data collection form in which more complex duration data can be collected.

Section D – Latency Measurement

As the previous chapter described, **latency** is the measurement of time between the appearance, presence, or presentation of a stimulus and a particular response. Low or reduced response latency is generally associated with skill fluency: the stronger a skill is established in a person's repertoire, the quicker they will respond. Conversely, high or increased response latency signifies the passage of more time between the stimulus and the response. Increased latency is generally associated with a weaker establishment of skills within a repertoire or with the presence of other variables – usually related to compliance or motivational factors.

Since latency can be a helpful dimension in determining the strength of a particular behavior (appropriate or inappropriate), it is important to have systems for measurement available. Any table that includes when the stimulus occurred and when the response was initiated will help organize information. It may also be helpful to record average or mean rates of response latency, similar to duration recording.

Figure 5.8

Name: ______________________

Behavior: ______________________

Date:	/ /	/ /	/ /
1	Start:	Start:	Start:
	Stop:	Stop:	Stop:
	Duration:	Duration:	Duration:
2	Start:	Start:	Start:
	Stop:	Stop:	Stop:
	Duration:	Duration:	Duration:
3	Start:	Start:	Start:
	Stop:	Stop:	Stop:
	Duration:	Duration:	Duration:
4	Start:	Start:	Start:
	Stop:	Stop:	Stop:
	Duration:	Duration:	Duration:
5	Start:	Start:	Start:
	Stop:	Stop:	Stop:
	Duration:	Duration:	Duration:
6	Start:	Start:	Start:
	Stop:	Stop:	Stop:
	Duration:	Duration:	Duration:
7	Start:	Start:	Start:
	Stop:	Stop:	Stop:
	Duration:	Duration:	Duration:
8	Start:	Start:	Start:
	Stop:	Stop:	Stop:
	Duration:	Duration:	Duration:
9	Start:	Start:	Start:
	Stop:	Stop:	Stop:
	Duration:	Duration:	Duration:
10	Start:	Start:	Start:
	Stop:	Stop:	Stop:
	Duration:	Duration:	Duration:

Accuracy Data

Response topography, or the actual form of the behavior itself, is also considered a dimension of human behavior. There are times when we are solely interested in the accuracy of a response, or the ability for a response to be carried out in a manner that meets specific criteria. When we look at a skill such as handwriting, or if we examine verbal repertoires concerning a particular subject matter (e.g., essay tests), we are concerned primarily with whether or not the behavior emitted meets the criteria we have established. As long as an operational definition of the behavior in question has been established, there are many ways by which we can measure learner performance.

Accuracy of topographic data is most often associated with skill acquisition, such as grading in school, or to mark progress in learning programs. An example of accuracy data collection would include counting the number of times, out of 10 opportunities, that a student correctly identifies a named object. Another example would be determining the number of correctly completed steps in a seven-step hand-washing program.

While there are no hard-and-fast rules for topography data, some guidelines apply. First, the criteria must be as precisely defined as any other target behavior. If a stranger to the situation can understand exactly what to look for, the criteria are clear. Second, a determination should be made whether the data will be analyzed in terms of percentage correct or rate of response. (This second point will be elaborated on when we discuss data analysis later in this chapter.)

Accuracy data can be collected as "**probes**," or simple tests that are conducted without teaching or prompting immediately preceding the test. In many instances, probe data have been found to be more accurate indicators of skill mastery than data collected immediately following prompting or instruction. Probes test the endurance of the skill, which is a key component of fluency.

Figure 5.9

Name: ______________________

Behavior: ______________________

Date:

	Start:	Start:	Start:	Start:	Number of occurences
	Stop:	Stop:	Stop:	Stop:	Total duration:
	Duration:	Duration:	Duration:	Duration:	Average duration:
	Start:	Start:	Start:	Start:	Number of occurences
	Stop:	Stop:	Stop:	Stop:	Total duration:
	Duration:	Duration:	Duration:	Duration:	Average duration:
	Start:	Start:	Start:	Start:	Number of occurences
	Stop:	Stop:	Stop:	Stop:	Total duration:
	Duration:	Duration:	Duration:	Duration:	Average duration:
	Start:	Start:	Start:	Start:	Number of occurences
	Stop:	Stop:	Stop:	Stop:	Total duration:
	Duration:	Duration:	Duration:	Duration:	Average duration:
	Start:	Start:	Start:	Start:	Number of occurences
	Stop:	Stop:	Stop:	Stop:	Total duration:
	Duration:	Duration:	Duration:	Duration:	Average duration:
	Start:	Start:	Start:	Start:	Number of occurences
	Stop:	Stop:	Stop:	Stop:	Total duration:
	Duration:	Duration:	Duration:	Duration:	Average duration:
	Start:	Start:	Start:	Start:	Number of occurences
	Stop:	Stop:	Stop:	Stop:	Total duration:
	Duration:	Duration:	Duration:	Duration:	Average duration:
	Start:	Start:	Start:	Start:	Number of occurences
	Stop:	Stop:	Stop:	Stop:	Total duration:
	Duration:	Duration:	Duration:	Duration:	Average duration:
	Start:	Start:	Start:	Start:	Number of occurences
	Stop:	Stop:	Stop:	Stop:	Total duration:
	Duration:	Duration:	Duration:	Duration:	Average duration:
	Start:	Start:	Start:	Start:	Number of occurences
	Stop:	Stop:	Stop:	Stop:	Total duration:
	Duration:	Duration:	Duration:	Duration:	Average duration:
	Start:	Start:	Start:	Start:	Number of occurences
	Stop:	Stop:	Stop:	Stop:	Total duration:
	Duration:	Duration:	Duration:	Duration:	Average duration:
	Start:	Start:	Start:	Start:	Number of occurences
	Stop:	Stop:	Stop:	Stop:	Total duration:
	Duration:	Duration:	Duration:	Duration:	Average duration:
	Start:	Start:	Start:	Start:	Number of occurences
	Stop:	Stop:	Stop:	Stop:	Total duration:
	Duration:	Duration:	Duration:	Duration:	Average duration:
	Start:	Start:	Start:	Start:	Number of occurences
	Stop:	Stop:	Stop:	Stop:	Total duration:
	Duration:	Duration:	Duration:	Duration:	Average duration:
	Start:	Start:	Start:	Start:	Number of occurences
	Stop:	Stop:	Stop:	Stop:	Total duration:
	Duration:	Duration:	Duration:	Duration:	Average duration:

Section E – Graphic Representation of Behavioral Data

Visual analysis, as opposed to statistical analysis, is a hallmark of applied behavior analysis. Almost every significant aspect of the effects of intervention can be analyzed by looking at a graphic display of the data. For this reason, all behavioral data eventually should be compiled into a graphic representation. There are many particular conventions associated with proper graphing of behavioral data; however, the goal of this manual is to simply introduce the reader to this important component of behavior measurement.

The most common type of graphic display utilized with behavior analysis is the **line graph**. These graphs consist of two axes that represent time and behaviors, a set of data points, and a data path drawn between them. Line graphs make it possible to quickly assess behaviors and interventions with precision. Trends become readily apparent, and an immediate, lasting, and easily accessible record is available at a glance.

Any behavior can be graphed, including adaptive behaviors that are taught, as well as maladaptive behaviors targeted for elimination. When constructing a behavioral graph, care should be taken to ensure that the dimension of behavior depicted is represented by the vertical axis, and that time (days or sessions) is represented by the horizontal axis. Also included on any well-constructed graph is a legend that briefly explains what the symbols on the graph represent. Phase or condition change lines, which indicate changes in intervention, are included, as well as labels describing the axes, baseline, and treatment conditions and the general title of the graph. Sample graphs are reproduced in Figures 5.10 and 5.11. (A more detailed discussion on the visual analysis of data is contained in Chapter 8.)

Figure 5.10

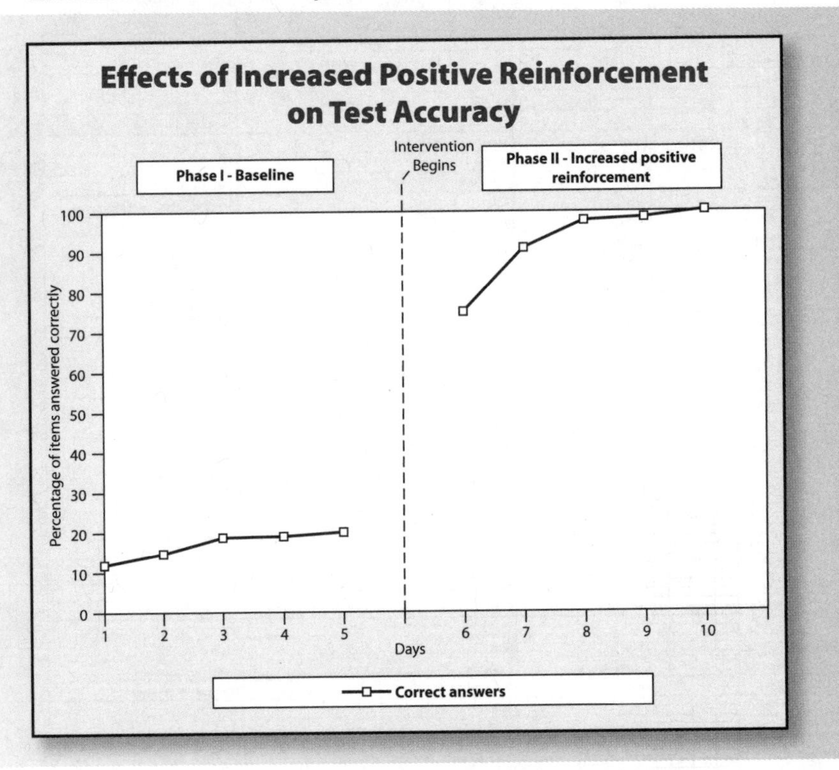

Data Analysis

Data, in their raw form, do not immediately provide us with the kind of meaningful information necessary to make decisions about effective behavioral treatment. In this basic state, data are quite often just a string of numbers that might, for example, relate to the frequency, latency, or duration of a particular target behavior. These individual numbers only describe something about the target behavior at a specific moment in time, without relating it to its environmental context – leaving us with only one piece of a much larger puzzle.

To be useful, data must be considered in relation to time and the individual's opportunity to respond. Simply saying that a child made 20 correct verbal responses, for example, tells us very little. Did it take him five minutes, or 20? In the same way, merely stating that a student spelled 10 words correctly is rather incomplete unless we are made aware of the total number of words presented on the spelling test.

How data are analyzed forms the critical next step in the measurement of behavior. Historically, behavior analysts have utilized three units of conversion to complete this analysis: frequency, rate, and percentage (Cooper et al., 1987). All other dimensions of behavior must be converted into these units if we want to effectively discuss them. An example of this is latency data based on a child's response to his teacher's instruction, collected per opportunity. Taken alone, in its raw form, this data might look something like this:

5 seconds
7 seconds
12 seconds
2 seconds
7 seconds
15 seconds

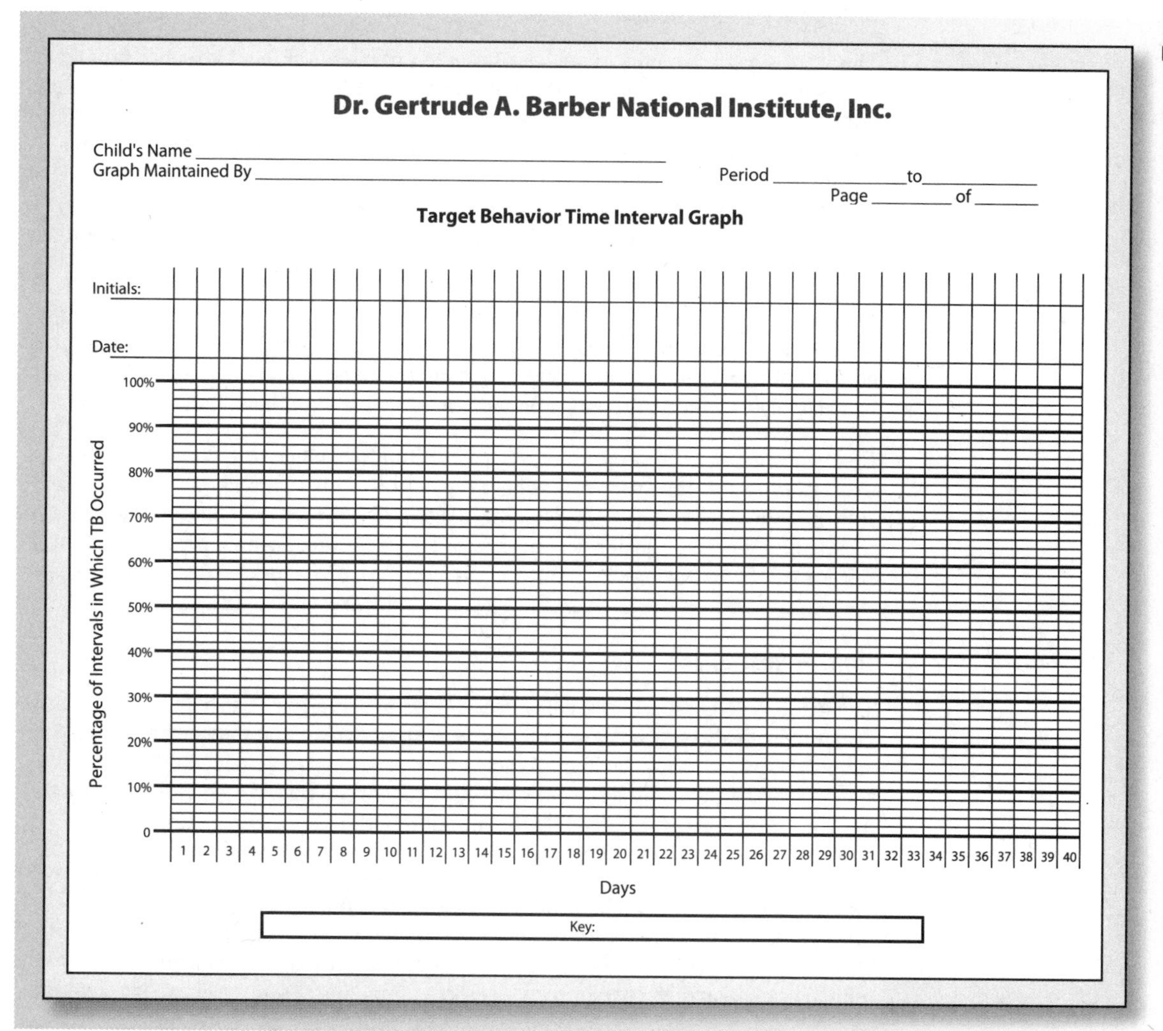

Dr. Gertrude A. Barber National Institute, Inc.

Child's Name ______________________________
Graph Maintained By ______________________________ Period __________ to __________
Page ______ of ______

Target Behavior Time Interval Graph

Initials:

Date:

Percentage of Intervals in Which TB Occurred: 100%, 90%, 80%, 70%, 60%, 50%, 40%, 30%, 20%, 10%, 0

Days: 1 2 3 4 5 6 7 8 9 10 11 12 13 14 15 16 17 18 19 20 21 22 23 24 25 26 27 28 29 30 31 32 33 34 35 36 37 38 39 40

Key:

Figure 5.11

To become useful, these data must be converted into units that relate to time or opportunity. This may involve adding up the total number of seconds, and then dividing that number by the total number of opportunities to respond that occurred during the observation period. In this example, such a calculation would yield an average latency of 6.2 seconds (37 total seconds divided by the six opportunities).

A slightly different approach would compare the child's responses over time to the class norm of five-second latency between teacher directive and child response. One way to analyze the data would be to take the total number of responses at or below the norm, then divide it by the total number of opportunities. Multiplying that quotient by 100 would yield a percentage correct figure of 33 percent. (In the example, two of the six recorded responses were at or below the five-second norm: 2 ÷ 6 = 0.33 x 100 = 33%.)

In both cases, the data were converted so that they could be expressed in terms of time or a percentage of opportunities. This allows us to compare the child's performance over time and within the context of the observational sessions. With this more complete analysis, we are in a better position to develop effective treatment and measure success over time.

Frequency of Response

There are several benefits of analysis based on frequency. First, frequency counts are relatively quick and easy to do. They do not significantly interfere with teaching, nor do they seriously impede the parent or caregiver from running the household if data collection is occurring at home. Second, when it becomes necessary to track a student's errors, a frequency-based analysis can be directed toward the counting of incorrect responses. Finally, an analysis of behavior based on frequency is very easy for both the child and the parent to understand. Even a fairly young student understands when he is told that he got "seven right" or "three wrong."

Frequency-based analyses are well suited for comparisons of data collected from observational sessions of equal duration, or from instructional tasks that possess equal opportunities for responding. One example of an appropriate use of frequency-based analysis would be a daily comparison of incidents of head-banging behavior.

Frequency is not an appropriate measure in situations where the duration of the observational sessions varies, or where the opportunities for responding fluctuate from session to session. If, for example, a child's responses are counted during a five-minute discrete trial session on one day and then counted again during a 15-minute session on the following day, a meaningful comparison cannot be made.

Rate of Response

The inability to compare frequency data across observational sessions that vary in duration is easily resolved if we utilize the second conversion unit – rate. Rate is simply the number of behaviors that occurs in relation to a specified unit of time. Usually expressed as *responses per minute*, rate is calculated by dividing the total number of responses observed by the duration of the observation, expressed in minutes.

To illustrate how rate can be used to analyze and compare data between observational sessions, return to the scenario involving the child receiving Discrete Trial Instruction (DTI). If the child provides 20 correct responses during a five-minute session and 45 correct responses in a 20-minute session, we can use rate to provide meaningful, comparative data. Using the standard *frequency divided by time* formula, we would perform the calculations found in Figure 5.12.

Rate allows us to convert simple frequencies into a unit of measure that allows us to compare the child's performance in both sessions. In session one, the child responded correctly at a rate of four responses per minute, while in session two, he responded correctly at a rate of three responses per minute. When viewed in terms of rate, this information not only allows us to equitably compare the child's performance across time, but it also tells us something very important about his proficiency or fluency with the task observed. A child that responds correctly four times per minute would be said to be more proficient or fluent with the task.

Session #1

20 responses ÷ 5 minutes = 4 responses per minute

Session #2

45 responses ÷ 15 minutes = 3 responses per minute

Figure 5.12

We will delve more deeply into the area of fluency, celeration, and rate of response in later chapters. For now, suffice it to say that rate is the most sensitive measure of behavior. It can reflect very minute changes in responding and, as such, can be an invaluable tool in determining skill mastery and deciding when to make procedural changes in our instruction (Skinner, 1966).

A few cautionary comments should be made. If the instructional or observational sessions being compared are of vastly different duration (e.g., comparing a five-minute time period to a 24-hour time period), we tend to see discrepancies in rate between the two sessions. This may be partially attributable to fatigue, in that a child's rate of responding will naturally trail off as he tires during instruction.

Second, rate remains an accurate comparative measure if the tasks being presented are of equal complexity or difficulty. Because of this, care should be taken to ensure continuity when assessing the materials being used across sessions.

Lastly, rate is tied closely to the notion of a **free operant**. Behaviors that can be emitted freely at nearly any time and (in terms of education) are not restricted by the presentation of materials or verbal instruction are considered to be free operants (Baer & Fowler, 1984). Examples of free operants with children include the number of animals a child can name, the number of words a child can read per minute, or the number of two-block structures a child can replicate within a certain time limit. The instructor's behavior does not control the student's rate of responding. The initial directive is given (e.g., "tell me the names of as many animals as you can") and from that point forward, the child is free to respond as quickly as he can without further guidance.

On the other hand, rates of **restricted operants** are obviously limited to the speed at which the instructor can present the materials or introduce the next trial. The concepts of free and restricted operants will be discussed in much greater detail when celeration and precision teaching are covered later in this manual.

The discussion of free and restricted operants is applicable to our discussion of rate measurement because the rate of response might be affected by the "freeness" of the operant. If the operant is restricted, rate might be limited in some way by the instructor. If the operant is free, then the rate is a more accurate picture of child performance. This is especially important to keep in mind if you are attempting to compare rates that are obtained under different conditions.

Percentage Correct

The final measure of comparison utilized in data analysis is **percentage correct**. When the frequency of a behavior is viewed in relation to how many opportunities the child had to emit it, we typically describe that relation as a percentage. Calculating percentage is easy and rather straightforward: the number of correct target behaviors is divided by the number of opportunities for response, and then multiplied by 100. The result is percentage.

The most common educational example of percentage is test scores, and how they pertain to the A-F grading system. A student's performance is measured by how many correct answers are given compared to the total number of questions (or points available) on the test. If, for example, the student correctly answers 78 of 100 questions, he would earn a 78 percent, or a "C" in most grading systems. An example of this calculation appears in Figure 5.13.

Figure 5.13

78 correct ÷ 100 possible points = 0.78 × 100 = 78%

Percentage correct is often used as a measure of a child's performance in Discrete Trial Instruction. When trial-by-trial data (event recording for each discrete trial) are collected, the number of correct responses is divided by the number of trials presented and multiplied by 100. A percentage correct analysis for a child's responses to a simple receptive command program is represented in figure 5.14.

Figure 5.14

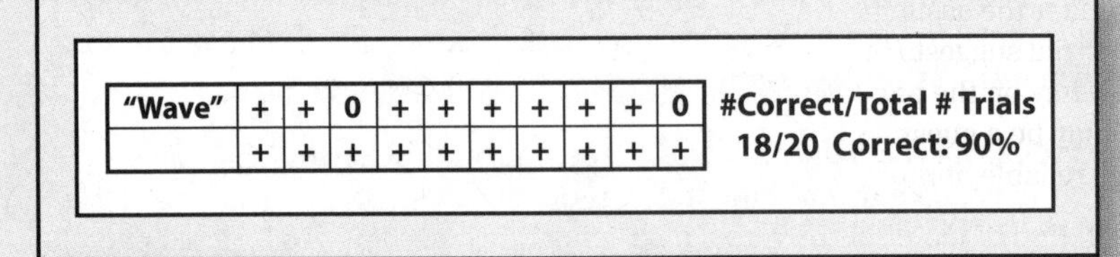

"Wave"	+	+	0	+	+	+	+	+	+	0	#Correct/Total # Trials
	+	+	+	+	+	+	+	+	+	+	18/20 Correct: 90%

One benefit of the percentage correct analysis is that it can be applied to training situations where the opportunity to respond fluctuates between observations. This flexibility is limited, however, to comparisons that do not involve significant variation in the number of opportunities to respond. When the number correct (or dividend) falls below 20, this method of analysis can result in gross over- or under-estimates of behavior change (Guilford, 1965).

For example, if instructional sessions were conducted with only four trials or opportunities to respond, and the child made only one correct response during the first session, her percentage correct score would have been 25 percent.

If, during the next session of four trials, she merely makes one more correct response she will have doubled her performance to a 50 percent correct status. Such a significant improvement would not have been seen if the sessions had consisted of 20 trials. In that instance, an improvement from 15 to 16 correct responses out of 20 opportunities would represent a progression from 75 to 80 percent – or a five-percentage point improvement.

While it is quite commonplace and accepted in the field, this type of data analysis has other limitations. Unlike rate-based analyses, percentage correct does not give us any indication of how fluent the child is with the skill. In the above example, we do not know how much time elapsed during the session. It may have taken the child five to six seconds to make each response – suggesting that, contrary to the ostensibly good score of 80 percent, the child may still be struggling with this task. Because percentage correct does not involve time in its analysis, it does not provide the type of sensitive measure that can be attained with rate.

In situations where fluency might not be as critical – such as during a behavioral assessment when data are being recorded on a specific problem behavior – a percentage analysis may suffice.

Section E – Probe Data

Teachers often disapprove of trial-by-trial data collection during instruction, due to the fact that it can interfere with the flow of the instruction. If the teacher must pause following every trial to make an entry on a data sheet, the pace of instruction is interrupted, and his or her attention is momentarily diverted from the student. This diversion can result in reduced student attention to task or engagement in undesirable behaviors.

One way that teachers can prevent data collection from "cramping their style" is to collect **probe data**. Strictly defined, a probe refers to a single trial of a skill that has not been directly taught. In this classic interpretation of a probe, data are collected to determine if the student is able to generalize from what has been taught to perform other related, but untaught, skills.

In Discrete Trial Instruction, the term probe data is often used (somewhat incorrectly) to describe data taken on the child's first exposure to the target skill taught each day. Better described as *first-trial data*, this method of data collection operates under the assumption that the child's consistent ability to respond correctly on the first trial suggests mastery of that skill. While a successful first trial may suggest fluency on the part of the child, there does exist the possibility that this first response may be a guess – particularly with discrimination tasks. For first-trial data to be more reliable, it must be conducted several times across several days so that replication can be attained before considering a skill mastered. Figure 5.15 is an example of a commonly used first-trial data sheet.

Figure 5.15

	Dates									
Antecedent										
Clap hands	Y N	Y N	Y N	Y N	Y N	Y N	Y N	Y N	Y N	Y N
Wave bye-bye	Y N	Y N	Y N	Y N	Y N	Y N	Y N	Y N	Y N	Y N
Stand up	Y N	Y N	Y N	Y N	Y N	Y N	Y N	Y N	Y N	Y N
Stomp feet	Y N	Y N	Y N	Y N	Y N	Y N	Y N	Y N	Y N	Y N

An acceptable and possibly superior alternative to first-trial probe data is the practice of conducting probes that consist of 10 trials of each skill. Using this approach, a child is provided with 10 opportunities to demonstrate the skill (with no prompting), and a percentage correct analysis is employed. An ongoing visual analysis of these data can then be accomplished by plotting the percentage correct data points on a standard line graph.

While this may resemble trial-by-trial data, it should be noted that the probes are conducted only once daily – typically at the start of the day. This leaves the teacher free to engage in instruction unencumbered by data collection for the remainder of the day.

The authors adopted such a system of data collection that melds accuracy and fluency probes after observing its implementation at The Carbone Clinic in Valley Cottage, New York. For the authors, it has since proven to be effective in creating a more accurate picture of a student's mastery of a given skill.

Finally, it should also be noted that data collection systems (particularly in DTI programs) that abandon rate as the primary datum used for making curricular decisions run the risk of underestimating the role of fluency in skill development. This can result in an inaccurate depiction of a child's level of proficiency with the skills being taught.

Establishing Fluency Criteria

Typically, to establish fluency criteria, we attempt to see how fluently typical children or adults can perform a given skill, and develop an aim similar to this. For example, if we were attempting to determine a criterion for fluent responses -to receptive commands (e.g. correct responses to "clap hands," "jump," or "wave"), we would conduct several timings with typical children or adults performing the same skill, and then determine the mean (average) rate of correct responding across these people. We would then establish a fluency criterion that is similar to this average rate.

Establishing Other Forms of Mastery Criteria

When establishing mastery criteria for skills that are being assessed via accuracy or percentage-correct data alone, we typically establish 80-90 percent correct responses across at least three consecutive sessions of at least 10 trials each. Further, we typically add a secondary criterion that the above level of performance must be attained across at least two instructors.

This added component introduces the concept of inter-observer agreement (IOA), which tells us that more than one person has verified that skills are being demonstrated to the specified criteria. Observed performance of the skill with a second instructor also shows a level of generalization on the part of the learner.

There are times, however, when a ten-trial data probe is not feasible or desirable, such as activities that take longer periods of time to complete. An example is the completion of a 30-piece puzzle, or rote counting to 100. In these cases, we often rely upon first-trial probes, and specify that the correct response (e.g. completion of the puzzle or 90 percent accuracy with counting) occur across at least three consecutive "first trials," utilizing at least two instructors.

Another type of criterion we can utilize is frequency of correct response in a given session, which may be the case when we assess skills such as requests for preferred items or activities. We may establish a minimum number of responses that we would like to see within an instructional session, and mastery would be determined contingent upon whether or not the learner has emitted the specified number of responses.

In Summary

Data collection is one of the most-often overlooked parts of autism intervention programs – but it is one of the most important. How can you gauge progress if you don't know the effect you are having on the child's performance? Without data, we are simply going on a "gut feeling," or allowing subjective and potentially erroneous information to guide our approaches.

Take the time to become familiar with the concepts presented in this chapter. Also know that we have only provided examples, both here in the text and on the accompanying DVD – feel free to design customized data collection tools that meet your needs. And remember this: if you can measure behavior, you can collect solid data. Just keep in mind what type of data will be most useful at each moment. When you're armed with the information provided by valid data, you're in a great position to make programming decisions.

Possible/Recommended Data Collection Methods

Behaviors	Duration	Latency	Frequency/ Rate	Whole interval recording	Partial interval recording	Percentage correct
Tantrum	*	*	*	*	*	
Head banging		*	*		*	
Receptive labeling		*	*			*
Time on task	*			*		
Social greeting		*	*			

References:

Baer, D.M., & Fowler, S.A. (1984). How should we measure the potential of self-control procedures for generalized educational outcomes? In W.L. Heward, T.E. Heron, D.S. Hill, & J. Trap-Porter (Eds.), *Focus on behavior analysis in education* (pp. 145-161). Columbus, OH: Charles E. Merrill.

Cooper, J. O., Heron, T. E., & Heward, W.L. (1987). *Applied behavior analysis.* Upper Saddle River: Prentice-Hall.

Guilford, J.P. (1965). *Fundamental statistics in psychology and education.* New York: McGraw-Hill.

Skinner, B.F. (1966). Operant behavior. In W.K. Honig (Ed.), *Operant behavior: Areas of research and application* (pp. 12-32). New York: Appleton-Century-Crofts.

Consequences and Their Role in Operant Conditioning

At a Glance

Chapter Points

- According to the operant conditioning model, consequences are the most influential determinants of future behavior.
- Reinforcement is the process that increases the future frequency of a behavior.
- Punishment is the process that decreases the future frequency of a behavior.
- Extinction is the withholding of reinforcement from a previously reinforced behavior.
- When and how consequences are delivered will have a bearing on their effectiveness.
- Punishment and extinction must be approached with caution.

Key Terms

Reinforcement

Response Class

Positive Reinforcement

Negative Reinforcement

Primary Reinforcers

Secondary Reinforcers

Generalized Reinforcers

Principle of Contingentcy

Satiation

Deprivation

Motivational Operation

Punishment

Positive Punishment

Negative Punishment

Primary Punishers

Conditioned Punishers

Sensitivity

Desensitization

Extinction

Extinction Burst

Intermittent Reinforcement

Consequences
And Their Role in Operant Conditioning

The effectiveness of any intervention is inextricably linked to the environmental events that follow a target behavior – also known as the consequences. It makes no difference whether the behavior is targeted for reduction (such as aggression or self-injury), or targeted for acquisition or improvement (such as the use of vocal speech). In either case, consequences play a key role in learning.

This chapter defines the three types of consequences involved in operant learning: reinforcement, punishment, and extinction. Beyond the formal definitions, we will provide real-life examples that hopefully will solidify the reader's understanding of these important concepts. In addition, each section will delve into the practical application of consequences, as well as factors that can either enhance or diminish their effectiveness.

Since it can be a politically charged issue, the authors have paid special attention to punishment as a consequence. Our intent here is to neither advocate for nor advise against its use, but merely to inform the reader about the nature and potential effects of punishment as a treatment option.

We will begin our discussion with an overview of operant reinforcement.

Section A – Reinforcement

Outside the field of psychology, the term **reinforcement** is typically used to describe the act of strengthening. Examples include reinforcing concrete, reinforcing an argument or reinforcing troops in battle – all of which involve augmenting a preexisting condition.

In our present discussion of human behavior and, more specifically, of how young children with autism learn, we define reinforcement in quite similar terms. Reinforcement strengthens behavior, increasing the future probability that it will occur.

More formally, *operant reinforcement* is said to occur when an environmental change following a behavior causes similar behavior to occur more frequently in the future. At this early stage in the discussion, it is important to stress that the strengthening that goes on during reinforcement always has to do with *future* displays of the behavior in question. Skinner was very clear in making the point that "It is not correct to say the operant reinforcement 'strengthens the response which precedes it.' The response has already occurred and cannot be changed. What is changed is the future probability of responses in the same class." (Skinner, 1953) We will see the importance of this concept later in this manual when we focus on how problem behavior is strengthened.

In this same statement, Skinner brings to light another important reinforcement concept: it is not the identical behavior that is strengthened by operant reinforcement, but rather a class of similar behaviors (Skinner, 1969). This notion of a **response class** – or a group of similar but somewhat different behavioral responses – is central to describing how new behaviors are acquired or shaped.

If operant reinforcement only pertained to identical behaviors and not classes of behavior, it could not account for the acquisition of any new behavior by an individual. This idea, which pertains to the concept of "shaping," will be further explained in Chapter 7.

Positive Reinforcement

Behavior can be reinforced in different ways. **Positive reinforcement** involves *adding* an environmental stimulus to a situation, or *magnifying* an existing stimulus. This results in an increase in future probability of responses in the same class as the behavior that preceded it. Generally speaking, positive reinforcement stimuli are pleasant or preferred stimuli.

Examples of positive reinforcement could include receiving an unexpected raise in salary, getting a pat on the back from the pastor as you leave church, or a smile from a friend after you offer a kind word. All of these examples involve the addition of something to an existing situation – the pay raise, the pat on the back, and the smile. If the frequency of working, attending church, or speaking kindly to your friend increases in the future, positive reinforcement has occurred.

Negative Reinforcement

Negative reinforcement involves *removing* an environmental stimulus from a situation or *reducing* an existing stimulus. Like positive reinforcement, the actions should result in an increase in probability of future responses in the same class as the behavior that preceded it. Generally speaking, the stimuli involved in the process of negative reinforcement are unpleasant or undesirable.

Examples of behaviors strengthened by negative reinforcement include asking a waiter if you can move to a table farther from the noisy kitchen door, putting on sunglasses as you drive into the setting sun, or providing your child with a toy in order to stop an embarrassing tantrum in the store. All of these examples involve the removal or reduction of an existing negative stimulus – the noisy kitchen, the glaring sun, and embarrassment about your child's behavior. If, in the future, you more frequently make requests to waiters, wear sunglasses, or give toys in the store, negative reinforcement has occurred.

Note that while negative reinforcement has historically been confused with punishment, they are two completely different things. The confusion is likely due to the word *negative*, which people misconstrue as meaning that the action involves something unpleasant. With reinforcement, it may be helpful to think of positive and negative as mathematical terms. Positive reinforcement involves *adding or increasing* something to the situation, while negative reinforcement involves *subtracting or taking something away* from the situation.

Reinforcement and Learning History

Chapter 4 discussed how *unlearned behaviors* originated in the evolutionary development of the species, while learned behaviors are a product of the individual's contact with his or her environment. Reinforcing stimuli can be classified in the same way.

Primary or **unconditioned reinforcers** are environmental stimuli that possess reinforcing qualities for all of us, regardless or age, gender, geographic origins, culture, or learning history. Inextricably linked to species survival, primary reinforcers include food, water, air, warmth, and sexual stimulation, as well as avoiding painful or harmful stimuli. Whether positive or negative, we do not have to learn to like or be motivated by primary reinforcers.

When primary reinforcers are paired with other, neutral environmental stimuli over time, the neutral events begin to take on the reinforcing value of the primary reinforcers with which they have been associated. For example, infants' access to food, water, and warmth is directly linked to their parents' attention. And although parental attention has no immediate value to a newborn, it quickly becomes reinforcing due to its pairing with access to primary reinforcement.

Stimuli that take on reinforcing qualities due to learning are called **secondary** or **conditioned reinforcers**. Examples of secondary reinforcers can include social attention, access to preferred items or activities, avoiding demands, or terminating activities that require effort. Unlike primary reinforcers, denying secondary reinforcers does not immediately compromise the survival of an individual or the propagation of the species. They are, however, critical to our social and emotional well-being and for that reason, are of great value.

Generalized reinforcers are previously neutral stimuli that, because of repeated pairings with primary and/or secondary reinforcers, become effective as conditioned reinforcers for a wide range of behaviors.

Generalized reinforcers, such as tokens or money, maintain their effectiveness in motivating individuals regardless of deprivation. For example, if food is used to motivate a child during an instructional session, the child's present state of hunger would directly impact food's effectiveness as a reinforcer. If the child had just consumed a large meal, the value and effectiveness of food as a reinforcer would be diminished.

The use of a generalized reinforcer like a token overcomes this problem, because no specific deprivation is required for it to remain effective. The token can be "cashed in" for a wide variety of primary or secondary reinforcers, the deprivation state of which may be very high for the child at that moment.

Automatic Reinforcement and Autism

Children with autism and other developmental disabilities typically engage in behaviors that professionals in the field call *stereotypic behavior*. Examples of this include hand flapping, body rocking, spinning objects, and toe walking.

In defining stereotypy, clinicians point out that these behaviors occur repetitively with no apparent social or communicative function. They are said to be *automatically reinforcing*, in that the behavior itself produces the necessary biological reward. As with primary reinforcers, the reinforcing effect comes from the immediate physiological input produced.

Automatic reinforcement can also be classified as positive and negative. With young children with autism, automatic *positive* reinforcers typically involve the repetitive body movements described above, but can also include more typical self-stimulation such as skin picking, teeth grinding, and masturbation.

Automatic *negative* reinforcers generally have to do with pain reduction. Children who engage in severe self-hitting as a means of lessening some internal discomfort – possibly due to an ear infection, headache, or gastrointestinal distress may be seeking automatic negative reinforcement. For example, Mary has a toothache but lacks the communicative skills to let her mother know that she is in pain.

Without any immediate recourse from this situation, Mary has learned that engaging in head hitting can provide a momentary distraction from the pain of the toothache.

Reinforcement – A Two-Way Street

Earlier in this chapter, an example of negative reinforcement involved a parent giving a toy to a child to stop an embarrassing tantrum in a store. This could also be construed as an example of positive reinforcement, since something is added to the child's condition that will likely serve to increase the future frequency of in-store tantrums. So which is it: positive or negative reinforcement?

The answer is that the example involves *both* positive and negative reinforcement contingencies. The parent's toy-giving behavior is negatively reinforced by the cessation of the child's tantrum – as long as the future frequency of toy giving (in the presence of tantrum) increases. An aversive condition (the social embarrassment of the public tantrum) is terminated following a class of behaviors (toy giving).

But if viewed from the standpoint of the child, this scenario describes a fairly clear positive reinforcement contingency. The child's tantrum behavior is positively reinforced by the presentation of a toy – as long as the future frequency of in-store tantrum (in the presence of the parent) increases.

What this bidirectional explanation demonstrates is the complex nature of the behavior/reinforcement relation. When we observe our children's behavior we must not only consider the possible reinforcement contingencies operating on the child, but we must also keep in mind that our behavior (as we deliver consequences) is also influenced by its own consequences.

Section B – Principles of Reinforcement

Decades of research have shown that the effectiveness of reinforcement is influenced by several factors. These factors must be taken into account as we begin to design effective instruction for young children with autism.

To begin with, a child's reinforcement history will affect how he or she responds to reinforcement in an instructional setting. We have observed children diagnosed with autism who, since birth, have consistently received large amounts of non-contingent reinforcement; that is, reinforcement delivered irrespective of specific responses. The parents of these children have made a habit of anticipating the child's needs and meeting them without requiring the child to first express the need. Additionally, a wide variety of reinforcers (toys and activities) are often freely accessible to the child in large quantities.

When such children are first brought into an instructional setting, they often appear lethargic and disinterested in the reinforcers that the therapist uses to teach new behavior. The children's long histories of non-contingent reinforcement and their ongoing free access to similar reinforcers have an adverse effect on the therapist-controlled reinforcers.

These effects can be diminished by altering the children's general access to reinforcement throughout the day, selecting novel reinforcers to be used in the instructional sessions, and working with the parents to develop contingencies that build the children's repertoire of requesting behaviors.

Since the children's reinforcement histories have already occurred, we tend to focus efforts on what can be changed in the present training environments that will allow reinforcement to be most effective. To that end, there are several basic principles of reinforcement that come into play when conducting instruction with children with autism.

The Principle of Immediacy

The **Principle of Immediacy** concerns the timing of reinforcement delivery. It has been found that delaying the presentation of a reinforcer can adversely affect the power of that consequence. The following example illustrates this principle:

A child is being taught to make verbal requests rather than tantrum for candy. During the first few training trials, the child begins to learn to verbalize "candy" with few prompts from the instructor. Following a break in the instruction, the instructor finds that he has run out of candy and retrieves a new supply of candy – these differing only in that they are individually wrapped. Following the child's next successful verbal response of "candy," the instructor must pause for a few seconds to unwrap the candy before handing it to the child. Over subsequent training trials, the instructor notices that the child's performance worsens and that more prompting is required for him or her to verbalize "candy."

The procedure is adjusted to ensure candies are unwrapped and held in the instructor's hand prior to the trial. This allows more immediate delivery following the child's verbalizing "candy," and the instructor notices increased frequency of verbal requesting over future training sessions.

This idea of *contiguity*, or the nearness in time of two events, is critical for maintaining the effectiveness of reinforcement. The closer reinforcement presentation can come to the child's response, the more satisfactory the results will be.

The Principle of Contingency

According to the **Principle of Contingency**, optimum reinforcement occurs if the reinforcer is delivered *only* when the target behavior occurs, and not at other times. Referring to the previous scenario, a new situation arises during the trials involving individually wrapped candies.

In the time it takes for the instructor to unwrap the candy, the child begins to whine. The candy is then delivered. Over subsequent training trials, the instructor notices that the child tends to whine following his verbal request. This suggests an accidental reinforcement effect – a behavior chain consisting of the verbal request followed by whining is actually being reinforced. An adjustment in procedure is then made that ensures candy is only presented following the child verbalizing "candy," and that candy is withheld during any trial involving whining behavior. After this change, the instructor notices that the frequency of verbal requesting increases, while whining behavior diminishes.

It should be noted that not having a clearly defined target behavior and accidentally reinforcing alternate behaviors can lead to diminished likelihood that the child will receive reinforcement for performing the correct behavior. Given a child's possible history of being reinforced for tantrum, such a situation may cause the tantrum to overtake the adaptive response and become even more deeply entrenched.

The Principle of Magnitude

The **Principle of Magnitude** relates to the amount of reinforcement provided following the target response. Generally stated, this principle indicates that the more reinforcement provided, the greater the effect on the future rate of the targeted behavior. It is necessary to adjust the amount of reinforcement provided based on two factors:

1) *The level of performance for a particular response.* For example, if the child has been responding with minimal prompting and all of a sudden responds without prompting, then increasing the size of the reinforcer for that particular trial is in order.

2) *The difficulty of the task.* Tasks of greater complexity or physical effort may require reinforcement of greater magnitude than that provided for lesser tasks.

The maxim in reinforcement delivery is "reinforce well, but don't give away the store." In other words, give enough of a meaningful reinforcer to increase the probability that the child will emit the target response on the next trial, but not so much that the child becomes overly satisfied and lacks the motivation to continue working.

Figure 6.1

Principles of Reinforcer Effectiveness

They Include:

1. **Immediacy**: reinforcers must be delivered quickly following the target response.

2. **Contingency:** reinforcers must be provided only following the target response and no other response.

3. **Magnitude:** reinforcers must be provided in sufficient amount to keep the child working to his best potential.

4. **Variability:** reinforcers must be varied from trial to trial in order to diminish satiation.

5. **Deprivation:** access to reinforcers must be controlled to maintain their value for the child.

The Principle of Deprivation

The **Principle of Deprivation** is related to a child's access to reinforcement. Many discussions of reinforcer effectiveness include the terms **satiation** and **deprivation**. Satiation refers to the diminished effectiveness of a reinforcer following repeated presentations. Deprivation refers to increased effectiveness of a reinforcer due to its being withheld. In order for learning to take place, a certain "need" for reinforcement, or a level of deprivation, must be present. The effectiveness of a reinforcer waxes and wanes depending on the child's exposure to it and other similar reinforcers.

The previous scenario also illustrates the principle of deprivation:

As the learning trials continue, the child is successful in verbally requesting candy, and continues to consume candy to the exclusion of all other edibles or drink. As the session progresses, the instructor notices that the rate of the child's requesting falters and gradually drops off to very low rates. A procedural adjustment is made, changing the verbal request to "water," as well as changing the reinforcer to a sip of water. Following the change and some quickly faded prompts, the child's rate of responding returns to the level previously observed with requesting candy.

What occurred was likely related to the child becoming satiated with candy. Following repeated presentations, its effectiveness as a reinforcer declined to the point where the child stopped requesting it. Guessing that the consumption of candy might create thirst, and also knowing that the child had not been given anything to drink during the session, the instructor switched reinforcers. Because the child's water deprivation was greater at that point, it was a more effective reinforcer.

A child's success during instruction often hinges on access to the reinforcers used. If, during the normal course of the day, he or she has free access to the same or similar tangible reinforcers used during instruction, their potency may be seriously compromised. For this reason, we usually recommend isolating certain tangible reinforcers – only permitting the child to engage with them during instruction, and then only when the child is performing well. Moreover, if the therapist reduces his or her reliance on tangibles and utilizes more social reinforcers (tickles, hugs, funny faces and noises), then the problem of tangible reinforcement satiation can be even further diminished.

Section C – Motivational Operations

The processes of satiation and deprivation impact a child's behavior throughout the day – during instruction, play, social interaction with parents or peers, or displays of problematic behavior.

Behavior analysts view these rather general concepts of satiation and deprivation quite differently than traditional psychology. Cognitive theories typically explain the behavior/motivation relationship in terms of internal "drive states." In other words, we engage in a behavior because we "want to," or because of the presence of an unobservable drive state that urges us on.

Unfortunately, the existence of these internal states is difficult to verify. Common statements like "I'm looking for food because I'm hungry," "I kicked my brother because I was mad," or "My child hits himself because he has autism" create circular reasoning and don't provide useful information about the real reasons behind the behaviors described. When it comes to intervening or treating such causes, we are faced with a dead end.

Rather than assigning these processes to internal states such as "drives" or "motives," the behavior analyst sees them in relation to the concepts of reinforcement and motivational operations.

A **motivational operation** (MO) is defined as an environmental event, operation or stimulus condition that affects an organism by momentarily altering (a) the reinforcing effectiveness of other events, and (b) the frequency of occurrence of the type of behavior that had been consequated by those other events (Michael, 1993). These are also known, respectively, as the value-altering effect and the frequency-altering effect. Other terms for the effects of MO's include, again respectively, the reinforcer establishing/abolishing effect and the behavior evocative or abative effect.

The reinforcer establishing effect of an MO is probably easiest to understand if we take the example of food deprivation. Given a healthy child without any pharmacological influences present such as Ritalin, the absence of food for three to five hours will result in hunger. From the standpoint of an MO, this "operation" of food deprivation will result in the momentary increase in the value of food as a reinforcer for that child.

If we are conducting an instructional session with this same child, we will find that edibles are very effective as reinforcement for a period of time. As the child works and consumes more and more food reinforcement, however, its value as a reinforcer will diminish. The consumption of food actually serves as another MO that acts in the reverse – abolishing the reinforcer effectiveness of food. So we see that motivational operations can work to either establish or abolish the effectiveness of a reinforcer.

The second effect of an MO is that it will evoke behaviors that have been previously reinforced by the reinforcer in question (in the above example, food). When the MO of food deprivation is in effect, any behavior that has ever been reinforced with access to food may be evoked: searching through kitchen cupboards or the refrigerator, calling restaurants to order take-out, driving near fast food restaurants, or cooking. All of these behaviors must have resulted in food reinforcement in our past or we would not engage in them when hungry.

We stated before that operant conditioning is a three-term contingency. The introduction of the MO actually adds a very important piece to the front end of the contingency. Now, with our understanding of the MO, we can look at a *four*-term contingency, consisting of the MO, then the stimulus, response, and consequence. (See Figure 6.3 and Figure 6.4) This new, expanded relation is particularly critical when it comes to conducting discrete-trial instruction with our young children with autism and will be discussed in more detail in our chapter on stimulus control (Chapter 7).

Figure 6.2

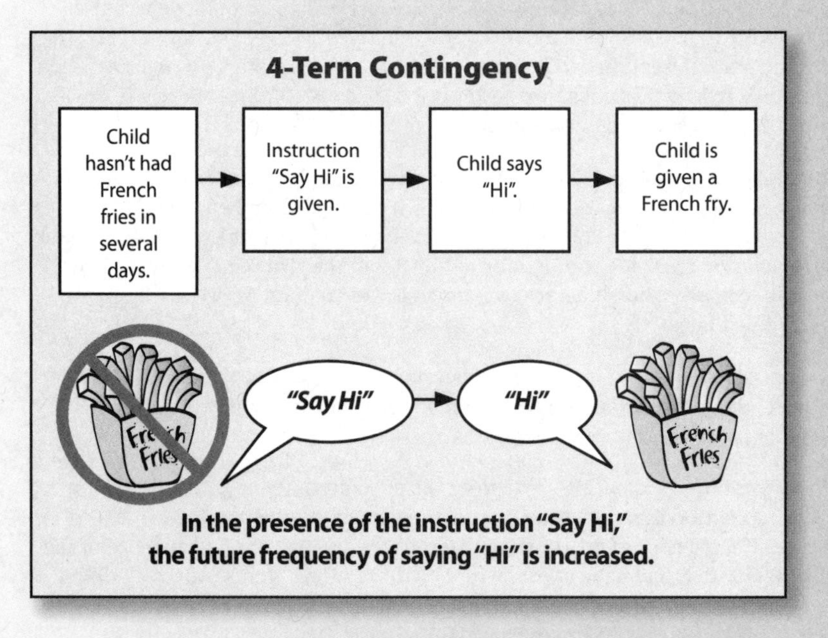

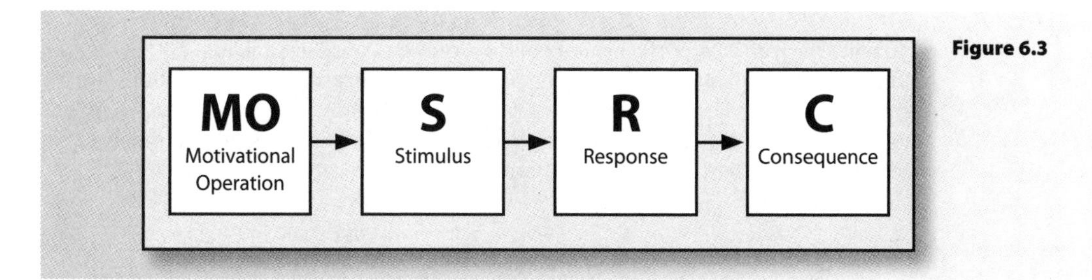

Figure 6.3

Many people fail to realize that motivational operations have two main effects that go in two different directions:

- the "establishing/abolishing effect," which either strengthens *or weakens* a stimulus as a reinforcer; and
- the "evocative/abative effect," which results in either increased *or decreased* rates of the behavior(s) associated with the reinforcing stimulus.

In our experience, most people talk only about the establishing and evocative effects of MO manipulation, which makes it extremely useful for intervention aimed at behavior acquisition. It's important to understand, however, that MO manipulation can be just as powerful a tool for behavior reduction.

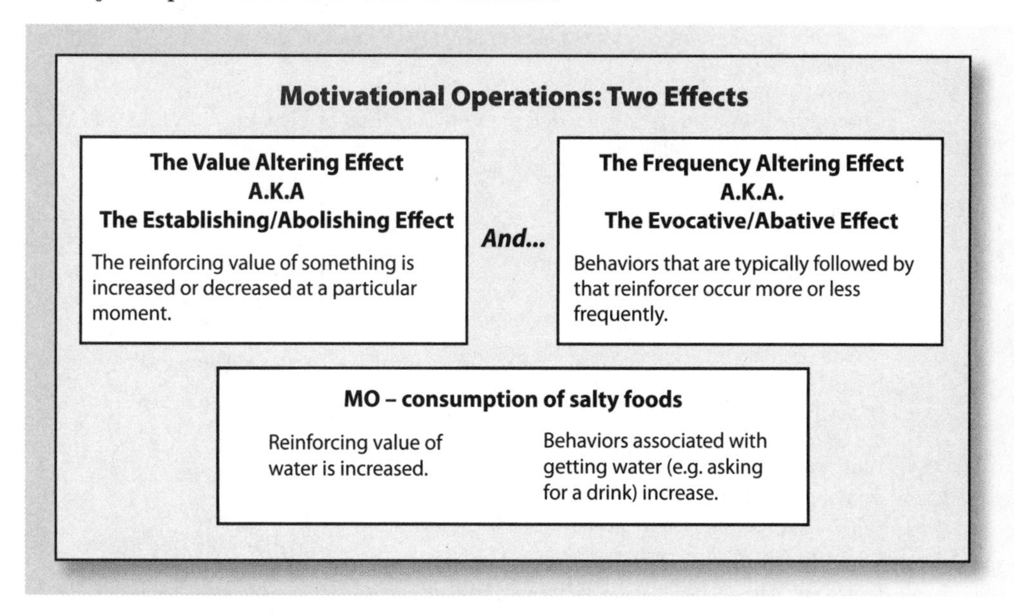

Section D – Punishment

The operant reinforcement model can be used to describe **operant punishment** with a few minor adjustments.

Many in the field will agree that the skillful application of *operant reinforcement* principles has been the hallmark of Applied Behavior Analysis (Sidman, 1989; Skinner, 1953). There seems to be an unnecessary reluctance, however, to discuss the converse of reinforcement, **punishment**. Punishment, by definition, is neither complex nor difficult to understand. It is any consequence or stimulus following a behavior that results in a decreased future frequency of that or similar behaviors.

Why then, is the topic considered taboo in many circles? Throughout this section, we will remove some of the mystery and secrecy surrounding punishment, illuminate and discuss some of the well-founded controversies regarding its application, and present an objective and logical analysis of its use. Finally, we will offer some ethical and legal considerations that must play a lead role in any discussion that involves the potential application of any type of punishing intervention.

Defining the Term

The first part of this discussion has to be an objective exploration of the term itself, and what it means. To many outside of the field of behavior analysis, the word arrives with the baggage of many pre-conceived notions, including spanking, verbal reprimands, and "time outs."

But over-generalizing any topic or event increases the risk of limiting the view of the category, or of stunting further knowledge or development. When this happens, it is usually the result of incomplete knowledge or a problem in understanding the concepts involved. When this type of overgeneralization is disseminated, the problem begins to perpetuate itself.

The predicament surrounding punishment illustrates all of the above. People who do not understand the core definition of the term tend to hold a very limited view of what it is and what it means. Compounding the problem is the extreme nature of most of the examples of punishment that come to mind when the topic is brought up in conversation.

Punishment has historically carried connotations that imply pain, suffering, or discomfort. Additionally, punishment has historically been used within moral contexts to imply retribution for acts that have been perpetrated wrongly against others.

From the standpoint of applied behavior analysis, punishment need not be any of these things, but is merely a consequence that decreases the likelihood of the preceding behavior's recurrence. Behavior analytic use of the term only refers to the function of the *consequence*, not the topography. (Remember that "topography" refers to the form of a response.) What this means is that we cannot think of punishment in terms of what form it takes *unless* we are aware of what effects it has on the future likelihood of the behavior it follows.

> *Punishment* is: A process in which a *consequence* to a behavior results in a *reduction of the future frequency* of that behavior or similar behaviors.

Using this functional definition, we can say that one particular type of response to a behavior could be reinforcing, punishing, both or neither, depending on how it affects the future frequency of the behavior.

Let's look at a very real-world example of this concept at work.

Mary has a history of slapping her head. On Tuesday, following a series of head-slaps, she is approached by an adult who asks her to do her work instead. This happens every time she engages in head slapping from that point forward. Throughout the day and the days to follow, Mary's rate of head slapping decreases dramatically.

The consequence of adult approach accompanied by redirection functions as punishment, because the frequency of the behavior decreases in the future.

In another example, Michael engages in head slapping. On Tuesday, following a series of head slaps, an adult approaches and asks him to do his work instead. Throughout the day and the days to follow, Michael's rate of head slapping increases dramatically.

> Punishment is defined by its effects, not its topography.
>
> What serves as a punisher for one person may serve as a reinforcer for another.

This example, while almost identical to the previous one, differs in one extremely important component – the effect of the consequence on the future frequency of the behavior. Because the behavior increases in the future, the same exact consequence (identical topography) that functioned as punishment in the previous example actually functions as reinforcement in the current example.

The preceding examples bring to light some very important distinctions that need to be made in any understanding of punishment from a behavioral standpoint. First, a consequence need not have any type of negative or harsh connotation to be considered punishment. Consequences that serve as punishers to some people may actually serve as reinforcers to others. Note that there was no reference to descriptors like "pleasant," "uncomfortable" or any other adjectives that infer value. While these terms certainly may be applicable in a discussion about reinforcement and punishment, they are not necessary. Second, neither "punishment" nor "reinforcement" can be used to identify a consequence unless there has been some type of change in the future frequency of the behavior.

It only takes a rather brief explanation to define punishment. Why, then, is such a seemingly simple concept enveloped in heated controversy? The confusion may be due to the fact that the term was selected to represent a process that is part of a rather new field. Scientists frequently walk the line between conveying new information in familiar terms and developing new terminology to prevent confusion. Punishment is a prime example of this process gone wrong!

In retrospect, we might be able to say that the problem started when Skinner chose the term to describe the type of consequence he was trying to explain. Because he did not invent the term, but borrowed it from the common vernacular, he had to accept that people would already have a common set of preconceived notions about its meaning. This situation makes a strong case for the need to understand both the common and scientific meaning of the word, and that they are quite different from one another.

The misunderstanding of the term is only the starting point for an exploration of the controversies surrounding punishing consequences, and this topic will be delved into in much greater detail later in this chapter. First, however, we must develop a framework for a more complete understanding of the process. Just as there are many considerations regarding types, selection, and delivery of *reinforcement* that have an impact on behavior change, there are similar considerations to be made regarding punishment. We will first explain the processes involved in punishment, and then we will return to the dilemmas and problems surrounding its use.

Principles of Punishment

In the following section, you will see that the principles of punishment virtually mimic those of reinforcement, except for the frequency-altering effect that it possesses. The fact that it is a stimulus means that it signifies an environmental change. Like reinforcement, it is a consequent stimulus, which means that it follows a behavioral response.

There are, however, finer points involved in a refined understanding of the principles of punishment. First, the topography of the punishing stimulus will allow us to determine what type of punishment has occurred. This could be *any* type of environmental change, whether it occurs naturally or as the result of planning. Similar to the terminology used to describe the processes of reinforcement, the terms "positive" and "negative" can be applied to punishment to describe how the it occurs.

Positive punishment refers to the addition of something to the environment following a behavior, which, in turn, decreases its future frequency. People often assume that this means introducing something unpleasant, harmful, or painful, but these types of adjectives reflect the perspective of the individual using them. In a strict behavioral sense, any change in the environment that is a result of something being added (and which results in decreased future frequency of the behavior) would be classified as a positive punisher.

For some individuals, the addition of attention following a behavior might serve as punishment. For others, it might be the introduction of other tasks, or it might be the introduction of any kind of physical touch. Likewise, it could include the introduction of certain sounds, certain conditions (such as temperature or humidity), or the presence of particular objects that a person would probably choose to escape or avoid. Remember, though, that what one person might choose to escape or avoid might be something that another person would seek out. This is where the frequency-altering effect is paramount in determining whether or not something can be classified as punishment.

It cannot be denied, however, that positive punishment does indeed include the introduction of harmful or painful stimuli. The introduction of pain, as exemplified by striking or the administration of electric shock, is an example of positive punishment. Likewise, the imposition of hard labor or the introduction of an unpleasant smell or noise would also be considered positive punishment, as long as the future frequency of the behavior decreases.

Types of Punishment

Positive (Type I):
Something aversive is *added* to the environment following a behavior

Negative (Type II):
Something "desirable" is *removed* from the environment following a behavior

Negative punishment describes a process in which a stimulus involves taking something away, which results in the reduction of future occurrences of the behavior. This can include removing a person from an enjoyable experience, imposing a fine of some sort, or removing things, events, or activities that the person would probably choose to access or retain. Again, this only would be called punishment if the future frequency of the behavior decreases following this stimulus.

Punishment can also be termed "Type I," or positive punishment, or "Type II," or negative punishment. This classification system may have been developed to help reduce some of the confusion that seems to surround the use of "negative" and "positive" when referring to reinforcement. Many people tend to look at the two terms from a valuation perspective (positive = "good" while negative = "bad"), as opposed to the scientific perspective from which they were derived (positive = addition; negative = subtraction). Using the Type I/Type II referential distinction eliminates some of this confusion.

Reinforcement and Punishment Matrix

	"GOOD THINGS"	*"UNPLEASANT" THINGS*
INTRODUCED	POSITIVE REINFORCEMENT *(increases behavior)*	POSITIVE PUNISHMENT *(decreases behavior)*
REMOVED	NEGATIVE PUNISHMENT *(decreases behavior)*	NEGATIVE REINFORCEMENT *(increases behavior)*

Also, like reinforcement, punishment can be classified as primary or conditioned, depending on the learning history that may be required in order for the stimulus to take on aversive or punishing characteristics. **Primary punishers** are stimuli that do *not* require any previous learning or exposure for them to be aversive. Similar to primary reinforcers, these are stimuli that are related to our evolutionary need for species survival.

Physical pain is an example of an unconditioned, primary punisher, if in fact it serves as a punisher for a particular person (there are those for whom pain does not serve as a punisher). We experience pain as a way for our bodies to indicate damage or the potential for damage. If we ignore pain, there is a good chance that we will inflict damage upon ourselves, which may result in risks to our survival. Therefore, our reactions to pain (recoil, cessation of the activities which cause us to feel pain, etc.) are programmed into us as a species survival mechanism.

Likewise, extremes in temperature can be considered primary punishers when they serve as such, as can deprivation of food. In relation to the early discussion in this section, it seems as if when most people are asked to describe punishment, they think of primary punishers.

However, much more common are **conditioned punishers**, or punishers that require some experience or learning in order for the stimuli to develop punishing qualities. The development of a stimulus into a conditioned punisher usually involves some type of pairing of the stimulus with an unconditioned punisher at some point. Likewise, the conditioned punisher may acquire its punishing qualities as a result of social learning.

Let's look at some rather typical examples of conditioned punishers, and how they are applied. People need to provide themselves with food, shelter, and clothing. These are primary reinforcers. If these items are taken away, their removal is negative punishment of the primary kind.

However, we live in a social world in which almost all communities of people gain access to these things through some form of a token economy. We earn paper notes that represent monetary value, which in turn can be exchanged for those primary reinforcers. Because we must be taught the symbolic meaning of currency, it is a conditioned reinforcer. When a fine is imposed, for example, or when someone takes money as a result of a specific behavior and the future frequency of that behavior decreases as a result, then conditioned punishment has been applied.

Conditioned punishment also happens unintentionally. When people learn that social contact with other people is terminated as a result of saying certain things, and they refrain from saying those things in the future, conditioned punishment has again been applied. For example, many people do not enjoy discussing politics or religion at social gatherings. If Bill begins to see that people walk away from him when he begins such discussions, and therefore avoids the topics in the future, his behavior has resulted in conditioned negative punishment.

Conditioned positive punishers include stimuli such as verbal reprimands, warnings, or even particular words, gestures, or looks from others. These are things that have little to no meaning or value initially, but once conditioned, signify that something "undesirable" is about to occur. Because they are added to the environment, they are positive punishers.

Everyday Examples of Reinforcement and Punishment

Positive Reinforcement
(give good things)

Give preferred edible

Provide access to preferred activity or toy

Provide preferred social interaction (hugs, tickles, play)

Positive Punishment
(give unpleasant things)

Give un-preferred item or substance

Present un-preferred task or activity

Provide un-preferred social interaction (spanking, reprimand)

Negative Punishment
(take away good things)

Remove access to preferred edible

Deny or terminate access to preferred activity or toy

Deny or terminate preferred social interaction

Negative Reinforcement
(take away unpleasant things)

Remove or terminate exposure to un-preferred item or substance

Remove un-preferred task

Terminate un-preferred social interaction

Factors Related to Punishment Effectiveness

In order for a punishment procedure or process to gain control over the frequency of a specific behavior, the same principles that govern reinforcer effectiveness must be in effect.

First, the Principle of Immediacy holds true for the application of punishment. The more immediately the punishing stimulus follows a target behavior, the greater effect the punisher will have in reducing future frequency of the behavior. By following the behavior as closely as possible, it is more likely that the person emitting the behavior will make the "connection" that the punisher is the result of the behavior.

If a large span of time is allowed to elapse between the behavior and the consequence, there is also greater opportunity for other behaviors to occur before the punishing consequence occurs. When this happens, the punisher may actually follow a different behavior, and affect its future frequency instead.

The Principle of Contingency also applies to punishment. If a particular aversive stimulus is presented only when a very specific target behavior occurs, every single time it occurs, the future frequency of the behavior will decrease quickly and drastically. This is due to the clarity of the contingency offered by very consistent pairing. To the person emitting the behavior, there is more certainty that a functional relationship exists between the behavior and the aversive consequence, and therefore the resultant behavior change is hastened.

The Principle of Size applies to punishment, as well. Common sense leads one to assume that the greater the magnitude or severity of the punishing stimulus, the more effective it becomes in reducing the future frequency of the behavior – and controlled studies have shown this to be the case. Many factors contribute to the determination of the "size" of a particular punisher, and they all have their roots in dimensional properties of behavior.

First, punishing stimuli of greater magnitude typically have more of a frequency-altering effect on behavior than those of lesser magnitude. Magnitude can refer to the strength of the stimulus, such as pressure or ability to cause pain, or to the amount of stimulus that is applied or removed. In a positive punishment scenario, a slight tingle as a result of accidentally touching water that is a bit too hot would be of much lesser magnitude than the severe burning sensation that would result from accidental contact with the heating element on a stove. Given these two examples, the punisher with the larger magnitude (the stove element) would certainly have a more immediate and lasting effect on the future frequency of behaviors that lead to contact with it.

In the case of negative punishment, magnitude plays a role as well. What would likely have more of an effect on the future frequency of speeding – a $10 fine, or the year-long revocation of a driver's license?

Punisher "size" effects can also be realized by the dimensional quality of duration. A punishing stimulus may be of moderate magnitude, but of an extremely long duration. When this is the case, the effect of the punishment on future frequency of the behavior may be as significant as if it were of greater magnitude.

Punishment and Motivational Operations

In most cases, the processes or conditions that influence and determine our behavior (such as reinforcement and punishment) possess some type of polar opposite. However, there also seem to be relationships between these opposites.

One example of just such a relationship is temperature control. When a person turns up the heat in a cold room, they might be doing so to add heat to the environment (which would be considered positive reinforcement), or to remove cold (which would be considered negative reinforcement). In either case, the condition that is increased is related to the condition that is attenuated.

Punishment and reinforcement can operate in the same type of relationship, which plays a role in motivation. When a person is paid for work performed, are they seeking reinforcement or avoiding punishment? Clearly, they would not be able to appreciate the reinforcement provided by earning money (the ability to buy food, clothing, or shelter) as fully if they had never experienced any of the punishing contingencies associated with not having these things.

In this way, punishment clearly plays a role in our motivation. Contingency structures that avoid punishment altogether and focus only on reinforcement often encounter difficulty finding reinforcers potent enough to influence the frequency of behaviors. This is particularly true when access to competing reinforcers (automatic reinforcement, some attention-related reinforcement) cannot be entirely controlled.

In these situations, the process of behavioral selection tends to be weakened. Any type of available consequence is as potent as the next, and reinforcement is likely to occur at some level regardless of the appropriateness of the behavior that is emitted. In other words, the available motivational operations have been either significantly diminished or completely neutralized.

When a punisher is introduced as a possible contingent consequence, however, the selection process becomes much more consistent. Think of it in these terms:

Josh's teacher has been trying to reinforce him for raising his hand when he has something to say, instead of simply blurting it out in class. A functional analysis has shown that Josh engages in the behavior as a means to obtain positive reinforcement in the form of attention. She has been providing M&M's and social praise each time he raises his hand. When he talks out, she ignores the behavior. When she ignores him, he continues to talk out until the other students are distracted. At this point, she provides a minute amount of attention to him by reminding the other children that they will earn extra recess for ignoring Josh. Her behavior specialist informed her that, as long as she reinforces him adequately with the things he wants, he will eventually stop talking out.

The teacher notices, however, that Josh likes the attention and M&M's that he receives every time he raises his hand. She is frustrated, though, because she cannot completely ignore his behavior when he talks out. Also, as much as he likes the attention and the candy, they don't seem to be powerful enough to consistently influence his behavior. There is simply too much competition coming from the minute amount of attention he receives in the form of bargaining with the other kids in his presence.

The teacher then decides that instead of ignoring the talk-out behavior, she will require Josh to practice writing the phrase "I will not talk out in class" 20 times every time he talks out. Now, Josh has a different contingency structure in operation, and a new set of alternatives. If he raises his hand, he still receives attention and candy. When he talked out before, there was no alternative to candy except for low-level reinforcement. There was also not much contrast between the consequences for engaging in either behavior. According to the new contingency structure, however, Josh's alternative to earning attention and candy for appropriate target behavior is the consequence of extra work for inappropriate target behavior. Josh begins to raise his hand more often, and he talks out less.

Josh's teacher has just manipulated motivational operations in a rather complex way. By implementing the above contingencies, she created a much greater contrast between the consequences for appropriate versus inappropriate behaviors. The presence or availability of a punisher increased the reinforcing value of the attention and M&M's at that moment, and the frequency of the reinforced behavior increased as well. At this point, Josh more consistently selects the behaviors that earn him candy and attention.

This process also helps to illuminate the bi-directionality of reinforcement or punishment. Whether we like to admit it or not, these processes happen naturally in our daily lives. Most of the things that reinforce our behaviors do so in contrast to a "flip side," or a group of contingencies that may punish our behaviors if the wrong one is selected. Primary reinforcers such as food, water, shelter, and general comfort are inextricably linked to hunger, thirst, exposure, and pain. To consider either to the exclusion of its relativity to the other oversimplifies the complexities of the relationships involved in human behavior.

Even nonhumans operate under punishing contingencies as significantly as under reinforcing contingencies. Birds avoid Monarch butterflies because of the foul taste that results (a positive primary punisher), and even learn to avoid all butterflies with similar color and markings (a generalized positive conditioned punisher). Likewise, many animals tend to alter their selection of home sites after initial placement in areas that leaves them vulnerable to predators.

The bottom line is that punishment will continue to shape our behavior, no matter how much we try to avoid it or move beyond its influence. It is an integral part of the behavioral equation, along with reinforcement, extinction (which will be discussed later in this chapter), and the environment itself.

Section E – Problems with Punishment as Treatment

Even if punishment never enters the realm of accepted interventions, it is going to occur naturally as a part of any organized society, and quite often at that. Therefore, anyone charged with the task of helping individuals with behavioral issues (such as those common with children with autism) should be familiar enough with punishment to be able to identify and correct punishing situations that might be occurring unintentionally, and to the detriment of a child's progress.

There may even be many situations where a well-developed, closely monitored, and highly regulated application of punishment is the least restrictive, most effective, and most ethical intervention option. But punishment has been "blacklisted" as an intervention by the human services field in the current climate of care, and there is good reason for this.

Punishment is susceptible to many problems – especially in the hands of the uneducated practitioner or parent. Some of the problems are the result of the processes and effects of punishment by their very nature. Some are the result of poor understanding and implementation of the processes by ethical and well-meaning but unprepared individuals. Still others are rooted in history and stem from uninformed and, unfortunately, completely unethical uses of punishment.

Sensitivity and Desensitization

The first problem associated with using punishment is very much related to the satiation and deprivation effects described in the discussion of reinforcement. However, when related to punishment, **sensitivity** and **desensitization** are more appropriate terms to use. Like all animals, we tend to adapt to our surroundings (to one degree or another), even when those surroundings become aversive. When a novel punisher is implemented, depending upon its magnitude, there is a tendency for only a temporary reduction in behavior. If the punisher is of a lesser magnitude, the punishing effects are also minimized, including the duration of the behavior reduction. Over time, the magnitude of the punisher must be increased in order to have the same reductive effect, to the point where it no longer has any "power" to reduce the future frequency of the behavior. Worse yet, the magnitude of the punisher has to be increased to the point that actual physical harm is possible.

To illustrate this, consider the systematic application of a loud, startling noise as a punisher for self-biting. For many children with developmental disabilities, this kind of sound is extremely aversive, and can be considered a punishing consequence to inappropriate behavior.

When Tyler bites his hand, his teacher immediately blows a whistle, which causes Tyler to startle and perhaps cry a bit. After doing this several times, Tyler bites his hand less frequently.

On the sixth hand bite, however, his teacher notices that Tyler doesn't react with crying, and even the startle seems to be losing its intensity. He winces, but doesn't jump. It appears as though he is becoming used to the noise, and the hand biting begins to rise slightly in frequency. After a few more exposures, Tyler no longer winces, and actually laughs when it is blown. Now, the hand-biting behavior begins to rise to levels at or above levels prior to intervention.

Tyler has become desensitized to the whistle, so his teacher has decided to use something louder and more abrupt. She picks up an air horn at the store, and uses it in place of the whistle the next day. On the very first occurrence of hand biting, she blows the air horn and Tyler responds with same reaction he had with the whistle on the first trial – he jumps and begins to cry.

The behavior temporarily decreases like it did before, but before long he is also used to the air horn. The process begins anew, with increasingly more aversive stimuli until there is nothing left that has any punishing power. At this point, there is nowhere left to go, short of painful stimuli, for which the same process might occur again.

For the purposes of illustration, the above scenario utilizes extreme and somewhat far-fetched examples of punishers. It is unlikey that one would ever encounter an air horn in a classroom. (At least the authors hope not!) However the process involved is very real, and presents perhaps the greatest single complication with using punishment. In order to counter the effects of desensitization, the target behavior has to be replaced with one that is functionally equivalent (more on this when we discuss functional analysis in later chapters), and one that can be heavily reinforced.

Another option, albeit one that must be made with *extraordinary* care, is to only select punishers that are quite potent from the outset, combined with a high level of reinforcement for desirable alternate behaviors. The idea behind this practice is that strong reinforcement, combined with equally potent punishment, will make the selection process much clearer for the person whose behavior is causing harm. As a result, the punisher should only have to be implemented a few times. The result of choosing weak punishers and minimally potent reinforcers is that the individual will likely have to come into contact with the punisher much more frequently, thus increasing the likelihood of desensitization and eventual program failure. Please note that this information is coming from a strictly behavioral standpoint, and is based on sound clinical practice by highly trained professionals.

The Lure of Punishment

The second problem with punishment is its very powerful and immediate effect. Because of this, it often lures parents and practitioners into its trap.

To the average parent or practitioner, using punishment requires much less thought and effort than a well-designed teaching program focused on using reinforcement to teach appropriate behaviors. In actuality, a punishment program requires far more care, expertise, and effort to ensure that undesirable side effects are avoided. There are simply too many things that can go wrong when people choose to punish indiscriminately.

Without teaching a replacement behavior that is a functional equivalent, punishment is likely to do no more than "buy time" for the person who implements it. In this way, it can be said that the use of punishment has some "addictive" qualities to it.

How does one avoid becoming overly dependent on punishment? Quite simply, by realizing that punishment by itself is rarely effective in the long run. Because of this, it should be avoided when possible and used only in a highly prescribed and well-planned way, in combination with a plan that focuses first on reinforcement for functionally equivalent behaviors. Punishment is nothing to dabble with!

An Inexact Method

A third problem related to punishment is the fact that it does not have to be based on the function of a behavior in order to be effective. It does nothing to address the reasons the behavior occurred in the first place. Because of this, the behavior might stop, but there is no guarantee that an equally undesirable behavior will not take its place. This can be addressed by conducting a thorough functional analysis prior to the development of any intervention plan. (Functional analysis will be discussed in great detail later in this manual.)

Punishment...or Reinforcement?

One of the most common application errors occurs when punishment is the only component of a behavior change plan, and when the plan has no basis in the function of the behavior. One example of this is a classroom or school management plan where the behavior's form (topography) dictates the punishment. When these types of behavior intervention plans are implemented in school, there is a strong chance that:

- punishment will not be severe enough to have any lasting effect on behavior;
- punishment will not address the reasons behind the behavior; and
- the "punisher" may actually be reinforcing to the child.

In the latter example, some students misbehave as a means to gain attention from supervising adults. Others misbehave to gain access to things or activities. Some do so as a means to escape unpleasant situations, and yet others engage in inappropriate behaviors as a way to gain sensory stimulation.

The second author was a consultant on a particular case where a child engaged in very disruptive behavior at lunchtime in the cafeteria. As "punishment," the student lost cafeteria privileges and had to consume his lunch in the classroom, under the close supervision of his teacher, followed by a writing assignment until the end of the lunch period. The student's functional analysis showed that attention and escape were very strong variables maintaining his inappropriate behavior. By sending him to the classroom for lunch, the school actually reinforced both of these functions. As a result of his misbehavior, the child gained one-to-one attention from his teacher and was able to escape the loud environment of the cafeteria, which was determined to be aversive.

This occurs far too often, and is one reason for discipline problems in schools and homes. Remember that it is not punishment unless the future frequency of the behavior decreases, even if the child cries, protests, or acts emotionally distraught. If behavior continues to increase or remains at the same levels, there is no question that it is being reinforced somewhere along the way, perhaps even by what is thought to be "punishment."

Problems with Punishment *as Treatment*

1. Punishment can lead to desensitization, which may induce the parent or practitioner to increase the magnitude of punishment.
2. Punishment may be "addictive" to parents or practitioners, thereby threatening its effectiveness (see # 1), or leading to blatant overuse.
3. Punishment is often not related to the function ("cause") of the behavior, and therefore does little or nothing to teach appropriate alternatives. The punished behavior is likely to be replaced by other undesirable behaviors that serve the same purpose.
4. Poor applications of punishment may produce no desirable effects, but may produce a large number of undesirable side effects and undue trauma to the person being punished.
5. Punishment, when delivered without a strong foundation in ethics and knowledge, can easily become abusive.

Section F – The Ethicality of Punishment

The fourth significant problem with punishment arises from its use when it is unnecessary, when it has been selected hastily, or when its use is of no benefit to the child.

In some instances, it can be argued that withholding punishment may be more unethical than implementing it. Take, for example, life-threatening behaviors. If a child engages in attempted escape from moving vehicles at high speeds, who can argue that something drastic should be done? We should find a functional alternative and reinforce that, but such teaching takes time.

In the meantime, there are several options, none of which are pleasant: should the individual be restrained mechanically with straps and shackles every time transport is necessary? Should they be shut in? Or should a potent punisher be used a few times to suppress the behavior, providing enough of a reprieve to teach the alternative through reinforcement? These choices must be decided on a case-by-case basis, but they present themselves very frequently to anyone working with the autistic or developmentally disabled population. Choices like this challenge our ethics, and require us to think critically.

Despite data and research results, the current climate in human services strongly and unequivocally advises against the use of punishment. At the heart of their message is an ideology that services must be designed to be unrestrictive. But what is more restrictive in the above car escape scenario – months of seclusion, indefinite mechanical or medical restraint, or one or two exposures to a punisher? Most people's common sense would lead them to conclude that an effective approach that takes the least amount of time and dignity away from a person's life would be a clear choice. In the above scenario, punishment certainly could meet that distinction.

The picture becomes extremely muddled, however, when the behavior is not immediately threatening and the alternatives aren't as restrictive. How should situations be handled when the behavior precludes social contact with others? A child with autism who tantrums every time something is asked of him or her is certainly not at risk of physical harm.

There are times when a behavior analyst could argue that short-term exposure to a "restrictive" intervention such as seclusion might be far more ethical and less restrictive in the life-picture of an individual if it is effective (Axelrod et al., 1993). What if inappropriate behaviors – like tantrums – prohibit a person from being included in society, and those inappropriate behaviors are shown to be maintained by attention?

Escalating behaviors must be attended to if they continue to escalate (even if only to maintain safety) – which makes it is difficult to control access to this type of reinforcer. At the same time, the behavior will continue to occur if it continues to be reinforced. Therefore, a program based solely on reinforcement is likely to fail or work very slowly at best.

In this case, seclusionary techniques could be the only way to effectively cut off reinforcement for the undesirable behavior. Because most policy categorically denies the use of seclusion in the field of developmental disabilities, it is not an option, even if it is functionally appropriate. Still, one should ask what is more restrictive in this case: short-term, monitored treatment with seclusion, or years of exclusion from societal activities?

Many in the field would argue that non-aggressive tantrums do not warrant a punishment procedure and could be dealt with through reinforcement alone. Others would argue that punishment allows a reinforcement program to be more effective (through effects on and of motivational operations), and that reinforcement programs might allow us to attain the desired outcomes eventually, but at the cost of efficiency. The result of a longer or inefficient behavior change process could be the countless missed opportunities to learn and to relate to others.

This therapeutic effect of punishment – specifically increasing the efficacy of a teaching program (functional communication training) was demonstrated clearly by Hagopian et al in an applied research study published in 1997. In this study, the treatment protocols for 21 individuals with mental retardation and severe problem behaviors were examined. It was found that functional communication training (FCT) without extinction or punishment was not an effective treatment. While FCT with extinction produced effective results in approximately 50 percent of the cases, FCT with punishment was effective in every application.

There is no valid way to project what the long-term, cumulative differences would be between someone who has had intervention that is more efficient than others and someone who has received effective but inefficient intervention. From preschool through adolescence, how can punishment to achieve quick results be compared with "softer" methods when working toward the same behavioral goals? How does one count every missed learning opportunity, or determine each opportunity's role in long-term abilities to function independently or responsibly?

There are certainly those who would argue that the chart in Figure 5.1 on page 61 might be applicable in this discussion of efficiency. As time goes by, and inappropriate behaviors are not addressed efficiently, there is more likelihood that the behaviors will interfere with learning. As a result, the life skill gap between the person with problem behavior and their typical peers inevitably grows larger. The opponents of punishment would argue that the cost of being so efficient might not be justifiable by the end alone. It is certainly a complex debate.

Essentially, there are no easy answers to these arguments. The only thing we can recommend with certainty is that the well-being of the child is the first consideration in all cases (when we describe the "well-being" of the child, we refer to both safety/physical well-being, and to the child's quality of life in the present, as well as in the future). Any program decisions must be individualized, made on a case-by-case basis, and made only by those who are knowledgeable and prepared enough to take a thorough approach to analysis and intervention. Further, any program that is designed to address problematic behaviors should be closely monitored. **Data should drive all instructional and intervention considerations.**

Equally important in any discussion of whether or not to implement a punishment procedure is the set of legal guidelines or restrictions that may be in place. Many state service systems (departments of education, mental health, or mental retardation services) impose mandates upon what types of procedures can and cannot be implemented within their systems of service. (Ironically, violation of these mandates places a provider of services at risk of losing funding or permission to operate – in other words, punishment is being used to enforce an anti-punishment stance.)

Further, state and federal governments may adopt policies that affect the ability to implement certain procedures. Many of these restrictions are necessary and act as safeguards against abuse. They also are designed to protect consumers of therapeutic services from potentially harmful practices.

It is important to note, however, that many policymakers and lawmakers are not experts in the field of behavior analysis, and are easily swayed by those who oppose scientific, behaviorally-based approaches. Policies are often forged and mandated by the influence of politically influential individuals with little or no regard for the rigor of research, to the efficacy of the intervention in question, or to the choice of the client served. In 2005, Hanley et al showed how, when presented with the choice, two children clearly preferred functional communication training protocols that included a punishment component. This particular study suggested "the treatment-selection process may be guided by both person-centered and evidence-based values" (Hanley, 2005).

The authors also recommend that any person dealing with the behavior of others should have a basic understanding of the processes of punishment. Even if one does not plan to consciously design programs that utilize punishment, he or she must be able to identify and correct punishing contingencies that impede progress.

Ultimately, it is our responsibility to provide opportunities to children. We also have to constantly make judgments based on the "big picture." Tough choices will eventually present themselves to anyone working in this field, and probably quite often. Our best advice is to be prepared with the skills and the right information to make ethical decisions when they do.

Section G – Extinction

We have offered somewhat detailed discussions of two types of consequent stimuli: reinforcers and punishers. Reinforcement increases the future frequency of a behavior, while punishment decreases the future frequency of a behavior. There is a third type of consequence to behavior that is also likely to decrease the future frequency of a behavior. This consequence, called **extinction**, can actually be more accurately defined as the lack of a reinforcing consequence. When extinction occurs, the reinforcement that historically has been provided following a behavior no longer occurs. When the behavior is no longer reinforced, it will become less frequent over time until it is extinguished, or no longer occurs.

The process of extinction is quite simple and logical. An example can be found in the typical behavior of getting a drink from a soda machine: when the correct amount of money is deposited in the machine and a button is pressed, these behaviors are reinforced by access to the drink. What happens when no drink is delivered following those behaviors? More often than not, the button will probably be pushed several more times, and one more round of coins may be deposited, but almost anyone in this situation will either press another button or walk away. If this chain of events continued to happen at this particular machine, the person would eventually stop using it and find another to serve the same purpose.

This example is a perfect "snapshot" that illustrates the effects of reinforcement and extinction. The behaviors that were previously reinforced by soda delivery are no longer reinforced, so they disappear or change.

There are many ways in which programs can be developed to systematically hasten behavior change, and later chapters will delve into this topic. It is important to realize, though, that extinction is usually at least a component of most of them.

In this typical example, a student's swearing behavior is maintained by negative reinforcement. Every time he swears during math assignments, he is sent to the principal's office, and so escapes math work. The behavior continues at steady rates over a period of time. Once the teacher realizes, however, that the student's escape from an undesirable task is contingent upon swearing, he attempts to rectify the situation through escape extinction. When the student swears, he is not allowed to leave the activity. This tends to lead to more swearing behavior initially, but the teacher holds fast and continues with the assignment. Over time, the student's swearing begins to occur at a decreased rate until eventually, it no longer occurs at all.

The example above occurs frequently in schools, where the concept and logic are simple: if the behavior no longer "works," it goes away. It is the same concept learned by anyone who has ever had an annoying brother or sister and remembers Mom saying, "Just ignore him and he'll go away." Extinction at work!

Unfortunately, extinction also works to extinguish desirable behaviors, often unwittingly. For example, a child who asks nicely for a quarter is more likely to get one than a child who has a tantrum if the answer is no. And yet, because we tend to expect appropriate behavior as the norm, we also take it for granted. If we are not careful, it becomes very easy to tell the child who asks nicely, "Not now. Maybe later."

If the requesting behavior is not reinforced eventually, and if the reason for the quarter remains as powerful as reinforcement, the child will no longer ask nicely. She will likely find a different way to get the quarter, adopting another way to appropriately request money or directing the request to someone else. It could also lead her to engage in inappropriate behaviors as a means to gain the quarter. The purpose of this example is simply to clarify for the reader that extinction can happen unknowingly, and can diminish behaviors that we want to retain.

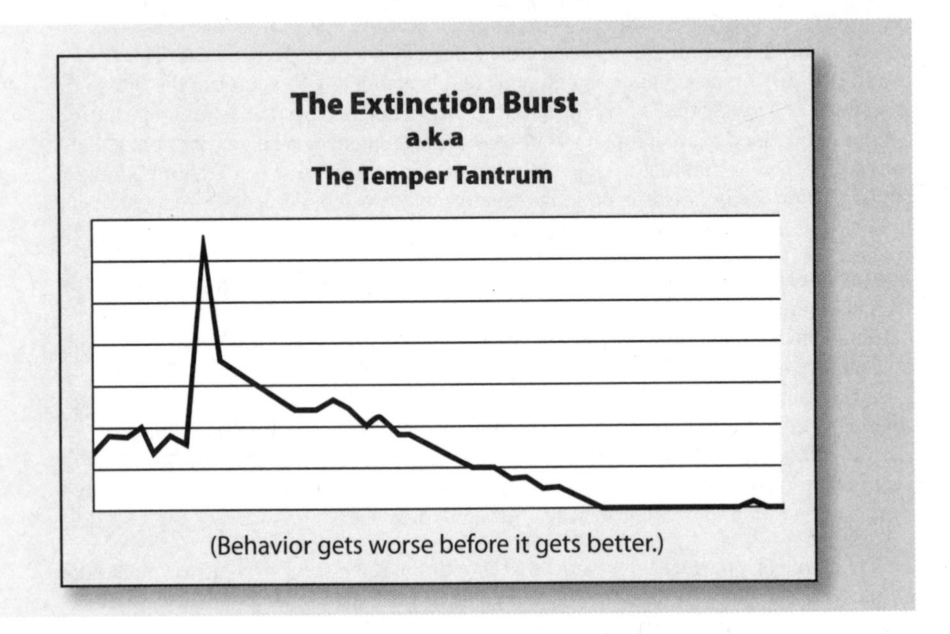

Challenges That Accompany Extinction

When it is used as part of a planned intervention, extinction, like punishment, presents a few problems. The first and most significant of these is a side effect known as the extinction burst. An **extinction burst** is the *temporary* increase in frequency, duration, or intensity of a behavior that is likely to occur shortly after extinction is introduced. Extinction bursts, in plain language, refer to the process that leads a person to "try harder" to make a previously effective behavior work before giving up.

To illustrate this, let's return to the soda machine scenario. In the past, every time someone places coins in the machine and presses a button corresponding to the desired drink, the drink is delivered. On one occasion, however, nothing comes out when the button is pressed. According to the principle of extinction, the behavior should stop. However, this is not likely to happen at first. The behavior has worked in the past, so there is no good reason to believe that it will not work now. Before giving up and walking away after the initial unsuccessful try, the person might press the button again. He or she might press the button several more times, a bit harder, and other (more intense) behaviors might be attempted. For example, the machine might be shaken or tapped. The tapping may progress to a moderate pounding, and perhaps even kicking. But eventually, the person will walk away.

It is important to note that extinction bursts often create serious problems when extinction is applied to tantrums, aggressive behaviors, or other problematic behaviors. This frequently results in the termination of a well-developed and effective plan, because many people see the increases of behavior as a sign that the plan may not be working.

The most important thing to realize is that extinction bursts are expected, and they are temporary. It could even be argued that the presence of an extinction burst is actually a sign that the plan is working, for it exemplifies the plan's success in identifying the reinforcer that maintained the behavior. (Following chapters will guide you in formulating a comprehensive plan that will help you change behavior.) At this point, it is important to know that precautions should be taken to ensure the safety of the individual exhibiting an extinction burst, while making accommodations to ensure adherence to the program.

Resistant Behaviors

Extinction bursts are not the only challenges faced by those who purposely use extinction as part of a behavior reduction program. Some behaviors are more **resistant** to extinction than others and may persist longer than anticipated. In other words, depending on variables between people, behaviors, or environments, extinction may not be as effective for reducing particular behaviors.

Several factors influence resistance to extinction, and most have to do with the reinforcement history of the person and the behavior. First, the weaker a behavior-consequence contingency is established, the more resistant it will be to extinction. This might seem counterintuitive at first, so we will explain. The strength of the behavior is related to how long it has been associated with reinforcement, how many times it has gained access to the maintaining reinforcer, and how often it occurs. The strength of the behavior is also related to the potency of the reinforcer it produces.

To explain a behavior's weakness in relation to resistance to extinction, we rely upon the Principle of Contingency. When the contingency of behavior-reinforcement is unclear, it means that the contingency has not been well established. When this is the case, it is likely that withholding reinforcement for a specific behavior will have little effect on it.

Intermittent Reinforcement

A well-established behavior's association with intermittent reinforcement presents another challenge to extinction. Schedules of reinforcement, including **intermittent reinforcement**, will be covered in later chapters. In the meantime, understand that intermittent reinforcement is reinforcement that occurs sometimes, not in a predictable way, and at random. Intermittent reinforcement schedules could also mean that a behavior could go on for quite some time before reinforcement occurs.

When a behavior is placed on extinction and an extinction burst occurs, there is a chance that the burst will escalate to the point where the plan implementation fails and people reinforce the behavior as a means to "de-escalate" the situation. The behavior is not reinforced when it first happens. However, once it continues for a certain extended length of time or increases in intensity to the point at which others feel the behavior should not be allowed to continue, the person implementing the plan frequently "gives in." The result is a new, intermittent schedule of reinforcement that unwittingly teaches the child that the behavior only has to endure longer, more frequently, or with greater intensity in order to gain access to reinforcement. Worse yet, it might teach the child that the behavior only needs to begin at a more intense level in order to be effective. This is one way in which tantrum behaviors can be quickly shaped into aggressive or self-injurious behaviors.

Intermittent reinforcement prolongs or increases the intensity of extinction bursts once extinction is implemented, and it also serves to strengthen the behavior across contexts. In this way, many plans based on principles of de-escalation actually make the behaviors more strongly established over time, and also risk increasing the intensity of rather mild and easy-to-deal-with behaviors to levels that jeopardize health and safety.

When Ignoring Resembles Rewarding

A final challenge associated with extinction is that sometimes an extinction process looks to the untrained eye like the person misbehaving is "getting away" with the behavior without a consequence. Extinction procedures can include ignoring if attention is the reinforcer that maintains the behavior, but they can also include specific attention if escape or avoidance are the maintaining reinforcers. So, in this way, a person who swears to gain attention may be completely ignored when swearing occurs, as opposed to a reprimand or other consequence. To some, it may look as though the behavior is not being dealt with, but ignoring in this case is an intentional procedure that may reduce the future occurrence of the swearing behavior.

In summary, extinction is simply the process of eliminating the contingency between a behavior and its reinforcing consequence. When we implement extinction, we no longer allow a behavior to "work," in any way, for the person who is behaving. It is a very effective process in most circumstances, albeit often somewhat slow.

If extinction is combined with an effective schedule of reinforcement for an alternate behavior, the process happens much more quickly. Extinction will surely work at some point, as long as intermittent reinforcement does not occur and as long as the extinction burst is planned for.

References:

Axelrod, S., Spreat, S., Berry, B., & Moyer, L. (1993). A decision-making model for selecting the optimal treatment procedure. In R. Van Houten & S. Axelrod (Eds.), *Behavior analysis and treatment* (pp.183-202). New York: Plenum Press.

Hagopian, L.P., Fisher, W.W., Thibault Sullivan, M., Acquisto, J., & LeBlanc, L.A. (1998). Effectiveness of functional communication training with and without extinction and punishment: A summary of 21 inpatient cases. *Journal of Applied Behavior Analysis, 31*, 211-235.

Hanley, G.P., Piazza, C.C., Fisher, W.W., & Maglieri, K.A. (2005). On the effectiveness of and preference for punishment and extinction components of function-based interventions. *Journal of Applied Behavior Analysis, 38*, 51-65.

Michael, J. (1993). Establishing operations. *The Behavior Analyst, 16*, 191-206.

Sidman, M. (1989). *Coercion and its fallout.* Sarasota: Authors Cooperative Inc.

Skinner, B.F. (1953). *Science and human behavior.* New York: MacMillan.

Stimulus Control and Shaping
At a Glance

Chapter Points

- Stimulus control is necessary if we want to make certain behaviors more predictable under certain conditions.
- A learner must know which behaviors will be reinforced under certain conditions.
- Behaviors are acquired through a shaping process.
- Prompts allow the learner to come into contact with reinforcement.
- Stimulus control must be transferred from one stimulus to others in many cases.
- Prompt dependency is likely if proper measures are not taken.

Key Terms

Stimulus Control

Discriminative Stimulus/S^D

S^Δ/S-Delta

Topographical Response Class

Functional Response Class

Method of Successive Approximations

Shaping

Terminal Behavior

Task Analysis

Shaping Across Response Classes

Shaping Within a Response Class

Prompt

Stimulus Prompts

Response Prompts

Transfer of Stimulus Control

Stimulus Generalization

Prompt Dependency

Stimulus Control and Shaping

In order to reach this point, it was important to gain a basic understanding of behavior, as well as how various types of consequences influence the future frequency of behaviors.

In this chapter, we will explain some of the processes involved in learning specific new behaviors, as well as the tremendous role played by reinforcement and other motivational factors. We will explore how learning is influenced by the setting and conditions in which a behavior will occur – as well as the conditions under which it is *not* likely to occur.

We'll introduce several concepts that explain why a particular behavior will occur at a specific point in time, and why others may not. Finally, we will identify key components that influence how behaviors become part of a person's behavioral repertoire.

Section A – Stimulus Control

When we teach skills to children with autism, we not only try to bring specific skills or behaviors into their repertoires, but we also try to ensure that they are exhibited under very specific conditions. For example, when a child sees something that he or she wants, it is appropriate to teach the child to ask for the item by gesturing, vocalizing, or using some other means to convey the information in a functional way. To do this, we first have to choose our desired pattern of response.

Let's say that the desired response topography for requesting the object is pointing with the index finger. First, we need to determine whether extending the index finger is one of the child's established skills. If it is not, we must task analyze the skill and teach it from its most established prerequisite – perhaps getting the child to simply put her entire arm in front of her. If it is an established skill, we must make sure that we can evoke the behavior with a specific stimulus (instruction, essentially).

This begins a process of shaping, or reinforcing responses that gradually come closer to the targeted response. Once we know that we can reliably evoke the pointing behavior and reinforce its occurrence under set conditions, we can transfer control of the behavior from our instruction to the mere presence of the preferred object. There can be many steps in this process, and each one of them requires careful consideration. The major steps involved in the above scenario are the focus of this chapter.

Shaping and the Principle of Contingency

The first thing to understand about shaping behavior relates to the Principle of Contingency introduced in Chapter 6: before a behavior can be reliably repeated or approximated, it must have a strong history of reinforcement. If the contingency is not obvious, the behavior will take longer to become established. Therefore, the shaping process must begin with a very clear "if-then" relationship between a behavior and its consequence.

In operant conditioning, a pivotal role is played by an antecedent (preceding) stimulus, which sends the child a signal that a particular behavior may result in reinforcement. While repeat behavior is dependent upon the consequence, the antecedent stimulus indicates that reinforcement is more likely to happen if the learned behavior is emitted.

When a particular stimulus reliably brings about a specific behavior, it is said that the behavior is under **stimulus control**. For example, it is unusual to hear the phrase, "please pass the salt," unless there is a specific stimulus or stimulus condition present. In this case, the stimulus is the presence of salt (albeit out of reach), the presence of another person to pass the salt, or a combination of both.

When food is present and salt has been deprived (see motivational operations in Chapter 6), the behavior of asking for salt comes under the stimulus control of both the presence of salt and another person. In other words, the asking behavior is unlikely to be reinforced (salt passed) unless there is salt present and a person available to hear the request and carry it out. Likewise, the person passing the salt is exhibiting behavior that is under the stimulus control of the request.

In terms of children with autism, we develop stimulus control when we engage in discrimination training. When teaching colors, for example, giving a blue object may come under the stimulus control of the presence of a blue object and the presence of an instruction to "give blue."

In most cases, any one human behavior is under the control of many stimuli or many stimulus conditions. When we teach a brand new skill, however, we attempt to make the relationship between stimulus and target behavior as discrete as possible. This enables us to be very specific with our reinforcement. Later chapters will discuss a practical application of this concept called Discrete Trial Instruction (DTI). For now, we will focus on the relationship between the stimulus and the behavior, and how this relationship interacts with reinforcement to bring about "tight" stimulus control.

Gaining Stimulus Control

Earlier chapters discussed the difference between antecedent stimuli (stimuli that precede a behavior) and consequent stimuli (stimuli that follow a behavior). The following section deals primarily with antecedent stimuli.

For a behavior to be considered under stimulus control, the stimulus in question must be consistently present when the subsequent behavior is reinforced. This makes two things happen:

- First, the stimulus begins to reliably evoke the behavior. This happens because the behavior was reinforced in the past while the stimulus was present.
- Second, the consequences (reinforcement, punishment, or extinction) that follow the behavior influence future frequency of the behavior.

Both of these factors, working together, help to determine the degree of stimulus control a particular stimulus has over a particular behavior.

The process of gaining stimulus control usually involves more complex relationships among stimuli, behaviors, and consequences. True stimulus control is gained when a stimulus serves as a **discriminative stimulus**, or $\mathbf{S^D}$. A discriminative stimulus is a stimulus, event, set of events, or environmental condition that is consistently present prior to a behavior that is reinforced. Further, this environmental condition is usually absent when the behavior is not reinforced (Cooper, Heron, & Heward, 1987).

To illustrate this, it may help to return to the salt-passing scenario. The salt and another person are consistently present when the request for salt is reinforced (by passing). In addition, when both stimuli are absent, the request for salt is usually not reinforced (it is not passed). Therefore, it is safe to assume that the presence of salt and the presence of another person are both discriminative stimuli for salt-asking behavior. There certainly may be more events or conditions that serve as discriminative stimuli in this case, but these are two of which we can be certain.

This helps explain why we exhibit particular behaviors to gain particular reinforcement. It is how we learn to understand the relationships between our actions and reinforcement, and how we learn when certain behaviors will be more effective than others, depending on the situation. Stimulus control goes a bit further, however.

It is one thing to know which stimuli or cues indicate that a response will be reinforced, but we must also identify stimuli that indicate a particular response will *not* be reinforced. Will a request for salt be reinforced if only pepper is present? Probably not. Will it be reinforced if no other people are present? Again, probably not. This is the heart of discrimination training, which allows us to actually teach these relationships to individuals with autism.

The S^D/ S^Δ Relationship

S^D:

A stimulus, event, set of events, or environmental condition that is consistently present prior to a behavior that is reinforced, and not present when the behavior is not reinforced

S^Δ:

An antecedent stimulus in the presence of which a particular behavior will not be reinforced

For children with autism who are just acquiring basic language concepts, we use such processes to teach the difference between item labels, such as "cup" and "shoe," for example. If I ask the child to give me the cup in the presence of a cup and a shoe, the cup is the only stimulus item that will result in "giving behavior" being reinforced. If the child gives me the shoe, reinforcement will not be delivered. In this case, we have turned the presence of the cup (in addition to our instruction) into a discriminative stimulus.

But what of the shoe? It is present during this task, so it is also a stimulus. However, we cannot call it a discriminative stimulus, or S^D, because its presence does not indicate that giving it in response to "give me cup" will be reinforced. Some would call this a distracter in this particular instance. However, in behavioral terminology, the presence of the shoe serves as an $\mathbf{S^\Delta}$, or **S-delta**. An S^Δ is an antecedent stimulus that, when present, does not indicate that a particular behavior will be reinforced. Likewise, "give me shoe" is an S^Δ for the behavior of giving the cup.

For those new to behavior analysis or discrimination training, the S^D/S^Δ relationship is very confusing and often misunderstood. One way to sort it out is to think of examples and identify which stimuli serve as discriminative (where the response will be reinforced), and which stimuli serve as S-delta (where the response will not be reinforced).

In the salt scenario, the presence of pepper serves as an S^{Δ} for asking for salt. If one wants salt, the presence of the salt is the S^{D}. The presence of the pepper instead of salt is the S^{Δ}. The person asking has to know what conditions will result in reinforcement:

- If he asks someone to pass the salt, and only pepper is present, the behavior will not be reinforced.
- If he asks for pepper, but really wants salt, the behavior will not be reinforced.
- If no one else is present, that condition serves as an S^{Δ} for asking someone to pass the salt, because salt cannot be passed if no one else is present.

Although later chapters will deal with Discrete Trial Instruction, it is important to know at this point that DTI and all other effective instructional techniques involve contriving situations to establish stimulus control. In other words, we set up scenarios that encourage the child to discriminate between stimuli to select the appropriate behavior for the conditions, which then results in reinforcement. This is the basis of teaching expressive communication skills, receptive language skills, functional life skills, and general knowledge.

Section B – Response Classes

In life, stimulus control is rarely limited to isolated, specific behaviors. More frequently, stimulus control is exerted over response classes, or groups of behaviors that share similarities (Cooper, Heron, & Heward, 1987).

We generally divide response classes into two main groups. First, there are behaviors that are related by the way they are performed. These behaviors become members of a **topographical response class**. Raising an arm to reach an object on a shelf, to offer an answer in class, or to apply underarm deodorant all involve the same exact response form (topography). Even though they are done for different reasons, they all look the same from a topography standpoint. In fact, a single operational definition for arm-raising could define the behavior in all three examples.

It is important to understand topographical response classes, because they are beneficial in guiding us through the initial stages of shaping. For example, it is impossible to teach a child to point to a particular stimulus item (such as "green" or "blue") if the topography of pointing has not been established. Likewise, it is impossible to teach speech repertoires, such as asking or labeling, if we cannot first shape the vocal topography of the learner.

Response Classes

Topographical Response Class:
Behaviors that are related by the way they are performed

Functional Response Class:
Behaviors that are related because they all serve the same or similar purpose

The other type of response class is the **functional response class**, or a group of behaviors that are related because they all serve the same or similar purpose. Members of a functional response class can have completely different forms or topographies. For example, one child may indicate the desire for a cookie by asking, "May I have a cookie, please?" A second child may point to a cookie, which usually results in delivery by the supervising adult. Yet another child may scream and cry because she has a history of cookies being presented to "calm" her every time she has a tantrum.

In all three of these examples, the response topography was completely different. In one case, we had vocal behavior. In another, we witnessed pointing. In the third, we saw tantrum behaviors. Because all three served the same purpose – to obtain a cookie – the behaviors were all part of the same functional response class.

An understanding of functional response classes is an important part of behavior shaping when it comes time to teach generalization. Discrimination training can be applied to teach skills that will result in functional applications of discrete skills. For example, pointing to objects, touching them, handing them to an instructor, or saying the name of the label vocally can all be used in the identification of labels. The child who can only use one response topography to demonstrate discrimination will be more limited than one who can use several response forms to serve the same purpose.

Section C – Instructional Prompts

The simple addition of prompts to instruction can diminish inconsistencies in a student's responses. A **prompt** is defined as any environmental stimulus that supplements the S^D and facilitates a correct response by the student (Snell, 1983). Before returning to shaping and discussing how prompts affect the process, we must first explore the two distinct categories of prompts.

Stimulus Prompts

Stimulus prompts involve changes in how the S^D is presented to the student. They often involve some form of manipulation of instructional materials to improve the probability of a correct response. An example of this is the **positional prompt**. Let's say we are trying to teach a child to discriminate between a "ball" and a "cup" when asked to "give me the [object]." Without the aid of prompts, the child may not quickly begin to make the receptive discrimination based on the auditory S^D of "give me the [object]."

Children with autism, when placed in such instructional situations, often resort to guessing, patterned responding (e.g., always selecting the object placed on the right), or relying on whatever inadvertent visual prompts might be present (e.g., picking up on the teacher's habit of alternating right and left placement of the objects).

When a teacher uses positional prompts, she is taking into account the young child with autism's reliance on visual cues, and is using that learning style to her advantage. In this example, the teacher might place the target object (i.e., the object that is currently being taught) closer to the child – thus increasing the probability that the child will select the target object. Thus, the *position* of an instructional object is altered to facilitate a correct response, and that prompt occurs as part of the S^D or stimulus condition.

Another type of a stimulus prompt that involves alteration in the instructional materials would be a **redundancy cue**. When we purposely alter some dimension of the instructional stimuli (color, size, shape, sound) to facilitate a correct response, we are using redundancy cues (Snell, 1983). A common example of a redundancy cue used during DTI is the **voice inflection prompt**. When training for color discrimination, we might set up a task where two objects are placed on a table in front of the child. The objects are identical in all dimensions except color; for example, two cups of identical form and size, differing only in that one is red and one is green. The verbal S^D of "give me the green cup" can be supplemented by the voice inflection prompt of "give me the GREEN cup" (with the word "green" spoken with magnified volume). In this way, a dimension (speaking volume) of the instructional stimuli is magnified to facilitate a correct response.

Another variety of stimulus prompt routinely employed in DTI is movement cues (Snell, 1983). Movement cues include tapping next to or pointing directly at the target object during a discrimination task, or placing an outstretched palm closer to the target object as we ask for it. Having the tap, point, or hand placement occur literally as part of the S^D is the critical characteristic that allows these movements to be defined as stimulus prompts.

Response Prompts

Response prompts are supplemental stimuli that are associated with the topography of the target response (Cooper, Heron, & Heward, 1987). Unlike stimulus prompts, which are concerned with how the S^D is delivered, response prompts are concerned more with ensuring that the form of the student's response is correct.

There are typically three varieties of response prompts. The first is **verbal prompts**, which, in their strictest sense, usually involve providing the student with additional verbal direction on how to complete the task. This can take the form of a simple, verbal description of the procedure (or portions of the procedure) the student must follow to be successful. For example, if we ask a child to imitate a block design, and he has difficulty responding solely to the S^D of "build this" paired with the visual model, we might find it necessary to tell him to "put the red triangle on top of the blue square" as the final step in the task. Because this supplemental verbal instruction occurs apart from the S^D and is designed to facilitate the target response, it is considered a response prompt.

Asking questions of the student as he completes the task is another form of verbal prompting that is often effective. If, using our previous example, the child routinely fails to put the red triangle block on top of the blue square, we can insert a verbal prompt, such as, "Do your blocks look like mine?" Follow-up questions, such as, "What's different?" "What's missing in your design?" or "How can you fix it?" might also be helpful.

The appropriateness of employing verbal prompts is of course dependent on a particular child's receptive language skills. We would not use verbal prompts for a child who has failed to demonstrate the ability to respond accurately and reliably to simple receptive commands such as "come here," "stand up," or "sit down." If the skill being taught requires more complex verbal commands than these, we would need to take into account the current level of the child's receptive language skills when deciding whether or not to use verbal prompting for a particular skill.

The second variety of response prompts are **modeling prompts**. Whether the task includes verbal or nonverbal action, the instructor demonstrates, or models, the target response to the student. This can involve portions of the response or the entire movement cycle.

We frequently utilize physical action modeling when we teach receptive language tasks that require a child to respond nonverbally to verbal instruction. Directing a child to "touch nose," "stand up," or "pretend you're a bunny" are all examples of receptive language tasks. As we will see, many children with autism have significant difficulty following a spoken direction when it is not paired with some form of visual cue. The use of modeling in these situations provides the child with just such a prompt – simultaneously saying, "touch nose" and modeling the action by touching your own nose.

Modeling prompts can also facilitate verbal responses. Often referred to as **echoic prompts**, verbal modeling prompts involve the instructor demonstrating the correct verbal response. Echoic prompts typically involve the command, "say…" and can be followed either by a portion of the verbal response or the entire target word or phrase.

Programs designed to teach children to label objects or actions, request reinforcers, or answer simple or complex questions can all benefit from the use of echoic prompts. For example, if a child is being taught to label a cup when asked, "What is it?" (with a cup present), the instructor quickly follows the initial question of "What is it?" with the echoic response prompt, "say cup." As the child progresses with identifying cup by saying, "cup," the prompt can be reduced by eliminating "say" and using only portions of the word, such as "cuh."

A child's ability to imitate the actions of others has an obvious influence on the effectiveness of modeling prompts. This is why Early, Intensive Behavioral Intervention (EIBI) programs place much of their initial focus on developing imitation skills. These programs often begin with teaching the child to imitate the instructor as he or she completes simple motor actions with objects (placing a block in a bucket, banging a toy hammer, or pushing a toy car). Then, good EIBI programs teach (in succession):

- Imitation of gross motor actions performed without objects (e.g., clapping hands, stomping feet, waving bye-bye).
- Imitation of fine motor actions without objects (e.g., touching nose, wiggling fingers, isolating index finger to point).
- Imitation of oral motor movements (e.g., open mouth, stick out tongue, put teeth together).
- Imitation of sounds, blends of sounds, full words, two-word combinations, short phrases, and eventually, complete sentences.

Experiencing this curricular sequence maximizes a child's ability to imitate the actions or words of others. It is critical for our children, because so much of our later efforts rely on the use of modeling prompts.

The final type of response prompt is physical prompting. **Physical prompts** entail hands-on guidance to ensure that the child responds correctly to instruction. As with modeling prompts, physical prompts can be provided in varying degrees, depending on the needs of the child. The instructor might provide a partial physical prompt, such as a light touch to a child's arm, to encourage a more complex movement cycle such as reaching across the table, grasping a target object from the table, and giving it to the instructor. If the child's skill is less developed, the instructor might provide a full physical prompt such as hand-over-hand guidance to reach across the table, grasp the target object, and release it into the hand of another instructor.

Physical prompts vary widely in topography – ranging from the subtle touch and movement of fingers when prompting the formation of a word in sign language, to the physical suspension of a child's entire body weight when prompting him to stand up and walk during a tantrum.

Unlike verbal prompting and modeling, the use of physical prompts does not require any prior learning or experience on the part of the child. While they are very helpful in facilitating nonverbal responses, physical prompts typically have limited applicability to teaching verbal responses.

The varieties of both stimulus and response prompts are virtually infinite. As an instructor works with individual children, she regularly modifies existing forms of prompting or finds it necessary to create new forms to address the idiosyncratic needs of each student. Simply as a means of providing a starting point for instructors new to EIBI programs, and as a means of organizing some of the more common forms of prompting, we have included two tables on the following two tables (Figures 7.1 and 7.2).

Stimulus Prompts

Prompt	Topography/Method	Common Application	Prerequisites	Limitations
Positional prompt	*Placing target object closer to the student*	*Receptive selection (point/touch/give) tasks*	*Basic attending skills*	*Not applicable when drill involves verbal responses*
Proximity prompt	*Positioning the instructor's body closer to or farther from the student*	*Receptive pronoun drills ("touch my nose")*	*Student must be able to verbally imitate*	*Limited to pronoun or possession drills*
Voice inflection prompt	*Magnifying or reducing the volume of the instructor's voice for a specific word*	*Magnification – Receptive selection (point/touch/give) tasks* *Reduction – Preventing echolalia*	*Basic attending skills*	*None encountered*
Gestural (tap/point)	*Tapping or pointing to target object*	*Discrimination tasks* *Visual performance tasks*	*Basic attending skills*	*Highly imitative students may mimic the tap/point*
Gestural (hand placement)	*Placing the instructor's outstretched hand nearer to the target object*	*Receptive selection (giving) tasks*	*Basic attending skills*	*None encountered*
Gestural (blocking)	*Shielding the non-target object or otherwise blocking access to it*	*Receptive selection (point/touch/give) tasks*	*Basic attending skills*	*None encountered*
Gestural (eye gaze or head nod)	*Directing instructor's eye gaze or nodding head toward the target object.*	*Receptive selection (point/touch/give) tasks*	*Well-developed attending skills*	*Requires student to be aware of subtle body cues.*
Highlighting	*Placing brightly colored paper or other marking on or in close proximity to the target object or location*	*Receptive selection (point/touch/give) tasks* *Receptive placement tasks (prepositions)*	*Basic attending skills*	*None encountered*
Size	*Increasing the size of the target object relative to the non-target object*	*Receptive selection (point/touch/give) tasks*	*Basic attending skills*	*None encountered*
Templates	*Placing paper templates on the table to indicate specific locations for placement of objects*	*Sequencing and seriation tasks*	*Basic attending skills*	*None encountered*
Dotted line prompt	*Providing dotted line or lightly drawn figures as guides for the student to complete a written or drawn response*	*Graphic imitation (drawing/copying/writing) skills*	*Basic attending skills* *Correct grasp of writing implement*	*None encountered*

Figure 7.1

Section D – Prompt Dependency

As we've learned, prompting is one of the most basic building blocks in shaping or gaining stimulus control over behaviors. There are many ways in which an instructor can "lead" a child with autism to perform target behaviors under target circumstances, and skill in prompting can be one of the most pivotal factors in a child's rate of progress. All too often, though, prompting can lead to instructional problems.

Prompt dependency tends to plague many children and therapists involved in intensive discrimination training. It occurs when a prompt acquires stimulus control

Response Prompts

Prompt	Topography/Method	Common Application	Prerequisites	Limitations
Verbal prompt (procedural)	*Providing verbal directions as to what the student must do to complete the task Provided either partially (in steps) or whole task*	*Tasks that have a physical/nonverbal response*	*Student must have sufficient receptive understanding of the words/concepts used*	*Can be confusing if used to prompt verbal responses – particularly with echolalic students*
Verbal prompt (questioning)	*Asking the student specific questions to prompt the completion of a (typically) complex task e.g., "What's missing?" "What did you forget to do?"*	*Complex verbal and nonverbal tasks*	*Student must have sufficient receptive understanding of the words/concepts used and, in most cases, should have question-answering skills*	*May evoke distracting verbal responses to the questions that could compete with completion of the physical task*
Echoic prompt (whole word/phrase/ sentence)	*Instructor models the entire verbal response – typically using the sentence form "Say [target verbal response]"*	*Verbal response tasks - tact or intraverbal*	*Student must be able to imitate the target verbal responses*	*Student may echo the prompt "say"*
Echoic prompt (partial word or phoneme)	*Instructor models a portion of the target word or the beginning sound (phoneme) of the target word*	*Single word echoic, tacting, or simple intraverbal (fill-in) tasks*	*Student must be able to imitate the target phoneme or portion of word*	*None encountered*
Physical modeling (whole task)	*Instructor models the entire physical response – can be paired with the phrase "do this"*	*Receptive commands (simple to complex)*	*Student must be able to imitate motor movements of similar complexity*	*None encountered*
Physical modeling(partial)	*Instructor models a portion of the physical response – typically the beginning of the movement cycle*	*Receptive selection (point/touch/give) tasks*	*Student must be able to imitate simple motor movements*	*None encountered*
Physical prompt (whole task)	*Instructor uses hands-on guidance to walk the student through the entire physical response*	*Receptive commands (simple to complex) Imitation tasks*	*None*	*Generally limited to physical actions Can be used for some rudimentary oral motor actions and phonemic production*
Physical prompt (partial)	*Instructor provides varying degrees of touch to facilitate the completion of a physical response*	*Receptive commands (simple to complex) Imitation tasks*	*None*	*Same as with whole task physical prompt*
Peer modeling	*Instructor has a peer or sibling physically or verbally model the target response in the presence of the student*	*Wide variety of verbal and nonverbal tasks*	*Student must be able to imitate similar verbal or nonverbal movements May be helpful to have the peer model be of similar age and same gender as student*	*Must establish compliance and interest of the peer Might require separate reinforce-ment contingency to motivate the peer*
Time delay prompt	*Instructor provides a short period of time (often paired with reinforcement) between steps of a multi-step task*	*Multi-step receptive commands Multi-step imitation tasks*	*Student must be skilled in the completion of component steps of multi-step task*	*None encountered*

Figure 7.2

over a behavior, and transferring that control to the desired stimulus fails. For example, we often try to teach children with autism to greet others spontaneously when a novel person enters a situation. In this case, the person's entrance to the environment should serve as the stimulus for the greeting, "Hi!" In order to show the child that reinforcement will be delivered contingent upon a greeting, we often resort to a modeling prompt, such as "say 'Hi!'" The child takes the prompt, receives reinforcement, and goes on his or her way.

The next opportunity for application of the skill looks just like this one – the instructor must give a verbal prompt before the child will greet the other person. Over time, the situation does not change, for the child consistently waits for the instructor's prompt.

In this case, the child has become prompt dependent in that the prompt is actually the discriminative stimulus for the greeting, and only the prompt has stimulus control over the response. However, the person's entrance alone should have stimulus control. To remedy this situation, the instructor must develop a strategy to transfer stimulus control from the prompt to the entrance of the other person. This process can involve extinction (i.e., no reinforcement is offered unless the behavior occurs without being prompted), differential reinforcement (a lesser amount of reinforcement occurs for prompted responses), prompt fading (described later in this chapter), a new prompting system, priming, etc. It is likely that the most effective approach would involve a combination of several strategies.

Prompt dependency can be quite a nuisance, and some children with autism seem to be especially prone to its occurrence. The situation can be avoided, however, if we select prompts that can be easily faded. We also need to be quick to identify cases of prompt dependency and begin the problem-solving process very early on. More often than not, skillful prompt-fading strategies, combined with reinforcement differentiation, will solve the problem.

Error correction strategies can also play a key role in the elimination of prompt dependency. Some formats, such as the NO-NO-PROMPT format, deal with prompt dependency by allowing a certain number of incorrect response opportunities (trials) to remain un-reinforced before a prompt is given. In this case, the child may "try harder" to be correct and independent in order to gain reinforcement. Error correction strategies will be described in great detail in later chapters.

The Power of Stimuli

Stimulus considerations are the driving forces behind skill selection – and no curriculum for teaching language and social skills to children with autism can be effective without them. Armed with a solid understanding of stimulus control, we're able to answer a wide range of questions, including:

- How are we going to present instructions?
- How are we going to understand why children act in predictable ways in the presence of certain conditions?
- How are we going to establish environmental conditions conducive to learning new skills and reducing previously learned inappropriate behaviors?

The truth is that without stimulus control, no learned behavior can exist. Our task, then, is to utilize what we know about the relationships between stimuli, responses, and reinforcement to teach new skills, strengthen weak skills, and ameliorate problem behaviors.

We do this through the shaping process, which involves shaping members of both topographical and functional response classes. Like all that has previously been discussed, there is a body of procedures and tools designed to take the principles of behavior into the practical realm. The following sections will deal with these proven, practical skills for behavior shaping.

Section E - Shaping and the Method of Successive Approximations

The **method of successive approximations** refers to a procedure that teaches new behavior to a child by reinforcing successive approximations of a terminal behavior. The action of the instructor or therapist involved in this process is referred to as **shaping** (Skinner, 1953).

It would be impossible to shape new behaviors within a child's repertoire without Skinner's concept of *response class* (see Chapter 6). This is because operant reinforcement affects not only the specific behavioral response that it follows, but also the future display of similar but somewhat different responses – i.e., behaviors within the same class as the originally reinforced behavior. If reinforcement only increases the future probability of the identical response it follows, the shaping of new or slightly different behaviors will never occur – or at best, the acquisition of new behaviors will have to wait until they are accidentally performed and then reinforced.

Additionally, shaping relies heavily on the concept of *response topography*. Also discussed in the previous chapter, topography refers to the form of a specific response. How does the behavior look, or how does the child carry it out? The successive approximations that are reinforced during the shaping process are actually different response topographies that lead up to the eventual goal or terminal behavior being taught.

To better illustrate shaping and the method of successive approximations, consider this well-known example within the field of applied behavior analysis. In 1964, Wolf, Risley, and Mees published a study that described the use of behavioral shaping to teach a young child with autism to wear his eyeglasses.

The child, Dickie, was three-and-a-half years old and had undergone cataract surgery that resulted in the bilateral removal of the lenses from his eyes. In order for Dickie to have any functional vision, he would need to wear prescription eyeglasses for the remainder of his life. Unfortunately, Dickie was very resistant to wearing them. Through typical means, his parents attempted to encourage him to wear his glasses for nearly a year following his surgery, to no avail.

The psychologists assigned to the case utilized a shaping procedure to reinforce successive approximations toward the terminal behavior of wearing the eyeglasses appropriately. Two to three 20-minute sessions were conducted daily, during which Dickie was provided with small bites of candy or fruit following display of the current target approximation. They began by reinforcing mere physical approaches to the eyeglasses that were lying on a table in the treatment room. Next, Dickie received reinforcement when he touched the eyeglasses. Steps progressed gradually from there: reinforcing picking up the eyeglasses, moving them toward his face, placing them on his face, and finally placing them correctly on his face. The entire process took five weeks to complete. Following training, Dickie continued to wear his eyeglasses for an average of 12 hours per day – which likely exceeded what the typical four year old with eyeglasses would be expected to do.

We selected this example precisely to make the point that behavioral shaping is central to *any* effective instructional program designed to teach young children with autism. The reader will quickly grasp that success in these various teaching modalities depends on expertise in effectively using behavioral shaping.

The Shaping Process

It's time to examine the actual "nuts and bolts" of the shaping process, including the steps involved and some helpful hints, as well as some of the common pitfalls encountered.

The obvious first step in any teaching situation is to identify what will be taught. Less obvious, however, are the problems that can be encountered if this selection process is not carried out in a systematic and objective fashion. For shaping to be effective, it is critical that a specific **terminal behavior** be identified and operationally defined so that the instructor (and any additional instructors involved with the child) is clear on what behavior is to be reinforced.

Failing to operationally define the terminal behavior can result in poor responding by the learner, and subsequent frustration for the instructor. For example, if we are teaching a young child to respond to the receptive command "touch head," we will need to define the correct response topography as something like this: *movement of either hand alone from a resting position on his lap or table upward and contacting it with the top of his head.*

Without such a precise definition, the instructor may be tempted to reinforce a variety of similar but different responses such as touching the face, two-handed touching of the head, or combining a previously learned command such as hand clapping with the touching of the head (resulting in a two-step response). While some of these alternatives may not initially appear to be "that far off" and possibly worthy of reinforcement, allowing "drifting" from the original definition of the target behavioral response undermines instructional control and results in an unacceptable level of imprecision that will likely come back to haunt the instructor when he or she tries to teach more complex discrimination tasks.

The child in this case is unclear about what he is precisely to do following the instruction, because he has had a variety of similar responses reinforced over time. If we would move on to finer discriminations of receptive identification of body parts, the child would likely have great difficulty responding accurately to alternating trials of "touch head" versus "touch face," because solid instructional control was never established with the initial task of touching his head.

Once the terminal behavior has been appropriately identified and defined, the next step in the use of shaping would be to *task analyze* the terminal behavior. A **task analysis** is conducted when we break a complex skill or series of behaviors into smaller, teachable units (Cooper, Heron, & Heward, 1987). When we speak of shaping, these steps of the task analysis become synonymous with the successive approximations that are eventually arranged in a systematic progression and reinforced as you shape the terminal behavior.

As an example, let us return to the receptive "touch head" command described above. The movement cycle that begins with the child lifting a single hand from his lap and ends with the placement of that same hand on the top of his head could potentially be broken down into an infinitesimal number of intermediate steps. However, for most instructional purposes (including this example), we want to limit the number of intermediate steps. This decision is typically made by the practitioner, and is based on the rate of progress the child displays at any given moment in the shaping process. Providing too many intermediate steps can actually slow the child's progress, as the potential exists to provide too much reinforcement at a given step. This, in turn, bogs the child down at that point in the process.

The Role of Extinction

If behavioral shaping is viewed as an exercise in differential reinforcement, it is easy to see the critical role that extinction plays in the process. Again, looking at the receptive command example, we can see that the progression of steps might begin with the instructor reinforcing any vertical movement of the single hand off of the child's lap. Once that behavior is reliably being displayed and reinforced, we wait for the next identified step in the sequence to occur – such as vertical movement of the hand more than three inches from his lap. Once that behavior is displayed, the previous step in the sequence (vertical movements of the hand less than three inches from the child's lap) is placed on extinction and no longer receives reinforcement. In this way, we differentially reinforce vertical hand movements of three inches or more.

When a child stalls at a given step in the shaping sequence, it can quite often be attributed to one of two occurrences:

a) Lingering too long on a given step. This can cause a particular response to become resistant to extinction and reduce the probability that the child will exhibit the next step's response.

b) Failing to use extinction properly once the child shows the ability to move on to the next step. This weakens instructional control by equally reinforcing the responses for both the previous and current steps.

The optimum number of steps in the shaping sequence will vary with the task and with the child. Generally speaking, an ongoing analysis of the child's progress is the best means of determining whether reinforcing is adequate, and that appropriate steps in the shaping sequence have been chosen. (This analysis can be accomplished through the close observation of the child during training, as well as an ongoing inspection of the data collected during training sessions.) Excessive errors on the part of the child may indicate that the steps are too large and that additional intermediate steps may be necessary. Stagnation at a particular step may indicate an improper use of extinction on the previous step's response and an overuse of reinforcement on the current step. A smooth, steady progression from step to step suggests that shaping is being used effectively.

It is also very important to be consistent when making the decision to move to the next step in the shaping sequence. To make this possible, objective criteria for the movement between steps in the shaping sequence should be established before the training begins. Data analyses that look at rate, percentage correct, or trials-to-criterion may be best suited for this purpose. In our example above, we might select as our criterion the unprompted completion of the target response (any vertical movement of the single hand off of the child's lap) for three consecutive trials.

Once the child completes the target response without any assistance from the instructor for three consecutive trials, the simple vertical movement ceases to be reinforced and only vertical movements of three inches or more receive reinforcement.

The Role of Prompting

Next, consider an example of how prompting can be used to speed up the shaping process, where the terminal behavior in question is head touching.

The instructor selects any *vertical movement of the student's single hand from his lap* as the initial step in the shaping process. The first instructional sessions involve providing a prompt (likely a partial physical prompt) to lift the hand from the lap, followed by the immediate delivery of meaningful reinforcement to the student. As the student begins to understand the contingency, he begins lifting his hand off of his lap without the prompt. Once these unprompted, low-level hand-lifting responses occur several times, the instructor provides a new level of prompting to ensure that the student lifts the hand at least three inches from his lap.

At this point in the shaping process, the instructor begins to use differential reinforcement. All previously reinforced responses (hand lifts of less than three inches from the lap) cease to be reinforced – i.e., these responses are placed on extinction. Only hand lifts of three inches or more receive reinforcement. Successive steps involve prompting and differential reinforcement of closer and closer approximations of the terminal behavior – i.e., lifting of the hand higher and higher until the student touches his head.

At each step along the way, it is imperative that the instructor cease reinforcing the previous step, so that the student makes smooth progress toward the terminal behavior.

Two Types of Shaping

So far, we have suggested that shaping can be used to teach a child a new form of a behavior from a different response class. For example, if a child is able to vocalize the individual phonemes that make up the word "cat" but is unable to say the word "cat," we can use shaping to teach the new behavior of saying "cat" – a member of a different response class. This type of shaping is often referred to as **shaping across response classes** (Cooper, Heron, & Heward, 1987).

Shaping can also teach the child to increase the duration or magnitude of a response. This form of shaping, known as **shaping within a response class**, takes responses of identical topography (e.g., whispering the word "cat" compared with speaking the word "cat" at conversational volume) and reinforces successive approximations of increased magnitude or duration. Examples of behavior found lacking in young children with autism that would be appropriate for shaping within a response class might include volume of speech, duration of eye contact, or duration of sitting still.

There are several advantages in using shaping to teach new skills to our children. First, shaping uses only positive reinforcement – no punitive components are included. Second, shaping is very effective in teaching skills that a child has never exhibited – as discussed previously, children with autism have long lists of skills that have never been displayed. Finally, shaping can be combined with other techniques to create an effective, custom-made intervention for a child. One popular example of melding shaping with another technique is the widespread use of shaping as an integral part of DTI.

While shaping has clear advantages, it also has several characteristics that may make it less than desirable for a particular child or a particular skill. Quite frequently, aside from the issues of improper differential reinforcement, a child just responds inconsistently. She may linger on one step longer than she should, or suddenly jump ahead several planned steps to a more difficult step.

Another disadvantage is that the subtle changes in behavior that must be recognized and reinforced during shaping are sometimes difficult to observe. Agreement between instructors or therapists as to whether a specific movement or sound was made is often difficult to come by. This is particularly problematic when teaching verbal imitation skills, where determining whether an accurate articulation of a specific speech sound was made typically requires close observation and a well-trained ear.

The two disadvantages noted above illuminate a third, potentially more problematic concern with shaping. Practitioners of shaping must be well trained and experienced enough to effectively deal with inconsistent student responding, and must have the well-honed observational skills necessary to pick up on slight variations in speech articulation. The average therapist-candidate entering an EIBI program does not initially have these practical skills strongly established in his or her repertoire, and requires extensive hands-on training to develop effective behavior-shaping skills.

Finally, as one might surmise from the examples used in this chapter, shaping can be both time-consuming and labor-intensive. Literally hundreds of trials may be required for a child to progress from the initial step to the terminal behavior. Along the way, impatience, frustration, distraction, and the overall amount of work required of the child can all negatively impact success with shaping.

Section F - Transfer of Stimulus Control

Transfer of stimulus control is a necessary part of any program that involves shaping or teaching new skills. Transfer of stimulus control can take many forms, but planned transfer usually involves superimposing stimuli or fading of some sort. It refers to the processes that allow us to somehow be able to take what the child can already do and bring it under the control of new stimuli, cues, instructions, etc.

For example, we would like to teach children with autism some basic language concepts, like categories. We begin with an obvious example, such as "cow." We assume that giving the cow (the target behavior) is already under the stimulus control of "give me cow." In other words, the child knows the receptive label for cow. To transfer the control of the giving behavior to "give me animal," we might "superimpose" the two stimuli on top of one another. This could be accomplished by saying, "give me animal…cow." Over time, we may fade the use of "cow" in the S^D until it is no longer existent. Eventually, we will fade in numerous examples from the category of animals, until the child can respond successfully to the S^D "give me animals." The response was initially under the control of the S^D "cow," but control was transferred to "animal" through the fading process.

Another example of this can be applied to a child whose work on pronoun acquisition has been largely ineffective. After many unsuccessful trials concerning fading of traditional prompts, it may be helpful to revise the skill program to include the pairing of a colored cue card with the spoken word "my," along with a physical prompt. Over time, the physical prompt can be faded out, allowing the behavior to come under the control of "my" and the colored card. After even more training and fading, the size or hue of the card can be faded to zero, bringing the target behavior under the control of the spoken word "my."

This is also the key concept in the establishment of **stimulus generalization** (Cooper, Heron, & Heward, 1987). Think about normal, everyday conversational skills that we call upon on a regular basis, and a great deal of stimulus generalization can be seen at work. There are many different types of question forms, comments, gestures, etc. that allow us to communicate with one another.

For example, my behavior of turning on a light may be under the control of:

1. Someone else saying, "It sure is dark in here!"
2. Someone saying, "Can you please turn on the light?"
3. A sign on the door that says, "Please turn on light when entering."
4. Another person yelling, "Turn it on!" and so forth.

The point is that there are many different types of stimuli that we respond to with similar behaviors. In order for all of these stimuli to gain control over the same type of behavior, there has to be some type of transfer from an initial stimulus or set of stimuli. Over time, through pairing or superimposition, fading, or some other way of associating new stimuli with already-established ones, control of our behavior can be transferred to many types of stimuli.

Like most of what we have discussed, these processes can happen inadvertently, as a part of everyday life, or they can occur as a result of careful planning. Knowledge of stimulus control is important, because we have to be able to identify how it happens in case the child with autism has learned to over-generalize (all people with brown hair are named "Paul," because one person they met who had brown hair was named Paul), or if the child is not showing enough stimulus generalization to be ultimately functional.

Parents and other caretakers can themselves serve as stimuli. In this case, a parent can be part of a stimulus condition that brings about either appropriate or inappropriate behaviors. When this happens, we tend to say that the parent for whom the child behaves appropriately has stimulus control over the child's general pattern of behaviors. It would be more accurate to say that the presence of the parent serves as a stimulus, and this stimulus has control over the child's general response characteristics.

This stimulus control is inevitably the result of consistent pairing with other stimuli and consequences, to the point that the mere presence of the parent takes on characteristics of the antecedent stimuli that have previously prompted the child's behaviors. On the down side, when a parent has consistently been in the presence of stimuli that prompt inappropriate behaviors for which the child has been reinforced, their presence gains an amount of stimulus control over negative behaviors.

In other words, Mom or Dad's presence has come to exert stimulus control over "good" or "bad" behavior.

In the above scenario, behavior analysts try to develop programs that allow a transfer of stimulus control from the person who has come to exert sufficient control over the child's appropriate behaviors to the person(s) who struggle to exert such control. This is usually a daunting task, but it can be accomplished quite successfully through well-planned use of extinction, reinforcement, prompting, pairing, and shaping.

References:

Cooper, J. O., Heron, T. E., & Heward, W.L. (1987). *Applied behavior analysis.* Upper Saddle River: Prentice-Hall.

Ferster, C.B., & Culbertson, S.A. (1982). *Behavior principles* (3rd ed.). Englewood Cliffs, NJ: Prentice-Hall.

Lovaas O.I., & Smith, T. (1989). A comprehensive behavioral theory of autistic children: Paradigm for research and treatment. *Journal of Behavior Therapy and Experimental Psychiatry, 20*, 23-24.

Rilling, M. (1977). Stimulus control and inhibitory processes. In W.K. Honig & J.E.R. Staddon (Eds.), *Handbook of operant behavior* (pp. 432-480). Englewood Cliffs, NJ: Prentice-Hall.

Skinner, B.F. (1953). *Science and human behavior.* New York: MacMillan.

Snell, M.E., (1983). Implementing and monitoring the IEP: Intervention strategies. In M.E. Snell (Ed.), *Systematic instruction of the moderately and severely handicapped* (2nd ed., pp. 113-145). Columbus, OH: Charles E. Merrill.

Wolf, M. M., Risley, T. R., & Mees, H.L., (1964). Application of operant conditioning procedures to the behavior problems of an autistic child. *Behaviour Research and Therapy, 1*, 305-312.

Functional Analysis of Problem Behavior
At a Glance

Chapter Points

- The consequences that maintain a type of behavior are known as "functions."
- Functions can include attention, escape, preferred items or activities, and self-stimulation.
- Identifying the function of a behavior allows us to tailor effective interventions.
- Interventions based on behavioral topography are not as effective as those based on function.
- Functional analysis includes many methods.
- Experimental analyses are the only way to establish functional relationships, as opposed to mere correlations.

Key Terms

Function

Functional Analysis

Indirect Methods

Direct Methods

Functional Analysis Interview

Motivational Assessment Scale (MAS)

Functional Analysis Screening Tool (FAST)

Descriptive Analyses

Anecdotal Reporting

A-B-C Analysis

Functional Behavior Assessment Observation Form

Structured A-B-C Analysis Form

Scatter Plot

Analogue Condition Functional Analysis

Maintaining Variables

Visual Analysis

Functional Analysis of Problem Behavior

It is Always Function Over Form

When people hear the word "autism," many different images or thoughts come to mind. Included in these are stereotypes from the film industry, such as Dustin Hoffman's Raymond from *Rain Man*; Simon, a child with autism who cracks top secret computer codes in the film *Mercury Rising*; or Molly, the character played by Elizabeth Shue in the film of the same name.

More often than not, what is portrayed on film and television is both an inaccurate distortion and magnification of characteristics that have their basis in reality. And while dramatic portrayals may be inaccurate in detail, most parents who live with a child with autism – as well as anyone who deeply cares for one – will agree that children with autism often pose behavioral challenges.

In addition to displaying significant skill deficits, children with autism often *do* engage in dangerous, aggressive, socially inappropriate, or otherwise challenging behaviors that can impact all areas of family life. As a result, they may be excluded from family or social events. Problem behaviors can interfere with a child's ability to receive and respond to instruction, and can also prevent other children from approaching. Parents feel the stress that stems from a child's misbehavior, coupled with uncertainty and debate over how to stop it. Teachers also feel frustration, wondering how much more effective they could be in teaching new skills if only they could get a firmer handle on problem behavior.

Even though these examples are all presented in relation to the topic of this manual, the issues presented are encountered by many families, regardless of the presence of a child with an autism spectrum disorder. Everyone knows someone who is struggling or has struggled with child behavior problems of some kind.

Despite this, there is a tendency for parents and professionals to try to "explain away" behavior problems as simply a manifestation of autism. In our work with children with autism and their families, and even when discussing these issues with other professionals, it is quite typical to hear or read comments like, "Paul engages in self-injurious behaviors as a result of his diagnosis of autism," or "Jenna frequently screams because she is autistic."

This viewpoint can actually do quite a bit of harm, for several reasons. First, it minimizes the role of external events in establishing and maintaining problem behaviors. This obscures our ability to alter the environment to encourage behavior change. Second, it serves as a fatalistic source of inaction that perpetuates the problems themselves. If we feel that problem behaviors are innate, we are wasting our time trying to address them. Finally, the circular argument that children with autism misbehave because they are autistic closes many doors of opportunity that can be opened through the application of operant conditioning.

While it is true that autism is a neurobiological disorder that ultimately has an effect on how individuals acquire and assimilate information, the diagnosis itself does not negate the effects of consequences on behavior. The future frequency of any behavior is determined, in part, by reinforcement, punishment, or the absence thereof when it (or similar behaviors) was displayed in the past. This is something that applies to all of us – autistic or not, child or adult.

This chapter explains how a basic knowledge of operant conditioning can be used to understand how problem behaviors are built and maintained. The goal is to empower the reader with the skills necessary to learn why behaviors really occur, which is prized information when building a program to make them stop. At the same time, readers will learn why conducting a functional analysis to answer these questions is not always as easy as it might appear – although it *is* possible in almost all cases.

Section A – Function of Behavior

School behavior plans and classroom management plans are the "rules" that govern children's behavior in school settings. Likewise, in legal and judiciary systems, rules of conduct are often stated, and consequences for infractions of these rules are also clearly defined.

The typical scenario goes something like this: "You are not allowed to [insert behavior of choice]. If you do [insert behavior of choice], we will [insert consequence]." This can be applied to any number of behaviors in any setting. For example, in most schools with a strict policy against fighting, the rule is often a variation of, "You are not allowed to fight. If you fight, we will suspend you for five days." Another example is littering: "You are not allowed to litter. If you litter, we will write you a citation and fine you $500."

It is safe to say that the above examples represent the status quo, because most common behavior management systems are built to be "one size fits all." At the same time, there are many people for whom the status quo fails miserably – especially when we are trying to influence the behavior of individuals with autism.

What are some potential problems with the above system, based on what has already been learned in this manual?

First, most of the behavior management programs in question do not take into account that behaviors are shaped over time by a reinforcement history. In other words, behaviors occur because they have been reinforced in the past – which is undeniably a unique chain of events for every individual. Because of this, these programs cannot possibly provide the custom fit that is necessary for real effectiveness and efficiency.

Second, most of the existing systems of behavior management rely on punishment (in its common understanding) as the main vehicle of behavior change. In Chapter 6, we discussed at length the correct definition of punishment – that it occurs after a behavior, and has a decreasing effect on the future frequency of behavior. Therefore, what is punishing to one person may not be to another, and may actually be reinforcing. We also know that punishment carries with it many warnings, because it can create many problems.

Third, behaviors may be similar in topography (form), but far different in terms of function (the purpose they serve). The **function** of a behavior is inherently related to the individual's history of reinforcement (Skinner, 1953). More precisely, the function of a behavior is essentially its reinforcement contingency.

Function, or purpose, is the core of any behavior. This is the *real* answer to the "why" question so often left out of behavioral discussions (at worst) or relegated to circular explanations (at best). It is the most important consideration when developing a system for behavior change, yet it is also the most ignored. This is where the real substance of this chapter begins.

The Role of Consequences

Our understanding of operant conditioning teaches us that voluntary behavior is maintained by its consequences. When the same behavior occurs often, it is likely that its consequences in the past have served a purpose.

Why, for example, do we flip a switch in a dark room? Because we learned in the past that doing so provides us with light. Would we be so inclined if flipping a switch had no result? Of course not, for extinction would have occurred. The same concept applies to most behaviors (good and bad). Think of the behavior as the "switch," and the consequence as the appliance that is operated. When a child does not want to go to bed and screams, flails, or argues (the switch), chances are that the bedtime will be at least temporarily postponed (the appliance). If the tantrum is especially effective, he or she will manage to squeeze a "Five more minutes, and *then* bed!" out of her parents. If this happens, chances are this will not be the last occurrence.

If we are to develop an effective approach to problem behaviors, we have to accomplish two main tasks. First, we must render the behavior powerless to influence the environment. Second, we have to understand that the function of most behaviors is indicative of a real need, and stopping a behavior rarely does much to take away the reason for its occurrence in the first place.

For children with autism or other developmental disorders, there are obviously great deficits in communication skills. As a result, maladaptive behavior often serves as a way for these children to effectively gain the things that they want or need. Screaming may result in escape from a task, as may a simple request for a break. Both serve the same function (escape), which is equally desirable in both situations. In other words, teaching a child not to scream will not make him or her want to escape any less. The answer is to teach replacement behaviors that will serve the same purpose for the child.

Common Functions of Problem Behavior

Rendering a behavior powerless to serve its purpose and teaching a replacement behavior are impossible without knowing what function the problem behavior serves in the first place. Before we can explain how this is accomplished, we must first understand a little bit about possible functions. The common functions of problem behavior can usually be categorized into four groups:

1. Attempts to gain some kind of ***attention*** *or response from another person.*

Attention, tangible/preferred activities, and automatic reinforcement are all examples of positive reinforcement, because they involve adding or presenting something after the behavior. Attention can be delivered by any kind of approach from another person, including a hug, a question, a verbal response, a reprimand, or even a glance.

2. Attempts to gain access to a ***tangible item or preferred activity.***

Tangible reinforcement can be represented by the presentation of food, toys, or any other items. Reinforcement in the form of preferred activities can include extra time to play a game or the opportunity to watch a favorite television show.

3. Attempts ***to escape*** *a demand or* ***to avoid*** *something or someone.*

Escape refers to behaviors that result in a demand being lifted or the removal of some environmental condition. Avoidance refers to behaviors that result in environmental conditions not being presented in the first place.

4. ***Automatically maintained behaviors,*** *where the behavior itself feels good (self-touching, nail biting, etc.).*

In these cases, the behavior creates its own consequence, rather than stimulating the environment to do so. Automatic reinforcement can involve any behavior that, in itself, creates a pleasurable feeling. These types of behaviors are generally self-stimulatory by nature.

Most problem behaviors in children are the result of attention, escape/avoidance, or preferred item/activity functions. These functions may work independently or in combination. By analyzing behaviors with the above functions in mind, there is a great chance that inappropriate behaviors can be minimized in a relatively short period of time.

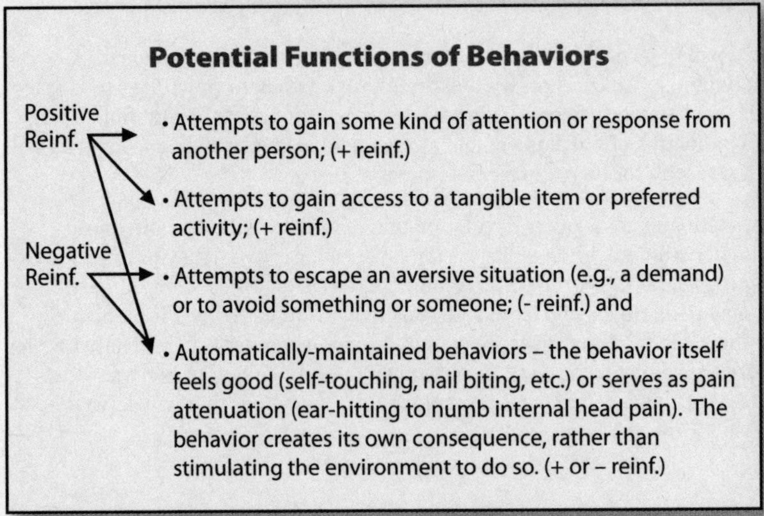

Potential Functions of Behaviors

Positive Reinf.

Negative Reinf.

- Attempts to gain some kind of attention or response from another person; (+ reinf.)
- Attempts to gain access to a tangible item or preferred activity; (+ reinf.)
- Attempts to escape an aversive situation (e.g., a demand) or to avoid something or someone; (- reinf.) and
- Automatically-maintained behaviors – the behavior itself feels good (self-touching, nail biting, etc.) or serves as pain attenuation (ear-hitting to numb internal head pain). The behavior creates its own consequence, rather than stimulating the environment to do so. (+ or – reinf.)

In summary, the first step of behavior change is finding out the purpose the behavior serves. Parents and/or professionals should always ask one simple question following a behavioral incident: "Did this behavior and my reaction make the child's situation better in any way?" If the answer is "yes," chances are the behavior is likely to recur. The next task is to figure out "how" or "why" the behavior made the situation better for the child.

Section B – Basics of Functional Analysis

Functional analysis is the process of gathering information and data to develop a hypothesis about the function a behavior serves for an individual (O'Neill et al., 1997). This process is also known as a *functional assessment or a functional behavioral assessment.*

Functional analysis takes into account the scientific approach of behavior analysis, where data is used to drive decisions. During functional analysis, events are observed and measured, and environmental variables are identified and manipulated to determine their effects.

When done correctly, functional analysis allows us to eliminate some of the guesswork in determining why a behavior occurs. This allows us to develop a plan that is almost sure to uncover the root of the problem and undertake an effective intervention. There are many different approaches to gathering this information, but we strongly feel that the most valid information comes from direct observation, combined with systematic manipulation of components of the environment.

As we will learn throughout the course of this chapter, functional analysis takes many different forms, and some applications are more valid than others. (Note that even some methods with questionable validity can be useful when developing a hypothesis about a behavior's function.)

There are two major categories of methods for performing functional analysis: **indirect methods** and **direct methods**. Indirect methods obtain their data through third party anecdotal reports from parents, teachers, and others who have observed a behavior first hand. The behavior does not occur in the presence of the analyst, and systematic or experimental manipulation is never performed. Direct methods, in contrast, obtain information by directly observing and recording events. They can be based on observation alone, or they can involve experimental or otherwise systematic manipulations of environmental variables.

Section C – Indirect Methods of Functional Analysis

Indirect methods of obtaining and analyzing third-party data are usually limited to rating scales or interviews that provide a more detailed description of events that surround and include the target behaviors. Typically, these methods provide more structure and a better "picture" of the behavior than simple anecdotal discussion alone.

Sometimes, a **functional analysis interview** is used to create a picture of how others perceive the individual's behavior. O'Neill et al. (1997) developed a **Functional Analysis Interview Form** that provides a very structured format for gathering relevant data. To complete the form, the analyst meets with parents, teachers, or others who witness the target behavior, and asks a series of questions that are organized into sections. The person for whom the functional analysis is being developed does not need to be present; in fact, depending on level of functioning, his or her absence is sometimes recommended.

The interview form, which takes roughly 30-45 minutes to complete, includes sections that help develop a clear operational definition of the behavior. This is done through questions that ask for precise descriptions of the topography of the behavior. The form also asks a series of questions that requires interviewees to describe the conditions under which the behavior is likely to occur or not occur. Some questions are geared toward identifying frequency or rate of target behaviors, while others ask for descriptions of magnitude or intensity. Finally, the form asks for information regarding underlying physical conditions that could influence motivational operations (MOs).

The form is relatively easy to complete, as are most interview forms developed for this purpose.

The **Motivation Assessment Scale** (MAS) (Durand & Crimmins, 1987) is a "16-item questionnaire that assesses the functions or motivations of behavior problems. The sixteen items are organized into four categories of reinforcement (attention, tangible, escape, and sensory). The MAS asks questions about the likelihood of a behavior problem occurring in a variety of situations (e.g., when presented with difficult tasks)."

As can be seen in Figure 8.1, the MAS is an indirect measure that utilizes a 6-point, Likert-type rating scale (0-5) for the interviewer to record the respondent's observations of the target problem behavior.

Figure 8.1

Motivational Assessment Scale

	Never					Always
1. Would the behavior occur continuously if the client was left alone for long periods of time (for example, one hour)?	0	1	2	3	4	5
2. Does the behavior occur following a command to perform a difficult task?	0	1	2	3	4	5
3. Does this behavior occur when you are talking to other people in the room?	0	1	2	3	4	5
4. Does this behavior ever occur to get an object, activity, food, or game that the client has been told that he/she can't have?	0	1	2	3	4	5

Durand, V.M. & Crimmins, D.B. (1988). Motivational Assessment Scale

Unfortunately, research on the MAS indicates that it is not always reliable. For example, Zarcone et al. (1991) indicated that when several observers completed the MAS regarding the same individual's target behavior, they only agreed on 20 percent of what they observed. Such poor reliability (good reliability would be 80 percent or better) would suggest that the MAS is best used as a screening tool, and should not be utilized to determine function of behavior.

The Florida Center on Self-Injury created the **Functional Analysis Screening Tool (FAST)**, which is similar to the MAS. The FAST is an indirect measure in the form of an 18-item questionnaire. Respondents are asked questions pertaining to when the target behavior occurs, across a variety of possible environmental conditions. Additional questions are used to determine if attending adults tend to respond to the child's problem behavior in certain ways, and how the child responds to the presentation of demands or the removal of attention or tangibles. See Figure 8.2 for a sample FAST.

The FAST is described as a means to identify factors that can influence the occurrence of behavior problems. The form's directions state very clearly that the FAST should be used *only* for screening purposes as part of a comprehensive functional analysis of the problem. They also suggest that the results be used "as a guide for conducting direct observations in several different situations to verify likely behavioral functions, clarify ambiguous functions, or identify factors not included in this instrument." (Florida Center on Self-Injury, 1996). However, the FAST has never been published in peer-reviewed literature, and, thus, has no available psychometric properties.

Some clinicians develop their own forms or procedures for conducting functional analysis interviews. Usually, these resemble the one described, but with more or less detail.

Inherent Problems with Indirect Methods

When indirect methods are used as the primary source of information regarding a behavior, some problems arise.

First, all information is gained through the perspective of others. With everyone coming from a different background and level of understanding, it is safe to assume that many of the people who respond to interviews do not have the scientific objectivity that behavior analysis requires. In addition, information can be subjective, making it unreliable or invalid. For example, parents who experience a significant emotional reaction in the presence of their child's misbehavior are likely to overestimate the frequency, intensity, or duration of such behaviors. Also, parents or teachers who are aware of the role they may play in maintaining the behavior may feel embarrassed by their contributions and may subsequently "bend" the reality of their report.

Figure 8.2

Functional Analysis Screening Tool (FAST)

1. The behavior usually occurs in your presence or the presence of other clients.	Yes	No
2. The behavior usually occurs soon after you or others interact with the client in some way such as delivering an instruction, walking away from the client (ignoring the behavior), taking away a preferred item, requiring the client to change activities, talking to someone else in the client's presence, etc.	Yes	No
3. The behavior is often accompanied by other "emotional" responses such as yelling or crying.	Yes	No
4. The behavior often occurs when the client has not received much attention.	Yes	No

The Florida Center on Self-Injury (1996)

Respondents offer less-than-accurate information for a number of other reasons. Sometimes they don't know the answer, remember incorrectly, or don't have experience with some of the situations mentioned in the questions. Because of this, the validity and integrity of the method can be compromised.

The second problem with the interview method is that it does not involve any kind of manipulation. Remember that one of the hallmarks of science is the manipulation of variables to test hypotheses. To claim that one has discovered the function of a behavior without any manipulation and measurement to test the hypothesis is not sound practice. Until the relationship between function and behavior has been even minimally demonstrated, all that is shown is a correlation. In light of this, it is not surprising that many programs based on anecdotal information ultimately fail to bring change.

Despite their shortcomings, indirect methods do serve a valuable role in the development of a functional analysis. As mentioned, analysts can utilize these tools to better understand the perspective of those who deal with the problematic behavior on a regular basis. Personal, face-to-face time with these individuals also gives analysts an idea of the reinforcement history that may be maintaining *caretaker* behavior. Additionally, it can provide a history of interventions that have been tried and failed, as well as those that may have been marginally successful.

Interviews can uncover important background information about the child that might otherwise be missed – including potential physical conditions (allergies, painful conditions, etc.) that may be contributing factors.

They can also be useful in situations where a behavior occurs with relative infrequency and at such a degree of intensity that direct observation is not possible or feasible. One example of this concerns Timothy Vollmer, Ph.D., at the University of Florida, who has been involved in projects aimed at addressing large-scale social issues such as teenage runaways. How does one gather baseline data for a behavior that happens only once or twice a year without relying upon the reports of others? In this context, indirect methods may be the only recourse.

And finally, indirect methods can have a positive professional impact. The time a behavior analyst spends conducting interviews with family members and teachers often serves as an opportunity to establish trust. This, in turn, can create a more receptive response to intervention ideas presented at a later date.

Section D – Direct Methods of Functional Analysis

Direct methods of functional analysis include any technique that collects data through direct observation of the behaviors as they occur. When they do not involve manipulation of antecedent or consequence variables, but rely on observation to *describe* the behavior as it occurs across a variety of situations, they are called **descriptive analyses**.

Anecdotal Reporting

Anecdotal reporting is a direct method that involves entering the individual's environment and recording events as they occur, or in retrospect. The observer simply writes down what happens in narrative format, often employing an organizational form that categorizes events by time or sequence. Afterward, the observer reviews all of the information and tries to identify trends, such as, "Every time Emily is redirected to work, she rips her paper." Several such trends may be identified, which the analyst uses to form a hypothesis regarding function of the behavior.

Even though anecdotal reporting data are gained through direct observation, their interpretation is relatively subjective. This is because all that can be obtained is a correlation between events; a functional relationship is only suggested.

The potential benefits of anecdotal methods of analysis include the first-hand gathering of information, which eliminates one of the inherent limitations of indirect methods. This process often allows the analyst to spend time watching the individual's behavior in his or her environment, and to experience the "big picture" surrounding his or her behavior. In addition, conditions that might play motivational roles can be highlighted and recorded as narrative data. Anecdotal reporting can also provide a great opportunity for behavior analysts to hone their skills of observation and adherence to operational definitions.

A-B-C Analysis

Another direct method is the **A-B-C analysis**. This method is similar to anecdotal reporting, but organizes observation data into sections related to their placement in the "three-term contingency" of antecedent, behavior, and consequence. Here's how it works: as events transpire in the environment, the observer writes information in the appropriate place on an organizational form. If a behavior is observed, it is recorded along with the event(s) immediately preceding it and the event(s) immediately following it. This information is then used to identify recurring themes, similar to anecdotal reporting. An example of a simple A-B-C analysis can be seen in Figure 8.3.

Although it is an improvement over indirect methods and unstructured reporting, A-B-C analysis still lacks a degree of validity. It does not move beyond showing correlations, and there is no manipulation involved to test the resulting hypotheses.

Even so, A-B-C recording does have its applications. It shares all of the strengths of anecdotal recording, with the added benefit that the structure inherent in the method leads to relatively easy establishment of correlations. Any of these methods are also useful sources of information to design experimental models, which will be discussed shortly.

Example of Simple ABC Analysis

Antecedent	Behavior	Consequence
Teacher is helping another student	Student leaves seat without permission	Teacher tells student to go back to her seat
Teacher directs students to complete independent work	Student throws pencil	Teacher reprimands student and stands with her to keep her from throwing the pencil again
Students are walking as a group to the cafeteria	Student drops to the floor	Teacher physically prompts student to the cafeteria

Interpretation

If several such observations reveal the same type of information, one might assume that a correlation has been established between the student's misbehavior and the provision of attention from the teacher. Possible interventions might include addressing antecedent factors to make attention less reinforcing at those times, as well as consequence-based interventions that sever the reinforcing contingency between the problem behavior and the attention that has been following it.

It must be noted, however, that we do not recommend this type of analysis for anything more than a step toward hypothesis development that will guide an experimental FA. Descriptive analyses do not demonstrate cause/effect relationships.

Figure 8.3

Advanced Tools

Further elaborations on the A-B-C data collection system have emerged in recent years. These instruments, which extend beyond the standard A-B-C format, are designed to:

- Gain more information regarding a subject's problem behavior.
- Facilitate the discernment of patterns of behavior relative to antecedent and consequence variables.
- Foster the development of reasonable hypotheses about those behaviors.

Due to the limitations inherent in correlational analyses, we are restricting our exploration of these tools to two prominent examples. The first is the **Functional Behavior Assessment Observation Form** developed by O'Neill and colleagues (1997). This form (see Figure 8.4) allows the observer to record not only the

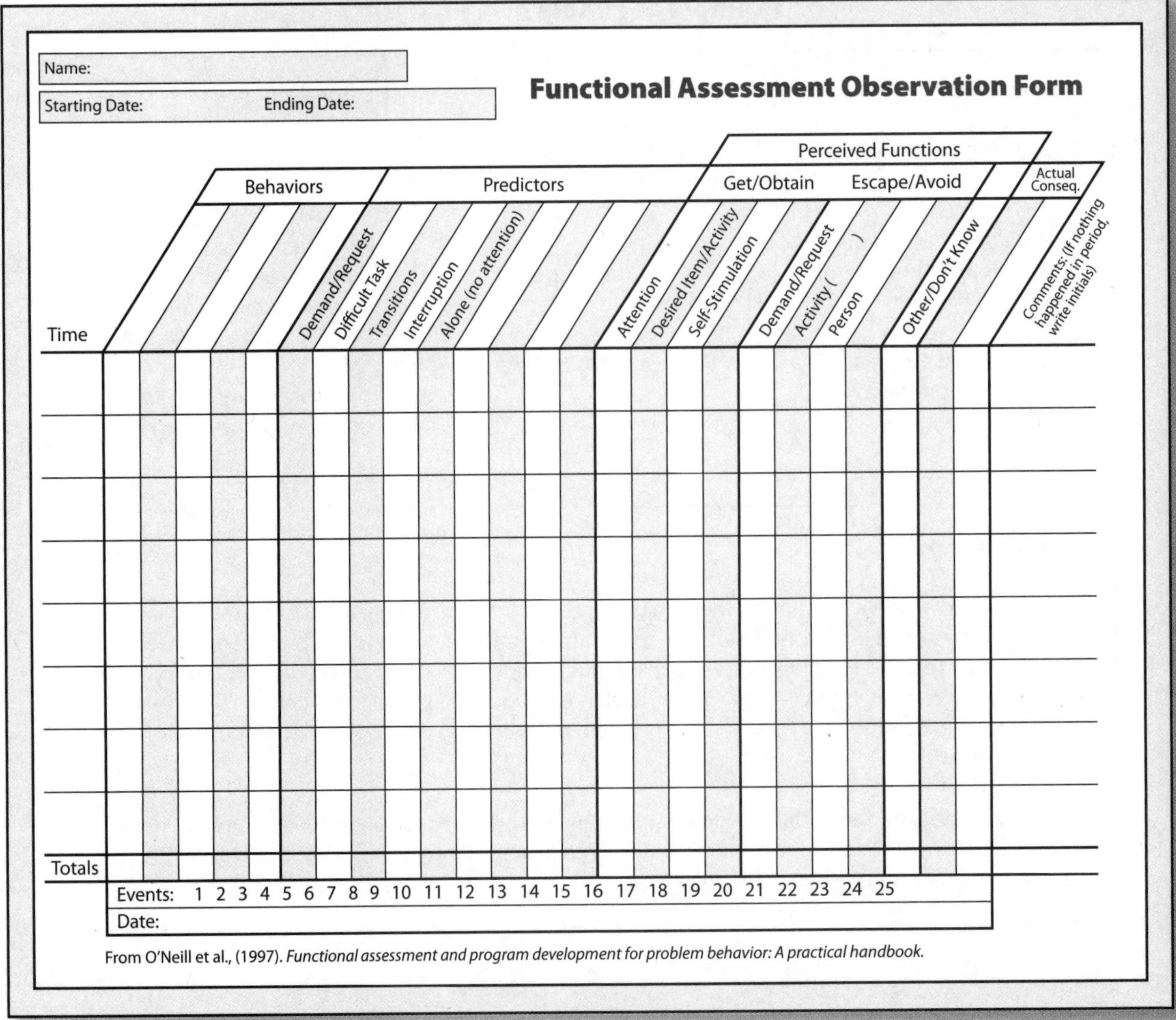

Name:

Starting Date: Ending Date:

Functional Assessment Observation Form

Behaviors

Predictors: Demand/Request, Difficult Task, Transitions, Interruption, Alone (no attention)

Perceived Functions

Get/Obtain: Attention, Desired Item/Activity, Self-Stimulation

Escape/Avoid: Demand/Request, Activity ( ), Person

Other/Don't Know

Actual Conseq.

Comments: (If nothing happened in period, write initials)

Time

Totals

Events: 1 2 3 4 5 6 7 8 9 10 11 12 13 14 15 16 17 18 19 20 21 22 23 24 25

Date:

From O'Neill et al., (1997). *Functional assessment and program development for problem behavior: A practical handbook.*

Figure 8.4

frequency of a problem behavior, but also to plot multiple occurrences of the behavior within the specific time intervals in which they occurred. This process reveals patterns of behavior that occur at certain times of day or during specific activities.

By recording what O'Neill et al. refer to as "setting events" (what we call MOs), as well as antecedent and consequence information for each incident of problem behavior, observers can accumulate correlational data pertaining to the behavior's function. A section on the form allows the observer to use this data to hypothesize about the "perceived function" of the target problem behavior(s).

One drawback is the complexity of information recorded on this one form, which creates a certain amount of confusion for observers new to using it. Given the example of the completed form in Figure 8.5 the first incident recorded on February 8 required the observer to make seven entries in five different sections of the form. Our experience with offering this form for use by direct-line staff – either

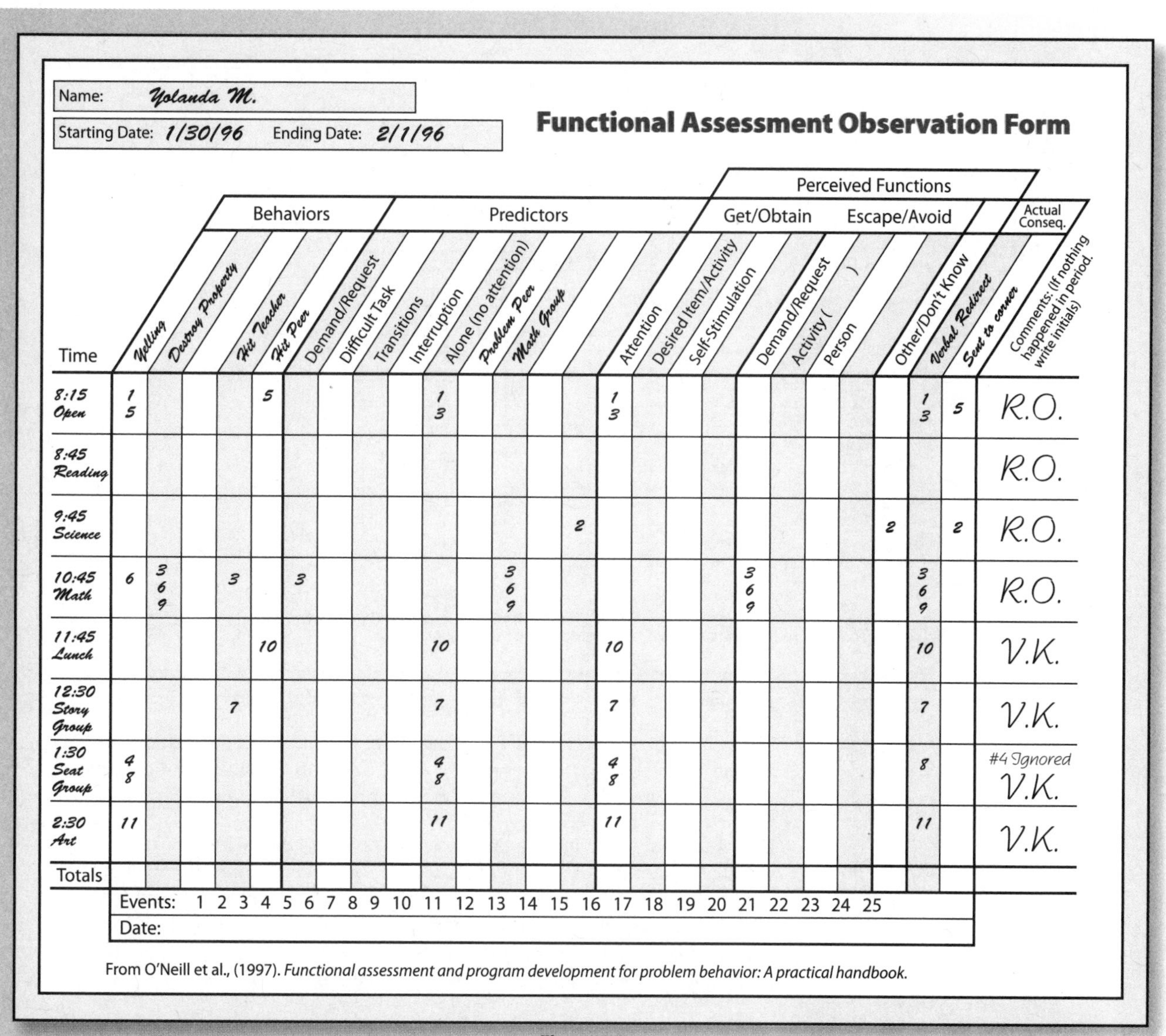

Name: *Yolanda M.*

Starting Date: *1/30/96* Ending Date: *2/1/96*

Functional Assessment Observation Form

	Behaviors					Predictors									Perceived Functions: Get/Obtain				Escape/Avoid					Actual Conseq.		
Time	*Yelling*	*Destroy Property*		*Hit Teacher*	*Hit Peer*	Demand/Request	Difficult Task	Transitions	Interruption	Alone (no attention)	*Problem Peer*	*Math Group*			Attention	Desired Item/Activity	Self-Stimulation		Demand/Request	Activity ( )	Person		Other/Don't Know	*Verbal Redirect*	*Sent to corner*	Comments: (If nothing happened in period, write initials)
8:15 Open	1 5				5					1 3					1 3									1 3	5	R.O.
8:45 Reading																										R.O.
9:45 Science														2									2		2	R.O.
10:45 Math	6	3 6 9		3		3						3 6 9							3 6 9					3 6 9		R.O.
11:45 Lunch					10					10					10									10		V.K.
12:30 Story Group				7						7					7									7		V.K.
1:30 Seat Group	4 8									4 8					4 8									8		#4 Ignored V.K.
2:30 Art	11									11					11									11		V.K.
Totals																										

Events: 1 2 3 4 5 6 7 8 9 10 11 12 13 14 15 16 17 18 19 20 21 22 23 24 25

Date:

From O'Neill et al., (1997). *Functional assessment and program development for problem behavior: A practical handbook.*

Figure 8.5

in schools or residential facilities – is that it can be visually overwhelming and somewhat impractical to use "on the run" during the often-hectic school day or residential shift.

It should also be pointed out that the data on this form continues to be correlational at best, with limited value in determining the function of the targeted behavior.

The second data collection tool that extends the use of the A-B-C chart is the **Structured A-B-C Analysis Form** developed at The Florida Center on Self-Injury. This form (see Figure 8.6) incorporates the MO, antecedent, and consequence information of the Functional Behavior Assessment Observation Form in a similar format so that the observer can make selections as to location, activity, and the immediate antecedent and consequence stimuli involved in each incident of problem behavior.

Figure 8.6

Structured ABC Analysis*

Date:
Time
Staff

Individual:

Classroom:

Behavior:

	Pos. Reinf. attn.	Pos. Reinf. tang.	Neg. Reinf. esc.	Auto. Reinf. sens.
General Activity in Progress:				
Leisure/solitary (music, TV, etc.- alone)				
Leisure/social (with another person)				
Lunch/Snack				
Academic, work, or training activity				
Immediate Antecedent:				
Staff was not directly interacting with individual				
A tangible/edible item or activity was removed/denied				
Given instruction/prompt to work				
Provoked by peer				
Individual was alone and not engaged in any activity				
Immediate Consequence:				
Attention, response block, told to stop				
Redirected to another area/activity				
Items or alternate reinforcers were offered				
Work requirement lessened or terminated				
Staff walked away				
Staff did nothing				

*Modified version of Structured ABC Analysis by The Florida Center on Self-Injury. (1996).

Differences between the FAST and the O'Neill form lie primarily in the absence of time intervals, and the presence of a more comprehensive list of possible antecedents and consequences in the Structured A-B-C Analysis Form.

Unfortunately, removing the time intervals prevents the observer from quickly visualizing patterns of problem behavior during specific times of the day. The Structured A-B-C Analysis Form does include a time-of-incident entry at the top of the form that allows the observer to perform a separate analysis of incidents related to time of day. It is questionable, however, whether any of our children's problem behaviors display a specific sensitivity to time of day.

On the positive side, the Structured A-B-C Analysis Form's inclusion of entries to track the location of each incident and the specific activity engaged in prior to the incident does allow the observer to analyze patterns of behavior that occur during routine activities (e.g., during lunch, math class, free time). These patterns, however, are not as visually apparent as those on the O'Neill et al. form.

A helpful addition in the FAST is the section located at the lower right of the form that allows the observer or analyst to summarize both the antecedent and consequence data in terms of maintaining variables. While the actual data are still rather uncontrolled and subjective, a more organized analysis can be used to develop correlations and hypotheses.

Finally, the FAST may be easier for untrained staff or parents to document. Because it is not as concerned with time-of-day patterning, it only requires a simple check mark in each of five categories arranged along a single vertical column that represents each incident. Moreover, it provides more options to choose from when recording antecedent and consequence events than those offered in the O'Neill et al. form.

Pros and cons aside, there are no published data on the validity of either of these tools, and both provide only correlational data that leave us with limited information concerning the function of any observed target behavior.

Scatter Plots

The **scatter plot** was adapted to tracking stimulus control of problem behavior by Touchette et al. (1985). It is a grid in which time intervals (usually 30 minutes) are blocked within and across days. Observers record occurrences of target behavior within these intervals across successive days in an attempt to identify time-correlated patterns of responding (Kahng et al., 1998). Figure 8.7 includes two examples of completed scatter plots from the Kahng study referenced above.

Figure 8.7

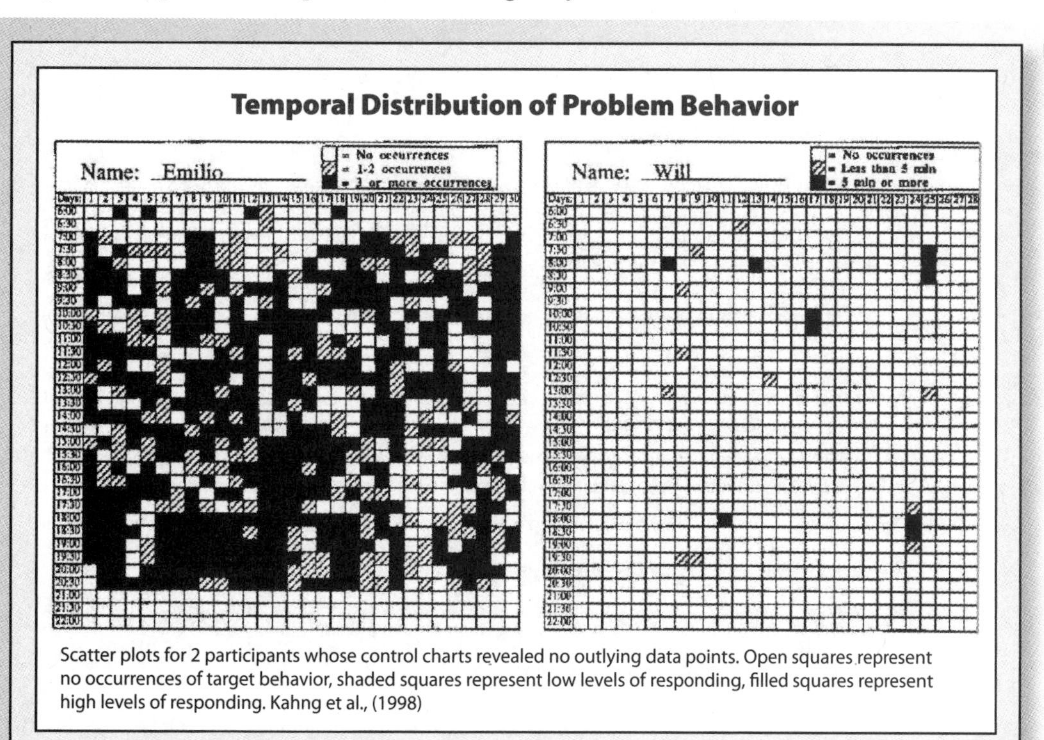

Scatter plots for 2 participants whose control charts revealed no outlying data points. Open squares represent no occurrences of target behavior, shaded squares represent low levels of responding, filled squares represent high levels of responding. Kahng et al., (1998)

Scatter plots can be visually analyzed to discern any patterns of responding that occur relative to specific times of day. Cross-referencing these temporal patterns with actual environmental events that occur at those times allows the observer to make correlations between how a child behaves and these routine changes in the environment.

The fact that scatter plots do little to provide information as to antecedent and consequent events suggests that they are significantly limited in revealing any solid functional relation between a child's target behavior and the environmental events that surround it (Axelrod, 1987). They are yet another example of a direct observation tool that establishes behavior/environment correlations but fails to divulge functional relations. Additionally, Kahng et al. (1998) showed no useful temporal patterns via scatter plot, which may be another reason to not use them.

General Limitations of Descriptive Analyses

A common theme underlies all of the functional assessment methods described so far. Whether direct or indirect, they provide the analyst with data that, at best, merely establishes correlations between a child's behavior and environmental events.

The advantages of direct methods over indirect methods are that they usually provide operational definitions of the target behavior, involve systematic observations that can be repeated across time and setting, and provide reliable quantitative data on the problem behavior. Even so, direct methods do not involve systematic manipulation of the child's environment to establish clear functional relations.

Relying solely on descriptive analysis to perform a functional assessment is not recommended, for the following reasons:

- It involves complex data collection procedures that are difficult for staff to consistently implement, and often yields subjective or inaccurate reporting of behavioral events.
- It does not allow for necessary control over the environmental variables involved.
- It often requires lengthy observations in order to capture intermittent but important information pertaining to function.
- Correlations revealed by a descriptive analysis may not indicate actual behavioral function.

In order to accurately identify the function of a child's problem behavior so that an effective intervention can be developed, behavior analysts must move beyond these initial screening tools. They must be able to conduct some form of systematic manipulation of the environmental variables that affect the child's behavior.

Section E – Experimental Methods of Functional Analysis

If there is one recurring theme in this chapter, it is the need for experimental methods of functional analysis, for which there is a strong base of support in the behavior analytic literature.

Chapter 3 discussed some of the basic principles of science and related them to the guiding principles of behavior analysis. This included establishing experimental control and the need to clearly define target behaviors. What was not covered, however, was the research model utilized by the sound practice of applied behavior analysis.

The basic premise of the experimental model is to choose a particular design that examines the effects of environmental manipulation on behavior. The primary concern is to establish a cause-effect relationship (experimental control) that is only accomplished by manipulating some element of the environment and measuring its effects on behavior. This can be done across subjects, environments, or conditions. Various phases of the experimental design allow us to describe, compare, contrast, predict, and validate information obtained in other phases.

For example, if we were testing to see if Michael head-slaps as a way to gain attention from others, we would do something similar to the following (but not necessarily in this order):

- We would start by setting up a control condition where everything is going his "way." Attention would be available, there would be no demands in place, and anything Michael wants would be available to him.
- We would test to see if the behavior is a way to escape from demands by changing the condition just a little bit so that everything is the same except for the introduction of some demands, which would be lifted when problem behavior occurred.
- To test for attention, we would keep everything the same as in the control, except that we would make attention unavailable until a problem behavior occurred.
- We would set up a condition to test for tangibles, by making preferred items or activities unavailable until a problem behavior occurred.
- We would test for automatic reinforcement by keeping everything the same as in control, except that attention would never be available.

After running these sessions a few times, we would compare data from each one. The sessions in which the highest rates of problem behavior occurs will likely represent the function. (The analysis described above is representative of a type of experimental method know as an analogue FA, which will be described in more detail shortly.)

When using experimental methods, it is important to establish tight procedures so that research can be validated or checked for reliability through replication. Finally, the hallmark of behavior analytic research is that it is subject to visual analysis, as opposed to statistical analysis. Collected data are represented visually, usually on a line graph. Because of this, changes between phases of the experimental design can be identified and analyzed on sight. This allows for quick and relatively accurate analysis of data.

The field of applied behavior analysis requires single-subject research design as a means to select and practice effective interventions. If this type of research does not support a particular intervention or technique, its implementation is a gamble. If it has support, there is a very good chance that it *is* going to work. When it comes to functional analysis or functional assessment of problem behaviors, experimental methods are the *only* methods that meet these rigorous criteria.

Functional Analysis (FA) Methods

Indirect Methods of FA (Not reliable):

Rating Scales (MAS, FAST)

Parent/Teacher Interviews (Functional Analysis Interview Form)

Learner Interviews (Counseling)

Direct Descriptive Methods of FA (Questionable reliability):

A-B-C Observation

Anecdotal Reporting

Functional Behavior Assessment Observation Form

Structured A-B-C Analysis

Scatter Plot

Direct Experimental Methods of FA (Most reliable):

Analogue Condition Functional Analysis

Systematic Manipulations

Brief Experimental Functional Analysis

Analogue Condition Functional Analysis

What do experimental methods of functional analysis look like? The fundamental experimental model comes from Dr. Brian Iwata, perhaps the world's foremost authority on self-injury and one of the most prolific researchers in behavior analysis today. In 1982, he and several colleagues published a paper outlining an experimental protocol for assessing the function, or purpose, of self-injury in students with whom they worked. The type of analysis described in this work is called an **analogue condition functional analysis**, which involves setting up experimental phases or conditions in which potentially *reinforcing* variables are manipulated.

The Iwata et al. article described procedures developed to experimentally control such variables as attention, tangibles, escape/avoidance, and automatic reinforcement. During each of the conditions, data on target behavior frequency were collected. These data were then compared to those collected in a control condition, in which the subjects were provided with relatively unrestricted access to reinforcement.

Because of the lasting influence of this work, we will describe the procedure in detail. First, the notion of "analogue" in the procedure's name refers to the idea that the experimental conditions are set up to be similar, or analogous, to conditions that might occur naturally surrounding specific behaviors. So, if it's suspected that a target behavior is maintained by a schedule of positive reinforcement in the form of attention, a condition is established that tries to provide a schedule of positive reinforcement for the behavior, while maintaining tight control over other variables.

Conditions Defined

In the classic design for analogue functional analysis, conditions are administered at random, although many behavior analysts choose to run a control condition first. In light of this, the order in which the conditions are described here is for illustration purposes only.

The **control condition**, like control conditions in any experiment, serves as a baseline or reference point for other conditions. The point of establishing this baseline is to describe the behavior under set conditions, predict what future baseline phases will look like, and provide a point to which treatment phases can be compared.

In theory, the control condition should be neutral in terms of level of demand, attention, or tangibles. A typical setup provides the child with access to tangible items in the environment, including edible items or preferred activities. Attention is provided for brief intervals, spaced perhaps 30 seconds apart. No demands are made upon the individual during this condition, but work materials may be present in the environment. Data on the target behavior is collected during this phase.

It's been suggested that target behaviors are displayed at relatively suppressed rates during control condition, because of the neutrality of the situation. Things are going relatively "well" for the individual, and care is taken not to load the environment with anything potentially aversive or overly reinforcing.

Example of Analogue Condition Functional Analysis (conditions may vary, dependent upon the learner)

Control Condition

Free access to tangibles and preferred activities

Attention available

No demands

Data are collected

Preferred Items/Activities Condition

Access to preferred items or activities is interrupted or denied, and granted contingent upon target behaviors

Attention available

No demands

Data are collected

Negative Reinforcement Condition

Free access to tangibles and preferred activities

Attention available

Demands are introduced and escape is granted contingent upon target behaviors

Data are collected

Attention Condition

Free access to tangibles and preferred activities

Attention is withheld, and granted contingent upon target behaviors

No demands

Data are collected

Alone/No Interaction Condition

Tangibles may be present (or may be absent, depending on whether or not false negatives are suspected)

Attention is withheld

No demands

Data are collected

Once this phase is complete, a small break can be offered, or the session can be terminated. The next session will occur at a later time (perhaps five minutes, but maybe a day or two). The sessions should be selected at random, but we will assume for our purposes that the next condition is the **attention condition.**

In this condition, all of the elements of the control condition remain intact, but the variable of attention from others is manipulated. In this scenario, attention is withheld *until* the target behavior occurs. If the individual engages in head slapping, for example, attention is delivered via a social approach, a reprimand, or even a look. The actual topography of "attention" in this condition can vary, dependent upon the individual's history. (This is where descriptive or indirect methods can serve a useful purpose.)

If attention is, in fact, a maintaining variable of the target behavior, than one would expect to see an increase in the frequency of the target behavior during the attention condition, relative to control condition rates.

In the **tangible condition**, the control condition remains intact, except for the individual's access to tangible items or preferred activities. In this case, tangibles are delivered only upon exhibition of the target behaviors. Attention is still available at pre-determined rates, and demands are kept low. If the child's behaviors were typically maintained by access to tangible reinforcement, we would expect to see an increase in rates of target behavior in this condition, relative to rates in the control condition.

The **escape condition** tests to see if escaping demands or avoiding conditions is a maintaining variable. To accomplish this, the only component of the control condition that is manipulated is the issuance of demands. In the control condition, demands were non-present. In the escape condition, some type of difficult demand or instruction is placed upon the child at 30-second intervals.

If the child engages in target behaviors, the demand is lifted until the beginning of the next 30-second interval. In this case, escape is delivered contingent upon presence of the target behaviors. If the individual's behaviors were maintained by negative reinforcement (escape), the rates of target behavior during this condition would show an increase over control condition rates.

A confound often exists when the presentation of a demand also means the postponement or termination of a preferred activity (i.e., "working" = "not playing"). To eliminate this, it is frequently helpful to make sure that the learner's access to preferred items is unimpeded.[1]

Finally, in the **automatic reinforcement condition**, the control condition remains intact except for the deletion of the social attention component. In this condition, the individual is left alone and observed. Tangibles are not present, because recent research has shown them to produce false-negatives (perhaps as a result of the provision of competing reinforcement), and demands are not made.

In this condition, we are trying to assess whether or not the behavior will occur regardless of socially mediated consequences. If this is the case, chances are that the behavior is occurring because something about it is reinforcing all by itself. It does not need to be followed by any type of consequence other than the sensation that the behavior itself provides. The question asked in this condition is, "Will the behavior

[1] Directed play as an escape condition to test for negative reinforcement as a maintaining variable: this may be accomplished with younger children, for example, by running the demand condition as a "directed play" condition instead. The child is permitted access to highly preferred activities, such as building blocks, but must use them in ways that are specified by the person implementing the condition.

occur when the individual is completely alone with no competing reinforcer available?" If the behavior is maintaining itself, or automatically reinforcing, rates will generally show similarity or an increase over control condition rates.

These conditions frequently last between five and ten minutes, but can be much longer or shorter, depending on the individual's history. Typically, sessions are set up to rotate through the conditions, with breaks in between, and the conditions may be repeated many times. The more often phases of a research design are repeated, the greater level of experimental control can be established. The end result is a very strong establishment of the behavior's **maintaining variables**, or the types of reinforcement that maintain a target behavior.

Additional Considerations

As mentioned, this type of analysis is most effective when the conditions can be repeated enough times to establish strong experimental control – one time through each of the conditions is usually not enough. Additionally, this type of analysis requires a great deal of planning and precision, so it is often reserved for applications in clinical settings. This need not be the case, however, for many practitioners have found success with the procedure in home and school environments. The key is training and practice. Once an analogue functional analysis has been run several times, the procedures themselves make more sense and become almost like second nature. For more detailed discussion of advanced issues in functional analysis, please refer to Figure 8.8.

In almost all cases, this type of analysis should be videotaped, because it is difficult to implement the conditions and track the behaviors at the same time. Additionally, consent should be provided, because we are setting up conditions in which we are actually trying to occasion the behaviors to see what types of naturally occurring variables are maintaining them. In other words, a successful analysis depends on exhibition of target behaviors. If we are evoking target behaviors, we should be prepared to take any safety precautions that may be necessary, and those responsible for the individual's care and well being should provide informed consent, demonstrating that they know how the procedure will be carried out.

An Alternative Approach

If time constraints, staffing issues, and the like make it impossible to follow these procedures, some type of systematic manipulation is still desirable. A functional assessment should answer two basic questions: "What makes the behavior occur?" and "What makes it stop?" Without going through the rigor required by a true analogue analysis, a scientific approach can still be taken. Practitioners should know precisely what behavior they are observing, establish a baseline, and manipulate the environment to evoke the behavior and to make it stop. The change in behavior should be measured and the procedure repeated several times. This is known as engaging in **systematic manipulations**, and is more effective than merely noting correlations through observation or indirect methods alone.

For example, all of our anecdotal information and observation data suggest that Michael engages in aggression as a means to escape particular demands, such as fine motor work. To test this hypothesis, we collect baseline data during typical school activities (excluding fine motor work). We present fine motor work on a regular basis, and see if the behavior occurs. If it does occur, we remove the work to see if the behavior will stop. All the while, we are collecting data to determine rates of behavior in each of the conditions.

Advanced Issues In Experimental Functional Analysis

This section deals with some pretty dense material. It is intended for those who are already practicing within the field, or who fully understand the basic concept of experimental functional analysis. Even those new to the topic may find that the following section can provide some valuable insight when discussing functional analysis with those responsible for conducting behavioral assessments. So, if you are interested in the topic at hand, if you don't mind sifting through some technical concepts, and you are up to the challenge, we offer this additional discussion of functional analysis in this box.

In our prior discussion of functional analysis, we said that there are ways to set up simple conditions to test for the type of reinforcement that is behind a particular behavior. Usually, one or two functions "pop out" as the culprit. However, it is also important to understand that functions of behaviors can be transient, and behaviors can also be multiply maintained.

Some behaviors begin as the result of one particular function, but the function of the behavior changes partway through. This is often the case in school environments, where behaviors often begin as a way to escape a demand, and the subsequent prompting that ensues provides a reinforcing attention component.

Functions can also be maintained in multiples, where behavior that shares the same topography (i.e., it looks the same, such as aggressive behaviors) serves multiple functions. If the behavior is strongly associated with reinforcement, and has been given the opportunity to occur often enough over time, it is not uncommon for it to become a "default" behavior that occurs for many reasons. A child may throw items to escape demands on one occasion, to gain attention on another, and to access desired items on a third.

Because of this, the set up of the actual conditions may require a bit of creativity to test for each of these hypotheses. For example, combination conditions can be developed that test for both escape and attention. (In some situations, demands actually serve as a motivational operation for attention. In this case, the presence of demands may actually increase the reinforcing value of attention, and therefore result in an increased frequency of behaviors that have gained reinforcement in the form of attention. In other words, what looks like a simple case of escape-related behavior at first glance is actually attention-maintained!) How would we test such a hypothesis in the context of an analogue condition FA?

To begin with, we have to keep in mind that a major consideration of this type of analysis is setting up conditions that will reliably evoke the behavior in question. Think of it this way – if a car is making a disturbing noise, there is little a mechanic can do to fix the problem without hearing it. When describing the problem to the mechanic, the conditions under which it occurs are also described so that the mechanic can replicate them in a controlled manner in a test-drive. With this scenario in mind, how can we set up an analogue condition that will likely evoke behavior that's been informally observed? We do it by combining elements of different analogue conditions.

The combination condition may look something like this: In condition "1," demands are presented at 30-second intervals. If the target behavior occurs, we continue to state the demand instead of lifting it, but also provide great amounts of social attention. This may include prompting, or even verbal interaction such as bargaining or questioning. In condition "2," we resort to the standard escape-from-demand condition, in which demands are lifted once behavior occurs. In condition "3," we might consider a condition in which demands are lifted but attention continues, contingent upon exhibition of target behavior.

Figure 8.8

While this is an extremely complicated set of test conditions, there are times when a "standard" or more simple functional analysis may appear to demonstrate multiple functions maintaining the problem behavior – when in fact, the contingencies maintaining the behavior are actually much more specific and subtle. For instance, attention may only be reinforcing within the context of demand. The standard attention condition would not reveal this, and the resulting data from the demand condition might lead to the false assumption that the behavior is escape-related.

What is actually happening may be the result of a complicated motivational operation, in which the presentation of demands makes attention more reinforcing. In this case, any intervention based on the presumption that the behavior is escape-related would likely make the behavior stronger, as opposed to weakening it. In order to avoid jumping to this kind of false conclusion, it is sometimes necessary to employ more advanced functional analysis methodologies.

With careful consideration, a condition can be devised to test for any of a number of combinations or reinforcer scenarios. The classic protocol may not be sufficient to test for complex functional relationships. When developing a more complex experimental analysis, MOs tend to play a large role. This is especially the case when the behavior occurs at relatively low rates (e.g., removing a jacket, in that once a person takes it off, he or she can't repeat the behavior without putting the jacket back on), or when the behaviors themselves would end the session before it could be completed (e.g., behaviors that are extremely dangerous).

Additional considerations must be incorporated into FA design when the behavior occurs at extremes of intensity. In these cases, the FA may measure latency as opposed to rate. The stronger a functional relation is between a reinforcer and the behavior, the lower the latency between the introduction of the stimulus condition portion of the analogue and the behavior. Latency is a viable option when people are concerned about the explicit reinforcement of problem behavior, or with a dangerous behavior, because sessions can be terminated shortly after the latency is recorded.

Potential Criticisms of Analogue Functional Analysis

Some critics of analogue functional analysis (according to the classic protocol) contend that the design itself could result in a shaping process within each of the conditions. If reinforcement is made contingent upon target behaviors, and placed on a schedule of 1:1 correspondence, a quick learner is likely to see in short time that the inappropriate behavior will be reinforced. Therefore, elevated rates of target behaviors can result from the analysis and not be an indication of the function outside of the analysis. However, this has not been demonstrated empirically.

To deal with the potential practice effects, or the shaping effects of the process itself, some researchers (Mace and Lalli, for example) have experimented with contingency strength issues. In these cases, they have provided reinforcement for target behaviors in relation to non-occurrence of target behaviors according to a schedule that may be more representative of naturally occurring scenarios. For an example, every occurrence of head slapping may not be reinforced in natural environments. So, during analogue condition, it won't be reinforced every time. Rather, it will be reinforced at random (as would occur in a more natural context) but on an average of every *x* time.

Still, in spite of the learning effects that can occur within the classic analogue condition functional analysis, the exaggeration of rates should remain consistent with regard to the conditions in which the variable manipulated is more reinforcing. In other words, the analysis will still demonstrate the conditions under which the problem behaviors are likely to occur. There have been thousands of replications of Iwata's initial protocol, and the treatment decisions that result have been shown to be highly effective. Because of this, we strongly endorse the use of such functional analysis procedures whenever possible.

If presentation of the demand evokes the behavior, and removal of it makes it stop, chances are the behavior is related to escape from that particular task. The downside of this method is that no real experimental control is established, so the resulting information could be described as a glorified correlation, as opposed to a true functional relationship. However, such methods are a step more reliable and scientific than non-experimental methods, and can yield useful information in a short amount of time.

Data Collection Within Analogue Condition Functional Analysis

Once an analogue functional analysis has begun, what type of data must be collected, and how is this best accomplished?

Since the ultimate goal is to compare a child's responding in the various analogues in order to determine the function of a target behavior, the selection should be limited to measuring one dimension of the behavior. Likewise, consistency should be maintained in the data collection methodology across all conditions. Vacillating between several different dimensions or using two different data collection methods will not allow a fair comparison of the child's responding across conditions, and will therefore compromise efforts to accurately determine function.

Generally speaking, many of the problem behaviors encountered in young children with autism are easily evoked in analogue conditions and are of relatively high frequency, making them conducive to frequency-based measurement. For this reason, frequency is selected for most functional analyses conducted with young children with autism.

Even so, the two most common dimensions of target behavior measured during an analogue functional analysis are *rate* and *latency*.

The clear advantages of rate-based analyses of data over simple frequency or percentage-based methods make it the most preferred dimension to study in experimental analyses. If rate is used as the datum for analysis of a problem behavior, it can easily be maintained during the treatment phase so that a sound comparison can be made between the child's rate of responding during the analysis, during treatment, and following treatment.

Latency measures are also helpful, particularly when analyzing low-frequency behaviors. If, for example, the target behavior of head hitting can only be evoked once during the five-minute attention conditions, it may not be very meaningful to compare that rate (0.2 responses per minute) if the same rate of head hitting in the demand conditions reliably displays one incident per each five-minute session (see Fig. 8.9).

If, however, the same behaviors are observed for latency – i.e., the time between the reinforcing stimuli being presented or removed and the onset of the target behavior, more differentiation between the conditions might be seen. Even with similarly low *rates* of target behavior between the two conditions in the above example, the child averaged 45 seconds from the moment adult attention was removed and he began exhibiting the target behavior in the attention condition. Conversely, his latency in the demand condition – i.e., the time between the presentation of a demand and the onset of target behavior, averaged five seconds. A visual display of the child's latency across several analogue sessions (see Fig. 8.10) demonstrates a much clearer differentiation between attention and demand conditions than in a rate-based analysis of the same child's analogue sessions.

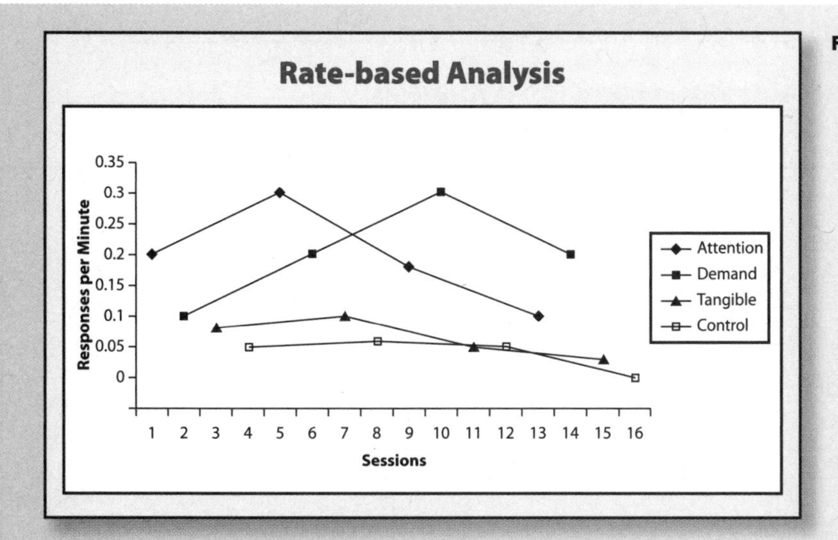

Figure 8.9

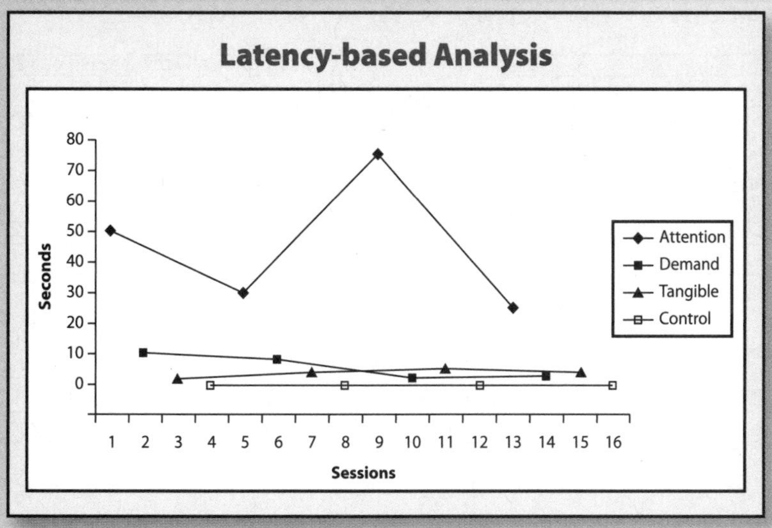

Figure 8.10

Collecting Data

Raw data are collected to provide either a rate (responses per minute), or a percentage of intervals in which the target behavior occurs. The two accepted methods for collecting functional analysis data split along these lines. Partial interval recording provides a percentage of intervals in which the target behavior is displayed (see Figure 8.11), while a strict frequency count within specified observational intervals provides a rate of responding. (Please refer to the discussion of data collection in Chapter 5 to review interval recording and continuous data collection.)

An additional way to maintain the accuracy of data recording is using a video camera to film the analogue conditions. Once the sessions are complete, the observer can view the videotape of each analogue and complete the data recording. Having the entire functional analysis on videotape also affords the observer the luxury of reviewing any session (or portion of session) repeatedly – thus decreasing the probability of error in data collection. A video camera also allows for several individuals to observe the analogues without actually being in the observation area. This reduces the potential for the child's responding to be influenced by the mere presence of several observers.

Analogue Functional Analysis
Partial Interval Recording Form

Child: ______________________________

Observer: Bob Gulick　　　　Date: 09/07/2005

Alone Condition　　Condition# 4　　Interval set at: 30 sec　　% of Intervals: 0%

1	2	3	4	5	6	7	8	9	10	11	12	13	14	15	16	17	18	19	20	21	22	23	24	25	26	27	28	29	30
0	0	0	0	0	0	0	0	0	0	0	0	0	0	0	0	0	0	0	0										

Attention Condition　　Condition# 2　　Interval set at: 30 sec　　% of Intervals: 25%

1	2	3	4	5	6	7	8	9	10	11	12	13	14	15	16	17	18	19	20	21	22	23	24	25	26	27	28	29	30
0	0	+	0	+	+	+	0	0	0	0	0	0	0	0	+	0	0	0	0										

Demand Condition　　Condition# 5　　Interval set at: 30 sec　　% of Intervals: 80%

1	2	3	4	5	6	7	8	9	10	11	12	13	14	15	16	17	18	19	20	21	22	23	24	25	26	27	28	29	30
0	+	+	+	+	+	0	0	+	+	+	+	+	+	+	0	+	+	+	+										

Tangible Condition　　Condition# 3　　Interval set at: 30 sec　　% of Intervals: 40%

1	2	3	4	5	6	7	8	9	10	11	12	13	14	15	16	17	18	19	20	21	22	23	24	25	26	27	28	29	30
0	0	+	+	+	0	0	0	0	0	0	0	+	0	+	+	+	0	+	0										

Play Condition　　Condition# 1　　Interval set at: 30 sec　　% of Intervals: 10%

1	2	3	4	5	6	7	8	9	10	11	12	13	14	15	16	17	18	19	20	21	22	23	24	25	26	27	28	29	30
0	0	0	0	0	0	0	+	0	0	0	0	0	+	0	0	0	0	0	0										

Figure 8.11

Section F – Visual Display/ Interpretation of Data

Once the data are recorded, and either a rate of behavior or a percentage of intervals that occurred for all analogue sessions is provided, the next step is to graph the results. This information is used to conduct a visual analysis or interpretation of the data.

Whether the data are expressed as responses per minute or as percentages of intervals, behavior analysts generally prefer to use *line graphs*. (The graph in Figure 8.12 is presented as an example of a functional analysis line graph.) This is because line graphs allow us to view trends in the child's responding across sessions of a single analogue condition. For example, in the graph in Figure 8.12, we might be interested in how the child's rate of responding increases in the attention condition as the analysis progressed from the first to the fourth session.

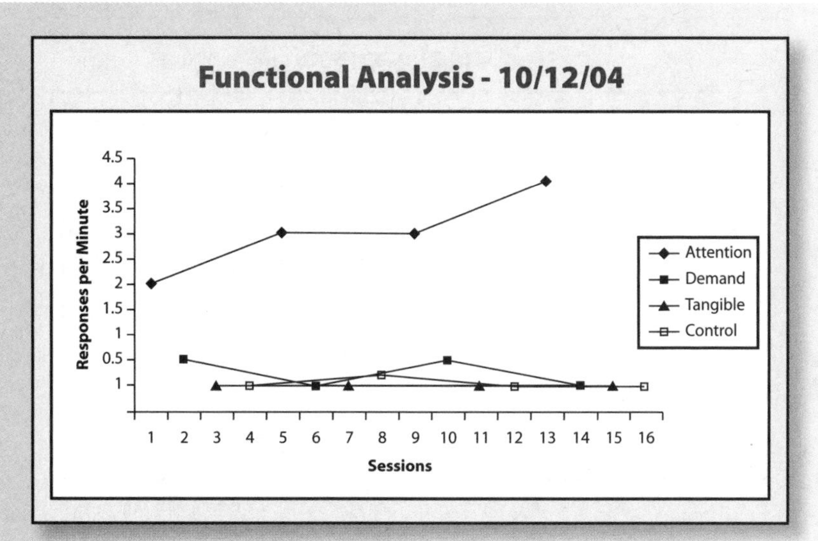

Figure 8.12

More importantly, the line graph provides us with a linear representation of the child's responding in each of the analogue conditions. A separate data path is available to view the child's responding in the attention condition, the demand condition, the tangible condition, and the control condition. The visual display set up by these four series of data allows us to compare responding *to the control* condition and interpret the results of the functional analysis.

Interpreting the Results

Interpreting the results of functional analyses graphs requires us to first develop an understanding of some of the basic principles and concepts of interpreting *any* graphic display of behavioral data.

Behavior analysts use an orderly inspection of the graphic display of behavioral data that is known as **visual analysis**. These analyses identify if significant or meaningful change in behavior has occurred (such as between baseline and treatment), and if that change can be attributed to any environmental changes engineered by the analyst (i.e., treatment) (Cooper, Heron, & Heward, 1987).

Using visual analysis, the behavior analyst tries to answer these questions about behavioral change, including whether a functional relationship exists between the behavior change and controlled environmental events. The analyst looks at four basic properties of data to assist in this process.

First, the analyst counts the number of data points available. In the functional analysis data collected, each session of each analogue condition yields a data point representing either the child's rate of responding or percentage of intervals in which the target behavior is observed, depending on which recording method was used.

It is generally accepted that the more data points there are or the longer the time period for data collection, the more accurate a statement about the trend in the data.

For example, if only two sets of analogue conditions are conducted, the analyst is less able to observe accelerating or decelerating trends than if five sets are conducted. The graphs in Figure 8.13 and 8.14 illustrate this situation. When it comes to visual analysis, more information is generally better.

Figure 8.13

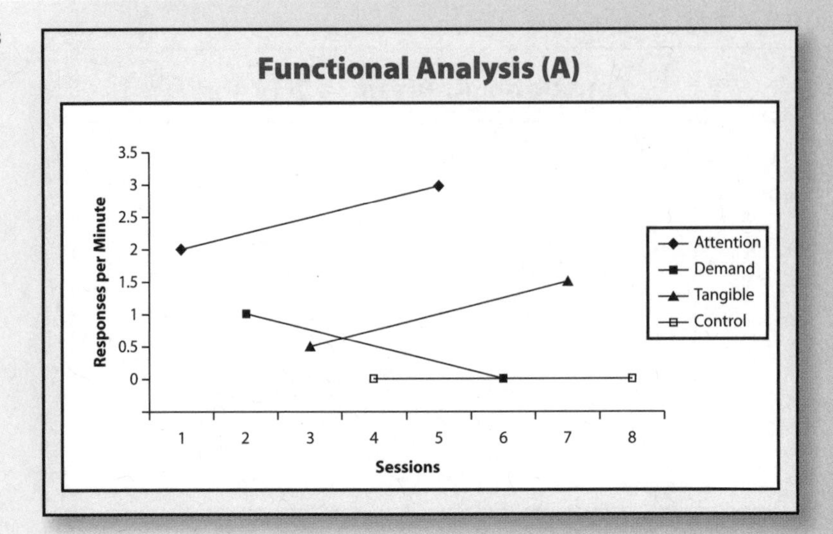

Figure 8.14

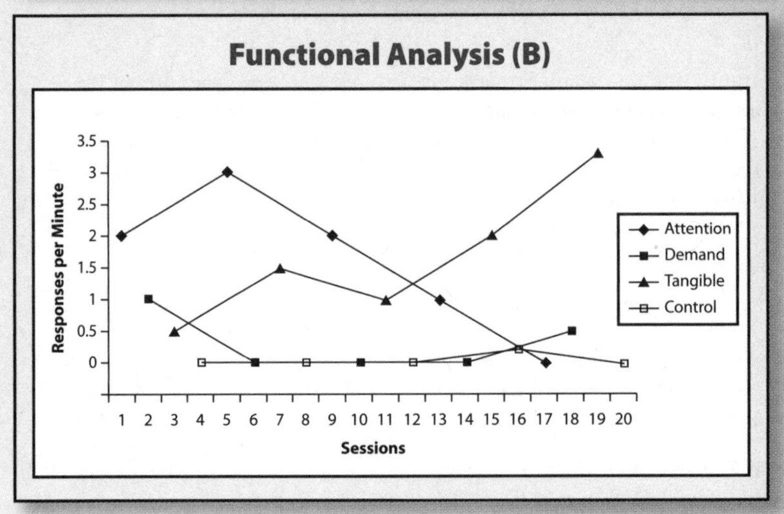

Second, the analyst looks for variability in the data path. **Variability** refers to the extent to which measures of behavior under the same environmental conditions differ from one another (Cooper, Heron, & Heward, 1987). With functional analysis data, we hope to see minimal variability within conditions. If the data points within a condition vary to the point where the resulting data path is an "up-and-down" fluctuating visual pattern, our likely interpretation is that there was little control of the behavior in that condition.

This might indicate procedural problems with the functional analysis, such as a poorly contrived MO, or the inconsistent delivery of reinforcement. A more stable data path would indicate steady responding and a properly controlled analogue. The graph in Figure 8.10 illustrates a highly variable data path (attention condition) and a more steady data path (demand condition).

Next, the **level** of the data path may be of interest to the behavior analyst conducting a functional analysis. Level refers to the value of the vertical axis scale around which a set of behavioral measures converges (Cooper, Heron, & Heward, 1987). Basically, this refers to where the data path lies in relation to the vertical (y) axis. Taken along with variability, level can be used to describe various types of data paths.

For example, in Figure 8.15, the attention condition's data path would be described as a low, highly unstable level of responding – i.e., the data path occurs relatively low on the vertical axis and is highly unstable.

Conversely, the demand condition's data path in the same example would be characterized as a high, stable level of responding.

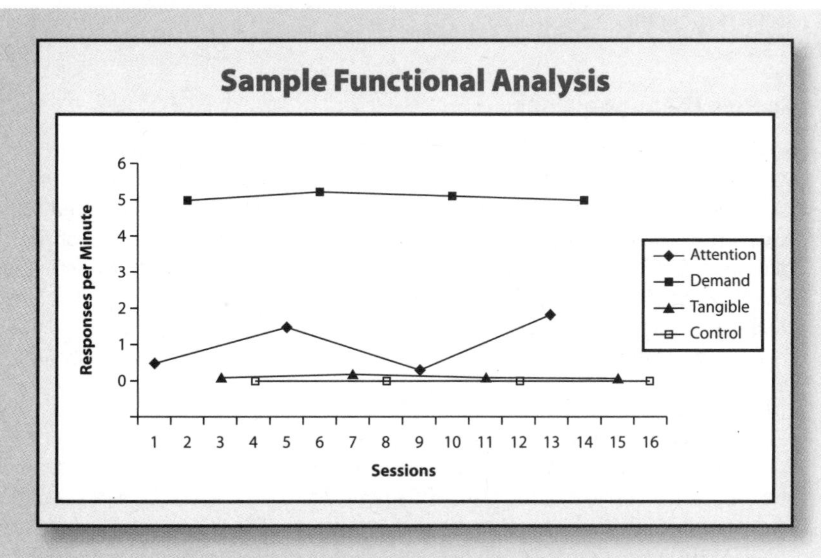

Figure 8.15

In interpreting functional analysis graphs, we are very interested in the level of the data paths in all analogues. High-level data paths suggest greater overall rates of responding by the child. Moreover, a relatively high, steady data path strongly indicates the presence of a functional relation between the variables manipulated in that analogue and the child's target behavior. Again, looking at the graph in Figure 8.15, a visual analysis of the data indicates two things:

- A functional relation between demands and the child's target behavior (due to the high, steady level of the data path).
- Control problems in the implementation of the attention condition (due to the high variability of the data path).

It is important to know that the most significant point of comparison in a functional analysis is between *each* test condition and the control condition, not between test conditions.

Finally, the behavior analyst might look at the **trend** or overall direction of the data path. Referring back to the functional analysis graph in Figure 8.14, the data path representing the tangible condition is characterized as following an ascending or **accelerating** trend. A descending or **decelerating** trend in data is seen in the attention condition of that same graph.

Accelerating trends in functional analysis data usually indicate a reinforcement effect, or that learning is occurring in that particular analogue condition or across/

between test conditions. The child's rate of responding is increasing, suggesting that whatever is being manipulated in the sessions is increasing the probability of the target behavior occurring in future sessions.

In contrast, a decelerating trend in functional analysis data might indicate that a "bogus" reinforcement effect or "bleed-over" effect from the preceding condition occurred in one of the earlier sessions, and was controlled out or otherwise ameliorated in subsequent sessions. Decelerating trends in such situations suggest a weak or nonexistent functional relation between that condition's maintaining variable and the child's target behavior. And finally, descending data paths might be indicative of the child's habituation to the analogue condition. Quite simply put, the child in these situations "figures out" what is going on in the analogue and stops responding.

Section G – Suggestions

When implemented correctly, experimental methods of functional analysis yield the most reliable results. To be most effective, experimental functional analyses are most appropriate for behaviors that are likely to be exhibited at least a few times within a five- to ten-minute condition. Otherwise, it is difficult to demonstrate a reinforcement effect. Also, we recommend ***not*** conducting an experimental functional analysis of a particularly dangerous behavior (such as those associated with severe self-injury), *unless* medical personnel are available and session termination criteria have been established prior to the start of the analysis procedures.

We also suggest that the functional analysis be adapted to the learner and his or her history of reinforcement. According to James Carr, Ph.D., BCBA, "One of the things that is particularly powerful about the experimental FA is the ability to customize new and idiosyncratic test conditions. The following elements are required for a test condition: an EO is in place (e.g., the reinforcer is unavailable) and the putative reinforcer is only delivered contingent on problem behavior. If the reader learns these requirements, he or she will be able to customize test conditions and not be confined to the 'attention-demand-tangible-alone' framework, which is not always relevant."

Further, we want to stress that for visual analysis of functional analysis data to be effective, the behavior analyst should look for a clear differentiation or split between the level of one (or two) data paths and the control condition. This indicates a functional relation.

Well-controlled implementation of the analogue conditions, followed by an accurate data collection and visual analysis will typically lead the behavior analyst to determine the function of the child's target behavior. Once this is achieved, selecting an effective treatment protocol that corresponds to the function of the target behavior can be more confidently accomplished.

References:

Axelrod, S. (1987). Functional and structural analyses of behavior: Approaches leading to reduced use of punishment procedures? *Research in Developmental Disabilities, 8*, 165-178.

Cooper, J.O., Heron, T.E., & Heward, W.L. (1987). *Applied behavior analysis.* Upper Saddle River: Prentice-Hall.

Durand, V. M., & Crimmins, D.B. (1988). Identifying the variables maintaining self-injurious behavior. *Journal of Autism and Developmental Disorders, 18*, 99-117.

Iwata, B.A., Dorsey, M., Slifer, K., Bauman, K., & Richman, G. (1982). Toward a functional analysis of self-injury. *Analysis and Intervention in Developmental Disabilities, 2*, 3-20.

Kahng, S., Iwata, B.A., Fischer, S.M., Page, T.J., Treadwell, K.R.H., Williams, D.E., & Smith, R.G. (1998). Temporal distributions of problem behavior based on scatter plot analysis. *Journal of Applied Behavior Analysis, 31*, 593-604.

O'Neill, R.E., Horner, R.H., Albin, R. W., Sprague, J.R., Storey, K., & Newton, J.S. (1997). *Functional assessment and program development for problem behavior: A practical handbook.* Pacific Grove, CA: Brooks/Cole.

Shabani, D.B., Carr, J.E., Petursdottir, A.I., Esch, B.E., & Gillett, J.N. (2004). Scholarly productivity in behavior analysis: The most prolific authors and institutions from 1992 to 2001. *The Behavior Analyst Today, 5*, 235-243.

Skinner, B.F. (1953). *Science and human behavior.* New York: MacMillan.

Touchette, P.E., MacDonald, R.F., & Langer, S.N. (1985). A scatter plot for identifying stimulus control of problem behavior. *Journal of Applied Behavior Analysis, 18*, 343-351.

Zarcone, J.R., Rodgers, T., Iwata, B.A., Rourke, D.A., & Dorsey, M.F. (1991). Reliability analysis of the motivation assessment scale: A failure to replicate. *Research in Developmental Disabilities, 12*, 336-49.

Introduction to Verbal Behavior and Relational Frame Theory At a Glance

Chapter Points

- Verbal behavior is any behavior that acts upon other people to act upon the environment.
- Specific verbal operants – or classes of verbal behavior – are based on the function of the behavior, the type of stimulus that controls it, or both the function and the stimulus controlling the behavior.
- Prompting and fading strategies can be used to transfer stimulus control from one verbal operant to another – thus teaching a child new ways to use language.
- Rule governance, stimulus equivalence, and derived relational responding both challenge and extend Skinner's work on human language and cognition.

Key Terms

Verbal Behavior

Verbal Operants

Mand

Tact

Echoic

Intraverbal

Receptive Language

Rule-Governed Behavior

Stimulus Equivalence

Symmetry

Reflexivity

Transitivity

Relational Frame Theory

Derived Relational Responding

Mutual Entailment

Combinatorial Entailment

Transformation of Stimulus Functions

Introduction to Verbal Behavior and Relational Frame Theory

A Behavioral Approach to Language

In the previous chapter, we learned that inappropriate behaviors often serve as a surrogate form of communication. This happens because individuals with autism have wants and needs that they try to meet – even if they are unable to do so in socially acceptable ways. For this and other reasons, any attempt to provide effective instruction for individuals with autism should focus on developing communication skills.

At the very severe end of the continuum of autism spectrum disorders, it is common to see children or adults who have acquired absolutely no language skills. Even at the high end of the spectrum, we see individuals who have developed a fantastic vocal repertoire, but still lack the ability to accurately perceive, interpret, or project *non-vocal* communication. These individuals, while obviously less impaired than those at the opposite end of the spectrum, still experience a great deal of frustration because of missed or botched social opportunities. It is very difficult to be effective socially without knowing how to solicit information or action from others, or not understanding when others are soliciting them from you.

B.F. Skinner and Verbal Behavior

In *The Behavior of Organisms* and *Science and Human Behavior*, B.F. Skinner provided a very detailed account of the roles consequences play in our future selection of behavior. Since then, the theory upon which Skinner based his claims has been validated repeatedly through controlled experimentation. What seemed to be missing, however, was the connection between his theory of operant conditioning and perhaps the most complex of all animal behaviors: verbal interaction.

Despite the growing acceptance of an operant theory of behavior, the world refused to accept Skinner's scientific principles when the subject in question was not merely survival behavior, but more complex *social* behavior, such as speaking, writing, gesturing, or reading. One of Skinner's colleagues eventually challenged him to develop a theoretical account of language. Skinner accepted, and worked more than 20 years to complete one of the most profound works of his career: *Verbal Behavior*. In this volume, Skinner attempted to apply the basic principles of operant conditioning to social and communicative behaviors.

This chapter will provide a brief introduction to the main concepts presented in Skinner's theory as well as an overview of more current theoretical developments in the area of human language and cognition – namely **Relational Frame Theory** (RFT). Some readers may find the material presented here rather difficult to grasp. To help guide the reader through these rather dense works, we have attempted to keep our discussion as simple as possible while remaining true to the original tenets of both RFT and Skinner's analysis of verbal behavior.

Before proceeding, however, it is important to point out several things. First, both RFT and Skinner's analysis of verbal behavior are, in fact, works of theory. Second, there are reasons to treat these theories within their own framework, related to but separate from the basic operant conditioning paradigm. Finally, while there are some valid objections to these theories, there have been many empirical validations of *Verbal Behavior* since 1957 (For a review of these studies, see Oah et al. 1989.) as well as a growing body of basic and applied work in recent years validating RFT.

Why present psychological theory in a practical manual? The answer is simple. Practitioners who are highly successful in teaching language to individuals with autism and other developmental disabilities have used these theoretical structures to guide curriculum development and to improve language outcomes. One of the most frequent criticisms of a behavioral approach to teaching language to young children with autism is that such strategies produce only rote language use and "robotic" speech patterns. A child's ability to respond to novel situations by generating language that has not been formally drilled and practiced is not seen as an outcome of most of these types of programs. This need not be the case.

A practitioner who is well-versed in the basic principles of *Verbal Behavior* and Relational Frame Theory will find him or herself not only better equipped to teach language skills, but capable of developing an effective language curriculum that goes beyond rote learning and results in children developing much more natural language repertoires. More concrete examples of how the theory ties into curriculum development will be discussed in Chapter 14.

Again, this material is complex. It may take several "read throughs," along with some help from a few of the resource texts listed in the reference section of this chapter before the average reader thoroughly understands the concepts presented here. It will be well worth the effort, though, as it will provide the reader with a heightened sensitivity to how language is learned — knowledge that will prove to be the difference between an average language program and an exceptional one.

Section A – Verbal Behavior

We know that any interaction between an organism and the environment constitutes behavior, and we know that this applies to talking, reading, writing, and gesturing. As behaviors, they are under the control of environmental stimuli and serve a purpose or function. Because they are voluntary, they also fall under the operant conditioning paradigm.

Going forward, we will refer to communicative behaviors like these as **verbal behavior.** Verbal behavior is defined as any behavior that acts upon other people to then act upon the environment, as opposed to behaviors that act upon the environment directly (Skinner, 1957).

In this chapter, we will discuss specific applications of verbal behavior theory, including behavior reduction and acceleration techniques, as well as their application in curriculum development. For now, it is enough to know that when children with autism experience difficulties in acquiring and using basic verbal skills, the results are often behavioral and instructional problems.

Verbal Operants: Beyond the Topography of Language

When we shape language, we often think that once expressive or receptive language is intact, our work is complete. However, if we analyze verbal behavior through a functional framework, we can achieve a much more detailed view of where language development is progressing or faltering. This framework takes shape in the form of **verbal operants**, or verbal behaviors that are based on the function of the response – in other words, the type of discriminative stimuli, motivational operations, and consequences that have acquired control over the response.

To understand the functional properties of verbal behavior, think about the many ways the word *water* can be used:

1. If a person hears the request, "say water," the word will probably be repeated back to the requester. This is often the case when learning a new language, where an example is given, and is then repeated by the student.

2. When water is present, we are apt to label it – in other words, the mere presence of the object can lead us to say "water," either alone or in combination with other words ("that's water," for example). We can also be given an instruction to name the item we see. It is likely that labeling the item in the presence of others will encourage them to look at the item as well.

3. We can say "water" as a means of identifying what we want or need. For example, if we are extremely thirsty, we say the word – not to identify what we see, but to request what we need.

4. When we read the word "w-a-t-e-r" in print, at the very least it indicates the thing to us. It can even lead us to do something with this information, depending upon where or who it came from, and the context surrounding its appearance.

5. We can print the word ourselves, which, depending on the context in which we write it, can be a way to communicate a function. It can relay factual information, it can request water, or it can be in response to a request from someone else.

6. We can use the term "water" to answer a question from another person. This is a situation in which the object (water) is neither present nor requested. In this case, the behavior of stating the word functions solely to answer or reciprocate the verbal behavior of another.

7. Finally, another person can present the word "water" to us, and we can select a behavior as a result. We can point to show identification of water, we can give the person water, or we can otherwise use the word as a basis for a response that does not in any way involve saying it. In this case, our use of the word serves a receptive purpose. We know what to do, or (more specifically) how to behave, when a certain word is heard.

Although a true analysis of verbal behavior goes much further than this cursory, one-word example, it serves as a "stepping off" point for deeper exploration. Next, we'll discuss the major classes of verbal behavior, along with individual verbal operants.

Mands

A **mand** is a verbal behavior that indicates a direct request for positive or negative reinforcement. (An example of a mand in the list above is the use of the word "water" to indicate a need or desire for it.) Because of their direct relationship with (often primary) reinforcement, mands are usually the first verbal operants to be shaped. They are arguably the most important of the verbal operants, for they are the basic ways in which we occasion behavior from others that will ultimately meet our needs (Skinner, 1957).

It is interesting to note that mands are almost always associated with getting something requested, or getting away from something aversive. Mands are not limited to requests for items or escape, though – mands for information are also incredibly common. Every time someone asks for an answer to a question, a mand is presented. Mands can also come in the form of a statement that *implies* a question, such as, "I need to know where you live, so that I can deliver your package."

For children with autism and other developmental disabilities, it is often impossible to communicate according to the rules and topographies of conventional language systems. These children often have a difficult time coordinating the musculature involved in precise vocal production, and also experience difficulty in learning the "rules" of formal language. As a result, inappropriate behaviors like tantrums, aggression, or self-injury take the place of formal language and serve as mands in their own right.

Chapter 8 showed how these kinds of inappropriate behaviors often become effective substitutes for requests that express wants and needs. What is often really at issue – particularly in cases where the child has a severe developmental disability – is a way to teach an appropriate mand repertoire that will be as effective as the inappropriate behaviors.

In fact, a useful and fluent mand repertoire is one of the most important things that we must provide for individuals with autism. At the very young or very severe end of the spectrum, mand fluency training can mean the difference between appropriate communication and problem behavior. At the very high end of the spectrum, a knowledge of how and when to ask for assistance, clarification, or further information can determine whether the individual can independently hold a job in the community, or work under a supported vocational training program.

At the most basic level, any child must be taught to mand (request) for basic tangible primary reinforcers, such as food and drink, and also for negative reinforcement, such as escape from unpleasant situations. It is important to realize, though, that inappropriate behaviors have probably become very efficient ways to meet these needs, so the mands we teach must be just as easy to perform, and must operate on the environment more effectively than the target behaviors.

From a motivational standpoint, mands are an important place from which to begin the process of instruction. Implicit in mand training (which will be discussed in future chapters) is an effort to follow the child's lead to center instruction upon asking for things that are important to him or her. This allows us to shape a behavior rather quickly, and to pair ourselves with meaningful reinforcement at the same time.

Tacts

A **tact** occurs when a person names, or labels, a nonverbal stimulus while in its presence. The stimulus can be an object, picture, event, or characteristic, and must be present in order for the behavior to be considered a tact. In the initial exercise with the word "water," for example, we stated that when a person is in the presence of water, he or she is apt to label it by saying, "water." Tacts can include item names, verbs to identify actions, adjectives, adverbs, etc. (Skinner, 1957).

Tact training allows an individual to acquire names and labels for things as simple as the objects in his or her environment, and as complex as emotions or adverbs. Keep in mind, though, that in order to be considered a tact, the response must be emitted vocally or via sign language.[1]

As with many of the verbal operants, tacts often occur in impure forms. A *pure* tact involves nothing more than the presence of a nonverbal stimulus and the vocal response to label it. While pure tacts are common in typically developing children, most cases of tacting rely not only upon the presence of the object, but also upon

[1] A picture exchange (PECS) would not qualify as a pure tact as it involves matching visual stimuli first – thus becoming a combined match-to-sample/tact response.

the presence of other stimuli – such as an instruction to respond, or some other environmental cue to label the object. In these cases, we may actually be dealing with complex operants, which will be discussed a bit further down the line.

The reinforcement that follows tacting is typically of the conditioned type. This can include joint attention, or a reward for responding when the object's presence as an S^D is accompanied by a verbal S^D that labels it.

In terms of educating children with autism, a tact repertoire is a crucial component of expressive vocabulary development. Because there is a tendency for children with language disabilities to have poor vocabulary development early on, we utilize tact training as one of the first and most enduring types of skill programs that we build into the "master plan" of the curriculum.

The Echoic

When a person's verbal stimulus brings about an identical verbal response from a second person – and an object, picture, or other nonverbal stimulus is not present – the second person's behavior is considered an **echoic** response. In the first water scenario, for example, the word "water" was spoken solely in response to an instruction to do so. The reinforcement that follows echoic responses is generally non-specific, or at least dependent upon the context in which it occurs (Skinner, 1957).

If the previous definition seems complex, it must be in order to consider both the controlling variable and the response itself. A more "common sense" definition is this: an echoic response occurs when someone repeats a word or sound emitted by another person.

The echoic repertoire falls within and is closely related to the imitative repertoire. **Imitation** occurs when a response is controlled by nothing more than the model of the same type of response by another person. The reinforcement is meaningful, but context dependent.

Understanding echoic responding also has a tremendous impact on our abilities to provide effective instruction for individuals with autism. Our section on curriculum development will draw connections between this verbal behavior repertoire and a number of practical skill applications, as well as prompting strategies. What must be stressed here is the notion that much of what we learn to do and say, while under the operant control of reinforcement, is also under the control of models we imitate.

Most children learn the topographical elements of speaking and language through imitation of models. When a model is presented, the child imitates it or attempts to do so, and consequences shape the behavior over time. At the same time, a model stimulus serves as the S^D for much of our initial behavior when we learn new skills. This is why we tend to use caution when speaking around young children, for fear that they will imitate adult phrases or words that can cause embarrassment!

Children with autism frequently present an additional challenge. For them, echoic and imitative responding are necessary skills that form the basis of many prompting strategies. Even so, some children have to be taught how to specifically imitate the actions and words of others, because this skill may not be established through naturally occurring contingencies.

In order to accomplish this, an echoic repertoire must be established. This will only be effective if the child has the necessary musculoskeletal prerequisites, and if reinforcement is meaningful.

There are times when the therapist, teacher, or parent should be aware that an imitative response is not an equal substitute for a tact, a mand, or other verbal behavior. There may be situations in which the echoic response serves the functional purpose of skill programming, but in most cases, it is not indicative of an appropriate or functional use of a word.

Consider the following example of a child engaged in programming to increase spontaneous use of verbal behavior, where mand training has been implemented as a starting point. Because the child has not yet had lunch, target behaviors typically occur in response to not having access to cookies. Therefore, cookies are kept in sight but out of reach as a manipulation of the already-strong MOs in place for cookies. The purpose of this program is to evoke manding from the child. When we say: "What do you want?" and then model "cookie," the child's resulting utterance of "cookie" cannot be considered a pure mand. Instead, it is an echoic. Further, if the cookies are present, it could also take on some qualities of a tact.

The above scenario does not represent an incorrect way to implement instruction in verbal operants. What it does, however, is illustrate the significance of understanding them, so that we can make programming decisions that ensure each operant is given its due. There is no guarantee that a spontaneous pure mand will ever occur unless the programming takes into account the fact that other operants may need to be controlled first.

The Intraverbal

How we acquire and apply words to modify our environment is heavily influenced by the functional characteristics of language. In all cases, verbal operants are controlled by the presence of environmental stimuli. With tacts, for example, the visual presence of the object itself serves as an S^D for saying the word. With mands, the response is the product of certain environmental stimuli, plus evocative motivational operations. The presence of certain conditions lets a person know that asking for a particular thing will likely be reinforced, and the MOs are established so that the thing is desirable at the moment. The echoic operant is under the control of the model provided.

But what controls verbal behavior when we answer questions? Suppose we were asked what sound the letter "p" makes. Obviously, "p" is not present as an object, for it is a sound. Additionally, we are not motivated to ask for "p." To answer the question, we cannot simply repeat the "p" that is given in the example. There must be another verbal operant to consider.

This operant is known as the **intraverbal**, or verbal behavior that is under the control of other verbal behavior. Any time one answers a question, fills in a blank, finishes someone's sentence, reciprocates a comment, or engages in a topical conversation, he or she is demonstrating the intraverbal as a form of verbal behavior (Skinner, 1957).

In the grand scheme of language use, the intraverbal is the most complex and most called upon of all the basic verbal operants. It is the behavior that allows us to communicate about things that are not physically present, and to engage in topical conversation with other people. In fact, most of what we refer to as social language is the product of a well-developed intraverbal repertoire.

Children with autism typically have a particularly difficult time with intraverbal skills. We know that they tend to be visual learners, so a tact (labeling) repertoire is usually not difficult to shape with basic operant procedures. We also know that formal, rule-oriented language comes rather easily to children with autism who speak, so it is usually not very difficult to teach them language tasks like labeling and categorization. Additionally, motivational factors make mand training rather successful in most cases.

In the case of the intraverbal, however, we have to make sure that we are teaching not only rule-governed responses, but also intraverbal responses that require generative thinking. In other words, we must move beyond asking a particular question in a particular way to achieve an answer that is always in a specific format, such as "Cows are animals" in response to "What are cows?" Instead, we must be able to ask more generalized questions, such as, "Tell me all of the things you can think of that are animals."

Intraverbal communication can be evoked in many ways, alone and in combination with other operants. For example:

- If a child is asked to name a piece of clothing to wear in the rain, he or she has to formulate a response based solely on the verbal behavior already exhibited by another person. In this case, the response is an intraverbal.
- If a raincoat is present, the response is an intraverbal/tact combination.
- If the child is standing uncomfortably in the rain, and the question is posed while the instructor is showing a raincoat (and the raincoat is offered following a correct response), we can easily demonstrate a mand/tact/intraverbal operant where all three come into play to control the response.

How does one acquire an intraverbal repertoire? Essentially, we must try to look at the various ways in which the same content information can be used to evoke responses from the learner. Take, for example, the skills involved with identifying the functions of a pen. In order to adequately teach this, we must first teach the tacting skills that will allow the learner to identify the object in question. In this case, he or she should be able to say "pen" when asked to name the item. Similarly, the learner should know the concept of "writing," since it is the pen's function. This can also be accomplished through tacting, by way of answering "writing" when presented with a physical example of someone writing.

Many programs seem to be satisfied leaving the instruction there, but that creates a huge gap between basic identification and functional use of the concept in communication. To create the link that is missing from the above scenario, we must teach a response to "What do you use for writing?" without the pen present, or the inverse: "What is a pen for?" We can also try to establish a fill-in response by saying, "A pen is for [_______]," and requiring the learner to fill in the missing word. By doing this, we have established the basic building blocks necessary for simple topical conversation regarding a pen.

Regardless of the topography that we are trying to shape (vocal speech, picture systems, sign language, augmentative devices, etc.), we have to be extremely careful to pay close attention to the development of strong intraverbal skills. When these are lacking, there is likely a tremendous deficit in overall ability to communicate. We will go into more detail on how to shape strong skill sets across verbal operants in future chapters. For now understanding these basic intraverbal concepts is enough.

Receptive Language

Receptive language is any nonverbal behavior that comes under the control of a verbal stimulus. In other words, other people's verbal behavior serves as a stimulus for the listener to nonverbally behave in some way. An example is a child's response of standing up when asked to do so. Note that standing up requires no verbal behavior on the part of the listener, but is dependent on the verbal instruction.

Receptive language is of paramount importance to any communicating person. Many children learn to follow certain instructions, but still cannot carry on any kind of conversation or express their wants and needs. Because receptive skills are usually a bit easier to teach, many programs heavily favor them, creating imbalance between the verbal operants.

Even though receptive language skills can be extremely basic (receptive identification of objects or compliance with receptive requests for action), solid programming in receptive language goes further. We often strive to teach a receptive response regarding classification, function identification, and object features skills. Receptive skills can also be parlayed into the introduction of abstract concepts such as absurdity, opposites, and a host of other more complex language skills.

Other Considerations

There are other verbal operants, such as the textual repertoire, which is utilized in reading, and the transcriptive repertoire, which involves writing. However, these operants differ primarily in topography from those already described while taking on similar functional characteristics of others. For example, a mand can be written, controlling a receptive response on the part of the reader. Likewise, an intraverbal response to a question can be written, as is the case when a written test is administered.

Further chapters will deal more specifically with how these verbal operants can be trained or shaped into a learner's communicative repertoire. The important thing to realize at this point is that there are many more considerations that will be incorporated into curriculum programs for building language than simply focusing upon receptive versus expressive skills.

Section B – Transfer of Stimulus Control Between Verbal Operants

Teaching young children with autism to use language in a functional way requires that they establish repertoires of verbal behavior that involve *all* of the verbal operants we have previously described.

Such a well-rounded use of language is rarely seen when we first assess a young child diagnosed with autism. Quite often, these children possess little or no language. If language *is* present, it may be limited to one or two of the verbal operants. A common situation involves children who possess an extensive tact vocabulary – i.e., children who spend the day ritualistically labeling objects that they encounter in the immediate environment, in books, and on television. These same children however, cannot use these same words as mands to make their basic wants and needs known to others.

Another frequently observed imbalance in language repertoire involves children who can echo any word presented to them but have never moved beyond simple echoics to use these same words as mands, tacts, or intraverbals.

Whether we are faced with a nonverbal child who has been taught a basic mand repertoire, or a more verbally adept child who is simultaneously developing several verbal operants, we are faced with the same difficulty. How can we effectively progress from limited repertoires to the more comprehensive and functional use of language that is demonstrated by typical children?

One answer lies within the concept of stimulus control and the processes involved in the transfer of that control. As noted previously, each of the verbal operants involves responses that are controlled by very specific antecedent conditions. A mand is controlled by a MO, a tact is controlled by the presence of the object, an echoic is controlled by the word/phrase/sentence being spoken (with point-to-point correspondence and formal similarity), an intraverbal is controlled by the word/phrase/sentence spoken (*without* point-to-point correspondence or formal similarity), and so forth.

If a child has developed the ability to mand for a variety of reinforcers using single, spoken words, but has not developed any tacts, we can use superimposition of stimuli and fading to transfer stimulus control from the established mand to the new tact response (Sundberg & Partington, 1998).

In such a training situation, an MO would need to be in effect for a specific reinforcer. For the above scenario involving cookies, the child is deprived of his favorite cookie and is generally hungry when entering the training session. With a cookie present on the worktable, the child requires no prompting to say "cookie" in order to receive a small piece of it.

At this point in time, the spoken response "cookie" is under the control of the MO and, most likely, the presence of the cookie. The word "cookie" is functioning as a mand for the child, in that it results in reinforcement with that same item. Saying "cookie" gets him a piece of cookie.

Transferring stimulus control from the MO and the presence of the cookie (the stimulus condition for evoking a mand) to just the presence of the cookie (the stimulus condition for evoking a tact) requires the therapist to:

- superimpose additional antecedent stimuli (such as asking the child, "What is it?");
- fade out certain antecedent conditions (by allowing the child to eat cookies to drive down the MO for cookies); and
- alter the form of the reinforcer (providing social praise rather than a piece of cookie as the consequence).

If done correctly, this process can be effective in teaching the child to tact "cookie" – in other words, in teaching the child to identify "cookie" without receiving a piece of cookie as the reinforcer.

Following several mand trials, where the child's spoken response of "cookie" is reinforced with the delivery of small pieces of cookie, the transfer process can begin. During these trials, it may be necessary to weaken the MO somewhat in order to facilitate the transfer process and to more quickly teach the tact. This is accomplished by conducting these preliminary mand trials so that the child begins to become satiated on cookies.

What needs to be superimposed or added to the mand stimulus condition is the question, "What is it?" rather than "What do you want?" With the weakened MO in effect (the child is not so keen on eating cookies at the moment) and the cookie present, the therapist superimposes the question "What is it?" *Note: An additional echoic prompt such as "say cookie" may be necessary early on in the training to facilitate a correct response.*

Once the child responds by saying "cookie," a non-specific reinforcer is delivered. The therapist tickles the child or gives some form of verbal praise, but she *does not* give him a piece of cookie. (If a piece of cookie *is* provided as reinforcement for saying "cookie," the trial ceases to be a tact trial and reverts back to being a mand trial.)

Prompt fading then needs to occur, in order to transfer stimulus control from any prompting that has been used (sometimes even including the question "What is it?") to the natural S^D – which is the presence of the cookie alone. When this occurs, the therapist has successfully used an existing mastered verbal operant (the mand) to teach the child how to use a new verbal operant (the tact). This process is illustrated in Figure 9.1.

With the appropriate use of stimulus superimposition and prompt fading, any verbal operant can be taught by bridging between it and another currently established verbal operant. The echoic, receptive, or intraverbal can be taught by transferring stimulus control from the mand. Likewise, the mand can be taught via one of these other established verbal operants.

Figure 9.1

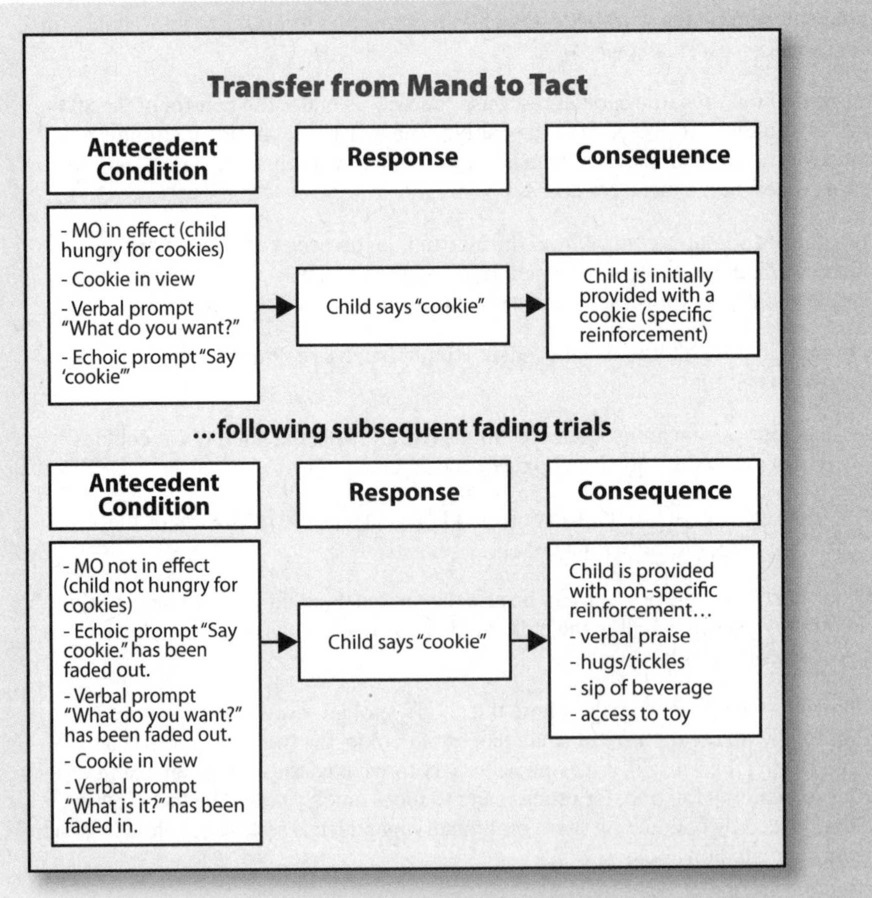

Limitations of Verbal Behavior

Almost immediately after its publication in 1957, *Verbal Behavior* came under the attack of linguists (most notably, Noam Chomsky) and cognitive psychologists alike. Skinner's critics generally argued that reducing human language to behaviors controlled by direct, external contingencies did not sufficiently account for the complexities of what occurs when humans communicate with one another. A notable cognitive psychologist, Steven Pinker, posits the following scenario in his book *How the Mind Works* as a means of questioning the validity of a purely behavioral account of language:

> Why did Sally run out of the building? Because she believed it was on fire and did not want to die. Her fleeing was not a predictable response to some stimulus that can be objectively described in the language of physics and chemistry. Perhaps she left because she saw smoke, but perhaps she left in response to a phone call telling her that the building was on fire, or to the sight of arriving fire trucks, or to the sound of the alarm. But none of these stimuli would *necessarily* have sent her out, either. She would *not* have left if she knew that the smoke was from an English muffin in a toaster, or that the phone call was from a friend practicing lines for a play, or that someone had pulled the alarm switch by accident or as a prank, or that the alarms were being tested by an electrician. The light and sound particles that physicists can measure do not lawfully predict a person's behavior. What does predict Sally's behavior, and predict it well, is whether she *believes* herself to be in danger. (Pinker, pg. 62)

As would any cognitive psychologist worth his salt, Pinker goes on to describe how language is a means of transferring beliefs, ideas, and thoughts from one person's *mind* to another's. This process is akin to how a computer deals with information. Viewing the brain as an information processor, cognitive psychology suggests that the brain encodes ideas or thoughts that are sent, via language, from one mind to another. There, they are decoded/processed in the receiver's brain.

The obvious appeal to internal, unobservable processes does not sit well with behavior analysts, because "information processing" theories of language leave no dependent variable that can be manipulated or tested via experimentation. Short of neurosurgery or psychopharmacology, systematic manipulation of the brain's internal workings to identify functional relations between physiology and language is impossible at this time.

From a behavior analytic point of view, then, cognitive psychologists and linguists have presented an untenable alternative to *Verbal Behavior*. This doesn't mean that the questions posed by Pinker, Chomsky and others should not be asked, or that challenges to Skinner's theory be ignored.

The fact is, that even though supported by a growing research program (see Oah et al., 1989) and effective clinical application, Skinner's theory of verbal behavior did seem incomplete – particularly in its analysis of more complex examples of human language and cognition.

Beginning in the 1970s, behavior analytic research began to delve into two areas that extended the Skinnerian view of language and ultimately provided a testable alternative to the direct-contingency explanation. These two behavioral processes were rule governed behavior and stimulus equivalence.

Section C – Rule-Governed Behavior

As early as 1953 in *Science and Human Behavior*, Skinner observed that society creates laws that govern our behavior. Specifically, he said that a law is actually "a rule of conduct in the sense that it specifies the consequences of certain actions which in turn 'rule' our behavior" (Skinner, 1953, pg. 339). In 1969, he referred to this process, by which laws or rules control behavior, as **rule-governed behavior** (Skinner, 1969).

Skinner went on to define rules as *contingency-specifying stimuli*. Just as a discriminative stimulus specifies the opportunity for reinforcement given a specific behavioral response, a rule operates as a verbal discriminative stimulus that specifies or tells us that a particular contingency is in effect. In real life, this usually takes the form of an *if-then* statement. "If you exceed the speed limit, you might get a ticket." "If you don't finish your lima beans, you won't get to play outside after dinner." The rule states the contingency in each of these examples: a specified behavior will result in a specified consequence.

When teaching language to young children with autism, early programmatic efforts are typically accomplished by the direct manipulation of contingencies, or shaping. We teach our children to request, to imitate, to match, to label, and to answer rote questions without ever departing from direct contingency-based instruction.

While this type of instruction is very effective in imparting basic, formal information to our children, we quickly realize that it is extremely limiting when it comes to establishing more complex or relational skills. An example of this would be teaching a child to tact "my" and "your" relations in the area of expressive possessive pronouns. This program is extremely difficult for our children, because the "rule" changes, depending on who is speaking. The child who has already learned to touch the instructor's leg when told, "touch *my* leg" struggles with the notion that when asked to tact that very same leg, he should respond "*your* leg."

The rather complex rule that underlies this seemingly simple task is, "If the teacher is pointing to herself and asking 'Who's…', then I say 'Your…' and if the teacher is pointing to me and asking 'Who's…?', then I say 'My…'" Teaching such a complicated relationship generally requires multiple examples and considerable trial randomization for the child to learn the rule. It is not amenable to a direct contingency-based form of instruction such as shaping.

Section D – Stimulus Equivalence

Prior to the work on rule-governance, Maury Sidman conducted considerable basic research at Massachusetts General Hospital in the 1970s. Although his initial investigation involved how reading comprehension might be taught better, Sidman ended up describing what would eventually be known as *equivalence relations*. This research played a pivotal role in how behavior analysts now view language development.

In 1971, Sidman's first experiment involved teaching the matching of spoken words to pictures, and spoken words to printed words. The subject of the study was a 17-year old boy with severe mental retardation, who then surprisingly proceeded to spontaneously match the printed words to the pictures – a task that had not been specifically trained during the experiment.

Sidman hypothesized that this untrained response occurred because the initial training – which involved repeated pairings of written words and pictures to spoken words – caused the pictures and written words to each become *equivalent* to the spoken words. Simply put, the boy learned that the pictures and written words meant the same thing as the spoken words. Because he had learned these equivalence relations, it wasn't much of a leap for him to see a similar relationship between the visual words and pictures. They became equivalent to each other.

Over the next 30 years, Sidman and colleagues replicated and tested this phenomenon that came to be known as stimulus equivalence. Simply put, **stimulus equivalence** occurs when a child is taught that A = B and that A = C (where A, B, and C are novel stimuli) and then, without direct teaching, the child derives that B = C. The triangular formula depicted in the figure below illustrates these equivalence relations (Sidman, 1994).

In the figure, the solid-lined arrows indicate relations that have been directly taught while the dotted-lined arrows indicate relations that have been derived instead of directly taught.

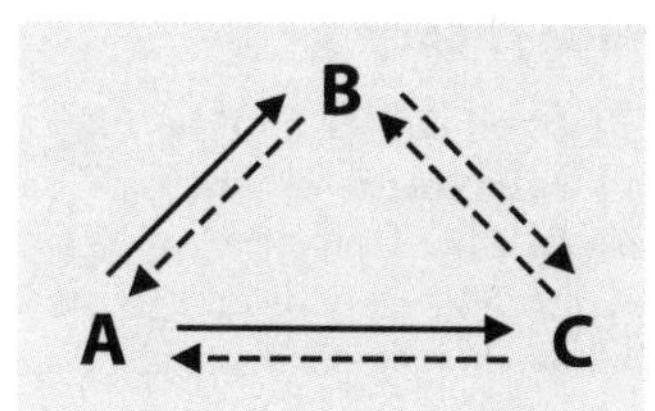

Stimulus equivalence has three distinct properties:

- **Reflexivity**, which is synonymous with identity matching. Given stimulus A, the child will pick stimulus A from an array.
- **Symmetry**, which refers to the reversibility of a conditioned discrimination – if A = B, then B = A.
- **Transitivity**, which involves the combination of relations described above – if A = B and A = C, then B = C (Sidman, 1994).

What was most surprising about the empirical evidence coming out of these studies was that the subjects reliably made discriminations without any direct operant or respondent conditioning having taken place relative to certain stimuli. While this process may seem obvious to the layperson, it has far-reaching ramifications for the field of behavior analysis.

The implications of stimulus equivalence within early intensive behavioral intervention (EIBI) programs are rather significant. As noted earlier in the chapter, much of our early programming efforts with young children with autism are directed toward teaching rote responses to very specific spoken or modeled instructions. Going beyond this acquisition of strictly formal knowledge to more relational concepts is often very difficult.

But when we incorporate stimulus equivalence theory into EIBI technology, we gain another means of ensuring that we are extending our instruction beyond the mere memorization of rote skills.

Using the concept of symmetry, we can design instructional programs that teach a skill or concept "in two directions." For example, when we teach a child to tact the function given the object (question: "What is a pencil for?" answer: "writing") we should also teach the skill in the opposite direction so that he can tact the object when given the function (question: "What do you write with?" answer: "a pencil"). If skills are consistently presented in this symmetrical fashion across most of the child's programs, we would expect that he will acquire the generalized skill of bidirectional responding.

Transitivity, when built into the EIBI curriculum, can make a significant impact on the child's ability to perform skills not directly taught to him, as well as aid in the teaching of abstract concepts. This is called generative learning.

For example, when teaching the categorization of objects (a cow is an animal), we can first teach matching the spoken word "cow" to the picture of a cow and then the picture of a cow to the spoken word "animal." Without any direct teaching, we would expect the child to match the spoken word "cow" to the spoken word "animal." A more practical example would be the child saying "animal" when asked, "What is a cow?"

Section E – Relational Frame Theory

Relational frame theory (RFT) was developed in the 1990s as a result of the long history of research associated with rule-governance and equivalence relations. Steven Hayes, a behavior analyst at the University of Nevada Reno, and his colleagues developed the RFT model as a response to the limitations of the Skinnerian model of verbal behavior. It was also an attempt to integrate the work already accomplished in equivalence and rule-governance into a cohesive theory of human language and cognition.

Even though RFT is over 10 years old, few professionals (including many behavior analysts) are aware of it. This may be due to the technical language used to describe RFT, its nontraditional approach to language and cognition, and the prejudicial attitude of most cognitive psychologists when considering any behavioral approach to the subject.

Delving deeply into RFT is a rather daunting task that exceeds the scope of this manual. What we hope to do, by way of the following summary, is give readers a taste of what RFT is, and hopefully stimulate further individual investigation into the theory and its application to EIBI programs for young children with autism. (A complete account of RFT can be found in *Relational Frame Theory: A Post-Skinnerian Account of Human Language and Cognition* by Hayes, Barnes-Holmes, & Roche, 2001).

At the very least, a rudimentary understanding of RFT and its theoretical explanations of how typical children acquire language will greatly benefit how we as practitioners develop language curricula for our young children with autism. As noted earlier in this chapter, the difficulties with establishing generative language can be reduced considerably by viewing language development through the lens of both Skinner's *Verbal Behavior* and Hayes' *Relational Frame Theory.*

An article by John T. Blackledge in *The Behavior Analyst Today* (2003) contained a particularly cogent explanation of RFT that overcomes some of the misunderstandings and confusion surrounding it. Blackledge accomplished this by using a similar cognitive model – Lang's fear network (1985) – to orient the reader to RFT.

This fear network is illustrated in Figure 9.2. It presents *stimulus propositions* (represented by ovals) that can best be described as antecedent or contextual stimuli, *response propositions* (represented by ovals connected with double lines) that refer to how the person responds in this context, and *meaning propositions* (represented by rectangles) that provide information defining the meaning of the stimulus and response data.

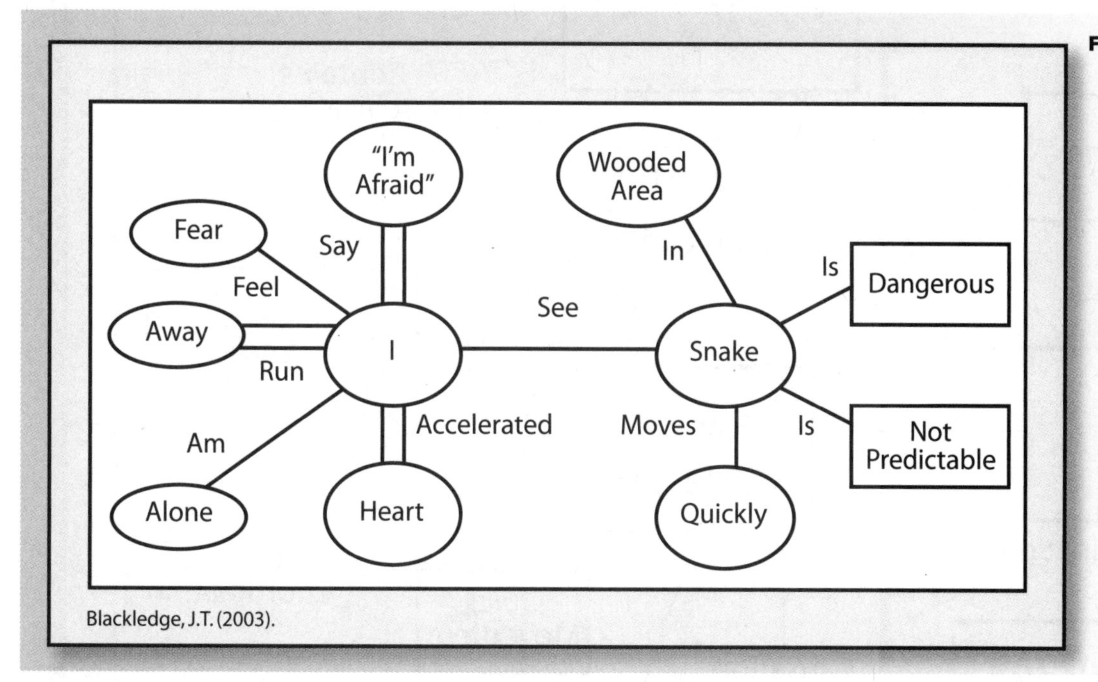

Figure 9.2

Figure 9.3 illustrates an RFT model for the same snake phobia described in Lang's fear network.

True to the cognitive approach, Lang viewed the fear network as a schema that exists in our long-term memory. The network is activated when only a few of the component stimuli are encountered. So, merely walking in the woods and seeing a quick movement in one's peripheral vision can be sufficient to cause someone's heart rate to accelerate, feel fear, and run away. The stimulus propositions provide the initial input, which is mediated by the meaning propositions present in the network (seeing quick movement in a wooded area implies danger and other unpredictable consequences) and result in the response propositions (increased heart rate, running away, and feeling afraid).

According to Lang, the components of the network can be learned directly (e.g., being bitten by a snake), through instruction (reading about snakes), or by modeling (watching others respond in fear to snakes or hearing others describe how afraid they are of snakes).

As can be seen, the RFT model is as visually complex as the cognitive example that precedes it. It is, however, more systematic and much more consistent with behavior analysis in many ways.

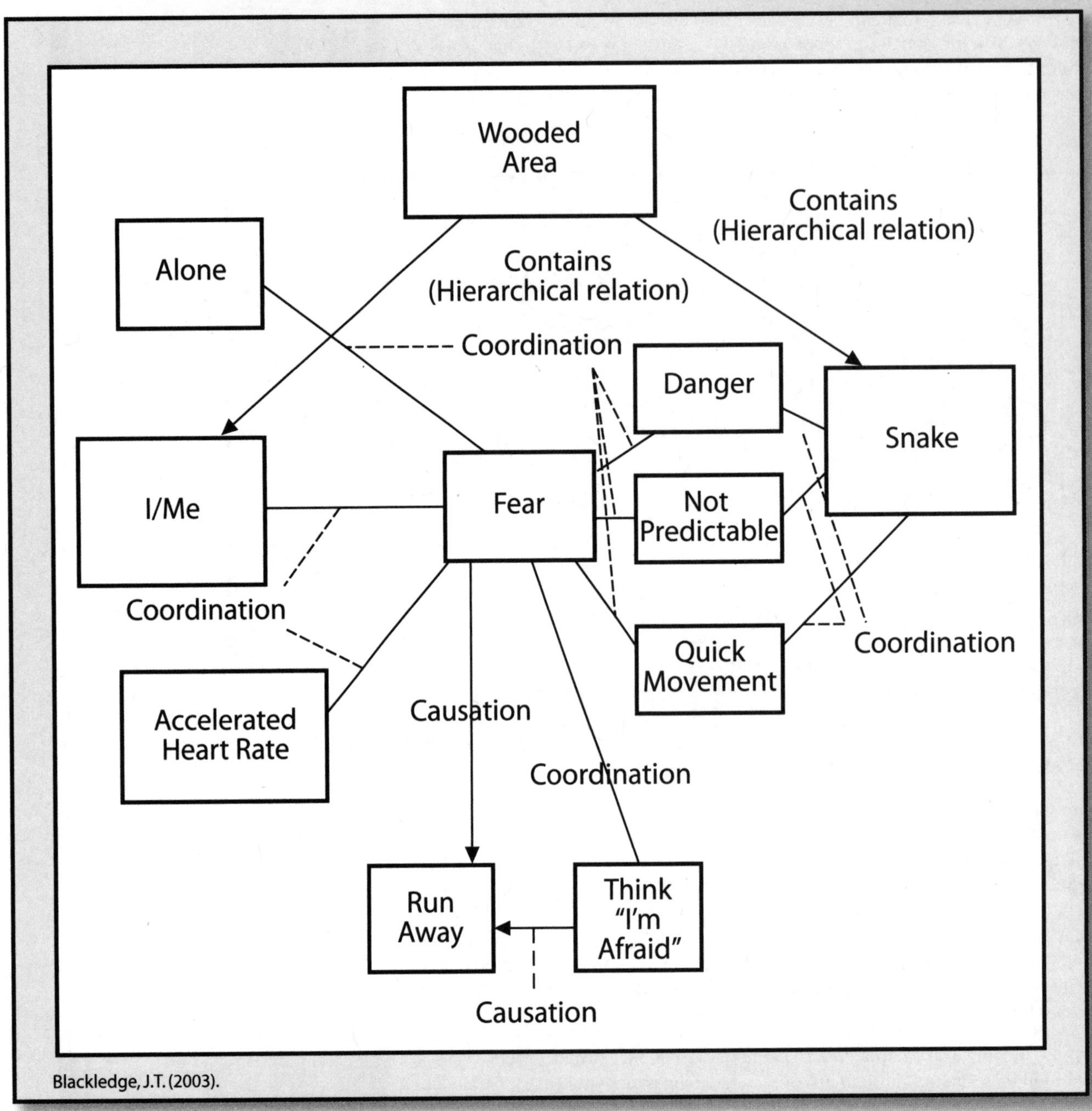
Wooded Area
Contains (Hierarchical relation)
Alone
Contains (Hierarchical relation)
Coordination
Danger
Snake
I/Me
Fear
Not Predictable
Coordination
Quick Movement
Coordination
Accelerated Heart Rate
Causation
Coordination
Run Away
Think "I'm Afraid"
Causation
Blackledge, J.T. (2003).

Figure 9.3

There are three distinct relationships between stimuli involved in RFT (these relationships are denoted by dashed lines in the diagram). These include hierarchical, coordinated, and causal relationships. Viewing the snake phobia phenomenon in terms of these relationships provides us with more information about the stimuli involved than if we had looked at them individually. Depending on the type of relationship present, we can also be made aware of how the functions of these stimuli can change (transformation of stimulus functions will be discussed at the end of the chapter).

Hierarchical relationships simply refer to the physical relationship between stimuli as parts to a whole. In Figure 9.3, a hierarchical relationship exists between "I/me" and the "wooded area" because I am in the wooded area (and the wooded area contains me). A similar hierarchical relationship is present between "snake" and "wooded area" since the snake is also in the wooded area (Blackledge, 2003).

Relationships of coordination exist between "snake" and the three stimuli "dangerous," "quick movement," and "not predictable." These three stimuli are also related coordinately to the stimulus "fear." Coordination in this sense refers to equivalence in that "snake" carries with it some of the functions associated with "dangerous," "quick movement," and "not predictable." Likewise, these three latter stimuli are equivalent – and because of this relationship, share some of the same functions as "fear." In common terms, when two stimuli have a coordinated relationship, they mean the same (or nearly) the same thing (Blackledge, 2003).

We typically learn to relate things based on how they look. As small children, we quickly learn that "this cookie" is equivalent to "that cookie." In behavior analytic terms, this is due to the process known as stimulus generalization that we introduced in Chapter 7. Over time, however, we learn that the spoken word "cookie"(the tact) is equivalent to the actual cookie, and move slowly away from formal similarity as the basis for establishing such relationships.

Relationships of causation indicate that one stimulus causes another stimulus to occur. In the diagram, causal relations exist between "fear" and "run away," because we commonly agree that fear can cause us to run away. In the same manner, a relationship of causation exists between "thinking that I am afraid" and "running away" (Blackledge, 2003).

Relational Responding

If you recall information in previous chapters regarding stimulus control and shaping, we stated very clearly that behavior analysis is quite often concerned with a child's ability to discriminate between individual stimuli. The concept of the discriminative stimulus or S^D demonstrates this point. Given a particular stimulus, and a learning history relative to that stimulus, a child is more likely to engage in behavior that has been reinforced in its presence, compared to the presence of a different stimulus (S^{Δ}).

In RFT, the focus is not so much on discrimination of individual stimuli but *on the relationships that exist between them.* This process of discriminating relationships between stimuli is called **relational responding** (Blackledge, 2003).

Relational responding allows us to gather more information from these related sets of stimuli than from the discrimination of individual members of those sets. In Blackledge's snake phobia example (2003), discriminating "a wooded area" (compared to a "city street") or "a snake" (instead of a "dog") tells me nothing about the hierarchical relationship between snakes and wooded areas (primarily, that snakes can be found there).

Furthermore, the coordinated relationship between "snake" and the three stimuli "dangerous," "not predictable," and "quick movement" can lead to other relationships of coordination, and the transfer of psychological functions between stimuli.
For example:

IF

1) If I am told that snakes (A) are dangerous, unpredictable, and move quickly (B).

AND

2) I already know that danger, unpredictability, and quick movement (B) are things to be afraid of (C).

THEN

3) I would be afraid (C) of snakes (A) even though I never encountered one before.

Removing the narrative elements to this example would leave us with the formula:

If A = B and B = C, then C = A

***Note: the = symbol in this and all future formulas within this chapter represents equivalence (and not necessarily equality).**

This formula should look familiar: it is the same schematic that appears in the standard description of stimulus equivalence. This is because, as noted earlier, relationships of coordination are equivalence relations. The person need not have any direct training or conditioning to make the "snake equals fear" relation.

Blackledge goes further to argue that this process of relational responding cannot be explained by standard behavioral principles. If operant or respondent conditioning were responsible for the phenomenon, direct contingencies would need to be present – i.e., the person would need to have had direct contact with a snake.

Stimulus generalization is likewise dismissed, as it would require that the person come in contact with formally similar stimuli, such as photographs of snakes, when she learned that snakes are dangerous. As noted in the example, the person was merely told that snakes are dangerous, unpredictable, and move quickly.

In summary, RFT is concerned with **derived relational responding**, which can be defined as the ability to relate stimuli in a variety of ways, even though the person has never been reinforced (directly trained) to relate those stimuli in those specific ways. As with stimulus equivalence, the untrained relation is *derived* from other relations. Fear of snakes is derived from the two relations 1) snake = dangerous and 2) danger = fear (Blackledge, 2003).

Mutual Entailment and Combinatorial Entailment

Controlled studies of RFT over the past 10 years have identified two distinct types of derived relational responding – mutual entailment and combinatorial entailment.

Mutual entailment is reminiscent of Sidman's property of *symmetry*, in that two stimuli are said to be mutually entailed when A = B and B = A. With mutual entailment, if A is related to B in a specific way, then B is related to A in a complementary way.

During Sidman's experiments with reading comprehension, the written word "bed" was seen as equivalent (meaning the same as) a picture of a bed. In this case, the symmetrical relation also holds true – a picture of a bed is equivalent to the word "bed."

With mutual entailment of more complex relations like comparison, the relationship is not so much a mirror image than it is complementary. For example, *if A is bigger than B*, it does not hold true that *B is bigger than A*. What does exist is a complementary relationship such that if *A is bigger than B, then B is smaller than A* (Blackledge, 2003).

This type of relational responding (with stimuli that are not visually similar) is not seen in non-human subjects (with one exception being a study with a sea lion in 1998), and typically is not seen with humans before the age of 18 months. It is also something that we have found we have to frequently teach to our young children with autism.

A common example occurs in the teaching of prepositions relative to physical location (see Figure 9.4). Discrete trial drills are conducted teaching the hierarchical relation between two objects such as a ball and a chair. The skill is typically taught unilaterally; the child is asked, "Where is the ball?" and the correct response is "The ball is on the chair." Young children with autism usually can learn this and other simple relations rather quickly (ball under the chair, ball next to the chair, etc.).

With typical children over the age of 18 months, the mutually entailed relation of "Where is the chair?" (with the correct response being "under the ball") does not have to be directly trained. The typical child derives the relation. The child with autism generally has to be taught this via multiple exemplars.

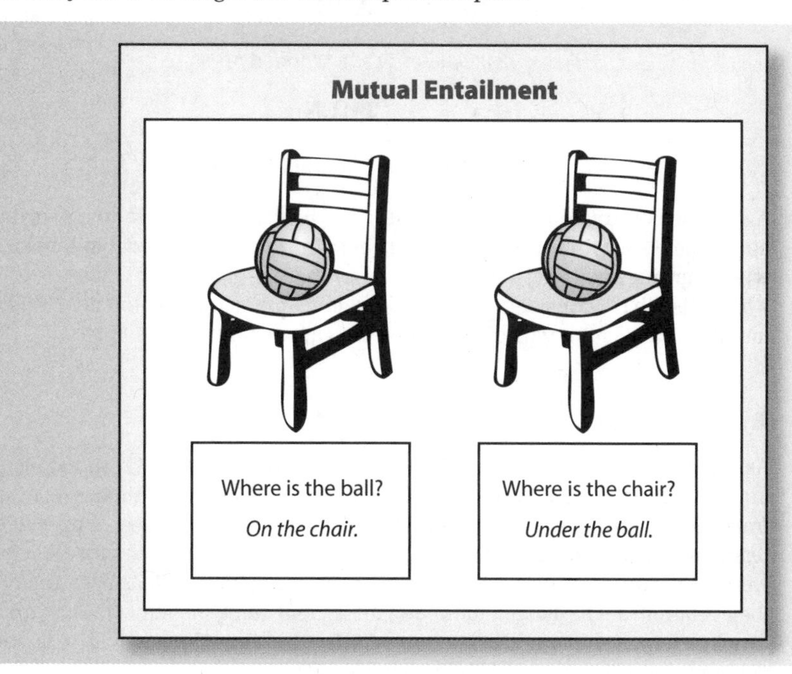

Figure 9.4

The second type of derived relational responding is **combinatorial entailment**. By definition, combinatorial entailment refers to reciprocal relationships that exist between two stimuli by virtue of how those stimuli are related to other, intermediary stimuli (Blackledge, 2003).

At least three stimuli must be present for combinatorial entailment to take place. Returning to Blackledge's snake phobia example, we can see how the "snake equals fear" relation is a product of combinatorial entailment:

IF

1) If I am told that snakes (A) are dangerous, unpredictable, and move quickly (B).

AND

2) I already know that danger, unpredictability, and quick movement (B) are things to be afraid of (C).

THEN

3) I would be afraid (C) of snakes (A) even though I never encountered one before.

This combination of three *coordinated* relations is said to be combinatorially entailed because the relationship between snake and fear exists by virtue of two other relations 1) snakes are related to danger and 2) danger is related to fear.

Other relations can also be involved in combinatorial entailment. The hierarchical relation of "I/me," "snake," and "wooded area" can be combinatorially entailed to produce derived relations. Consider the following:

IF

1) I am in wooded area.

AND

2) Snakes are in wooded areas.

THEN

3) There may be a snake near me.

Again, the controlled RFT studies that have been conducted over the past decade have reliably shown that combinatorial entailment does not occur automatically when learning language, but develops as a *function* of learning language. Children with autism have considerable difficulty with combinatorial entailment, and as with mutual entailment, it typically has to be taught via multiple exemplars.

Transformation of Stimulus Functions

As can be seen in the snake phobia example, derived relational responding quite often results in changes in the function of stimuli involved within the relational frame. The coordinated relationship established between snakes, danger, and fear results in a transformation of the snake's functions. Where before snakes were unknown, or at best neutral, they now are an object of fear by virtue of their relationship to danger, unpredictability, and quick movement. This process is referred to as the **transformation of stimulus functions**, which is another defining characteristic of RFT (Blackledge, 2003).

When derived relations are continually experienced across multiple exemplars, words begin to take on the function of objects, actions, people, and events. At first, this is accomplished via direct contingencies (discrete trial training via massed trials) and along formal stimulus dimensions; for example, the word "cat" is related only to one picture of cat. As training and experience proceeds, the exemplars become more and more *arbitrary* (less formally similar). The word "cat" is related to different looking cats, to other feline species, to the general category of animals, etc.

Through this process, the ability to derive relational responses between stimuli is extended to use arbitrary properties of stimuli. Non-human subjects have been taught to discriminate along the lines of formal properties (selection based on color, size, or shape), but there have yet to be any species other than man capable of being taught to select based on arbitrary or non-formal properties of stimuli.

Blackledge (2003) gives the example of selecting "the bigger one" when presented with the President of the United States, a retail clerk, and a hobo. The formal properties of the three choices would lead to the selection of the one that is physically larger. However, when a verbal human is presented with this array, *he* is likely to select based on the arbitrary property of "bigger" – as it refers to importance. This relation of *bigger = important* has been given arbitrary significance by the socio-verbal community. Our young children with autism (and many of our older children and adults) would have great difficulty seeing that relationship.

Finally, RFT asserts that these arbitrarily applied, derived relational responses are applied in a non-arbitrary fashion. This means that the socio-verbal community only reinforces certain arbitrary stimulus properties in given contexts, and not in others. The language community ultimately approves of how we relate specific things (Blackledge, 2003). For example, the relation of *bigger = important* noted above is established by society because it "makes sense" in the context of comparing people of varying fame or notoriety. Conversely, the socio-verbal community may give the word *bigger* an entirely different meaning when the context changes and we are comparing defensive linemen of the NFL. The use and meaning of the word varies arbitrarily from context to context – and the socio-verbal community determines which meaning is appropriate for the context.

This last piece of the RFT puzzle brings us back around to its accepted definition. With relational frame theory, the core of language is "arbitrarily applicable derived relational responding that is not arbitrarily applied." To better understand this rather complicated definition, consider its components:

1) *Relational responding* – the ability to respond to relations between stimuli rather than each stimulus separately.

2) *Derived* – relations need not be directly learned (the learning occurs via mutual and combinatorial entailment).

3) *Arbitrary* – the process can occur with stimuli that do not share formal properties.

4) *Non-arbitrarily applied* – the socio-verbal community approves of how we relate specific stimuli within specific contexts.

As with *Verbal Behavior*, relational frame theory is just that – a theory in need of testing and replication in both basic and applied disciplines. It appears from the current research being conducted on RFT that its basic premise has merit, and that application to EIBI programs may be very promising.

Final Thoughts Regarding RFT

Much of the criticism leveled at DTI and EIBI programs relates to issues of generative language and relational responding. Critics see children from EIBI programs with expert formal language skills, wielding 1,000-word tact vocabularies, but possessing little ability to dynamically use the language.

RFT can serve EIBI if it forces therapists to look beyond programs that teach mere formal language relations and consider arbitrary relational responding as a teachable skill.

In Summary

To sum up this rather theoretical chapter, it would be fair to say that treatment approaches based on *Verbal Behavior* (Sundberg, Partington, Carbone) are currently enjoying widespread application with great success – although the basic research connected to it continues to be difficult to engineer.

Perhaps a synthesis of the two models (verbal behavior and relational frame theory) can be accomplished in the near future. Evidence that this may be in the works exists in some recent writings on the subject. Most notable is an article that appeared in a 2000 issue of *The Behavior Analyst* by Barnes-Holmes et al., entitled "Relational frame theory and Skinner's *Verbal Behavior*: A possible synthesis," which provides a systematic RFT analysis of Skinner's verbal operants. It is hopeful that behavior analysts are looking to glean valuable information from both theories so that effective treatment modalities can be developed to improve the lives of children diagnosed with autism.

References:

Barnes-Holmes, D., Barnes-Holmes, Y. & Cullinan, V. (2000). Relational frame theory and Skinner's Verbal Behavior: A possible synthesis. *The Behavior Analyst, 23*, 69-84.

Blackledge, J.T. (2003). An introduction to relational frame theory: Basics and applications. *The Behavior Analyst Today, 3* (4), 421-433.

Hayes, S.C., Barnes-Holmes, D. & Roche, B. (2001). *Relational frame theory: A post-skinnerian account of human language and cognition.* New York: Plenum.

Oah, S., & Dickinson, A.M., (1989). A review of empirical studies of verbal behavior. *The Analysis of Verbal Behavior, 7*, 53-68.

Pinker, S. (1997). *How the mind works.* New York: W.W. Norton & Co. Ltd.

Skinner, B.F. (1953). *Science and human behavior.* New York: MacMillan.

Skinner, B.F. (1957). *Verbal behavior.* Acton, MA: Copley.

Skinner, B.F. (1969). *Contingencies of reinforcement: A theoretical analysis.* New York: Appleton-Century Crofts.

Skinner, B.F. (1985). *The evolution of verbal behavior.* Paper delivered at the annual meeting of the Association for Behavior Analysis, Columbus, OH.

Sundberg M. L., & Partington, J.W. (1998). *Teaching language to Children with Autism and Other Developmental Disabilities.* Pleasant Hill, CA: Behavior Analysts, Inc.

Chapter 10

Procedures to Increase Behavior At a Glance

Chapter Points

- Differential reinforcement procedures are commonly utilized to teach new or replacement behaviors
- Discrete Trial Instruction (DTI) breaks functional tasks into their smallest component behaviors and teaches/shapes them via a clearly delineated Stimulus – Response – Consequence contingency.
- Natural Environment Training (NET) is driven by the student's motivation and is carried out in natural environments.
- Token economies are very effective systems of reinforcement delivery that involve generalized conditioned reinforcers (tokens) that are cashed in for back-up reinforcers.
- Visual systems for setting contingencies or establishing a schedule of activities for the child may capitalize on his or her propensity for visual learning.

Key Terms

Differentiation
Discrimination
DRH
Schedules of Reinforcement
CRF
EXT
INT
Schedule Thinning
Ratio Schedules
Interval Schedules
Fixed Ratio/ Interval Schedules
Variable Ratio/ Interval Schedules
Token Economy
Discrete Trial Instruction
Inter-Trial Interval (ITI)
Response Requirement
Mass Trial
Trial Interspersal
Expanded Trials
Collapsing Trials
Random Trial Distribution
Errorless Learning
Transfer Trial
No-No-Prompt
4-Step Error Correction
Natural Environment Training
Incidental Teaching
Video Self-Modeling

Procedures to Increase Behavior

Behavior Analytic Approaches to Teaching New Skills and Building Positive Behavior

While many intervention programs seek to merely reduce problem behaviors, *successful* programs work to replace them with functional abilities – typically through the skillful use of reinforcement.

This chapter deals with specific approaches designed to make desirable behaviors more likely to reoccur. It demonstrates how a comprehensive program for a child with autism involves many components – all of which must be in sync with one another – as well as many approaches that are utilized simultaneously. For these reasons, we will rely heavily on some of the terminology and processes described in earlier chapters.

When creating these programs, it's important to utilize instructional methods that play to the strengths that accompany autism. Rule learning, visual performance and visual perception should be heavily utilized, and weaknesses should be temporarily bypassed. Simple and predictable methods are best, and visual aids should be used whenever possible.

The procedures in this chapter, and their explanations, may seem complex. Even so, we ask that the reader pay close attention, because these procedures form the basis of instructional interactions. Readers will also find that effective instruction for children with autism is powerful for teaching *anyone*.

Once you have learned the principles behind solid skill instruction, you will be nearly ready to go about the processes of assessment and subsequent curriculum planning. That is where these principles will be put to use.

But before programs for teaching replacement skills can be discussed in detail, we first need to set some groundwork.

Behavioral change programs, by their very nature, involve engineering the child's environment by contriving contingencies of reinforcement. How these initially contrived contingencies are managed – and how they are eventually brought into line with more natural contingencies that exist in the child's life – requires knowledge of the schedules of reinforcement.

Section A – Schedules of Reinforcement

A **schedule of reinforcement**, simply stated, is a set rule that determines which instances of a target behavior will be reinforced, and which will not (Cooper, Heron, & Heward, 1987).

Although this topic has filled volumes, we will simply provide a basic overview of what schedules are and how they can affect a child's behavior.

Continuous Schedule of Reinforcement

With a **continuous schedule of reinforcement (CRF)**, all instances of a target behavior are reinforced (Cooper, Heron, & Heward, 1987). For example, if Jasmine bites her hand in an effort to gain access to computer time, a typical approach might involve teaching her to use a picture to request the computer instead. To begin the process of teaching her this alternative, we no longer respond when Jasmine bites her hand, but we grant her access to the computer *every time* she exchanges a picture.

These schedules are typically used when we teach new skills or try to strengthen existing, but weakly established skills. In Jasmine's case, the use of pictures is a new skill that we are trying to establish in her repertoire.

In real life, CRF schedules are usually limited to behaviors that are less socially mediated. Examples include turning on light switches, flushing toilets, or answering the telephone when it rings. All of these examples usually result in immediate reinforcement every time we engage in the behavior.

Extinction Schedule

The direct opposite of a CRF schedule is an **extinction schedule (EXT)**, in which all instances of a targeted behavior *do not* result in reinforcement (Cooper, Heron, & Heward, 1987). In Jasmine's case, hand-biting behavior was placed on an extinction schedule in that its display did not result in access to the computer. (For a review of extinction and its associated issues, please refer to Chapter 6.)

Intermittent Schedule of Reinforcement

In most socially mediated (verbal behavior) situations, our behaviors are maintained by less *dense* schedules. For example, when teaching reading, an instructor typically does not stop a child at each word and praise him or her. Instead, fluent and accurate reading is praised when the child finishes the passage.

When reinforcement occurs at some rate that falls between a CRF and an EXT schedule, it is said to occur on an **intermittent schedule of reinforcement (INT)** (Cooper, Heron, & Heward, 1987). Intermittent schedules are used primarily to maintain existing behaviors in our repertoire. In fact, the vast majority of human verbal and nonverbal behavior is maintained by INT schedules.

Schedule Thinning

When we teach new skills to our children with autism, we usually start with a CRF schedule that enables us to bring the new skill to a certain strength. In order to maintain the skill over time, we progress from a CRF to an INT schedule through a transitional process referred to as **schedule thinning**. The term *thin* stands as an opposite concept to *dense* when we refer to schedules of reinforcement. The thinner the schedule, the less frequently reinforcement is delivered – and the denser the schedule, the more frequently reinforcement is delivered. A CRF schedule is the densest schedule possible.

The process of schedule thinning should be approached with caution, so as to not "pull the rug out" from under the child. A child who is accustomed to being reinforced for every response may initially be a little hesitant to respond when the schedule is thinned slightly – such as reinforcing every other response. This is to be expected. If, however, too large of a transition is made from the CRF schedule (such as to an INT schedule whereby reinforcement is delivered on every fourth response), the child's performance may unnecessarily suffer.

This phenomenon, known as **ratio strain,** occurs when a schedule is thinned too quickly and results in an extinction effect – i.e., the child stops responding as expected (Cooper, Heron, & Heward, 1987). Backing up temporarily to a denser schedule of reinforcement is usually all that is necessary to rectify the problem.

There are several reasons why progressing from a CRF to an INT schedule is desirable. The most obvious benefit is the practicalities involved – CRF schedules are labor-intensive and require the type of diligence that is generally not possible in the home or classroom setting. Teachers would get very little teaching done if they had to reinforce every behavior of every student in their class.

Secondly, basic and applied research has shown that CRF schedules are particularly susceptible to extinction. (Lerman & Iwata, 1996) An example of a CRF schedule in action is the behavior of turning on a light switch. Every time we perform the behavior (flip the switch), we are reinforced with the appearance of light. If, however, the light bulb is burned out on a particular occasion, we flip the switch once, or maybe twice. Faced with extinction (no reinforcement – i.e., no light) our behavior stops nearly immediately.

If, however, our learning history with that particular light switch is based on an INT schedule of reinforcement, our response to extinction is quite different. Suppose the light switch has a loose wire that we have not had time to repair, and we can only turn the light on by flipping the switch up and down several times before an electrical connection is made. In this case, our intermittent schedule of reinforcement will cause us to remain there flipping the switch up and down far longer than with the previous example of a CRF schedule.

By their very nature, intermittent schedules result in behaviors that are far more resistant to extinction. **Resistance to extinction** is the persistence of a person's responding even when reinforcement is not immediately forthcoming. The classic example of this is a slot machine. A person will engage in this behavior for hours without any direct reinforcement, because the machine's pay-off is set on an extremely thin schedule of intermittent reinforcement. (Note that this is why INT schedules are used for maintaining behavior.)

A third benefit of INT schedules is that they are better at avoiding reinforcer satiation than CRF schedules. When a particular reinforcer is continuously delivered, the constant exposure leads to satiation. An intermittent schedule provides the reinforcer at a lower rate, which diminishes satiation effects. The thinner the schedule, the less likely satiation will occur.

And finally, INT schedules are more in line with naturally occurring schedules of reinforcement. Consider a child who begins the school year on a CRF schedule, where candy is delivered for every correct response to teacher directives. This process is not only labor intensive (possibly requiring the assignment of a 1:1 aide), but it is far from the typical reward system set up in an elementary school classroom. If the CRF schedule can be quickly thinned to an INT schedule, the INT schedule can be gradually thinned over the course of the school year. Eventually, it will approximate the daily or weekly reward system established for the entire class.

Ratio and Interval Schedules

With our young children with autism, we build skill repertoires by establishing myriad new behaviors. We want our children to display these verbal and social behaviors in a variety of settings where reinforcement occurs naturally – not according to a contrived continuous schedule. This can only be accomplished by moving from CRF to INT schedules and then continuing to thin the INT schedules to approximate natural schedules of reinforcement.

Two varieties of intermittent schedules are based on how the reinforcer is delivered – either on the passage of time, or on the number of responses performed by the individual.

Ratio schedules require that a certain number of responses be emitted before one response is reinforced (Reynolds, 1968). An example of this is a discrete trial session with a child learning to tact common household objects. In this case, a break from the instructional session is provided after every 10 correct tact responses. This example meets the definition of an INT schedule because negative reinforcement (the break) is not provided for every correct response, but rather is reserved for every tenth correct response. It also qualifies as a ratio schedule, since the reinforcement delivery is based on a pre-specified number of child responses, and not on the mere passage of time.

Ratio schedules increase the rate of responding because the faster the child responds, the sooner he will come into contact with the reinforcer. In other words, the child actually controls reinforcement delivery.

Interval schedules require that a pre-specified interval of time pass before a response is reinforced (Cooper, Heron, & Heward, 1987). During the same discrete trial session described above, the child would be reinforced with a break following the first correct response that occurred after a five-minute interval elapsed. This is an INT schedule because each individual response does not result in reinforcement. It is an interval schedule because the passage of time dictates when reinforcement is available, instead of the number of responses the child makes.

Interval schedules do not typically increase rate, because the speed at which the child responds has no effect on when reinforcement is delivered. Time, not the child, controls when reinforcement occurs. It should also be noted that the mere ending of the interval does not result in the delivery of reinforcement. Only the first correct response following the end of the interval is reinforced – if the child responds incorrectly, reinforcement is withheld (extinction).

Application of Ratio or Interval Schedules

Ratio or interval schedules can be applied in a variety of ways; however, for the purposes of this manual, we will briefly discuss the two general variations that apply to both.

Intermittent schedules can be **fixed** or **variable**. With a fixed schedule, the ratio and the interval remain constant. In a variable schedule, the ratio and the interval vary from one response to the next.

Ratio schedules can therefore be either fixed or variable. A **fixed ratio schedule** keeps the number of correct responses at a constant. A fixed ratio schedule where every response is reinforced is referred to as a FR1 schedule. A fixed ratio schedule where every two responses are reinforced would be a FR2, and so forth.

One noteworthy effect of a fixed ratio schedule is the **post-reinforcement pause**. Children who become accustomed to a fixed ratio schedule will respond steadily until reinforcement is delivered. Immediately following the delivery of reinforcement, however, the child will stop responding. The duration of this pause is related to the size of the ratio. A large ratio requirement results in a longer pause, and a small ratio requirement is followed by a shorter pause. For example, the post reinforcement pause during an FR 10 schedule (reinforcement provided following every tenth response) would be expected to be much longer than that during an FR2 (reinforcement provided following every other response) schedule.

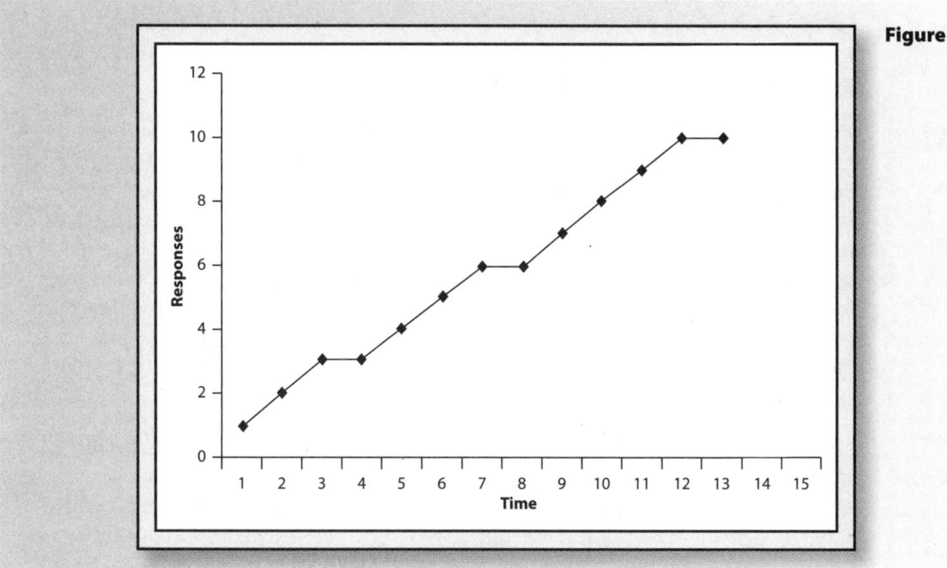

Figure 10.1

A visual representation of this can be seen in Figure 10.1

A **variable ratio schedule** bases reinforcement delivery on an average number of correct responses. The variable ratio counterpart of the FR2 is the VR2, where reinforcement is delivered *on average* after every two correct responses. The actual number of responses between reinforcement delivery varies each time (it is not always every two responses), but the overall average number will equal two. For example, for eight correct responses, reinforcement would be provided after responses one, five, six, and eight. Reinforcement would not occur following responses two, three, four, and seven. Figure 10.2 demonstrates how reinforcement would be delivered according to a VR2 (assuming all responses are correct).

1	2	3	4	5	6	7	8
Sr+	EXT	EXT	EXT	Sr+	Sr+	EXT	Sr+

Figure 10.2

In this example, reinforcement occurs on response number one (after one response), number five (after four more responses), number six (after one more response), and finally, following number eight (after two more responses). If the numbers of responses between reinforcement delivery are totaled (1 + 4 + 1 + 2 = 8) and divided by the total number of times reinforcement is delivered (8 ÷ 4 = 2), the average is every two responses.

Variable ratio schedules do not produce the post-reinforcement pause seen in FR schedules, because the child typically cannot anticipate when the next reinforcer will be delivered.

Interval schedules can also be either fixed or variable in their application. With a **fixed interval schedule**, reinforcement is delivered following the first correct response at the end of a set time interval. For example, an FI2 schedule provides reinforcement for the first correct response that occurs after every two minutes elapse. Children who become accustomed to an FI schedule begin to discern the fixed time pattern and realize that once a response is reinforced, the subsequent responses until the end of the interval never gain reinforcement. As a result, their performance typically tails off following reinforcement and produces a "scallop effect" on the cumulative graph.

Finally, an interval schedule can be set up so that the length of the time intervals varies between opportunities for reinforcement. This is called a **variable interval schedule**. Like the variable ratio schedule, the time intervals within the variable interval schedule occur in near-random fashion. Calculating an average length of interval is similarly accomplished by taking the *average* length of intervals that occur across time. For example, a VI-10 minute schedule provides reinforcement for the first correct response that occurs following intervals of varying lengths – but the overall average duration of intervals would equal 10 minutes. Time intervals of 10 minutes, 7 minutes, 12 minutes, and 11 minutes would average out to 10 minutes (10 + 7 + 12 + 11 = 40 ÷ 4 = 10 minutes).

Much of the power of the variable interval schedule lies in the unpredictability of reinforcement. The child never "knows[1]" when reinforcement will come, and since the next time interval may be very short, the scallop effect seen in variable ratio schedules or the post-reinforcement pause seen in fixed schedules typically do not occur. In fact, once the child acclimates to a variable interval schedule, we usually see some of the most steady and stable responding, compared to the other types of schedules discussed in this chapter.

Now that we have established a basic understanding of the schedules of reinforcement and extinction, we are ready to move forward with our discussion of procedures for increasing behavior.

Section B – Procedures For Increasing Behavior

Differential Reinforcement of High Rates of Responding (DRH) is a version of differential reinforcement[2] used to increase behavior by reinforcing a minimal number of responses that occur within a pre-specified time period. DRH procedures are quite often implemented in educational settings where fluency of responding is a goal.

If a behavior targeted for increase is occurring at relatively low rates – for example, a child is reading only 60 words per minute – a DRH procedure is an appropriate means of systematically increasing the target behavior.

In this instance, a criterion for DRH is set by taking the child's average baseline rate and highest rate recorded during baseline, and then selecting a mid-point between

[1] "Knows" is a mentalistic term. We used it only to illustrate a point in lay terminology. There needs to be no comprehension on the part of the learner whatsoever for operant effects of reinforcement contingencies to occur.

[2] Differential reinforcement refers to placing one member of a response class on extinction while reinforcing one or more other members of the response class. Please see sections in Chapters 7 (Stimulus Control and Shaping) and 12 (Procedures to Reduce Behavior) for more thorough discussions of differential reinforcement.

the two. For example, if the child's average baseline rate for reading is 60 words per minute, and her highest rate during this same baseline is 80 words per minute, the criterion for the DRH is set at 70 words per minute.

The teacher puts the DRH procedure into effect by setting a time interval and having the child begin reading. At the end of the time interval, the child's behavior is reinforced only if she reads at or above the rate of 70 words per minute. If, at the end of the time interval, the child's rate is found to be less than the 70 words per minute criterion, she does not receive reinforcement (extinction). The interval is then reset and the child is provided with another trial.

Section C – Discrete Trial Instruction

When Skinner first put forth a cogent argument for a scientific and environmental approach to understanding behavior, the result was a great deal of controversy. However, as the scientific community conducted test after test of applied behavioral theory, and data began to accumulate, behavior analysis gained a level of prominence within the field of psychology.

Then, developmental and cognitive psychology dealt a blow to behavior analysis by viewing it merely as a "fringe" group within the field. Despite repeated controlled studies and mounting evidence as to its effects, behavior analysis could not shake the image that it was a dying science.

This discussion is important for two reasons: first, because recent changes in public awareness and acceptance have breathed new life into behavioral analysis, and second, it illustrates why the field may continue to be misunderstood.

History

Any further discussion about applied behavior analysis, its new public prominence, and its association with autism must include the work of Norwegian-born researcher and psychologist O. Ivar Lovaas at UCLA.

Lovaas' groundbreaking work began in the late 1960s, when he realized that a variety of environmentally based interventions could be used to shape the learning behaviors of severely developmentally disabled individuals, while reducing behaviors that were deemed problematic. Applying the core principles of behavior analysis (observation, data collection, and manipulation of environmental variables to demonstrate experimental control), Lovaas was able to teach skills to learners that were severely impaired.

As autism became better known in the 1970s and 1980s, Lovaas found that his treatment and teaching methods seemed to be particularly beneficial to individuals with autism. Language skills could be taught at the same time that general compliance to instructional requests was being shaped. The children he treated often learned to communicate effectively, to follow instructions, and to show fewer instances of misbehavior.

Because Lovaas was one of the only practitioners who relied heavily upon the principles of applied behavior analysis to guide his treatment of children with autism, these techniques became known to the general public as "The Lovaas Method," "The Lovaas Approach," and "Lovaas Therapy," among others. In 1981, he and several colleagues wrote *The ME Book*, in which he outlined, in procedural format, the specific interventions used to teach language skills to young children with autism in a home-based program. It was the first time a behaviorally based, "how-to" manual was available for anyone who was interested in teaching skills to these children. *The ME Book* armed parents and families with a new sense of empowerment that they could, in fact, undertake a teaching program that would allow their children to achieve more than most initially thought.

Lovaas continued to publish in peer-reviewed behavioral and psychological journals. His research interests included skill instruction for the developmentally disabled, and the use of behavior reduction techniques (including the use of aversive stimuli) to ameliorate problem behavior.

As he began to see predictable and consistent results in many of the children with whom he worked, Lovaas instituted the UCLA Young Autism Project as a way to put his overall treatment package to the rigorous test of controlled investigation. The resulting study, which was published in 1987, showed that 47 percent of the children who received his protocol of intensive treatment demonstrated gains that placed them in the "normal" range of functioning, in terms of IQ and other standardized measures of cognitive and behavioral functioning (Lovaas, 1987).

This study spawned considerable debate both inside and outside the autism community that rages to this day. Critics attacked the study from all angles, citing weaknesses in experimental and procedural methodology, as well as ethical considerations concerning such intensive treatment for young children. In addition, there have been difficulties replicating the study precisely, because certain components of treatment (such as the use of aversives) are no longer considered socially acceptable, and have not been included in the treatment protocols of recent replication efforts.

However, several replication studies *are* showing reliable findings. Many more replication sites are operating worldwide, supporting the notion that many children improve significantly, even if not the proportion cited to have achieved "normalcy" in Lovaas' original study.

It has become increasingly apparent that when it comes to an ABA intervention approach for children with autism, conclusive support in a single study will continue to be quite elusive. This is not to say that ABA approaches to autism treatment do not carry solid and convincing evidence of their efficacy. On the contrary, countless studies have shown that smaller components of an ABA intervention reliably and consistently bring about positive changes in the behaviors of individuals with autism and other developmental disabilities. A thorough review of peer-reviewed literature in which experimental principles are upheld clearly demonstrates that ABA techniques have empirical support.

The key is to not get caught in the controversy. Keep in mind that the success of an intervention should be based upon improvement of each individual, and how this improvement translates into greater independence and functionality in his or her life. Trying to argue over percentages of children who achieve normal functioning, or attempting to refute selection processes in a large-scale study accomplish nothing.

In fact, focusing on the arguments undermines the significance of data that show, on a continual basis, that behavioral approaches to instruction, combined with data-based decision making and a focus on intensity, *will* lead to positive changes.

Regardless of the controversy surrounding his research, Lovaas laid quite a bit of groundwork for the teaching methods used effectively today with children with autism. Principally, he is known as the first to implement the concept of Discrete Trial Instruction with children with autism. Discrete Trial Instruction (DTI) has been wrongly used as a replacement term for "ABA," but nonetheless remains a viable component of many effective ABA-based treatment packages.

Mechanics of Discrete Trial Instruction

Discrete Trial Instruction (DTI) is a behaviorally based type of teaching that breaks functional tasks into their smallest component behaviors and teaches/shapes these behaviors by providing a clearly delineated Stimulus – Response – Consequence contingency. Discrete Trial Instruction can also be viewed as a deliberate instructional adaptation of the **four-term contingency** that drives all operant responding. First, the MO is in place. A stimulus occasions a behavioral response, and a consequence to the behavior either strengthens or weakens it. In short, DTI is a way to train discriminative responding.

The operant conditioning paradigm itself implies that most of what we do voluntarily is the result of a selection, based on past contact with reinforcement (or lack thereof) and given similar stimulus conditions or circumstances. Therefore, when someone says the word "green," we select a green object based on a stimulus condition (the word "green," the presence of something green), and our history of being reinforced for doing so.

In a previous chapter, we discussed the idea of the discriminative stimulus, or S^D, as the stimulus whose presence signifies that reinforcement is available if a particular behavior is selected. We also discussed the relevance of the S-Delta (S^Δ), in the presence of which the behavior will not be reinforced. These two concepts are at the heart of systematic discrimination training, which is what DTI provides.

How does this look in practice? The environment for DTI should be tailored to meet the needs of the learner. If a child is new to instruction and easily distractible, it might be helpful to gain instructional control in an environment that is relatively quiet and stark. The instructor should be with the child, close enough to reach him or her for physical prompting and reinforcement. If the child will remain in the instructional area without escaping or requiring many prompts to remain seated, instruction can happen from any seated location (on the floor, on a couch, at a table, etc.). Unfortunately, this is often not the case.

Children who are new to instruction are also often new to any type of adult-directed contingent reinforcement. For this reason, instructional control is the first issue that must be dealt with. Instructional control is typically established through a combination of reinforcement pairing (creating a clear association between the instructor and the delivery of reinforcement), contingent access to reinforcement, and simple compliance training.

When poorly established compliance is an issue, it is often best to begin instruction (after pairing and manding trials) in a structured setting. This could mean that the instructor and the learner are seated in chairs at a table, either across from one another or perpendicular to one another. However, the same type of instruction can happen anywhere.

Keep in mind that this contrived, isolated type of environment is a starting point, not an end. Any quality instruction (short of academic or school environment training) should aim to move instruction into generalized or naturally occurring environmental conditions as quickly as possible. *(It is important to note that the authors are presenting DTI in the way they incorporate it into EIBI. While not technically a part of the DTI format, we see instructional control as a beneficial focal point early on.)*

DTI and the Four-Term Contingency

Once the instructional environment has been identified and modified, if necessary, it is time to begin instruction. As a guiding principle, the instructor must realize the integral role of the word "discrete" in the concept of DTI. The word implies that instructional components and processes must be kept separate, distinct, or extremely clear. Technically, "discrete" refers to the fact that each trial is separate from each other; i.e., a restricted rather than free operant. Here's how the concept applies to the four-term contingency (MO – S^D – R – Cons.):

- First, an effective instructor captures the learner's MO. In other words, the instructor effectively identifies the things that are reinforcing for the learner at that moment, and modifies the environment in such a way that this effect is heightened. This environmental modification might involve isolating a toy that the instructor has just observed the child playing with, bringing the toy to the instructional area and making its further access contingent upon the child's correct responses to the instruction. As a result, a powerful reinforcer is captured and made available for use.

- Second, a very clear stimulus is offered. This is the S^D. The stimulus can be vocal ("touch shoe"), gestural (pointing to an object), modeled, etc. No matter what form the stimulus takes, it is made very clear to the learner that this is a signal – something is happening that requires a response of some sort.

- Third, a very specific behavior on the part of the learner must occur. In early discrimination training, this implies that there is only one correct way in which the learner can respond, and only responses that meet these topographical requirements will be reinforced.

- Fourth, the instructor provides a consequence to the behavior. If the behavior is the desired behavior (i.e. the child touches his or her nose, given the instruction to do so), the consequence is one of reinforcement. If the response/behavior is not the desired behavior, the consequence is either one of extinction (no reinforcement provided) or punishment (a negation or otherwise punishing consequence).

Each cycle through this four-term contingency constitutes one learning trial, or one discrete trial. A **discrete trial**, then, consists of one cycle of stimulus presentation or opportunity to respond, the response, and the consequence. (See Figure 10.3) By keeping the components of instruction this isolated, it is possible to home in on very specific response topographies and offer countless opportunities for the behavior to be met with reinforcement, which will strengthen it. Additionally, opportunities are built into the learning trial that force the learner to make a selection between the target response and those that are erroneous or that will not be met with reinforcement. In this way, consistent selection of correct responses and weakened selection of incorrect responses can be hastened.

The following example illustrates a "textbook" DTI procedure:

When learning to identify colors, the learner is taught to show discrimination of the color blue by pointing to a blue rectangle when the words, "touch blue" are heard. Discrimination is not considered attained unless there are also rectangles of other colors present – so an array of rectangles of differing colors is placed in front of the learner. The instructor is aware of the learner's affinity for chocolate chip cookies, and restricts access to them prior to the DTI session. When it begins, pieces of chocolate chip cookies are placed within view of the learner.

The S^D is delivered in the form of "touch blue" and the presence of the blue rectangle within the array. The learner touches the blue rectangle, and is given a small piece of cookie as a reward. On the next trial, the same thing occurs. On the third trial, the learner touches a red rectangle after the stimulus is presented. To this, the instructor responds by stating "no," and diverts attention from the learner while clearing the array from the table. Because a reinforcer (the cookie) is not delivered when red is touched, the error signals that reinforcement is not available for such a response. On subsequent trials, the learner successfully touches blue when asked to do so, and commits no further errors.

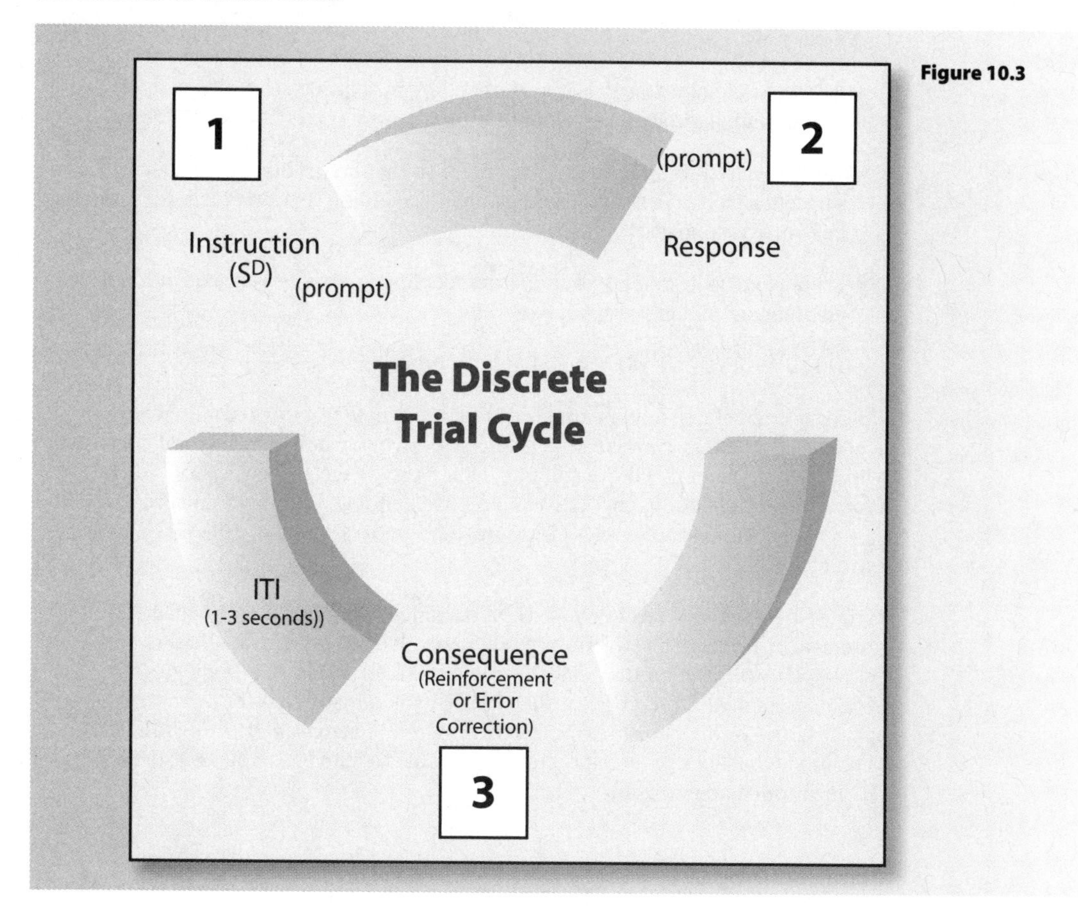

Figure 10.3

While the above scenario is simple, it highlights the main elements of the discrete trial.

- First, salient reinforcement was identified and based on the current MO. (Note that the reinforcement need not be related in any way to the task at hand – cookies certainly have nothing to do with the color blue!)
- A very specific and consistent stimulus was presented, in the form of "touch blue," and the presence of the array. There were no additional features of the stimulus items that could lead to a discriminative relationship (inflection of the instruction, colored items of different sizes/shapes/forms, etc.).

- A very specific response was necessary in order for reinforcement to be delivered.
- Reinforcement was delivered based on correct responding. A non-reinforcing consequence was delivered in the event of incorrect responding.

In the early stages of DTI, instruction is kept as clear, consistent, and uncluttered as possible. Many children with autism who begin intensive treatment programs have one very glaring commonality: they frequently have very few functional or social behaviors that are under tight stimulus control, and even fewer that are under tight instructional control.[3]

While DTI is a highly formalized and contrived approach to instruction, it is not always implemented as simply as our initial description. In addition to the care involved in keeping the main parts of the contingency intact and discrete, the instructor must also:

- Be aware of changing MOs, data collection, prompting strategies and prompt fading procedures, and appropriate error correction procedures.
- Take care to differentiate reinforcement so that behaviors are "shaped up" through successive approximations, while avoiding reinforcement for mixed or hybrid responses.
- Employ some systematic way of interspersing known versus acquisition tasks, and manage all instructional materials.
- Do all of the above while maintaining a brisk pace.

When all of the above factors are considered, a simple four-term contingency becomes much more complicated. Anthony Castrogiovanni, a behavioral consultant with Pyramid Educational Consultants, observed, "Discrete Trial Instruction is a funny thing. Just about anybody can do it well enough to make some progress. It is rare and difficult to mess it up completely, but it is rare and difficult to do it extremely well."

In the years since the authors have been training others in DTI techniques, this statement continues to resonate with accuracy. We often see practitioners in the field implementing what they call Discrete Trial Instruction with some degree of competence. At the very least, they are providing many trials or learning opportunities during work sessions with children. It is extremely rare, however, to be in the presence of an instructor who is able to manage all of the aspects of DTI mentioned above.

Deconstructing DTI

In this section, we describe each of the components of DTI in point-by-point fashion. The goal is to help the reader become more aware of all of the elements involved in effective DTI implementation. The exceptions are error correction and data collection, which are addressed in separate sections of this chapter, and prompting and stimulus control, which appear elsewhere in this manual.

---

[3] **Instructional control** is a form of stimulus control in which the stimuli that occasion behaviors are intentionally delivered. For example, children who go to bed when asked to do so are exhibiting behavior that is under the type of stimulus control known as instructional control. This is so because the behavior is one that has been specifically requested.

The remaining instructor responsibilities are presented in rather generic terms, to serve as a type of "checklist" for DTI presentation.

1. Keep components separate.

First and foremost, each component of the discrete trial must be kept discrete, or separate. This also applies to the idea that trials themselves are separate events.

How does this occur? Primarily, the instructor must be prepared to identify each element of an instructional interaction. This means that he or she should know exactly what the antecedent stimuli will be, and exactly what type of response will be consequated with reinforcement. Further, he or she must be able to identify where prompting and error correction fit within the trial itself. By keeping all of these considerations in mind, the instructor can then quasi-define a type of movement cycle that makes up an entire trial. In this case, however, the movement cycle is actually a chain of behaviors exhibited by both the instructor and the learner.

Why is this important? By identifying each part of the learning trial, the instructor has acquired the knowledge to also identify the beginning and end of one complete trial. This allows him or her to take measures to keep this single trial as discrete as necessary, or as free from "muddling" with other contingencies as possible. It is this discreteness that allows the learner to make the connection between his or her behavior and the subsequent presence or absence of reinforcement.

2. Wait briefly at the conclusion of one trial before beginning another.

This pause, which is known as the **Inter-Trial Interval (ITI)**, is a critical element in keeping trials discrete from one trial to the next. In the past, leaders in the field recommended a three- to five-second ITI. In this way, the instructor could be sure that the learner was also aware of the end of one opportunity to be reinforced for a response. More recently, others have favored much shorter ITI times, such as one to three seconds (Lovaas, 2003).

Keeping the ITI present but very brief yields many additional benefits. First, skills that are fluent are skills that can be performed with accuracy at a very quick pace – which implies a level of automaticity. Proponents of fluency-based instruction assert that increased fluency results in increased retention, endurance, automaticity, generalization, and ultimate functionality of a skill. Therefore, any efforts to build fluency, such as reduction of the ITI, will likely result in better and more meaningful skill acquisition.

Second, reduction of the ITI picks up the pace of skill instruction overall, allowing many more learning trials to be completed during the same session length. This results in more practice of the skill, more exposure to the S^D, more contact with reinforcement as a result of correct responding, and ultimately, greater fluency with the skill. Finally, there have been studies that have shown that a brisk instructional pace actually increases student accuracy and on-task behavior (Carnine, 1976). So, despite the leanings of the "old guard," research and refined practice have led most of today's most successful practitioners to shorten the ITI to increase the pace of instruction.

There are times, however, when the exact opposite must occur in order to stress the independence of each trial. Particularly at the onset of instruction with a new learner, it may be very important to stretch the ITI so that the relationship between stimulus, response, and reinforcement becomes very clear. As skills progress, and fluency becomes a target, the ITI is shortened. In order to make an appropriate decision regarding this matter, always consult the data. If the child is making adequate progress toward his or her aim, then an adjustment may not be in order. If he or she is not, the instructor must consider whether the trials are kept discrete enough, and whether the ITI is the issue.

3. Establish and use a written program plan.

Another important consideration in maintaining tight, discrete separation of learning trials is the establishment and use of a written program plan. Essentially, this is a one- or two-page document that takes some of the guesswork out of skill instruction by very clearly spelling out the parts of the trial for a particular skill that is in acquisition. Included are the specific stimulus conditions, the specific response topography that will be reinforced, and a simple procedure for implementing the program. Usually, recommendations for prompting and prompt fading are included on this form, as well as future targets within the same skill class.

4. Capture MO's and provide reinforcement.

When we pair ourselves with reinforcement, we encourage the child to allow us into his or her world. Providing reinforcement for taking prompts or following instructions sets up an instructional relationship that ultimately propels the child to do his or her best – even if the instructional content is extremely difficult.

Conversely, almost every instructional issue that serves as an impediment to learning also has a connection to reinforcement. Simply put, without meaningful reinforcement there can be no effective teaching interaction. This is perhaps the single greatest problem that the authors encounter when approaching discrete trial programs as consultants.

Fortunately, problems with reinforcement are usually amenable to change once they're identified, and once direction is provided on how to remediate them. Some basic rules apply here. First, the instructor has to realize that reinforcement is not dictated by anything other than its effect on behavior. Remember this. It means that what serves as reinforcement for one child may not serve as reinforcement for another.

Likewise, preferred items or activities may not serve as reinforcement in all contexts. Some children are very much "into" toys that light up, move, or make noise. When no demands are placed upon them, these types of toys may very well serve as an enjoyable way to pass the time. However, in the face of an increased MO for escape, such as when heavy demands or very difficult tasks are placed upon a child, the toy may not serve as reinforcement at all. This is because it does not lead to increased rates of responding. In this particular case, the MO at the time has elevated the value of negative reinforcement, and an effective instructor will recognize this and adjust accordingly.

It is also possible to provide effective reinforcement when the context of the situation is accounted for, in terms of its effects on the MO of the learner. MO's can be manipulated in many ways to make certain types of reinforcement more or less valuable at any moment. But, ultimately, the instructor must be able to identify these elements, manipulate them when possible, and adapt reinforcement delivery to reflect them. Additionally, the instructor should make efforts, whenever possible, to create competition between any negative or tangible reinforcement and positive social reinforcement. Again, DTI works best when instructors are able to establish themselves as reinforcers in their own right.

5. Collect data.

Every highly effective behavior change procedure has a strong data collection system as its main decision-making tool. DTI is no different. There are many programs that appear to do a fairly reasonable job of providing skill instruction to children with autism, despite deficiencies in data collection. However, even these programs would be much more efficient if they included a way to track learner progress through skill programs.

The tighter the data collection system, the easier it is to identify the need for changes, and, in most instances, even the nature of the necessary changes. We will explore data collection methods specific to DTI in later sections of this chapter, but for now, it is important to know that the instructor must consider data collection when providing skill instruction. Therefore, it is important to devise a system that will not interfere with progress or the ability to provide an adequate number of learning opportunities, while also providing enough information to drive changes in programming.

6. Incorporate prompting.

We know that prompting is necessary in order to shape certain response topographies (for a complete discussion of prompting and prompt-fading strategies, please see Chapter 7). But where does a prompt fit within DTI? The stimulus occurs, a response occurs, and a consequence occurs. While it might appear that there is no room within this equation for prompting, this is not true.

Prompting can occur as part of the S^D, as is the case with redundancy prompts such as inflection cues, visual cues, proximity prompts, etc. Additionally, response prompts (such as physical prompting, gestures, etc.) can be utilized to encourage the targeted response. When response prompts are utilized within a discrete trial, they occur immediately following the delivery of the S^D, and precede the response. The desired response still must occur, followed by reinforcement or error correction.

Some instructors get "thrown off" when prompting is introduced to the discrete trial format. Typically, they leave the four-term contingency at the prompt, and fail to return. This signifies the importance of maintaining an awareness of all parts of the discrete trial at all times, so that one trial does not become blurred with another.

7. Correct errors.

How does the instructor respond if an incorrect response is given? This seemingly simple question has been at the center of much debate within the autism treatment field. It has caused infighting within the ranks of behavior analytical autism practitioners, and has turned many people off to the whole idea of behavior analytic approaches to autism treatment.

An in-depth analysis of several options for error correction is included later in this chapter, At this point, it's important to understand that this question must be answered prior to implementing Discrete Trial Instruction, and that the answer will be dependent upon the learner, his or her needs and history, the context in which the skill is being presented, and the data that have been collected. Without providing too much detail prematurely, suffice it to say that error correction procedures must be considered at all times during a Discrete Trial Instruction interaction.

8. Provide differential reinforcement.

At this point, differential reinforcement should not be a novel term. Essentially, it refers to the process of providing reinforcement for particular members of a response class while placing others on extinction. In the case of DTI, it is the instructor's responsibility to shape new behaviors through differential reinforcement, and to use these procedures to "push the envelope" of the child's skill level further each session. In order to do this, the instructor must always be aware of the target topography of the skill, the learner's current level of progress, and whether or not the current stimulus involved a prompt.

As the learner becomes more proficient with particular skills, the response requirement is raised prior to earning reinforcement. **Response requirement** refers to the level of effort, particular topography, or extenuating circumstances under which a response must occur in order to be followed by reinforcing consequences. When training is rather new to a child, the response requirement is rather low. For example, a child who is just learning to speak may simply have to say, "coo" in order to gain access to a cookie. As his skills improve, access to the cookie is not provided until the whole word "cookie" is emitted. Finally, the response requirement may be raised to the point at which a full sentence, in the form of, "Mommy, may I please have a cookie?" is the only type of response that will result in the delivery of a cookie.

To a DTI instructor, the current level of response requirement for a particular skill determines the level of reinforcement given a certain response. The effective instructor provides a lesser degree of reinforcement for responses that reflect a lesser level of response. The importance of reinforcement differentiation within skill instruction cannot be understated, for it is a critical determinant of how quickly a learner will progress, and the degree to which he or she will progress.

As a result, effective instructors walk a very fine line when it comes to differentiation. They must raise the bar as high a possible and still maintain a level of response requirement that will allow the learner to experience success – as well as subsequent contact with reinforcement.

9. Manage all materials.

As if all of the above wasn't enough to be concerned with, DTI instructors must also be adept at organizing, managing, and maintaining a plethora of instructional materials. In order to be able to access items quickly and provide an effective pace of instruction, the instructional area must be neat and clean, and materials should be available and organized so that they are "at the ready" the moment they are to be used.

In addition, an effective instructor is acutely aware of how object presentation can affect student performance. For example, there may be certain discriminative features of instructional items that serve as bogus cues for selection. In this scenario, a child may be learning to identify a truck based on a picture card. Each time he is asked to point to the truck, success is experienced. However, the instructor notices that the child only responds successfully when a particular picture is used. This picture also has a crease in the middle of it, due to its age.

The instructor notices on the following day that the learner selected a picture of a shoe, also with a crease, when asked for the truck. In this case, it is likely that the crease became the discriminative stimulus for "truck," and because the instructor was not immediately aware of this, selection of the crease was reinforced.

Materials issues can also be encountered when determining how many items appear in an array, or where target items are placed within an array.

Materials handling and management is usually a learned skill. Some instructors find it helpful to rely upon index systems to organize picture cards, clear plastic storage bins to house manipulative items, and "cubby" systems to organize all materials for each student. Data forms are easily accessible if placed on clipboards, and writing instruments should be readily available.

10. Implement effective trial interspersals and target ratios.

The final major responsibility of the instructor within a Discrete Trial Instruction program is making sure that learning trials are interspersed effectively. **Trial interspersal** refers to the way in which trials of target skills are mixed with trials that require known responses. Trials of target skills can also be interspersed with one another.

There are several ways to identify types of trial interspersal, which is also referred to as trial distribution. In the classic, Lovaas-type presentation, instruction on acquisition targets is provided in **mass trial** format, where the same target skill is repeated time and again in similar trials. No distractors (non-target or known skills) are presented during these receptive discrimination tasks. For example, a mass trial format for teaching receptive commands is as follows:

Trial one

Instructor: "Touch nose."
Response: Learner touches nose.
Instructor: (provides reinforcement)

Trial two

Instructor: "Touch nose."
Response: Learner touches nose.
Instructor: (provides reinforcement)

Trial three

Instructor: "Touch nose."
Response: Learner touches nose
Instructor: (provides reinforcement)

...And so on.

One of the benefits of employing mass trials is that the practice may be the only way to gain sufficient exposure to the contingency without interruption. This decreases the time it takes to shape the response topography.

One of the issues frequently encountered when employing mass trialing is that the student is not forced to discriminate amongst stimuli in many cases, and responding may become over-selective or over-generalized. This is the classic scenario in which a child is asked to perform a task (i.e. "touch nose") many times in succession. When the discriminative stimulus is changed (i.e. "touch belly"), the student continues to respond in the same way that last gained reinforcement, touching his nose instead of his belly.

While overuse can result in "drill learning" and resistance to skill generalization – as opposed to true skill or concept learning – mass trials are still the most effective way (when used judiciously) to shape brand new responses under the control of new instructions. However, they can also lead to "false mastery" if a child misses the first trial, but imitates the error correction response on subsequent trials.

After mass trialing, the goal of any instruction should be to maintain levels of responding, even if instructions change and tasks are varied within a session. Skill fluency can be marked by a learner's ability to "switch gears," leave a type of task, and return to it later with success. Trial distribution or interspersal is how this is accomplished within DTI. How trials are interspersed can be the result of a highly systematic or a random process. There may be a need to do both.

Collapsing Trials

One way to systematically intersperse trials is a method of trial distribution known as **collapsing trials**. In a collapsing trial format, distracter trials are introduced via a fading process, beginning with mass trials and eventually ending up by alternating between the target and distracter trials. An example of collapsing trials follows:

A = target skill (i.e., "Touch cup")

B = random distracters (i.e., "Give me five," "Say 'Hi.'")

AAAAA B AAAA B AAA B AA B A B A B A B. . . . .

Another approach to collapsing trials is as follows:

AAAAA BBBBB AAAA BBBB AAA BBB AA BB A B . . .

Given the above format, it is easy to see how the mass trial format "collapses" until the target skill is alternating with the distracters.

Collapsing trials do not necessarily need to be as precise as this. In the above example, the ratio of targets to distracters was 5:1, then 4:1, then 3:1, and so on. In practice, one can be effective while being a bit less exact. The main point is to gradually decrease the number of consecutive target skill trials following each trial of the distracter skill.

Expanding Trials

Once the response is strong within an alternating format, there is still a need to fade in more distracter trials, so that the target response will occur after the number of distracters has increased. To accomplish this, an **expanding trial** format is often called upon. In expanding trials, instruction begins with an alternating ratio of targets to distracters. Increasing numbers of distracters are then introduced. Essentially, this is the opposite process of collapsing trials. An example of expanding trial format appears below:

A = target skill (i.e., "Touch cup")

B = random distracters (i.e., "Give me five," "Say 'Hi.'")

A B A B A BB A BBB A BBBB A BBBBB...

Another approach to expanding trials is as follows:

A B AA BB AAA BBB AAAA BBBB AAAAA BBBBB...

As with collapsing trials, the fading process within expanding trials need not be so precise. The main idea behind this procedure is to gradually introduce more distracter trials following each target skill trial.

Random Trial Distribution

Finally, there is a type of trial distribution that is completely random. **Random trial distribution** – in which trials of target skill responses and distracter responses are interspersed at random – is a fairly simple concept to understand.

This interspersal is invaluable when a skill is moved into generalization, because it mimics the type of interspersal that we encounter during our everyday lives. When, for example, was the last time that someone asked you your name 30 times in a row? Likewise, when was the last time that you were asked your name in an expanded or collapsing format?

Even so, it is quite common in situations like dinner parties to be asked your name several times throughout the course of an evening, with the name request interspersed between countless other opportunities to respond in some way.

Distributed Trials

Expanded Trials
- Gradually increase number of distracters between target skill trials

A= Target skill
(receptive response to "give blue")
B= Distracter
(any other known skills, related or not)
A B A BB A BBB A BBBB A BBBBB A
and so on …

Distributed Trials

Collapsing Trials
- Gradually introduce distractors to mass trials

A= Target skill
(receptive response to "give blue")
B= Distracter
(any other known skills, related or not)
AAAAA B AAAA B AAA B AA B A
and so on …

The Importance of Trial Interspersal

When it comes to autism, one of the greatest challenges we face is the fact that many of our children learn to do a great number of things within the highly controlled and obviously deliberate nature of our instruction. However, when opportunities to

Distributed Trials

Randomly Distributed Trials
- Promote fluent, "spur of the moment" responding
- Exaggerated model of "real world" conditions

A= Target skill
(receptive response to "give blue")
B= Distracter
(any other known skills, related or not)
ABBAABABABBBBBBBABBBBAABBABBBB

apply the skills in real-life scenarios present themselves, our children fail to emit the correct responses in a timely manner.

For this reason, trial interspersal should happen as early as possible in the skill acquisition process, and it should always eventually move into the random distribution format.

Typically, we recommend beginning with the first collapsing trial format described, followed by the first expanding trial format described, although, as noted, absolute precision is not necessary.

Criticisms of Discrete Trial Instruction

Despite its effectiveness in teaching skills, DTI is constantly under attack by critics. Some of the criticisms are well founded and merited. The majority, however, are simply based on faulty notions about teaching and learning that are propagated by schools of education and not founded in evidence-based practice. Remember that DTI is a behavioral, science-based intervention, and may not be very creative in nature.[4] For this reason, many of the same factors regarding science and behavior analysis discussed in Chapter 3 have influenced widespread acceptance of Discrete Trial Instruction.

In this section, we will explore some of the unfounded criticisms of DTI, and try to explain how they came to be and how we can reconcile with them.

Criticism #1: DTI is overly punitive and inappropriate for young children.

This is one of the most prominent criticisms of DTI; namely, that it is unfair because it is so intense, and is no fun. There are good reasons for this type of criticism. When DTI was in its formative years, aversive techniques were often combined with instruction. Some practitioners used pain as a deterrent to inappropriate responding, and some even went so far as to inflict pain for incorrect responses. This is certainly not the case now. If the science of ABA has shown us one thing throughout the years, it is that reinforcement is the single most important consideration in behavior change. Simply put, an individual will not voluntarily do something unless he or she has been reinforced for similar behaviors in the past.

In order for us to be effective with young children with autism, we *must* be able to pair ourselves and compliance to our requests with reinforcement. Although it may not be uncommon for the first week or two of instruction to be marked by tantrum (because it is likely the first time that things have been made contingent for the child), an effective instructor will turn this scenario into a very reinforcing one in very short order. Most well known experts in the field today would agree that effective DTI has to be based on reinforcement, and their practices reflect this philosophy.

Criticism #2: Drill and practice are a detriment to true learning.

Another popular criticism is that drill and practice do not lead to real skills, and are themselves a detriment to true learning. This is simply not true. No research supports this claim – in fact, most research states just the opposite (Heward, 2003). Practically speaking, without drill and practice, there would be very few musicians, athletes, warriors, or even readers.

[4] Not being creative, in this sense, refers to the fact that the instructional format is very rigid. There are not many opportunities for the instructor to stray from it while maintaining efficacy. There is room for creativity, however, in the instructor's presentation of materials, the content of the skill programs, and the selection/delivery of reinforcement.

Even so, this misconception continues to be a real problem. To address it, we must accept the fact that children with autism will not learn the vast amount of information they are deficient in unless they are provided with sufficient opportunities to practice the related skills – and receive reinforcement for doing so. However, we must also make sure that we do not endlessly drill the same information after it has been acquired, or if we are not making progress toward its acquisition. Data-based decision making will serve as a preventative measure in both of these circumstances.

Criticism #3: DTI stifles creativity.

Yet another criticism leveled at Discrete Trial Instruction is that it stifles the creativity of both instructor and learner. There has been a tremendous movement within education over the last half century that has favored creative approaches to education over efficacy-based approaches. Frankly, while there is a time and a place for creativity, a creative approach to education does not imply that it is effective. Also, efforts to be creative in instructional delivery often have the negative effect of taking away from the discrete nature of a simple instruction. When this happens, as we have already discussed, instructional contingencies become less clear, and instructional progress may be slowed.

Is there room for creativity within a direct instruction or DTI format? Absolutely! However, this creativity shifts its focus from the delivery of instructional content to the creative delivery of reinforcement following desired responses. A successful instructor will have a myriad of reinforcer options, as well as the ability to capture and create reinforcing interactions "on the spot."

Criticism #4: Everything DTI accomplishes is the result of adult direction.

This series of criticisms may be a bit more relevant. Basically, the point is that because everything accomplished during a DTI interaction is the result of adult or instructor direction, DTI doesn't truly capture the child's MO, teach an immediately functional repertoire of skills, or encourage spontaneity.

Much of this is true of less-than-ideal programs. To truly capture the MO of the learner, discrete trial responses lead to functionally related reinforcement. For example, the reinforcement (cookie) would be related to the response (asking for a cookie). In this way, we are not truly following the child's lead. In fact, we are usually providing reinforcement that is in no way a functionally related consequence to the response. For example, we probably give a cookie for the child's response of clapping hands upon request.

DTI also falters at times in its ability to encourage spontaneity. This occurs because of the very nature of the instructional format. Before a response occurs, there must be an overt stimulus. If we contrive to deliver a stimulus, the subsequent response is based on our actions. Therefore, it is not spontaneous.

However cogent these criticisms may be, they alone should not discourage the use of Discrete Trial Instruction when appropriate. They should, however, point out some of the limitations of this type of instruction. Rather than abandoning it (there are far too many benefits to do so), we should realize that the needs expressed above can be met through other behaviorally sound instructional procedures. We will discuss some of these procedures, such as Natural Environment Training, video self-modeling, and scheduling systems in subsequent sections of this chapter.

Section D – Error Correction During Discrete Trial Instruction

To teach new skills to a young child with autism, we present him or her with combinations of materials and forms of verbal interaction that are often quite alien. Given his or her poverty of skills, limited reinforcement history with such new situations, and propensity toward repetitive or inappropriate responses, it would seem highly unlikely that the child with autism would make the correct response to our S^D on the very first trial.

The improbability of a correct response leads to one of two alternate possibilities.

1) The child may refuse to respond at all. He or she may just sit and stare back (granted, staring back at you is responding – albeit at an extremely low amplitude).

or

2) The child may engage in a response that deviates either greatly or subtly from the target response being taught.

In both instances, it is fair to say that the child has made an error. From a behavior analytic viewpoint, however, the child has not *failed*. This situation is better described in terms of *our* failure as teachers to provide adequate instruction to guarantee a correct response. As with most explanatory fictions, blaming the child or the diagnostic label attached to the child does little to solve the problem. The challenge is to change the *will* of the child, or alter his or her neurobiological makeup.

If, on the other hand, we look at the teaching environment – i.e., our methodology or approach to instruction, possibilities for change and improvement are quickly revealed.

Instructional technologies that have sprung from applied behavior analysis have struggled with the dilemma surrounding error correction for decades. How we respond to student error, or how we design instruction that reduces or eliminates student error are at the heart of the debate.

One can clearly argue that making errors can have a positive effect on learning. The old adage "learning from your mistakes" demonstrates the common sense view that coming in contact with natural contingencies of extinction and/or punishment plays an important role in determining how each of us has learned to function independently in the real world. If, for example, our first grade math teacher had praised us equally for correct as well as incorrect answers to simple addition problems, our learning of basic math facts would have suffered terribly. The praise we received for answering correctly, contact with extinction, or, in some cases, mild punishers (being told "no" or "that's incorrect") assisted us greatly in learning to add.

On the other hand is the argument that making errors has several significant negative effects on learning. Martin and Pear (1983) noted that errors decrease the time available for instruction, and the extinction or punishment that the child encounters following an error can elicit emotional reactions or, in some cases, tantrum or aggressive behavior.

Errorless Learning

In pursuing the goal of error reduction, basic researchers have developed a procedure known as errorless learning. Using immediate prompting and fading, **errorless learning** gradually transfers stimulus control from prompts to the S^D. If done well, this process can occur without the child making any mistakes.

The seminal study describing errorless learning was conducted by Terrace (1963). In his experiment, Terrace set out to teach color discrimination to a pigeon. At that time, standard discrimination training with pigeons usually involved teaching the animal to peck an illuminated colored disc by providing reinforcement following each correct response. Once the pigeon learned to select one color, the experimenter presented the discriminative stimulus in an array with another stimulus – in this case, a different colored disc. The pigeon would then be reinforced with an edible, contingent on pecking the target disc (S^D). An extinction schedule would also be in place for any pecking of the non-target disc (S^Δ) – i.e., the pigeon would not receive an edible when it pecked the incorrect disc.

Figure 10.4

Terrace's experiment was unique to discrimination training in that, rather than presenting the array of two stimuli (the S^D and S^Δ) in the standard fashion, he diminished the salience of the S^Δ by reducing both its magnitude and duration. The pigeon, having learned to select the green disc (pecking the green disc was reinforced with an edible), began the discrimination trials with the red disc (S^Δ) being presented very briefly and with low illumination. As the learning trials progressed, Terrace slowly increased the illumination of the red disc and the duration at which it appeared in the array. In this way, the pigeon was provided with an immediate stimulus prompt (the red disk was more faint and only remained lit for a brief period of time) that nearly guaranteed its pecking of the green disc. Over time, with the fading in of the intensity and duration of the red disc, the pigeon learned to discriminate between two discs that differed only in color. The illustration in Figure 10.4 shows how the stimulus fading occurred in Terrace's errorless procedure.

Terrace's experiment was an example of basic research (i.e., not *applied* research), using animals, not people. This basic research, however, led to an understanding of learning principles that have since been applied with great effect to the typical discriminative training we present during Discrete Trial Instruction.

When we conduct the errorless procedure for discrimination training with a child, we provide a prompt immediately following the S^D on the initial trials. In this way, the child is nearly prevented from making an error, because his or her response is preceded by the prompt. As trials progress, prompts are faded and unprompted responses are differentially reinforced.

Receptive discrimination of objects is an example of a language program that better explains this somewhat technical process. A target object (cup) is placed on the table and the child is instructed to "touch cup." True to the errorless approach, on the first trial a prompt is provided simultaneously with the delivery of the S^D – such as taking the child's hand gently and touching the cup. On the very next trial, the instructor performs what is known as a **transfer trial**, where he or she tries to fade out some of the prompting – in effect, beginning to transfer control of the child's response from the prompt to the S^D. The child's hand might be taken toward the cup but released before he or she reaches it, in the hope that the child would continue on to actually touch the cup without assistance.

Over subsequent trials, the level of prompting provided is systematically reduced until the child touches the cup with only the verbal instruction to "touch cup."

A critical element in this process is the use of differential reinforcement, with the instructor's ability to fade prompts directly affected by how the trials are reinforced. As we've discussed, over-reinforcing a particular step in the shaping process can cause a child to stall out and become prompt dependent at that level. Much in the same way, providing undifferentiated reinforcement for all discrimination trials – regardless of the level of prompting required by the child – will cause the response (touching cup) to become strongly controlled by the prompt.

Prompting should be limited to the least amount necessary for the child to touch the cup. If, on the previous trial, the instructor merely tapped next to the cup before the child touched it, the current response *would not be* reinforced if the child required a more intrusive prompt – such as physically guiding his hand to the cup. As with shaping, over-reinforcing a lesser approximation (the response tied to physical guidance) should be avoided, and the more advanced response (the response tied to a slight gestural prompt) should be displayed before reinforcement is provided. Figure 10.5 presents this scenario of differential reinforcement in a visual mode.

Figure 10.5

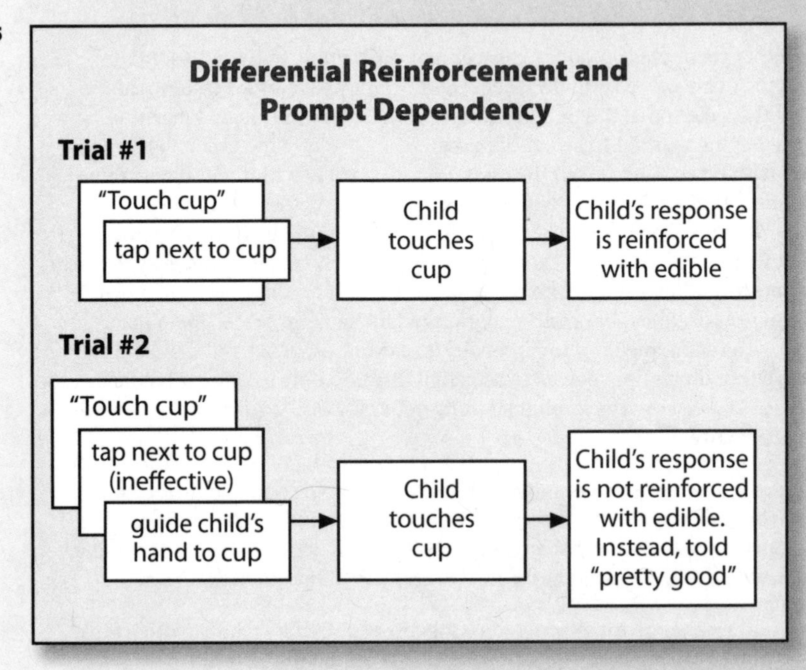

Another critical issue with errorless learning is the timing of prompt delivery. Waiting for the child to make a selection between two objects may result in the child choosing the wrong object – in effect, making an error. To avoid this, it is important that initial trials incorporate a prompt very close to, if not simultaneously with, the S^D. Transfer trials follow the initial trial and utilize a brief wait before presenting the prompt. In effect, the addition of a brief period of time between the S^D and the prompt challenges the child to eventually respond *before* the prompt is delivered – providing the instructor with a very effective prompt-fading method called **time delay prompting**.

Stimulus prompts that involve the positioning of materials on the table lend themselves especially well to the errorless approach. These prompts are part of the stimulus condition and, as such, are present well *before* the verbal instruction is given. Fading stimulus prompts is often easier to accomplish than fading more complex response prompts (such as verbal or physical modeling), and they do not require that the instructor keep track of the passage of time – as is necessary when using time-delay prompting.

A Standard Implementation Procedure

To recap the errorless learning approach, we offer the following as the standard procedure for implementation:

1) Present the S^D with immediate prompting so that the child makes the correct response.

2) Reinforce the correct response.

3) Follow the initial trial with a transfer trial, where the same S^D is presented either a with brief time delay or a less intrusive level of prompting.

4) If the child responds correctly without prompting or with less prompting, reinforce with a more potent/valued reinforcer than was used for the first, prompted response.

5) If the child begins to respond incorrectly, prompt the correct response and reinforce *less* than if the child had responded independently. Move on to other material, but be sure to return to this skill within several trials to attempt the transfer process again – prompted trial followed by a transfer trial.

Arguments Against Errorless Learning

Returning to our discussion of "learning from our mistakes," there exists a group of behavior analysts (Lovaas for one) who have taken exception to a purely errorless approach to Discrete Trial Instruction. Of particular concern is the extension of errorless learning to the maintenance of skills that might already be established (i.e., the child has demonstrated the ability to perform the skill without prompting), or to situations where the child's lack of proper responding is based not on skill mastery but on motivation.

Providing prompts to the child in these situations does seem ill advised. The errorless learning approach, however, does not discriminate between the skilled child, the non-compliant child, and the unskilled child. All three are prompted if they fail to respond correctly to an S^D.

In the case of a child who has demonstrated the ability to perform a skill without prompting, the errorless approach runs the risk of unnecessarily helping the child and putting him at risk of becoming prompt dependent. In order to avoid this problem, the teacher must be highly skilled in assessing the child's skill level and in striking the balance between prompt fading and differential reinforcement previously outlined.

The non-compliant child typically has shown the ability to perform the target skill repeatedly in previous training sessions. Due to environmental factors such as the use of ineffective reinforcement, failure to maintain the salience of the reinforcer, or the presence of competing reinforcement, the child lacks the motivation to respond as directed.

Providing prompting in this situation may inadvertently reinforce non-compliance by following the misbehavior with the addition of prompting. On one hand, the child's non-compliant behavior(s) may be strengthened by negative reinforcement in that the prompting reduces the response requirement of the target task. On the other hand, the addition of prompts may provide a form of contingent attention, thus maintaining the non-compliant behavior(s) with positive reinforcement.

Often, this difficulty in finding reinforcement to compete with deeply entrenched automatic reinforcers creates a critical situation in the instruction. Contrived positive and negative reinforcers are ineffective, and capturing an MO for the automatic reinforcers is nearly impossible. Movement forward is stalled because the child is "shutting down" during instruction and either refusing to respond or merely going through the motions.

At this point, we often find it necessary to introduce a punishment contingency to both reduce the non-compliant behavior(s) and to enhance the value of our social and tangible reinforcers (as an MO would). The most commonly used punishing stimulus is the teacher telling the child "no" following an incorrect response.

The No-No-Prompt Feedback Loop

The **No-No-Prompt** feedback loop was developed in keeping with the notion that, at a certain point, a child's learning can be positively affected by allowing errors to occur, When implemented correctly, No-No-Prompt (NNP) incorporates a great deal of errorless learning into its procedure. Simply stated, NNP uses the exact same protocol for teaching new skills as outlined above for errorless learning. Responses are immediately prompted to minimize errors and to maximize contact with reinforcement. Prompts are also systematically faded using the same methods described in the discussion on transfer trials.

Where NNP differs from errorless learning is that it ceases to provide prompts following errors once the target skill has been demonstrated at the independent level. If we return to our original example of teaching the child to select "cup," our implementation of NNP follows the same path in establishing the skill. The physical and gestural prompting occurs during initial trials, so that the child can be immediately successful in touching the cup.

Transfer trials – where prompts are faded out until the child begins making independent responses (i.e., touching the cup when directed to "touch cup") – immediately follow the initial, fully prompted trial.

Once the child responds without a prompt, however, the procedure shifts to NNP. Errors that occur from this point forward (such as not responding or touching the S^{Δ} object in the array) are not followed by a prompt. Instead, the teacher says "no" in a flat, informational tone. Simultaneously with the vocal "no," the teacher averts eye contact from the child and removes the cup and distracter object from the table. The spoken "no" serves as a conditioned positive punisher.

Most children, even those with autism, have a learning history with the word "no" and perceive it as an unpleasant stimulus. The removal of eye contact serves as a conditioned negative punisher – in effect, momentarily timing the child out from teacher attention. The removal of the materials simply makes it visually clear to the child that the trial has ended.

Following the inter-trial interval, the same S^D is represented, and a correct response is reinforced as usual. A second incorrect response receives the same consequence as the first trial – the spoken "no," averted eye contact, and removal of drill materials from the table.

Following two incorrect responses, the third consecutive trial is conducted. Here, the teacher returns to the errorless procedure and provides an immediate prompt following the S^D. The level of prompt should be sufficient to ensure a correct response by the child. Reinforcement is provided – but much less than what the child has been accustomed to – using differential reinforcement, since the response required prompting.

Immediately following the inter-trial interval, a transfer trial is conducted that involves a complete fading out of the prompt. If the child responds correctly, his or her response is followed by potent/meaningful reinforcement, and the teacher moves on to a different target skill. If the child responds incorrectly, the NNP feedback loop resumes. Figure 10.6 illustrates this loop.

Compliance problems aside, if the child fails to respond to the transfer trial following two consecutive cycles of the NNP procedure, the teacher should reassess whether the target skill is actually at mastery level for the child. It might be that the single independent response that prompted the teacher to move on to NNP was an accidental occurrence, and the skill has not been established well enough to begin NNP. Backing up and resuming the errorless procedure is generally recommended in such situations.

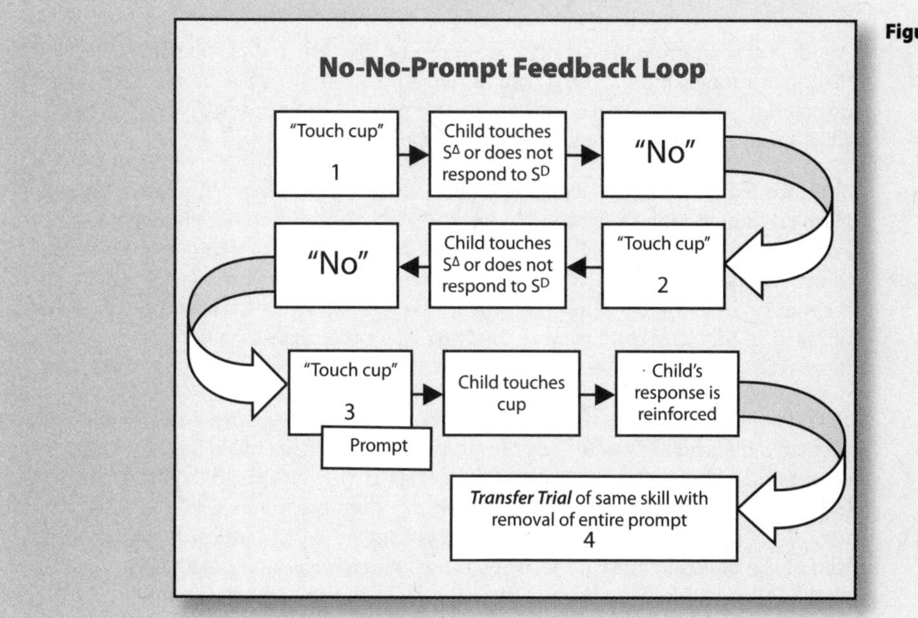

Figure 10.6

Potential Pitfalls with the No-No-Prompt

When there are compliance or motivational problems, NNP can be deleterious to instruction. As described in the section on errorless learning, children with autism can engage in significant stereotypic behaviors maintained by automatic reinforcement – and can do so for long periods of time. Presented with NNP, the child who prefers to "shut down" rather than respond to the instructional cue may simply wait out the two "no" trials, accept the prompt on the third trial, and still not consistently respond correctly to the transfer trial.

The problem here, as with errorless learning, is competing reinforcement. In both approaches, the selection of potent and meaningful reinforcers is critical to competing with the child's pool of automatic reinforcers. Again, it is not always possible to identify or access stimuli that are sufficiently potent to compete with these automatic reinforcers. In some situations the spoken "no" is not of sufficient punitive value, and more extensive procedures may have to be considered (these will be discussed in more detail in Chapter 12).

Another potential pitfall of NNP and errorless learning occurs with the child whose problem behavior is maintained by positive reinforcement in the form of physical/social attention. Both the physical prompting that we use to assist the child through the task *and* the spoken "no" can operate as positive reinforcement. What we often see in these situations is a child who stops responding and can be clearly observed waiting for the prompt – e.g., even going so far as to extend their hand to the teacher as a request for the prompt. The answer to this dilemma resides again in the selection of a reinforcer that can compete with the social attention provided by the teacher during prompting, or in the selection of a significant punisher to reduce the non-compliant behavior(s).

In some instances, persisting with the spoken "no" beyond the second incorrect response has been effective, as it creates a lengthy, mildly aversive condition from which the child eventually wants to escape. This kind of negative reinforcement scenario can demand a great deal of time of the teacher who must present literally dozens of trials of the same target skill. If this "waiting game" or "battle of wills" persists, it should be analyzed and options considered, because it monopolizes a great deal of valuable instructional time.

Another glaring problem can arise from use of NNP when it is specifically applied to discrimination training. With a field of two stimuli on the table, or with two possible intraverbal responses to a question, the use of NNP can reinforce what Lovaas (2003) refers to as a "lose-shift" type of responding.

Take, for example, a child learning to discriminate between a "cup" and a "spoon." If we are conducting distributed trials of the two targets and the child makes an error (e.g., touches "spoon" when asked to touch "cup"), he is told "no." According to Lovaas, the child has "lost" on that first trial – i.e., he has missed his opportunity for reinforcement due to his error. Given the loss following his selection of "spoon" on the first trial, the child is more likely to select the remaining item, "cup," on the next trial.

This "lose-shift" method of responding can, to the untrained eye, look a lot like receptive discrimination. It *is* discrimination, but the learning is based on a pattern of responding set up by the instructor, *not* based on what we are trying to teach (which is the child responding to the auditory stimulus "touch cup"). A simple way of testing whether this phenomenon is happening is to follow the error with a trial of the opposite item in the array. If the child is responding with the lose-shift method, he will likely make another error (because he will have shifted to the object requested on the first trial).

The use of NNP in this scenario will allow the child to be reinforced on every other trial, but will do little to actually teach him to discriminate based on a spoken S^D.

A common remedy is to insert some time or distraction between the error-response and the next trial. Bondy and Frost (1996) have developed a procedure called **model-prompt-switch-repeat (or 4-step error correction)** that addresses this problem nicely. When the child makes an error, the teacher follows it by *modeling* the correct response. The trial is then repeated with the teacher providing *prompting* so that the child can respond correctly. Following the prompted trial, the teacher can either have the child perform an unrelated "*switch* task," or allow a certain amount of time to pass before *repeating* the original trial.

Given our example of receptive selection of "cup," model-prompt-switch-repeat would look something like what is shown in Figure 10.7.

Another way to eliminate the lose-shift pattern of responding is to always teach receptive discrimination with a field of three. In this format, responding is conditional in nature, chance responding is lowered, and the probability of the lose-shift pattern is reduced.

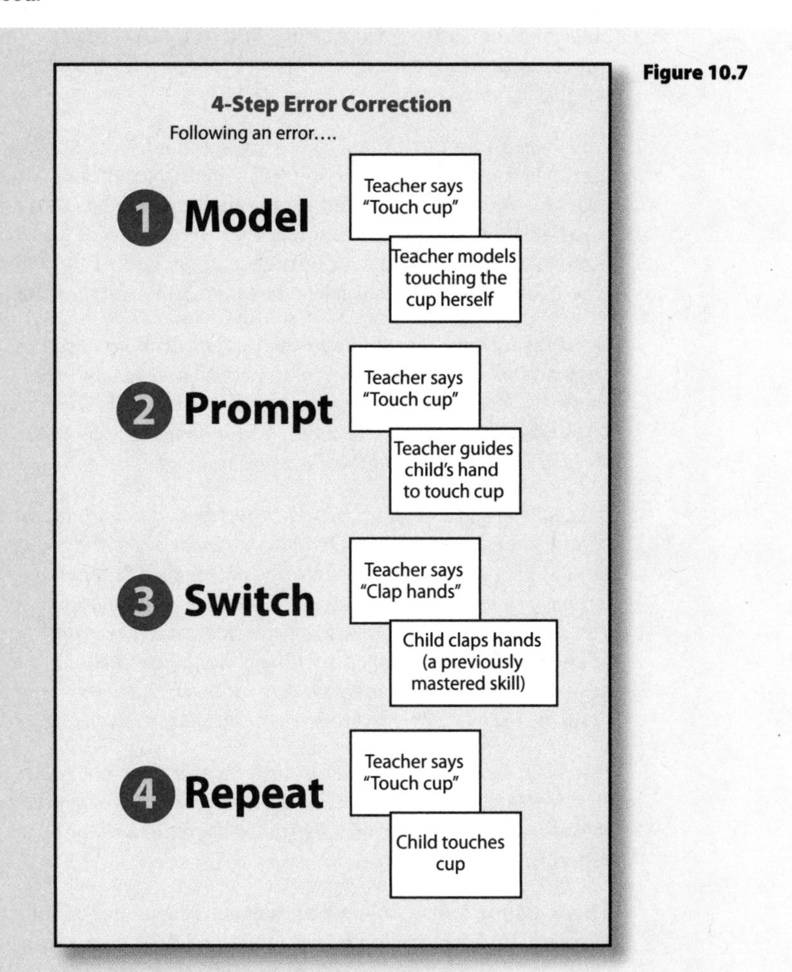

Figure 10.7

In Summary

Children can make many types of errors during instruction. Thankfully, there are just as many different types of error correction strategies available to the teacher. We have included here three strategies that we have found to be the most effective in designing instruction for young children with autism.

No one strategy appears to have all the answers for all children. Research comparing the efficacy of these methods is difficult to design, but it is slowly being accomplished and is beginning to appear in the literature. Until we have more definitive answers, it remains prudent to tailor error correction strategy to the needs of individual children, the method of instruction being used, and the particular skill being taught.

Section E – Natural Environment Training

Most of the information we have provided regarding direct instructional techniques has involved intensive teaching or Discrete Trial Instruction methods. Given their very controllable nature, these methods are the most efficient ways to isolate skills and maximize learning time. Within DTI, there are more instructions, more opportunities to respond, and more opportunities for instruction than with less precise formats.

However, as we mentioned, there are some inherent limitations presented by these methods. Because of their completely instructor-driven nature, they are marked by a lackluster ability to promote spontaneity, as well as by a need to move beyond the "drill" scenario if generalization is ever to take place. The following illustration is fictional, but it is one the authors repeatedly encounter when they consult on cases where Discrete Trial Instruction has been the primary vehicle for skill programming.

Jamie is a four-year-old boy with autism who has been receiving Discrete Trial Instruction in his home for two years. When his services started, he had minimal receptive language skills, no expressive language skills, and very rarely interacted with others in his environment. When he wanted something, he would tantrum or simply pull someone to the object he wanted.

At first, his discrete trial program focused, as most do, on teaching basic compliance to receptive instructions and simple discrimination tasks. As time passed, he began to work on more complex skills, such as programs requiring expressive verbal responses, pretend play, classification, and pre-academic skills. Two years into the program, Jamie possesses an expressive vocabulary (i.e., tacts) of close to 2,000 words, can follow complex directions, and can even decode some simple words. He can label objects by their categories and functions, and he can describe them with attributes such as color, shape, size, etc.

However, away from the drill table, he still does not interact with others very often. In addition, he still engages in tantrum behaviors or pulls others by the hand when he wants things, and he rarely displays any of the skills from his impressive repertoire in a spontaneous way.

This situation exists for several reasons. Fortunately, Jamie has shown us that Discrete Trial Instruction is, without any doubt, a very effective way to teach new skills. In fact, the time and effort put into teaching these skills has laid a rock-solid foundation upon which his future success as a communicator and social being will rely.

What has not occurred, however, is a planned and consistent program of generalization and provision of opportunities to apply the skills taught in a functional manner. This is an absolutely critical element of any behaviorally based program of instruction.

Think of it like this: most of the behaviors we emit are controlled by loose contingencies that vary in form and presentation from one situation to the next. In essence, we are surrounded at all times by a very dynamic, shifting, changing collection of stimuli. Our histories of reinforcement provide us with the abilities to select stimuli to which we will respond, and also the responses that will likely gain us the most reinforcement and the least amount of punishment. In other words, the contingencies that result in reinforcing and punishing consequences throughout most of our waking hours are not very discrete at all.

This is particularly the case when we approach the subject of verbal behavior, or any type of social behavior. When we use language to move others to act upon our environments, we are always reciprocating as the listener at times, and the speaker at others. For example, when a speaker says, "Please close the door," the listener hears this and responds in a way that is appropriate, given his or her reinforcement history for doing so in the past.

The speaker may initiate the interaction, or may use language in response to the behavior of others. In Discrete Trial Instruction, the learner very rarely is given the opportunity to initiate his or her turn as the speaker, so skills in spontaneously emitting verbal behaviors tend to be quite limited.

If this is the case, there must be some other way to arrange the instructional environment to evoke the desired response topography. The first step is to conceptualize DTI as a process based on a very simple, four-term contingency (MO – stimulus – response – consequence). By doing this, we can clearly see that a discrete trial (or one cycle through this contingency) can be carried out in almost any environment, natural or contrived.

Second, we must look to another teaching paradigm that can complement any discrete skills training. This is where the methodology known as **Natural Environment Training (NET)** comes into play. Natural Environment Training refers to instruction that is both driven by the student's motivation and carried out in environments that closely resemble natural environments, while being highly structured with regard to the learner's access to reinforcement.

When employing NET, the instructor capitalizes on the momentary MO of the learner, and uses it to arrange the environment in such a way that access to reinforcers is granted only when certain verbal responses occur. Additionally, sufficient prompting is provided to quickly occasion the reinforcement-getting behaviors. Take, for example, the following instructional scenario:

Becky's instructor is trying to shape the vocal response of "cookie." She knows that Becky really enjoys cookies, particularly chocolate chip cookies. In the past, Becky has been given relatively free access to cookies when she comes home from Grandma's house. They are kept in an open cupboard at her level. To access the cookies, all she has to do is open the door, access the bag, and eat. She never eats more than a few, and weight is not an issue. Becky's mom, until now, has seen her self-sufficiency as a positive trait, and has done nothing but encourage her.

After reading an article on language training for children with autism, the instructor determines that a NET approach will be utilized to shape the production of the word, "cookie." Now, care is taken to place the cookies out of

Becky's reach, but fully within her sight. Becky's grandma is given instructions to restrict cookies at her house, so that she will be hungry for them when she comes home. When Becky comes home on the first day, she goes to the kitchen, opens the cupboard, and realizes that there are no cookies in their usual place. She spots them on top of the refrigerator, and looks longingly at them.

At this point, the instructor prompts Becky by saying: "coo…". Becky makes the requested sound, and then is given a single piece of a cookie. After 10 minutes have passed, Becky is now spontaneously making an attempt to say "cookie," without any prompting from the instructor.

While this is a very simple example of NET, it illustrates how the environment was modified to boost, or at least capture the MO of the learner, and how to prompt for the desired response. It is important to note that Becky's ability to comply with the vocal instruction to "say coo…" is likely the result of instructional control established through more intensive instruction (i.e. DTI). But this type of manipulation of the natural environment was far less contrived than the isolation typically arranged for during Discrete Trial Instruction.

Note also that part of the contingency arranged during NET involved the running of a discrete trial (stimulus – cookie presence and "say coo…"; response – "coo"; consequence – cookie provided).

Natural Environment Training promotes generalization, because the natural environment is a stimulus condition in which component elements are constantly changing. Certain people, sights, sounds, activities, etc. may or may not be present from one moment to the next. Additionally, since the environment itself is not contrived, there is no need to program specifically to make it less contrived. With DTI, there must be procedures in place that move the skills taught from the DTI condition into the natural environment. So, in a way, NET allows us to bypass this step.

One of the difficult parts of running a Natural Environment Training program is that it takes quite a bit of thought to plan this type of instruction. It also takes a great deal of thought to develop data collection systems, skills progress monitoring protocols, and skill mastery criteria. However, this can all be accomplished, and later chapters will discuss these elements in greater detail. In addition, implementers of NET instructional techniques face significant challenges, because they must be aware of the changing MO of the learner, and must be ready to adapt instruction at a moment's notice to ensure that the MO remains high for instructional materials.

One last consideration is that, when compared to DTI programs, NET programs are marked by a bit less intensity. It is simply impossible to provide the same number of learning trials in NET and DTI sessions of the same length. However, the payoff of not having to develop as many procedures to teach generalization may nullify this point.

In our opinion, and in the opinion of many who are leading the field of autism intervention, the learner's instructional routine should ideally be divided between the two approaches (Sundberg & Partington, 1998). DTI is a wonderful way to teach the isolated skills that are necessary for language development, and it truly shines in the establishment of instructional control. It provides ample opportunities to respond, and is quite efficient. NET, on the other hand, is by far the strongest approach for teaching spontaneity, and particularly the communicative exchange necessary for manding. It is also a way to move discrete skills into the generalized or functional repertoires of children with autism. Both have their limitations, as well as their strengths.

Combining NET and DTI

There have been strong advocates of the use of a combined NET/DTI approach (Sundberg & Partington, 1998). When combining the two approaches, it is necessary to look at the learner on a case-by-case basis in terms of what the ratio of NET to DTI should be. Early on, when the emphasis is on both establishing instructional control and teaching the most basic communicative exchanges, we believe that this should be almost a 1:1 ratio. Discrete Trial Instruction will lay the foundation of compliance and instructional control that will be necessary for intensive teaching of more advanced skills. Additionally, it will shape some of the early discrimination skills that are so critical in any kind of later learning.

At the same time, a strong emphasis on NET will establish a mand repertoire and help pair the instructor with reinforcement. NET is often the vehicle through which children with autism first realize that they do, in fact, have a voice that can allow them to access reinforcement in the environments where they spend the majority of their time. Additionally, it helps capture the interests of the child and promotes spontaneous use of verbal behavior.

As time passes and skills develop, the mand repertoire usually becomes quite strong. At this time, the instructional focus tends to shift to more advanced discrimination tasks, such as reciprocal language, topical conversation, etc. When this level is reached, it may be helpful to place a slightly stronger emphasis on DTI, while retaining NET for the purposes of skill generalization and skill extension. Once sufficient skills have been learned to make it possible for inclusion in less restrictive environments for education, the emphasis should move toward NET. This enables us to ensure that all of the skills learned so far are called upon when the natural environment requires them.

Incidental Teaching

Stemming from the concept of Natural Environment Training is the instructional strategy called **incidental teaching**. Incidental teaching is similar to NET, but involves capitalizing on opportunities that present themselves in the natural environment, without prior arrangement of the environment.

Incidental teaching is a way to utilize virtually every waking hour of the child's day as a way to promote skill acquisition and use, and to provide reinforcement for doing so. For example, upon entering a playroom with the light off, the instructor can implement a quick mand trial to reinforce the learner for asking for the light to be turned on. As these types of opportunities for incidental teaching present themselves throughout the day, the astute instructor will capitalize on as many of them as possible.

Section F – Visual Systems

Visual systems are commonly used to tell young children with autism when more remotely deferred reinforcing activities will be available in their day. It is another example of an intermittent, albeit more natural, schedule of reinforcement.

With visual systems, visual or pictorial schedules employ a time-based sequence of icons representing the child's daily activities. The child typically is involved in setting up the schedule, selecting which reinforcing activities are available for the day and, in some cases, when these activities will occur. As the child moves through her day, she removes icons from her "list" and places them in the Current Activity section of the schedule. Once the current activity is completed, the child removes that icon, places it in a done envelope, selects the icon for the next activity, and replaces it in the *Current Activity* slot. Figure 10.8 shows us an example of a pictorial schedule used for a portion of a young child's preschool routine.

Figure 10.8

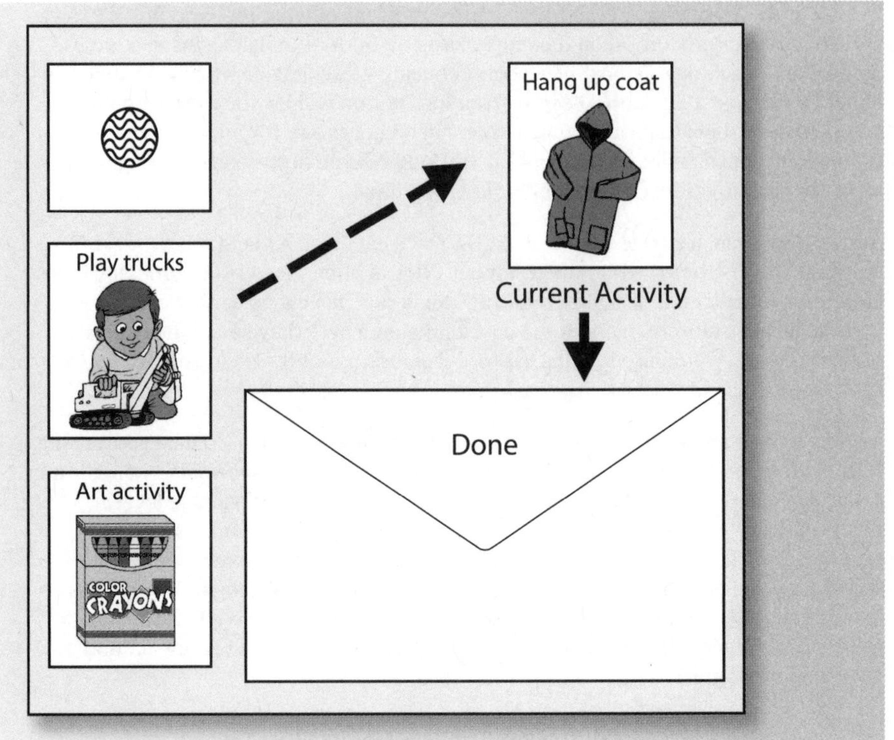

This same type of visual schedule can be employed in a more focused fashion within a child's instructional session. Rather than depicting the sequence of activities across her day, these *mini-schedules* (Hodgdon, 1995) take individual activities, break them down into their component parts, and then present those parts as a temporal sequence. This is an exceptionally effective means of reducing within-task prompting and eventually deferring reinforcement (INT schedule) until the end of a multi-step task.

The graphic in Figure 10.9 gives an example of a mini-schedule for an arts and crafts project in a preschool setting.

An excellent presentation of visual schedules, particularly photographic activity schedules, can be found in *Activity Schedules for Children with Autism* (McClannahan & Krantz, 1999). In our opinion, this book's description of visual schedules is second to none. It provides examples of how to incorporate social activities, token economies, and increasing levels of independence into visual systems, as well as a very clear, step-by-step teaching procedure for their design and implementation.

The representation system adopted for use in these schedules can vary, depending on the skill level of the child with autism:

- For the more skilled child, who may have the ability to read simple sight words, the schedule can utilize printed word representations of the activities.
- For non-reading children, simple icons paired with the corresponding printed words (such as those in Figures 10.8 and 10.9) are typically used.

- For children with visual impairments, the activities can be represented in Braille (for the reading student) or actual objects affixed to the card (for the non-reading student).

Finally, depending on the needs of the student and the environment in which the schedule may be used, the format can vary widely. Schedules can be as large as a poster, or actually be written on the classroom blackboard. Conversely, they can be the size of an index card that can be kept at the child's desk or folded into his or her pocket. With our older, more skilled children and adolescents, the schedule can take the form of a "To Do" list or be organized in a personal planner or PDA.

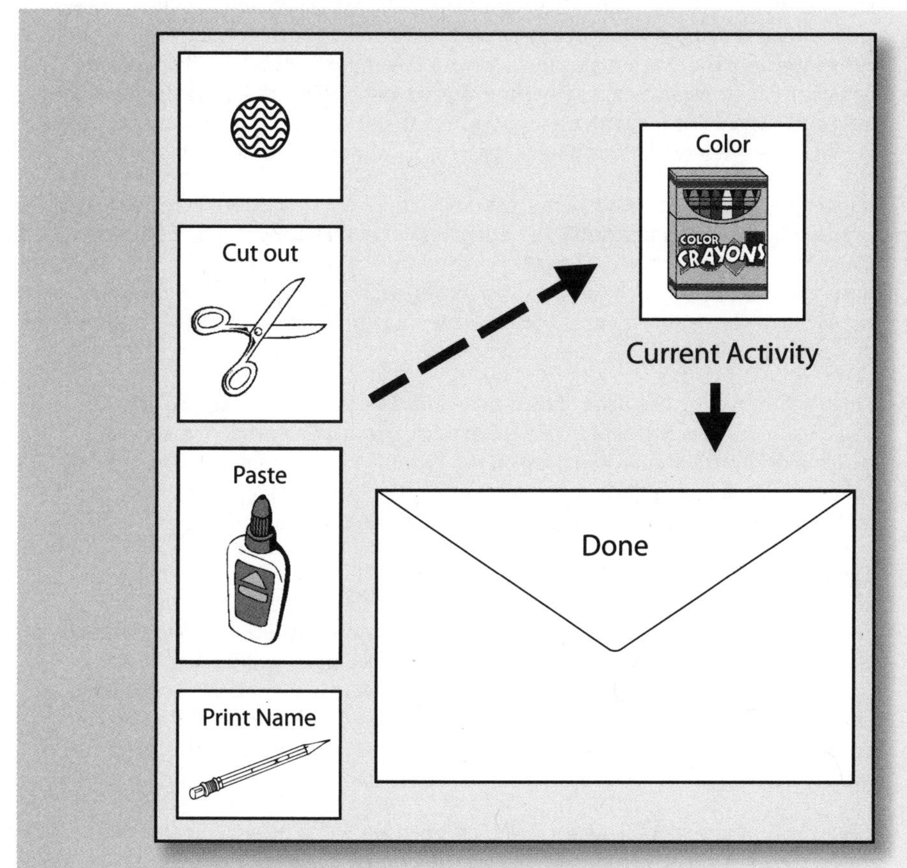

Figure 10.9

Section G – Video Self-Modeling

Many children with autism quickly pick up an imitative repertoire. In fact, many of them tend to be quite echolalic, which means that they repeat the words of others. When this happens, the words serve a self-stimulatory function more often than they do a communicative or skill application function.

In our work, we have seen quite a few children who cannot interact functionally with others, yet they can repeat – with great precision – songs, dialogue, or actions they have seen or heard on television or radio. This phenomenon may be due to the repetitive nature of a program on video, where a captured image or sound remains unchanged from one presentation to the next. In this case, each exposure to the image or sound is exactly like the previous one. There are no changes in inflection to deal with, nor are there changes in the subtleties of the presentation.

In a particular video, for example, the backgrounds, weather, dialogue, and characters, are *always* the same. This provides an element of repetition, which also allows for very tight stimulus presentation. After repeated exposures, the children are often able to repeat the sounds or words they hear, or perform the actions being presented.

If these types of responses can occur without any planning or instruction on our part, and if they can involve very detailed routines, we should be able use our behavioral "eye" to turn them into meaningful tools for learning functional skills like communication and social interaction. This is possible through a technique known as Video Self-Modeling. **Video Self-Modeling (VSM)** is a technique that involves videotaping approximations of a desired behavior, and then carefully editing the videotape until the finished product shows a fluent performance of the desired behavior. The learner then watches the altered video. After repeated viewings, the learner is then provided with the opportunity to use the skill. In this way, the video model serves as a type of priming activity, or a prompt used prior to instruction.

When taping these video segments, prompts can be used, scripts can be employed, errors can occur, and performance can be less than fluent. By using "Hollywood magic" to splice, cut, paste, and otherwise edit the audio and video tracks, all of the prompts, errors, and less-fluent responses disappear. When the final video is produced, it shows an example of the learner performing behaviors at a greater level of skill than that which has been observed.

Video self-modeling has been shown to be effective in several research articles. Since its initial development in the 1970s to treat stuttering problems, its use with children with autism has been on the upsurge since the early 1990s. Several leaders in the field regularly rely on VSM as a way to promote peer interaction, independence with self-care routines, and language fluency.

The success of VSM may be attributable to several factors. First, we already know that individuals with autism are visual learners, and video is certainly a visual medium. Second, we know that repetition and sameness lead to efficient skill development. Third, at the common-sense level, many children with autism thoroughly enjoy watching any type of video, and seeing themselves as the main characters can heighten the reinforcing value of watching. Finally, the video can be played for the student as part of leisure activities, which can allow us to squeeze even more therapeutic time into an already busy day.

Regardless of any specific factor, VSM has been shown to be a viable technique that can complement any kind of behaviorally based instruction.

Section H – Token Economy

A common method for systematically delivering reinforcement to young children with autism is the **token economy**. First discussed in the applied literature in 1968 (Ayllon & Azrin), the token economy involves the delivery of generalized conditioned reinforcers (tokens) following the child's meeting a pre-specified criterion (e.g., performing a target skill, whole-task completion, or the non-exhibition of problem behavior). Tokens are saved over time and later cashed in for back-up primary or secondary reinforcers.

In the case of a token economy, immediate delivery of the child's most valued reinforcers does not occur for all target responses. Instead, he or she must continue to perform, collecting tokens, until a predetermined "cash-in" time.

The token economy provides the child with a token that serves as a "reminder" of the ultimate reinforcer awaiting him or her at cash in. It allows the child to move from a continuous to intermittent schedule without the difficulties inherent in the schedule thinning process (see *ratio strain*). It also allows reinforcement delivery to occur in a setting away from instruction, so that a child can collect tokens for good behavior in school, which can be cashed in later when the child is at home. In addition, unlike primary and typical conditioned reinforcers, generalized conditioned reinforcers such as tokens are not affected by satiation and deprivation.

In the book *Applied Behavior Analysis*, John O. Cooper (1987) outlines the basic procedural guidelines for a token economy. He divides the process into a preparatory stage and a training stage.

Preparation for implementing a token economy requires the following steps:

1. Select the type of token. The therapist should ensure that tokens are:

    a. Safe for the child, in that they do not pose a choking risk for young children.

    b. Therapist-controlled, so that bootleg tokens cannot enter the system.

    c. Durable (made of materials that will hold-up to repeated handling through the exchange and cash-in processes).

    d. Readily accessible to the therapist and storable by the child. Ideally, they should be small enough to be kept in the therapist's pocket or hip-pouch, and stored by the child without interfering in his functioning.

    e. Not highly distractible (i.e., not constructed in such a way as to have significant reinforcing qualities of their own).

2. Define the rules and behaviors for the child:

    a. Target behaviors should be observable and measurable.

    b. Specific criteria must be set for the delivery of a token, such as the performance of a specific skill, level of prompting allowed, etc.

    c. Incorporate from the start a plan that addresses how the task criteria will be increased and the tokens faded.

    d. Ensure the child's success by making sure that he or she possesses all prerequisite skills necessary for performing the target behavior.

3. If implementing the system with several children in a classroom, set individual criteria and target behaviors. Consider the functioning level and reinforcement needs of each individual student and adjust for differences.

4. Select back-up reinforcers:

    a. Try to rely primarily on naturally occurring activities or events in the home or classroom as the cash-in reinforcers.

    b. Keep the system positive in nature by having back-up reinforcers as extra or "bonus" activities. Avoid using meals, normal opportunities for communication, and access to general comforts as the back-up reinforcers.

5. Establish a ratio of exchange:

   a. Begin with a small ratio of exchange – in other words, the back-up reinforcers can initially be purchased with a relatively small number of tokens.

   b. Once established, this ratio of exchange can be gradually increased, which in turn increases the "price" of the back-up reinforcers.

6. Establish general procedures of token delivery:

   a. Determine how the tokens will be dispensed and how the child will store them.

   b. Determine how the tokens will be exchanged. Will the child be presented with a written or pictorial menu of back-up reinforcers? Or will a physical "store" of back-up reinforcers be established where the child can "shop?"

   c. Determine the frequency of cash-in exchanges. This includes setting the time of day or, as the system is faded, the days of the week that tokens are cashed in.

   d. Determine how to interact with the child when he or she does not earn a token or, later on in the system-fading process, when he or she does not earn enough tokens to cash in for a specific preferred item.

   e. Determine whether a response cost (token removal for the display of specific problem behaviors) will be employed.

7. Field test the system. Conduct the token economy for three to five days without actually dispensing tokens. Make tally marks to represent when tokens would have been earned. This preliminary test should provide information as to the skill level of the participants and whether sufficient (or excessive) numbers of tokens will be earned by all of the students involved. Adjustments in target behavior definitions, token delivery, and pricing of backup reinforcers can be made following the field test. (Cooper, Heron, & Heward, 1987, pp. 489-493)

Training the token economy system requires the following steps:

For the higher-functioning, verbally receptive child, the system can be explained in simple language accompanied by modeling. Such a child can usually be trained in the token system within 30 minutes.

1. A verbal explanation of the system takes place.

2. The therapist physically models the delivery of a token, and then the immediate exchange of that single token for a back-up reinforcer.

3. Once the child can reliably perform the target behavior, receive a single token, and cash in that token for a back-up reinforcer, the system is ready to go.

4. The initial ratio of exchange is then explained to the child, pointing out that the ratio of "1 token = cash in" used during training will no longer be in effect, and that back-up items will now cost several tokens (Cooper, Heron, & Heward, 1987).

For the lower-functioning child, a more intense training procedure is usually necessary. In the book *Systematic Instruction of the Moderately and Severely Handicapped Children* (1983), Snell suggests that this process follow an eight-step procedure:

1. Select and operationally define a target skill that the child *has already mastered.*
2. Select back-up reinforcers, the type of token to be used, and a token storage container.
3. Require the child to perform the targeted skill (prompting as necessary). Reinforce the completion of the targeted skill with praise and a token.
4. Immediately hold out your hand and guide the child in giving you the token. Immediately present the back-up reinforcers on a tray, and allow the child to select one.
5. Repeat steps three and four until all prompts can be faded out and the child begins to show an "association between the tokens and the back-up reinforcers" (e.g., the child begins to reach for the tokens before you are ready to deliver them). Begin thinning token delivery to where the child must earn four to five tokens in order to make an exchange for back-up reinforcement.
6. Introduce the token container and teach the child to begin collecting earned tokens in the container. The container should also be used to transport earned tokens to the cash-in location (e.g., *token store*) for the exchange process.
7. Gradually increase the ratio of exchange to the point where it can be easily conducted in the classroom or at home.
8. Move the entire token economy into instruction sessions (classroom or home-based sessions), and adopt it as the child's reinforcement system.

See Figures 10.12 and 10.13 at the end of this chapter for a graphic representation of the token preparation and implementation process.

Regardless of how the system is trained, once the child has learned the basic procedure and contingencies of the token economy, it can then be maintained in the child's learning environment. In order for the system to remain effective, the basic principles of reinforcement described in earlier chapters of this manual should be closely followed. These include ensuring that token delivery is contingent on the child's performance of the targeted skill, that token delivery occurs immediately following the performance of the targeted skill, and that all staff involved are consistently following the procedures set up for token delivery and exchange.

Fading and Eventual Termination

As we were careful to point out in our discussion of schedules of reinforcement, it is critical to the development of our children that we continually move from contrived schedules of reinforcement to those that occur more naturally. To that end, any token economy system must have a plan for fading and eventual termination.

Again, returning to Cooper's treatment of token economies in *Applied Behavior Analysis* (1987), some standard guidelines must be considered when fading out a token system.

- Failing to pair social praise with token delivery may hinder the fading process, as the child will not have acquired the token as a conditioned reinforcer. If the instructor then tries to replace tokens with more naturally occurring social praise statements, the child may not respond as well as he or she did when tokens were used. Pairing social praise with every token delivery will allow praise to take on the reinforcing value of the tokens, and will go a long way toward preventing this problem.

- One of the most obvious ways of fading out the token economy is to increase the number of responses required of the child before a token can be delivered. This process was described in the training procedure for both high and low-functioning children, where a single response is no longer reinforced with a token. Over subsequent trials, the child is required to complete two, three, four, or more responses before earning a token. As the system is established and maintained over time, this thinning process can progress. Any good token system will therefore have, right from the start, thinning as an integral component.

- The length of time that the token system is in effect during the child's day can also be reduced over time. Replacement of the token system during these off-implementation times can be made with naturally occurring contingencies.

- Any contrived back-up reinforcers can be replaced with naturally occurring reinforcers. For example, rather than providing toy access as a back-up reinforcer in a third-grade classroom, the teacher may substitute access to computer games instead.

- Adjusting the price of back-up reinforcers can also assist in fading the token economy. While 10 minutes of computer time might initially cost 10 tokens – which could be earned in a single school day – it can gradually be increased to a value of 50 tokens, so that it can only be purchased once per week. In this manner, the system can be faded from a daily to weekly cash in.

- Finally, the physical evidence of tokens can be faded over time. Cooper (1987) describes an example where physical tokens such as poker chips can be replaced by slips of paper, then tally marks on a single index card which the child carries with him, to tally marks on an index card taped to the child's desk, to tally marks on an index card held by the teacher which the child can check at will, to tally marks on an index card held by the teacher that can only be checked at the end of the school day, to the same system with the child only allowed to check every two days, every four days, etc., until the system is entirely faded out.

As with any formalized behavior program, our ultimate goal is to improve the independent functioning of the child and to bring those behaviors under the control of naturally occurring contingencies of reinforcement.

Disadvantages of Token Economies

The token economy is a tried-and-true method for providing intermittent positive reinforcement to improve behavior, and to manage the behavior of groups of students simultaneously within the classroom. Even so, it does have a few characteristics that might cause hesitation before selecting it as a treatment option.

The imposition of a formal economic system into a classroom can be viewed as intrusive. Granted, if the behavior of a select group of students is capable of coming under the direct control of existing, natural reinforcement contingencies, then the addition of a contrived system of tokens and cash-in reinforcers may be unnecessary.

Second, token systems often work so well that therapists and teachers are hesitant to remove them. They become very reinforcing to us! They can bring the behavior of the group under such good control, that the negatively reinforcing qualities of the system can be great for the teacher. Unfortunately, keeping the learner on such a contrived, controlled system of reinforcement is not in keeping with our ultimate goal of independence brought under the control of natural classroom contingencies. However, when token economies are appropriately faded, much of the artificiality is removed.

Finally, tokens, token boards, token containers, cash-in menus, and back-up reinforcers are extraneous materials that must be brought to the classroom and, in some cases, must follow the child as he or she moves through the day. This entire process might be cumbersome for both the child and the teacher/therapist, as they require additional time and effort to manage.

Ultimately, the decision on whether or not to utilize a token economy depends on its "fit" for the individual child within his or her particular learning environment. If skill acquisition and displays of problem behavior seem to be unfazed by natural contingencies, or if movement from a continuous to a more intermittent schedule of reinforcement is desirable, a token economy may be the means to that end.

Other Visual Systems

The tokens used in a token economy are, at their core, *visual reminders* of deferred contingencies of reinforcement. This use of visual stimuli to aid the child with autism in contacting reinforcement is just one example of how visual systems can be used to improve the lives of these children.

An entire technology exists that utilizes visual materials to capitalize on the propensity for visual learning in children with autism. We will briefly review a few commonly used examples of these visual systems.

Visual reinforcement systems such as the "I am working for..." card developed by Andrew Bondy (Pyramid Educational Consultants) are similar, if not identical, to the token economies described above. The "I am working for..." card is a small, portable, visual contract that the child establishes with the teacher/therapist *before* beginning a task or series of tasks.

A pictorial representation of a child-selected back-up reinforcer is affixed to the card with Velcro, symbolizing what the child is, in fact, "working for." Tokens are then provided according to a pre-determined criterion (such as following every response, every third response, etc...), and are likewise affixed to the card. When the child fills the card with a certain number of tokens (per the current ratio of exchange), he or she can cash in for the back-up reinforcer. Figure 10.10 shows an example of an "I am working for..." card with the darkened circles representing tokens.

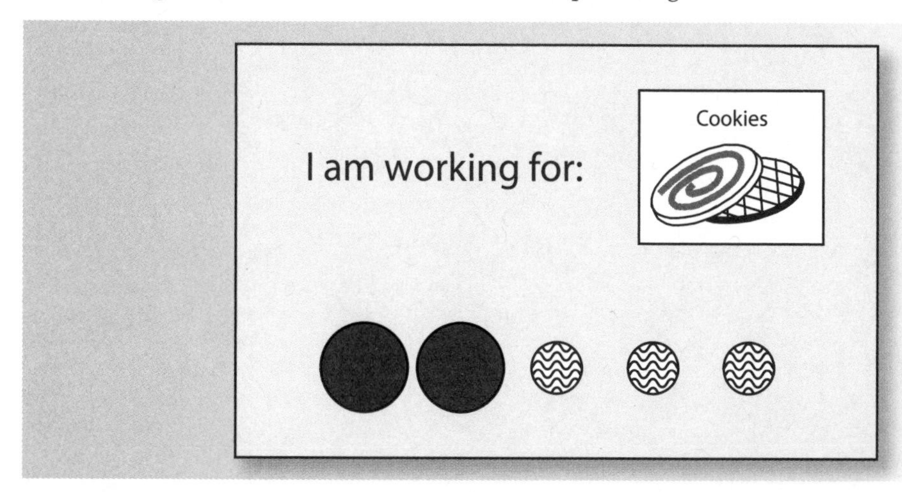

Figure 10.10

In the figure, the card indicates that two tokens of a five-token contingency for cookies have been earned. Once the child meets the requirements for earning the remaining three tokens, he or she will be able to "cash in" the card for some cookies.

It cannot be stressed enough that this "deal" set with the child must occur *before* the onset of the task. Tokens are awarded following correct responding by the child (according to a schedule of reinforcement). Any display of noncompliance or other problem behavior that occurs when the child is faced with the task do not result in earning a token. More importantly, however, if the therapist waits until after the task begins to set the deal, the potential exists for the deal-setting process to follow some display of problem behavior – potentially reinforcing that behavior.

Additionally, it would be highly inappropriate for the teacher to either refer to the deal card or "remind" the child of his deal once problem behavior starts. In both cases, the problem behavior has occasioned some reference to reinforcement – at best, interfering with any attempts at extinction and, at worse, directly reinforcing problem behavior with the promise of good things to come.

Implementing a Token Economy System

(Cooper et al, 1987)

Preparation:

1. Select the type of token
- a. Safe
- b. Therapist controlled
- c. Durable
- d. Readily accessible
- e. Not highly distractible

2. Define the rules and behaviors for the child
- a. Observable/measurable target behavior
- b. Set specific criterion for token delivery
- c. Plan how task criteria will be increased and tokens faded
- d. Insure child has all prerequisite skills for target behavior

3. If implemented in a classroom with several children, set individual criteria and select individualized target behavior
- a. Consider functioning level
- b. Consider reinforcement needs
- c. Adjust for differences

4. Select back-up reinforcers
- a. Try to rely on naturally occurring activities or events
- b. Select "bonus" or extra activities rather than meals, opportunities for communication, or access to general comforts.

5. Establish a ratio of exchange
- a. Begin with a small ratio
- b. Once established, gradually increase.

6. Establish general procedures of token delivery
- a. How tokens will be dispensed by adult
- b. How tokens will be stored by child
- c. How tokens will be exchanged
- d. Frequency of cash-in exchanges
- e. How to interact with the child when he does not earn a token or fails to earn enough for cash-in
- f. Decide if a response cost will be used

7. Field test the system

Implementation:

1. Field test the system
- a. Conduct the system for 3-5 days without actual dispensing of tokens
- b. Use tally marks instead of tokens to gauge system's success
- c. Adjustments in target behavior definitions, token delivery, and pricing of back-up reinforcers can be made following the test.

2. Train the token economy system (mildly disabled students)
- a. Simple verbal explanation
- b. Physical modeling
- c. Typically can be taught in about 30 minutes.

3. Train the token economy system (severely disabled students*)
- a. Select target skill that has already been mastered
- b. Select back-up reinforcers and type of token
- c. Require the child to perform the target skill and reinforce with praise and a token
- d. Immediately prompt the token exchange for a back-up reinforcer
- e. Repeat steps c and d until prompts are faded and child begins to reach for the tokens before you are ready to deliver them
- f. Begin thinning the token delivery to where the child must earn 4 to 5 tokens before cashing in
- g. Introduce token board or container and teach the child to store earned tokens
- h. Gradually increase the ratio of exchange to the point where it can be easily conducted in the classroom
- i. Move the system into the classroom/home environment and adopt it as his reinforcement system.

* from M.E. Snell's Systematic Instruction of the Moderately and Severly Handicapped Children (1983)

Figure 10.11

References:

Allyon, T., & Azrin, N.H. (1968). *The token economy: A motivational system for therapy and rehabilitation.* New York: Appleton-Century-Crofts.

Binder, C. (1993). Behavioral fluency: A new paradigm. *Educational Technology.* October, 8-14.

Bondy, A.S. (1996). *The pyramid approach to education.* Newark, DE: Pyramid Educational Consultants, Inc.

Cooper, J.O., Heron, T.E., & Heward, W.L. (1987). *Applied behavior analysis.* Upper Saddle River: Prentice-Hall.

Hanley, G.P., Iwata, B.A., & Thompson, R.H. (2001). Reinforcement schedule thinning following treatment with functional communication training. *Journal of Applied Behavior Analysis, 34*, 17-38.

Hodgdon, L.A. (1995). *Visual strategies for improving communication: Practical supports for school and home.* Troy, MI: Quirk Roberts.

Lerman, D.C., & Iwata, B.A. (1996). Developing a technology for the use of operant extinction in clinical settings: An examination of basic and applied research. *Journal of Applied Behavior Analysis, 29*, 345-382.

Lovaas, O.I. (1987). Behavioral treatment and normal educational and intellectual functioning in young children with autism. *Journal of Consulting and Clinical Psychology, 55*, 3-9.

Lovaas, O.I. (2003). *Teaching individuals with developmental delays: Basic intervention techniques.* Austin, TX: Pro-Ed.

Martin, G., & Pear, J. (1983). *Behavior modification: What it is and how to do it.* Englewood Cliffs, NJ: Prentice-Hall.

McClannahan, L.E. & Krantz, P.J. (1999). *Activity schedules for children with autism.* Bethesda, MD: Woodbine House.

Reynolds, G.S. (1968). *A primer of operant conditioning.* Glenview, IL: Scott, Foresman.

Snell, M.E. (1983). *Systematic instruction of the moderately and severely handicapped* (2nd edition). Columbus, OH: Charles E. Merrill.

Sundberg, M.L., & Partington, J.W. (1998). *Teaching language to children with autism or other developmental disabilities.* Pleasant Hill, CA: Behavior Analysts, Inc.

Terrace, H.S., (1963). Errorless transfer of a discrimination across two continua. *Journal of the Experimental Analysis of Behavior, 6*, 223-232.

Fluency-Based Instruction and Precision Teaching At a Glance

Chapter Points

- The idea that rate of responding or fluency may be a better indication of skill mastery was brought to education by Ogden Lindsley in the form of Precision Teaching.
- Precision Teaching focuses on observable, countable behavior.
- Frequency in Precision Teaching is usually described in terms of counts per minute, and provides a level of sensitivity in measurement not seen in percent correct or other standard measures of mastery.
- Precision Teaching utilizes the Standard Celeration Chart as a means of graphically displaying student learning and, more importantly, as a tool for making data-based decisions as to methodology and curriculum.
- Precision Teaching has much to offer EIBI programs – including more precise measurement, better skill retention, resistance to distraction, and more rapid acquisition of complex behaviors.

Key Terms

Fluency

Precision Teaching

Standard Celeration Chart (SCC)

Celeration

Daily Timings

Fluency Aims

Learning Channels

Phase Line

Timing Bar

Aim Line

Learning Ceiling

Tool Skills

Fluency-Based Instruction and Precision Teaching

A Step Beyond Accuracy

Anyone who has attempted to learn a foreign language knows that while basic vocabulary and sentence structure can be grasped relatively quickly, it takes considerable practice and experience before the language can be used in any kind of functional manner. Our efforts to speak are halting, slow, and awkward – until we have had enough practice to become *fluent* in the new language.

Our children with autism are faced with the same dilemma: learning a new language. If a child is not fluent with language responses, he or she will be at a serious social disadvantage during routine interactions with peers. Typical four-year-olds, for example, will probably not hang around for very long if their requests to play are met with silence.

With a discrete trial approach, our children can learn mands, tacts, and intraverbal responses. Learning to use these verbal operants in a functional and fluent fashion, however, requires that we take our drill and practice approach to a new level.

Free Operants

Free operants are ideal instructional targets, because they signify that students can respond in an unrestricted fashion. In Chapter 5, a *free operant* is defined as a behavior that can be emitted freely at nearly any time and (in terms of education) is not restricted by the instructor's presentation of materials or verbal instruction.

In the 1950s, Ogden Lindsley, a student of B.F. Skinner at Harvard, began what came to be known as a free-operant conditioning laboratory. Lindsley initially worked with psychotic children and adults, focusing his efforts on measuring the rate of behavior. Whether his patients were receiving psychotropic medication or behavioral programming, his early work showed that rate of responding was a much more sensitive measure of treatment success.

By the mid-1960s, Lindsley moved to the University of Kansas and focused his work on free operant responding in the field of education. Then, as now, the standard measure of academic success was the percentage of correct student responses. Lindsley introduced the idea that rate of responding, or **fluency**, may be a better indication of skill mastery. He called this approach **Precision Teaching (PT)**.

Lindsley defined Precision Teaching as "basing educational decisions on changes in continuous self-monitored performance frequencies displayed on Standard Celeration Charts" (Lindsley, 1992 p.1). He was very clear in stating that PT does not prescribe what should be taught or even how to teach it. Rather, PT is more a method of evaluating how well existing teaching strategies and curricula are working. The information derived from a PT approach allows instructors to make solid, data-based decisions as to how instruction should progress.

The Four Principles of Precision Teaching

Lindsley summarized PT according to four guiding principles:

1. Focus on directly observable behavior

Precision Teaching requires that we operationally define the target skills we are trying to teach. For that reason, it is extremely important that the learner's behavior be defined in measurable and observable terms. It has been recommended (McGreevy, 1983) that the task be a physical movement or permanent product of that movement that can be readily observed and counted.

In order to ensure that observation cycles are clear, the teacher will probably be required to make some adjustments in how he or she defines the target skill. In addition, private events such as silent reading may initially have to be made "public" to allow for observation and measurement.

In addition, tasks need to be defined in terms of *doing* something, as opposed to *not doing* something. Consider Lindsley's *Dead Man's Rule* for selecting a target behavior: if you are considering a specific target behavior to teach to your child, you need first ask yourself, "Can a dead man do it?" If the answer is "yes," then the target behavior (as you have defined it) is not a *behavior*.

A common example of this is the problem of student noncompliance – or, more specifically, the student not following teacher directives. Applying the Dead Man's Rule to this behavior, you would ask, "Can a dead man be noncompliant?" or, "Can a dead man not follow a teacher's directive?" Because the answer to both is "yes," your target behavior definition fails the Dead Man's Rule.

Redefining the target behavior in terms of what you want the child to *do* easily solves this problem. Compliance, or following teacher directions, can be clearly observed, counted, *and* meets the requirements of the Dead Man's Rule.

Assigning subjective labels to the student's behavior is also strongly discouraged. As pointed out in Chapter 10, labeling a child's behavior according to his diagnosis or other subjective descriptions can be detrimental in our efforts to measure both the frequency of the behavior and the effects of our teaching.

Saying that the child is "hyperactive," or that we are going to work on reducing "hyperactive behavior" doesn't provide a consistent means of knowing when the behavior is or is not occurring – or how to count its frequency. In this situation, the teacher may have her own definition of hyperactive behavior, while her assistant may have an entirely different take. Due to this observer disagreement, accurate frequency counts will be nearly impossible to obtain.

This problem can easily be resolved by defining hyperactive behavior in more clearly observable terms, such as "getting out of the chair" or "talking out when not called upon."

2. Frequency as a measure of performance

In strict scientific terms, *frequency* refers to the number of cycles or completed alterations per unit of time. In more general terms, frequency is usually thought of as some count, or number of occurrences, per unit of time. Behavior analysts have narrowed the term to mean the number of responses per minute, which they typically refer to as rate.

While behavior analysts use rate and frequency interchangeably, practitioners of Precision Teaching use frequency exclusively to mean responses per minute.

They usually describe frequency in terms of **counts per minute**.

Why is frequency important? Returning to our initial example of learning a foreign language, a first-year French language student could just as easily score a 100 percent in matching French words to pictures as a native-born Parisian. From a percentage-correct standpoint, both of these individuals are equally skilled.

If, however, we measure the frequency or counts per minute of both participants, we will likely see a very different comparison. The time that it takes for the novice French-speaker to complete the matching activity will likely be far longer than that of the person who speaks French fluently.

In other words, the level of sensitivity provided by a frequency or fluency-based measure provides us with a more accurate assessment of skill mastery.

Using frequency as a performance measure also provides a teacher with a very accurate means of assessing a student's progress on a daily basis, as well as assessing the instructional program being used. If our novice French-language student continues to score 100 percent on the word-picture matching activity, his teacher does not have any indication of his progress toward fluency. If, on the other hand, a frequency-based measurement is taken on this activity each day, the teacher is provided with information as to the student's rate of responding. If the teacher sees that this rate is improving, she has a better sense that the student is progressing toward fluency in the activity. If the rate is not improving after several days, the teacher might be prompted to make an adjustment in the instructional program to facilitate the student's progress.

3. The Standard Celeration Chart

When Lindsley began working with special education teachers in the mid-1960's, he found that each teacher came up with his or her own customized graph to describe student progress. This lack of uniformity – which made it nearly impossible to compare progress from teacher to teacher – led Lindsley to develop the **Standard Celeration Chart (SCC)**.

Drawing on his background as an engineer, Lindsley adapted the semi-logarithmic graph used in engineering to a new purpose. With this graph, the y-axis is set up on a *multiply scale* to accommodate behavior frequencies ranging from 1 per day to 1,000 per minute. Unlike the y-axis on a typical *add scale* graph that is divided into equal intervals, the multiply scale is divided into unequal intervals – an arrangement that provides the Standard Celeration Chart with several distinct advantages over the equal-interval graph.[1]

In addition, the x-axis on the Standard Celeration Chart is set up on an add scale to accommodate 140 successive calendar days, which is equivalent to one school semester.

The SCC is designed to display **celeration**, or the count per minute of a particular behavior over time. The logarithmic y-axis is used to plot very frequent behaviors (up to 1000 per minute) and very infrequent behaviors (down to one per day), and allows variations in behavior to be tracked over an entire school semester.

When behavioral data are plotted on a Standard Celeration Chart, the slope of the data path, or celeration, is less steep than the slope of the same data plotted on

[1] Equal interval graphs, most commonly used in applied behavior analysis differ from the SCC in that the y-axis is divided into equal intervals – progressing up from 0 in an arithmetic or additive function (e.g., 0, 5, 10, 15…).

an equal interval graph. Precision Teaching holds that this less-acute slope is a more accurate "index of learning." It is more sensitive to the actual increases and decreases in learning speed that a child might experience during a given period of time.

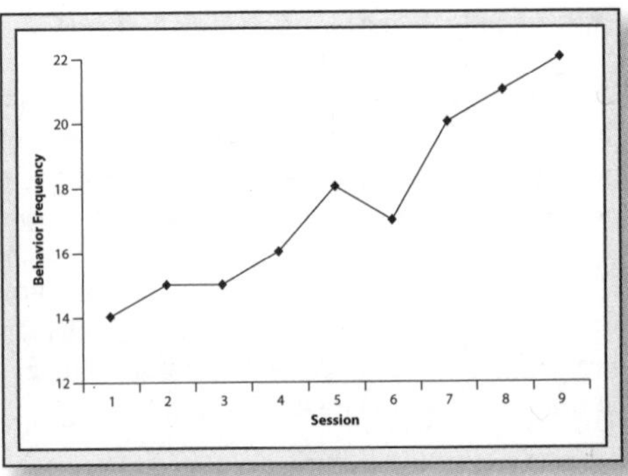

Figure 11.1

Depending on how the y-axis is set up on the typical equal interval graph, it can visually depict the same level of student performance in very different ways. Figures 11.1 and 11.2 illustrate this potential problem.

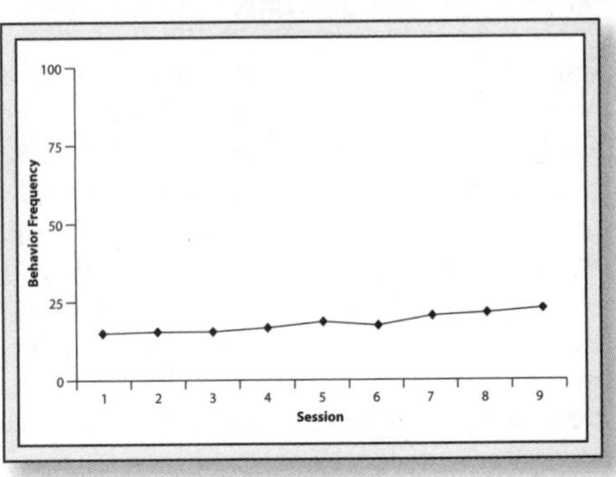

Figure 11.2

The graph in Figure 11.1 seems to indicate a much more rapid celeration in learning than the graph in Figure 11.2 – even though both graphs have the exact same data set plotted. Note the difference in the scale of the y-axis between the two graphs. The simple manipulation of this scale accounts for the significant difference between the two visual displays.

The Standard Celeration Chart avoids these inconsistencies, because the logarithmic scale along the y-axis provides a more sensitive and accurate depiction of a child's learning curve. When frequency doubles, such as when the child increases from six correct responses per minute on one occasion to 12 correct responses per minute on the next, it is said to be accelerating at "times 2" (abbreviated x2). When frequency is reduced by one-half between sessions, such as when a child's incidents of tantrum reduce from 12 per day to 6 per day between two consecutive data points, it is said to be decelerating at "divided by 2" (abbreviated /2).

The chart standardizes celeration, in that equal ratios of performance change appear as equal slopes on the chart, regardless of the starting frequency of the behavior. For example, the slope of a change from 1 to 2 (x2) looks similar to the slope of a change from 50 to 100 (also a x2 change). Because the ratio of change remains the same between the two situations (x2), the child's learning curve is the same.

4 Basic Principles of Precision Teaching

1. Focus on directly observable behavior
2. Use *frequency* as a measure of performance
3. Use the Standard Celeration Chart to track progress
4. "The learner knows best"

On the equal-interval chart, this same scenario would look very different. The change from 1 to 2 would be accelerating at an "add 1" or +1. In contrast, the change from 50 to 100 would be accelerating at an "add 50" or +50. The difference between the two slopes would be significant, but more importantly, would not accurately represent the similarity in celeration depicted in the SCC. The charts in Figures 11.3 and 11.4 illustrate the disparity between these two charting systems.

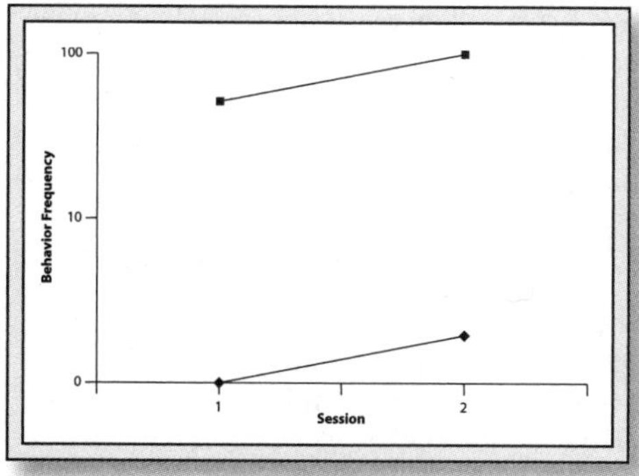

Figure 11.3

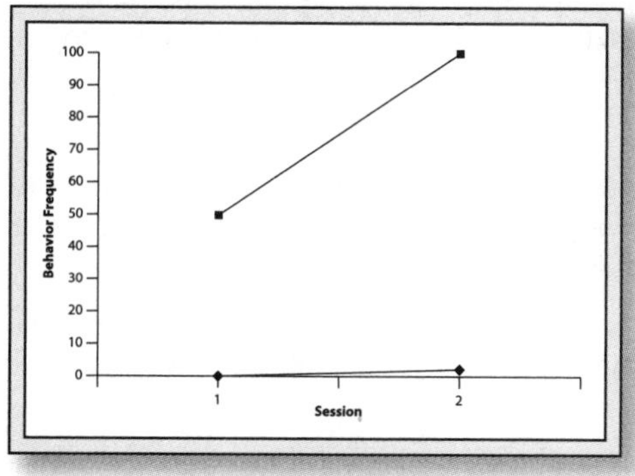

Figure 11.4

4. The learner knows best

While Ogden Lindsley was a Harvard University graduate student studying under Skinner, he approached Skinner with a cumulative record of an experiment he had conducted.

The subject of the experiment, a rat, had not responded as Skinner had described in his book *Behavior of Organisms*. When Lindsley challenged Skinner that his book must be wrong, Skinner replied, "In this case, the book is wrong. The rat knows best! That's why we still have him in the experiment!"

Lindsley loved this comment by Skinner so much, he adapted it to children as one of the four basic tenets of Precision Teaching.

In Precision Teaching, if a student is progressing according to plan, the teaching strategy is deemed appropriate for that student. If the student is not performing according to plan, there is a flaw in the teaching strategy. In such a case, the student is responding according to the contingencies set up by the teacher. If performance falls short of expectations, the teaching program needs to be modified in some fashion. As with the rat in Lindsley's experiment, *the fault never lies with the student.*

Learning as a Two-Fold Process

How is precise measurement and evaluation of student progress applied to a language acquisition program designed for young children with autism? The accepted use of Precision Teaching within an EIBI program generally involves viewing learning as a two-fold process.

Skills are initially taught to the child via some form of direct instruction or discrete trial training. This *acquisition phase*, which involves drill and practice, continues until prompts can be faded out and the child begins to respond accurately and consistently to the S^D.

The second phase of the learning process begins when we start to build fluency with the acquired target skill. This is accomplished by conducting **daily timings**, where the child is required to practice the target skill as rapidly and accurately as he or she can within a pre-specified time period. Timings can vary from 15 seconds to several minutes in duration; however, they are usually kept as brief as possible to reduce the potential for poor performance due to fatigue.

The results of these timings are usually recorded in terms of the *number of correct* responses and the *number of errors*. These data are plotted daily on the Standard Celeration Chart. As noted earlier, the *y-axis* of the SCC tracks responses per minute, so the number of correct responses and the number of errors are converted to rate by expressing them as the *number of correct/minute* and *the number of errors/minute.*

The accepted graphing conventions on SCC's are a filled dot to represent the acceleration data (number of correct responses) and an X to represent the deceleration data (number of errors). Over a period of days or weeks, these individual data points form a path or a trend line that indicates celeration – ideally, *acceleration* for the behavior targeted for fluency and *deceleration* for errors.

Fluency Aims

Mastery of any given skill is, as should be expected, expressed in time-based language. The predetermined performance standards utilized in Precision Teaching are expressed as responses per minute. These standards are also referred to as **fluency aims**. A fluency aim for a given skill is typically established when several normally functioning adults perform the skill under strict timing conditions and an average time is established. In order to account for variability, fluency aims are always denoted as a range. For example, the accepted fluency aim for oral reading of prose words in context is between 200-250 words per minute.

Precision Teaching researchers (most notably Kunzelmann et al., 1970) have worked to establish count-per-minute fluency standards for a wide variety of academic skills. A few examples of these can be found in Figure 11.5.

Several things are apparent from these few examples – most notably, the wide variety of skills that can be brought under the PT system of measurement. With a fluency-based approach, skills ranging from rudimentary speaking behavior (saying phonemes) to abstract language concepts (generating ideas) can be practiced, counted, and greatly improved.

Skill	Fluency aim
See/Say letter sounds	120-100 sounds/minute
See/Write numbers (random)	150-100 digits/minute
Hear/Write dictated words	100-80 letters/minute
Free/write upper case letters	80-60 letters/minute
Put together parts of a puzzle	15-30 parts/minute
Say or Write words that are opposite	20 opposite words/minute
Write or Say how people can help each other	20 ways/minute

Figure 11.5

Second, the table shows that PT practitioners describe skills in terms of **learning channels**, or "paths" of input and output. In this case, "input" is the sensory modality involved with the stimulus (e.g., sees digits), while "output" is the behavior contained in the response (Haughton, 1980). A learning channel is a combination of both.

For example, the skill of copying numbers from a model is referred to as "See/Write digits," because the input is seeing a model, and the output is writing the digits. Precision Teaching research has shown that speaking of behavior in terms of learning channels provides precise additional information to teachers, which in turn makes it easier to devise successful curricula and gauge student success.

The fluency aim for a given target skill is shown on the SCC as a line that runs horizontally at the level that corresponds to that particular rate on the y-axis. Skill mastery is based solely on the very accurate, time-based data collected on a daily basis. When a child's performance meets the fluency aim and continues at or above that level for several days, the skill is considered mastered, and a vertical **phase line** is drawn on the chart to indicate the completion of that curricular step. The example in Figure 11.6 should help solidify your understanding of this process.

This example chart includes a considerable amount of important information. For our purposes, however, we will limit our discussion to pointing out the basic chart conventions already covered earlier in this chapter.

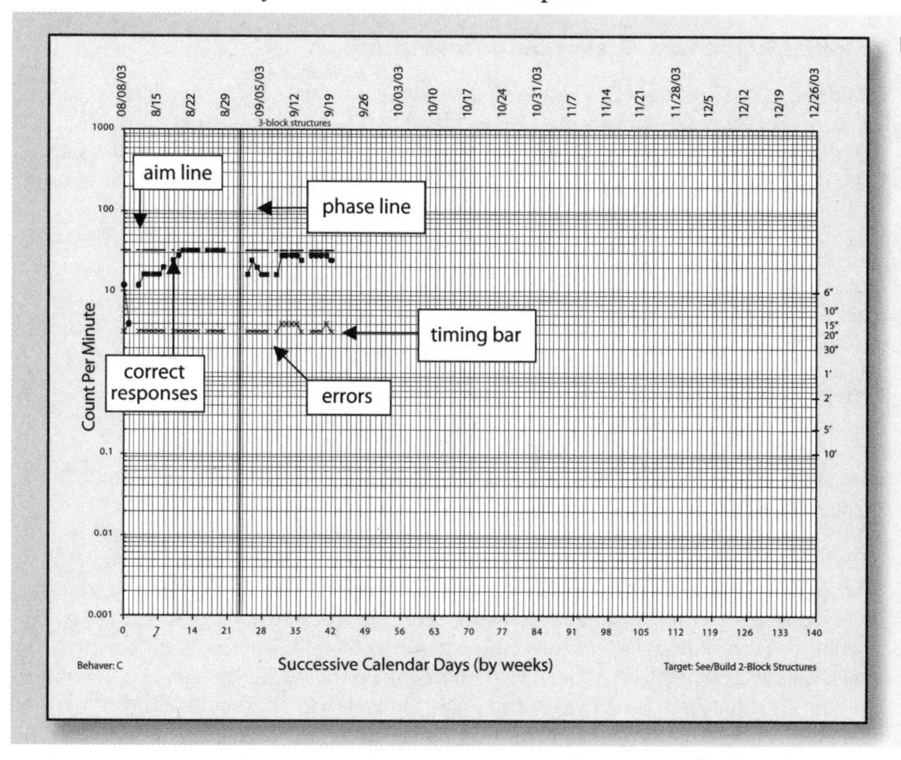

Figure 11.6

The skill that is initially taught is "building two-block structures" (see the bottom right-hand corner of Figure 11.6 for **Target**). This involves the child's ability to imitate pre-built block designs with his or her own set of building blocks.

Data were collected starting on August 08, 2003 (see the top left-hand corner of Figure 11.6) and proceeded with the two-block structures until August 28, 2003. Correct responses (accurate imitation of modeled two-block structures) are denoted by *filled-dots*, and errors (incorrect imitation of modeled two-block structures) are denoted by *x's*.

Acceleration of the child's correct responding can be seen by the upward trend in data points until they reach and stabilize at the *aim fluency line* (horizontal line drawn at the 32 responses-per-minute level) for several days.

A *phase-change* line was then drawn to indicate that the instruction proceeded (based on the child's success with the two-block structures) to building three-block structures. This phase change line can be seen as the vertical line drawn between the dates of August 31 and September 01, 2003. A label for the new target skill (three-block structures) is written above the graph following the phase change line. The child's progress with the second phase is somewhat variable at first, but quickly accelerates to meet the fluency aim by September 19, 2003.

Throughout the instruction that took place during this 42-day period, you can also track the child's rate of making errors. You can see that the number of errors, denoted by x's, remain at zero for the entire first phase. This is indicated by their location beneath the **timing bar** (the timing bar indicates the length of the timed practice sessions conducted). It is the lower horizontal line located at the 15-second level, as denoted on the right y-axis. During the three-block structure timings, single errors were noted on five separate days.

Studies Supporting Fluency-Based Instruction

The use of the Standard Celeration Chart – along with the other guidelines of Precision Teaching – has produced considerable research supporting the notion of fluency-based instruction. According to Binder, (1987), PT research findings are divided into three broad categories:

1) Studies that link speed of responding to improved retention or maintenance of skills and knowledge.

2) Studies showing that increased speed improves attention span or resistance to distraction.

3) Studies that indicate fluency in prerequisite skills or knowledge supports the application of new learning to more advanced or complex performance.

In addition, these studies also suggest the importance of practice in order to attain fluency.

One of the most commonly cited uses of PT was the Precision Teaching Project in the Great Falls, Montana school district in the early 1970s. Over a four-year period, students took part in 20–30 minutes of timed practice per day. Results were recorded on Standard Celeration Charts, and corresponding curricular decisions were made. The results demonstrated improvements between 19 and 44 percentile points on subtests of the Iowa Test of Basic Skills. For such a small outlay of time and effort (20 minutes per day), these students made phenomenal gains in their academic skills.

Unfortunately, despite these findings, few schools that we come in contact with have adopted a Precision Teaching model. In fact, most traditional educational technologies (materials and techniques) actually prevent students from ever achieving fluency. Opportunities for drill and practice are limited in most classrooms. And, other than timed tests in basic math facts, one would be hard pressed to identify many materials that offer ample opportunity for students to freely respond.

Similar limitations are readily seen in many EIBI programs, where skill mastery is often based on single probes or a percentage of correct responses. The children are moved through a curriculum of drills without ever reaching fluency in even the most rudimentary skills.

Most recently, PT practitioners (notably Fabrizio and Moors) have entered the EIBI arena, bringing with them the benefits of the SCC and time-based criteria. Precision Teaching's two-tiered approach – an acquisition phase followed by a fluency-building phase – seems to fit the discrete trial format quite well. As a precise method of measurement and evaluation, PT can be easily overlaid onto an existing Discrete Trial Instruction program.

A Fluency-Based Data Collection System for EIBI

One EIBI practitioner who has embraced the value of fluency is Dr. Vincent Carbone. In his clinic, he utilizes a data collection system that marries the traditional discrete trial probe data with daily timings. The authors have adopted this method in their clinical practice and have found that, although it surrenders some of the precision afforded by the Standard Celeration Chart, it does provide valuable daily data as to accuracy and fluency.

This data collection system makes it easy for teachers and therapists to make curriculum and methodology decisions – without having to wait for a lead therapist or consultant to observe the child and make the changes. In the short time that the authors have utilized it, they have found that their individual therapists and teachers are more in tune with their students' progress, and feel empowered to make confident programmatic decisions based on data, rather than on subjective opinion.

Here's how the system works. First, daily "cold probe" timings are conducted for each of the child's language programs. Once a target skill has been acquired (demonstrated by 90 percent accuracy across three consecutive sessions of accuracy probes), fluency probes begin. With fluency probes, the specific target skills are presented to the child in the standard discrete trial format, with an emphasis on speed of responding.

The therapist utilizes a digital timer and two tally counters to track the number of correct responses and the number of errors that occur within a pre-specified time period. As with PT, most timings are kept at a minimum (30 – 60 seconds) in order to control student fatigue. Because they are probes, no prompts are provided to the student during the timing. Responses during all probes (for either accuracy or fluency) are consequated with a neutral "okay." No reinforcement is provided if the child responds correctly, nor correction if the child responds in error.

The child's progress is then charted on an equal interval graph[2] that has as its y-axis a measure of *responses per minute*. Fluency aims are established much in the same fashion as with PT and an **aim line** is drawn horizontally across the graph at its corresponding level. Mastery criterion for most skills is attained when the child's responding can be plotted at or above the aim line for three consecutive probe sessions.

Figure 11.7 provides an example of an equal interval graph. In the graph, the data represent trials conducted on a Receptive Verb program that asked the child to "show me" a variety of actions. Starting at the far left, the data show responses to the "show me turning around" S^D. The fluency aim line is set at 13 responses per minute (a slightly thicker horizontal aim line can be seen running along the length of the graph at the 13 rpm level). On March 1st, the child completed her third consecutive session responding at or above the aim line, at which point movement to the next target "show me touching nose" was initiated (note vertical phase-change line at that point).

Errors are noted with x's and are generally located below the series representing the number correct.

Since these probes are conducted in the standard discrete trial format, it should be apparent that we are ultimately dealing with restricted operants. From a PT viewpoint, this is one of the major drawbacks of this data collection system – namely, that it does not allow for free responding by the student. What we have seen, though, is that consistent implementation and monitoring can lead to the attainment of a degree of *relative* fluency across several therapists. As our children progress through the skill curriculum, opportunities for free-operant responding become more frequent, and can be incorporated into the child's programming.

---

[2] We utilize an equal interval graph, as opposed to the Standard Celeration Chart, as we are tracking fluency rather than celeration. In addition, the equal interval graph is more in keeping with the standardized accuracy graphs used by our staff in the skill acquisition phase of instruction.

Figure 11.7

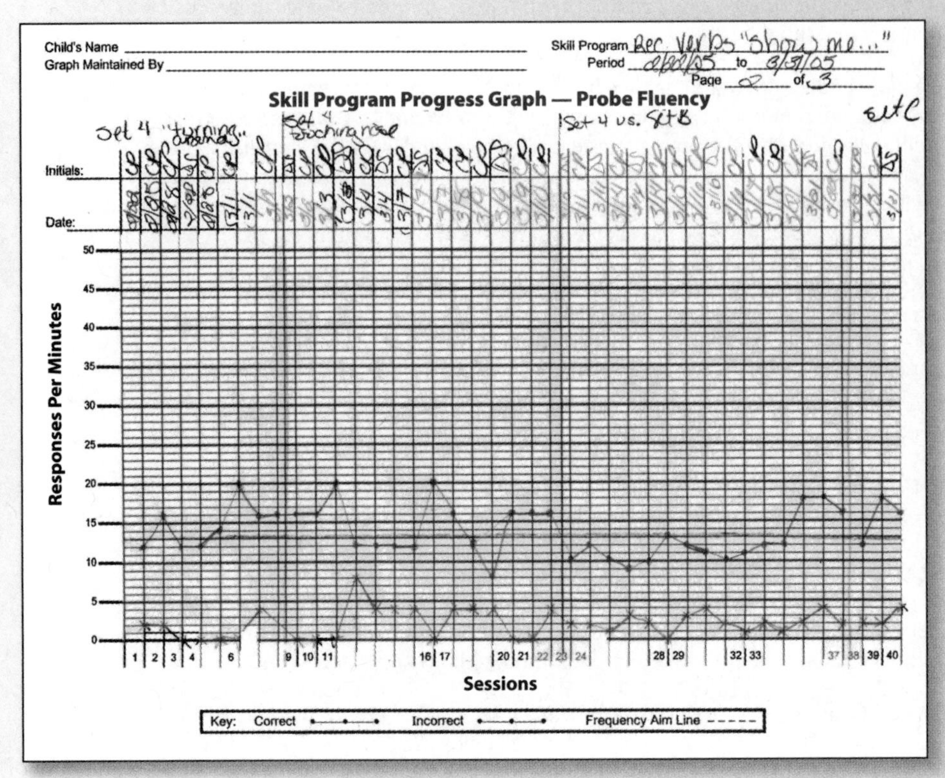

Learning Ceilings

Discrete trial instruction is full of "roadblocks" to free responding that PT practitioners call **learning ceilings**. Precision Teaching defines a learning ceiling as any component of instruction that hinders free responding. The most glaring example would be the standard verbal S^D. For each response opportunity, the child must *wait* for the therapist to give the S^D before he can respond. In that way, his rate of responding is seriously limited by the speed at which the therapist gives the instruction. The same problem exists with the use of flash cards or other instructional materials that must be manipulated by the therapist before the next trial can begin.

There are a few common methods for removing learning ceilings from traditional discrete trial approaches to learning. Presenting the child with a large field of manipulatives that allow for repeated practice trials of matching or block imitation drills can allow unimpeded responding. The child typically has to first be taught how to respond freely in such situations, particularly if she has had a long history of waiting for adult instruction in a DTI program. This usually does not take long to rectify, and the child can quickly become comfortable completing repeated trials without adult direction.

With block imitation, for example, we might set up 10 sets of two-block structures with corresponding sets of component blocks. The child would be given the initial S^D "build this" and then would be free to build all 10 structures as fast as she could.

Within tact programs, the materials can again be placed in a large field on the table as the child is given a single, starting S^D such as "What do you see?" She is then free to tact each object in the field as fast as she can.

Intraverbal programs can likewise be adapted to reduce or eliminate learning ceilings. A good example is the generating category-members drill. As no materials are generally needed for an intraverbal drill, the therapist might just give the starting S^D "Tell me as many animals as you can." The child would then be required to generate as many animal names as he can within the allotted timing. An alternate prompting device can be used with this same drill to help the child fluently generate category members. Preliminary fluency timings of naming animals from pictures (a See/Say learning channel) or reading a list of animal names (a Read/Say learning channel) can be conducted for several days prior to working on the intraverbal category generation drill. We have found that a child's ability to generate words intraverbally is positively affected by his fluency in simple tacting of those same words.

This last point alludes to what PT practitioners refer to as **tool skills**. These are the fundamental prerequisite skills that make up more complex behaviors. It has been shown repeatedly in the PT literature and research that a child's ability to fluently perform complex behaviors can be significantly improved by *first* teaching that skill's component parts.

A good task analysis of the complex behavior begins by identifying its most basic rudiments (viewing it as a movement cycle helps!). For example, a *See/Write single-digit addition facts* skill may have to be broken down into practice timings of just *See/Write single digits* or even *See/Write vertical and horizontal strokes*. If the child is not fluent in either of these fundamental skills, it seems unrealistic for us to expect her to be fluent in the more complex skill of solving single-digit addition problems.

In Summary

Fluency-based instruction (which includes Precision Teaching) has much to offer existing EIBI programs. The two most significant benefits are:

1) The introduction of a more precise system of measuring child progress.

2) All of the benefits of improved fluency, including better retention of skills, resistance to distraction, and more rapid and effective acquisition of complex behaviors.

The material covered in this chapter represents the *basics* of fluency-based instruction. Obviously, a discipline so rich in literature and applied research cannot be fairly represented within the scope of this book. Our hope is to whet the readers' appetite for fluency-based instruction, and to motivate them to seek more extensive information* on the subject.

*An excellent follow-up source for information on fluency-based instruction, Standard Celeration charting, and Precision Teaching can be found in Graff and Lindsley's 2002 book *Standard Celeration Charting*

References:

Binder, C.V. (1987). *Fluency building: Research background.* Nonantum, MA: Precision Teaching and Management Systems, Inc.

Graf, S.A. & Lindsley, O.R., (2002) *Standard Celeration Charting 2002.* Poland, OH: Graf Implements.

Haughton, E.C. (1980). Practicing practices: Learning by activity. *Journal of Precision Teaching, 1*, 3-20.

Kunzelman, H.P., Cohen, M.A., Hulten, W.J., Martin, G.L., & Mingo, A.R. (1970). *Precision teaching: An initial training sequence.* Seattle, WA: Special Child Publications.

Lindsley, O.R. (1991). Precision teaching's unique legacy from B.F. Skinner. *Journal of Behavioral Education, 1*, 253-266.

Lindsley, O.R. (1992). Precision teaching: Discoveries and effects. *Journal of Applied Behavior Analysis, 25*, 51-57.

McGreevy, P. (1983). *Teaching and learning in plain English.* Kansas City, MO: Plain English Publications.

Procedures to Reduce Behaviors
At a Glance

Chapter Points

- When targeting behavior(s) for reduction, one should precisely define target behaviors, collect baseline data, consider less restrictive options, conduct a functional analysis of the target behavior, and gain informed consent before proceeding with reductive techniques.
- Reductive programs should be based on the function of the target behavior.
- Problem behavior is always relevant, effective, and efficient for the learner.
- Extinction can be used to reduce problem behavior, but including it within a differential reinforcement procedure that also teaches replacement skills can enhance its effects.
- Punishment, though effective in reducing behavior, has potential risks and side effects.

Key Terms

Non-Contingent Reinforcement (NCR)

Differentiated Reinforcement of Alternative Behavior (DRA)

Differential Negative Reinforcement of Alternative Behavior (DNRA)

Differential Reinforcement of Incompatible Behavior (DRI)

Differential Reinforcement of Low Rates of Behavior (DRL)

Differential Reinforcement of Other Behavior (DRO)

Exclusion Time-Out

Nonexclusion Time-Out

Time-Out Ribbon

Contingent Observation

Planned Ignoring

Response Cost

Overcorrection

Contingent Effort

Contingent Restraint

Application of Painful or Noxious Stimuli

Procedures to Reduce Behaviors

Options for Problem Behaviors

Professionals who work with children with autism can expect to encounter a number of common problematic response topographies. Each of these, in turn, presents unique difficulties:

- Aggressive behaviors can create physical harm to both the aggressor and the person(s) to whom the aggression is directed.
- Tantrums can create barriers to independent social functioning that can, in turn, have a long-term negative impact on quality of life.
- Self-stimulatory behaviors can result in the same types of consequences as tantrums, possibly stifling opportunities to engage in social interaction.
- Non-compliant behaviors can impede a child's ability to develop skills through instruction.
- Disruptive behaviors can impede other children's abilities to prosper from the instruction provided to them.

A common thread runs through all of these examples: children engaged in problem behaviors are probably not engaged in behaviors that will help them become more independent and self-sufficient.

For these and other reasons, inappropriate behaviors must be dealt with. The more efficiently we can eliminate them, the less likely they are to cause long-term harm to the child's abilities to function effectively as a part of society. Conversely, given what we know about reinforcement history, continued exhibition (and reinforcement) of inappropriate behaviors makes them much more resistant to change.

In this chapter, we will discuss specific options that become available when we target behaviors for reduction. We'll begin with some basic, all-encompassing rules, and then move into specific examples of techniques – starting with the least intrusive or restrictive, and graduating to more restrictive and potentially controversial techniques.

5 Basic "Rules" of Behavior Reduction

1. Precisely define all target behavior
2. Collect data at every step of the way
3. Gain informed consent from parents/guardians
4. Consider less-restrictive options
5. Conduct a functional analysis of the target behavior

Section A – "Rules" of Behavior Reduction

To anyone who has read this manual from the beginning, the first part of this section should come as no surprise; in fact, it should serve as a review of previous material.

Rule #1: Precisely define all behaviors targeted for reduction.

When developing a precise definition for target behavior, make sure to include every part of the movement cycle. Most specifically, it is important to delineate the onset of the behavior, as well as the offset. With tantrums, for example, note what the behavior looks like when it begins. By identifying the offset or inter-response time (i.e., discrete incidents recorded when 30 seconds pass in which target behaviors do not occur), we ensure that the behavior can be counted.

Far too often, the authors have encountered situations in which behavior reduction procedures have been implemented without any solid or precise definition of target behaviors. For example, "non-compliance" may be all that is listed, with no definition of the movement cycle.

If no clear definition exists, one person may count a behavior as an incident of target behavior, while a second observer would not. Additionally, a person who counts the behavior is likely to implement a reduction technique (which may not be a pleasant experience for the child), while the second person would not.

What are the consequences of such imprecision? First, it becomes next to impossible to know if the intervention technique has the desired effect, because almost all data can be considered unreliable. Second, even if the intervention is effective in theory, its effectiveness will be limited by the consistency of its implementation. A potential side effect of such inconsistent implementation could also be the establishment of an S^D / S^Δ relationship. In this case, the person who does not implement the procedure might become associated with reinforcement for inappropriate behavior, while the person who is consistent in implementation does not.

Rule #2: Collect data at every step of the way, and graph it often.

If the behavior is worth the time and effort to target for change, it is also worth the time and effort to track. Data let us know how often the behavior occurs, how severe it may be, and its rate of occurrence. While definition gives us the ability to measure, data collection gives us the tools to measure and the ability to record these measurements for reference.

Data collection also provides us with standards for comparison. We cannot know if our intervention has been effective if we do not know the state of the behavior's performance at baseline, during, and after intervention. Graphic display of data, via a line graph, is the most effective way to analyze the data that are collected, so that the intervention program can be monitored and changed as needed.

The bottom line is that it is irresponsible to implement any kind of behavior reduction technique when there is no way to tell (via data analysis) if the technique is having the desired effect. Children can be exposed to ineffective techniques that may be questionable to begin with, and time spent on an ineffective approach inevitably translates to time not spent on another approach that would work more effectively.

Rule #3: Gain informed consent from parents or guardians prior to the implementation of behavior reduction techniques beyond differential reinforcement.

As we will explain ahead, there are times when it may be necessary to introduce aversive consequences. It is the responsibility of anyone who implements these techniques to gain approval and informed consent from the person(s) responsible for the child's welfare. Informed consent involves clearly defining the particular strategies that will be used – including techniques that may temporarily escalate behaviors (e.g., extinction), result in the loss of reinforcers, or result in the introduction of punishers. In addition, the potential risks and benefits involved should always be discussed. The person granting informed consent must never be subjected to persuasive tactics, and must be given the full right to veto the treatment approach at any point. Consent must be granted in writing, and preferably be subject to review by a human rights or behavioral review committee.

Rule #4: Consider less restrictive options before more restrictive ones.

The authors frequently make the point that as practitioners, we should never rely on extinction or punishment to do work that reinforcement can accomplish just as effectively. As we've discussed, there are several reasons why punishment-based techniques hold a certain type of favor for some people. The primary reasons are that punishing and other reduction-geared techniques usually work relatively quickly, and they provide somewhat immediate relief for the person implementing them.

We know, though, that punishment is usually only a temporary solution, and the behavior usually experiences an eventual return to baseline. Therefore, we must determine if our efforts would be best spent developing programs based on reinforcement, for that is where the most lasting effects will be realized.

Rule #5: Conduct a functional analysis of the target behavior.

A functional analysis – particularly one conducted experimentally – is an effective guide through the process of developing an intervention plan that will work. It identifies contingencies that maintain inappropriate behaviors, which is the first step in gaining control over them. Functional analyses also serve to let us know what types of consequences are reinforcing to the individual. They include information that can be used to effectively reinforce, implement extinction, and (if no other course is effective) punish in a way that will produce the most effect in the shortest amount of time possible.

Guiding Principles for Behavior Reduction

In addition to the above rules, there are some guiding principles to consider when dealing with programs to reduce behaviors. First, the program should be based on the function of the behavior as closely as possible. Granted, there are times when the intervention is not related to the function of the behavior (such is the case at times when positive punishment is used), but we can usually find a way to tie it to the function of the targeted behavior.

Second, we should remember that the target behavior is occurring because it serves the purpose of making the learner's situation better. At some level, the inappropriate behavior is relevant, effective, and efficient:

- It is **relevant** because of MO issues. Certain conditions drive the MO up or down, creating a favorable context for the behavior to be evoked.
- It is **effective**, because its demonstration in the past ultimately resulted in an environmental change that signified a "betterment" of the previous condition.
- It is **efficient** because it is probably not the only behavior that could have gained a similar change in the environment – just the one with the best chance of effecting the change fastest.

In order to effectively reduce inappropriate behaviors, we must make the behavior irrelevant to the greatest extent possible. This can be accomplished through manipulations of the MO, so that the reasons for the behavior's occurrence are minimized at the environmental level. For instance, behaviors maintained by escape from academic tasks may be related to skill deficits. In this case, a child who screams when asked to read aloud may do so because the task itself is difficult, compared to his or her skill level in fluent decoding.

By training necessary skills and remediating weakness, or by making sure that reading sessions are kept short, we may be able to drive down the MO for escape from reading. This will make escape less reinforcing, and the behaviors associated with escape less probable. By changing these elements, we have changed the context to make the behavior somewhat irrelevant.

We must also strive to make the behavior ineffective. This is accomplished through extinction. If we know that reinforcement has typically followed behaviors within a particular response class, we can do our best to guarantee that the reinforcement no longer occurs. This is directly related to the accuracy of the functional analysis of the target behaviors. If reinforcement no longer follows the target behavior, it has been rendered ineffective.

Finally, we can also render the behavior inefficient. Even if there are some times when reinforcement follows the inappropriate behavior, it is our challenge to find replacement behaviors that will gain the same reinforcement, but with far less effort on the part of the child. In other words, we can build a program that reinforces a simple, one-step exchange of a picture to ask for a break, which is certainly much more efficient than engaging in tantrum behaviors for five to ten minutes before a break is given. When given the choice between two behaviors, most learners will select the one that will gain reinforcement in the most efficient manner.

Now that some ground rules have been established, we'll move on to specific methods for reducing inappropriate behaviors.

Section B – Reduction of Behaviors Through Antecedent Manipulation

Sometimes, a functional analysis of problem behavior indicates a socially mediated function, such as access to attention or tangibles, or escape from demands. When this is the case, it often helps to consider the impact of motivational variables and the methods for manipulating them as a means of reducing the probability that the problem behavior will occur.

We know that the function of a behavior involves not only its consequences (in this case, the delivery of attention/tangibles/escape), but also the discriminative stimuli and MOs that are present before the behavior occurs. It stands to reason, then, that manipulation of these *antecedent variables* may be an effective way of reducing the relevant behavior.

Motivational operations for problem behavior often involve deprivation – for example, a child may find herself in a situation where levels of either adult attention or access to preferred tangibles are limited. We know that MO's have two effects: first, they momentarily increase the value of certain stimuli as reinforcers; and second, they evoke behavior that has been consequated by these same stimuli.

Given a situation where a child experiences reduced adult attention, the MO for attention may be in effect. This will increase the value of attention and evoke behaviors that have been reinforced by attention in the past. A similar MO could also be in effect for preferred tangibles, typically by reducing the child's access to these items.

Motivational operations for escape or avoidance work in a similar manner. Given a situation where a child is exposed to non-preferred tasks or activities (e.g., having to eat his broccoli), the MO for escape from the non-preferred stimulus may be in effect. This will increase the value of escape as a reinforcer and evoke behavior that has been followed by escape in the past.

If problem behavior is historically followed by escape from non-preferred situations, there will be an increased probability that the problem behavior will be displayed. In our broccoli example above, the prospect of eating broccoli (the non-preferred task) might be an MO for escape. Faced with this task, the value of escape from the dinner table is momentarily increased. In addition, the probability of any behavior (such as a severe tantrum) that has previously resulted in escape is likewise increased.

It would seem reasonable, then, that if the antecedent situation could be manipulated in such a way as to reduce the MO for the desired reinforcers (attention/tangibles/escape), we might be successful in reducing the probability for problem behavior.

Non-Contingent Reinforcement

One method for driving down the MO for desired reinforcers is **non-contingent reinforcement (NCR)**. Sometimes referred to as *environmental enrichment*, NCR procedures typically provide the child with access to the relevant reinforcer according to a predetermined schedule (usually a fixed or variable interval schedule). The reinforcement is considered non-contingent because it is delivered according to the passage of time, rather than the display of any particular behavior. The intent of NCR is to provide the child with levels of reinforcement sufficient to diminish or neutralize the MO. In doing so, the need to engage in the related problem behavior is reduced.

In the case of positive reinforcers, the child would be provided with attention or tangibles according to a time-based schedule, and at a rate sufficient to drive down the MO for either.

With a negative reinforcement scenario, the child would be provided with non-contingent breaks from the non-preferred task or activity; reducing both the MO for escape and the probability that escape-maintained problem behavior will be evoked. For a more comprehensive overview of NCR, as well as a review of the basic and applied research that has been conducted on NCR, see Carr et al., 2000.

Other Methods

Along the same lines as non-contingent breaks, there has been a good deal of applied research in the area of antecedent task modification (Dunlap, 1984), (Winterling et al., 1987), (Mace et al., 1988), (Dunlap et al., 1991), (Horner et al., 1991), (Lannie & Martens, 2004), and (Green et al., 2005).

Several methods have been shown to be effective in reducing problem behavior related to escape from demands. These include stimulus-fading procedures (Pace et al., 1993), where demands are slowly introduced into the instructional setting in increments. For example, during Discrete Trial Instruction sessions, we might begin by requiring the child to perform only one trial before offering a break. Once the child has met a predetermined criterion (such as three consecutive sessions without display of problem behavior), we would add a single trial to the work requirement – so that the child would have to complete two trials before gaining a break. Work would then be added accordingly, until the child reached an acceptable level with momentary pauses in the fading process occurring following increases in problem behavior.

Research has shown, however, that stimulus fading alone is not quite as effective as when it is used in conjunction with extinction procedures. Zarcone demonstrated in a 1994 study that when stimulus fading was used alone, it was initially very effective in reducing escape-maintained, self-injurious behavior. However, maintenance of these effects over time was not observed, and durable effects were achieved when stimulus fading was combined with extinction (Zarcone et al., 1994).

Other antecedent techniques used to reduce problem behavior include high-p/low-p sequences (where a series of high probability tasks are followed by a low-probability task that increases the probability of compliance to the low-p task), as well as systematic adjustment of instructional session length or the pace of instruction.

Section C – Reduction of Behaviors Through Differential Reinforcement

In previous chapters, we discussed the importance of conducting a thorough functional analysis of a child's problem behavior, and how a great deal of maladaptive behavior is related to communication. In Chapter 9, we concluded that problem behavior can sometimes be defined as verbal behavior, albeit faulty behavior. This is the case when a tantrum behavior acts on the environment through others to provide reinforcers.

Consider the following scenario:

James is a three-year-old boy diagnosed with PDD – NOS. Being functionally nonverbal, James does not use words to mand for reinforcement, nor can he tact objects in his environment. Imitative and motor abilities are likewise poorly developed. His receptive language skills are considered fair in that he can follow simple spoken instructions for routine tasks (single-step). He attends an inclusive daycare three days a week for three hours each day, and has a 1:1 aide assigned to him during this time.

From the beginning of his enrollment in daycare, James engaged in severe head banging in the form of striking his head forcefully against the floor. The daycare staff noticed that this behavior typically occurred during transitions between activities, or when another child was playing with one of James' preferred toys. In order to reduce the likelihood that James would engage in this behavior (since it appeared that he could be hurting himself), the daycare staff allowed James extra time during transitions and placed his favorite toys out of the reach of other children.

Following several months of this "walking on eggshells" approach, the daycare staff noticed that James' behavior was not improving. In fact, they were beginning to see the head banging behavior occur at other times of the day, such as when non-preferred tasks or foods were presented to him. Concerned that his behavior would continue to spiral out of control, the daycare director obtained the services of a contracted behavioral consultant to assess James and to offer suggestions regarding his problem behavior.

A functional analysis of James' problem behavior found that the primary maintaining variable for his head banging was access to positive reinforcement in the form of preferred tangibles or activities. Escape from demands was found to be a secondary variable, but the data on escape were not as pronounced as that seen with tangibles.

The consultant recommended a simple program designed to teach James to make requests for his preferred toys and activities via the Picture Exchange Communication System (PECS). [1] *Initially, every time PECS was used to mand for preferred toys or activities, reinforcement (the delivery of the requested item) was immediate. When James engaged in head banging, the daycare staff was instructed to prompt James through the transition and to begin the new activity. Head banging no longer was to result in a delay in transition or special access to preferred toys.*

James' preferred toys were likewise made available to all children. If James engaged in head banging when another child had one of these toys, the other child would not be required to give it to James. The head banging would be blocked (by use of a cushioned mat) to prevent injury, and no redirection to alternate toys would occur during the incident.

Over ensuing weeks, the daycare staff noticed a slow, steady decline in James' head banging behavior. He would occasionally have days with multiple outbursts but, by and large, he was using his PECS to make requests and his incidents of head banging were diminished.

Differential Reinforcement: "How-To"

The behavioral process described in James' treatment program should be recognizable as *differential reinforcement.* As defined in Chapter 7, differential reinforcement involves the reinforcement of one member of a response class while placing another member (or members) of that same response class on extinction. In James' situation (and in most cases of differential reinforcement) the behaviors in question are all members of the same *functional response class.*

If you remember, a functional response class is a group of behaviors that all serve the same function for the child. Both head banging and the use of PECS serve to gain James access to preferred tangibles or activities – therefore, they are both members of the same functional response class. As with most problematic behavior, the head banging serves James as a socially unacceptable or "faulty" mand.

With any differential reinforcement procedure, some form of behavior is being increased or strengthened while another form of behavior is being decreased or weakened. Even within the process of shaping, closer approximations to the terminal behavior are being strengthened while the previous steps in the shaping process are being weakened. Viewing differential reinforcement only as a means to increase or decrease behavior would therefore be incorrect.

There are two possible results of differential reinforcement. If it consists of reinforcing some responses and not others it leads to **differentiation** (Cooper, Heron, & Heward, 1987). If, on the other hand, it involves the reinforcement of a response when certain stimuli (S^D's) are present and not reinforcing the same response when those stimuli are not present (S^Δ), it leads to **discrimination** (Cooper, Heron, & Heward, 1987).

In the "James" scenario, the differential reinforcement process occurred when the daycare staff reinforced PECS-use by immediately delivering the requested toy – and withheld preferred toys (extinction) when head banging was observed. Use of PECS became the member of the functional response class that was reinforced, while head banging became the member of the same class that was placed on extinction.

[1] PECS is an augmentative/alternative communication system that teaches the exchange of pictorial icons as a means of communicating.

The fact that PECS-use functioned the same for James as head banging – getting him tangibles – we would typically say that PECS-use is the *functional equivalent* to head banging. **Functionally equivalent skills**, then, are alternate behaviors that serve the same function as the problem behaviors that they replace.

Differential Reinforcement of Alternate Behavior (DRA)

The procedure outlined for James in the above example is actually best described as **Differential Reinforcement of Alternate Behavior (DRA)**. In a DRA procedure, a target behavior (often a functional equivalent) is selected as an alternate to the targeted problem behavior, and then reinforced. The behavior targeted for reduction is conversely placed on extinction. In James' program, PECS-use was the alternate behavior that was strengthened, while head banging was placed on extinction.

With DRA, the existing target problem behavior has a history of reinforcement with the child, and as such, will naturally compete with the new target behavior for reinforcement. This makes it necessary to carefully choose an alternate behavior with qualities that will allow it to compete and eventually "win out" over the problem behavior. When selecting an alternate behavior for a DRA procedure, several requirements or guidelines should be followed.

1. Functional Equivalence

As already stated, the alternate behavior will be more easily adopted into the child's repertoire if it is functionally equivalent. However, while recommended, this is not strictly required. According to the basic definition of a DRA, it may be sufficient to select a behavior that will leave the child with less time to engage in the targeted problem behavior.

Also, the alternate behavior does not need to be topographically equivalent to the problem behavior. Adding an entirely new behavior or group of behaviors to a child's repertoire can, in and of itself, reduce the likelihood of the target problem behavior being displayed.

That being said, the selection of a functional equivalent as the alternate behavior still has one major advantage.

Suppose James' behavior consultant had chosen an alternate behavior from a different functional response class – such as completing puzzles. It may be true that once James became adept at puzzle building, he would have had less time to engage in head banging behavior. It would also be true, however, that a contrived reinforcer would have had to be delivered following each puzzle-building session, since there were no preexisting contingencies to reinforce puzzle-building in the daycare environment.

This relationship between the alternate behavior and a contrived, unnatural reinforcer is tenuous. It relies on the daycare staff going out of their way to provide extraneous reinforcement to James for the completion of puzzles. Moreover, the fact that James learned to build puzzles does not guarantee that he would not head bang when he had to transition from puzzle building to another activity. Nor would it ensure that similar behavioral outbursts would not occur if another child attempted to work on one of James' puzzles. Most importantly, a nonfunctional DRA sets up a competition situation in which the alternative behavior will occur when its MO is strongest; otherwise, we're likely to see problem behavior.

On the other hand, since James' problem behavior typically came under the control of natural contingencies in his environment (delivery of tangibles), other members of the same response class would more likely come under the control of those same natural consequences. By selecting an alternate *mand* rather than an arbitrary behavior, the consultant was better able to ensure that the new/alternate behavior would find naturally occurring reinforcement in the daycare environment, and therefore would continue to be maintained long after the formal program had been faded out.

2. Efficiency or Response Requirement

Another variable to consider when selecting an alternate behavior is *efficiency* or *response requirement.*

Children come to us with problem behavior histories of months, if not years. These behaviors are highly adaptable. They have been reliably reinforced for long periods of time, and have usually become very efficient means of operating on their environments. In these situations, it is important to select a functional equivalent that is *more efficient* or presents less of a *response requirement* to the child than his/her problem behavior.

In the example with little James, there was a specific reason the behavioral consultant decided on PECS as the mode of communication for the alternate behavior, rather than suggesting sign language or vocal speech. Recall that James had no functional vocal speech and poorly developed imitative and motor skills. Because of this, choosing vocal speech or sign language would have required extensive instruction that might have taken months. The first phases of PECS, on the other hand, can usually be taught to a child within an afternoon – making it a much more efficient approach.

Remember that when an alternate behavior requires more effort to complete than the problem behavior, it is highly unlikely that the new behavior will ever replace the entrenched inappropriate behavior.

3. Continuous Schedule of Reinforcement

Finally, the alternate behavior in a DRA must initially be reinforced according to a *Continuous Schedule of Reinforcement (CRF).* As noted in James' hypothetical program, "Initially, every time PECS was used to mand for preferred toys or activities, reinforcement (the delivery of the requested item) was immediate."

This is done to establish the alternate behavior as quickly as possible and maximize the effects of differential reinforcement. If we can demonstrate to a child that an appropriate mand will be honored *every time* it is produced, it will compete well against a strongly established faulty mand.

Once it has been established with a continuous schedule of reinforcement, the alternate behavior can then be maintained on more of an intermittent schedule. *Thinning out* the schedule of reinforcement usually involves increasing the time between reinforcement. This can be done by either increasing the time interval that occurs between reinforcement, or by increasing the ratio of responses to reinforcement. The latter involves progressing from a continuous schedule that involves reinforcement for every response to a ratio that involves reinforcement of *every other response.*

The most effective way to thin a reinforcement schedule for the alternative response is to use a graduated multiple-schedule arrangement, in which signaled periods of continuous rates of reinforcement and extinction are alternated (Hanley et al., 2001). To review in-depth information about schedules of reinforcement, please refer to Chapter 10.

Differential Negative Reinforcement of Alternate Behavior (DNRA)

Sometimes, functional analysis reveals that negative reinforcement is the maintaining variable for a child's problem behavior, and we are faced with teaching an appropriate functional equivalent.

With an escape-maintained behavior, the response (head banging) occurs with the onset of demands or presentation of an aversive or non-preferred stimulus. Reinforcement occurs when the demand or presentation of aversive or non-preferred stimulus is delayed or removed. This relationship increases the probability that head banging will occur with greater frequency in the future.

Again, head banging serves a communicative function – this time as a faulty mand for escape. It has become the child's way of asking for a "break" from the task demand, or to have an aversive stimulus "taken away."

Differential negative reinforcement of alternate behavior (DNRA) would be used in this situation. DNRA is identical to DRA in nearly every aspect, except for two significant differences.

First, the alternate behavior *must* function as a mand for escape. A spoken request ("I need a break"), formation of the word "break" in sign language, or the selection of a PECS icon representing a request for "break" is differentially reinforced, while the target problem behavior is placed on extinction.

Second, in DNRA the extinction process must be *escape extinction.* Rather than denying a tangible or removing attention, an escape-maintained behavior is placed on extinction by withholding the reinforcer that has typically followed the display of the behavior. In this case, it is escape from the task or removal of the aversive stimulus. By withholding escape, we keep the task in place and prompt the child through to its completion. (Ideally, the task will be completed without display of problem behavior – specifically, tantrum behavior.) We likewise keep an aversive in place until the problem behavior ceases.

All other requirements described in the section on DRA apply to DNRA. The alternate behavior should be a functional equivalent (an escape mand), it should be able to compete with the problem behavior in terms of efficiency and response requirement, and it should be reinforced initially according to a CRF schedule (with schedule thinning planned).

Differential Reinforcement of Incompatible Behavior

Another type of differential reinforcement program that operates in a similar manner is known as **Differential Reinforcement of Incompatible Behavior (DRI)**. Like DRA, DRI places one behavior on extinction while a functionally equivalent behavior is reinforced. However, in DRI the behavior selected for reinforcement is incompatible (Deitz & Repp, 1983). For example, a child whose hitting behaviors have been maintained by positive reinforcement can be taught to clap in order to gain reinforcement. Hitting and clapping are physically incompatible behaviors, so the increase in one may have an automatic effect on the reduction of the other. In addition, because it is a program based on differential reinforcement, it is implied that the hitting behavior will no longer serve to gain attention.

Differential Reinforcement of Low Rates of Behavior

The type of differential reinforcement program most often associated with the reduction of inappropriate behaviors is **Differential Reinforcement of Low Rates of Behavior (DRL)**. DRL programs essentially place a limit on the number of times a behavior can occur within a specified time period in order to gain reinforcement (Dietz, 1977). For example, a child who engages in approximately three talk-outs per minute as a means to gain escape from a group lesson may be placed on a DRL program.

In this particular program, a break (escape) is granted only after a certain number of minutes in which two talk-outs per minute or less occurs. The individual is allowed access to reinforcement, even after the target behavior has occurred, as long as the rate or frequency of the target behavior does not exceed a specified criterion.

The DRL procedure is recommended when the target behavior identified for reduction can be tolerated at low frequency, such as the talking out behavior noted in the above example. DRL would not be an appropriate treatment selection for problem behaviors like aggression or self-injury that present a danger to the child or others.

DRL programs usually establish criteria that are slightly below baseline rates. Once the behavior is reduced, new criteria are established, gradually decreasing the rate of the behavior over time. This approach can be used across full sessions (i.e., an entire group lesson), known as a **full-session DRL**, or across intervals, (i.e., reinforcement delivered at each x-minute interval within the lesson in which the behavior did not exceed the target criterion), known as **interval DRL**.

Another procedure involves **spaced-responding DRL**, where reinforcement occurs after an inter-response time (IRT) of a set limit. For example, reinforcement is delivered if a child can separate his talk-outs by at least 20 seconds, then 30 seconds, then 40, and so on. While this looks much like a DRO (which appears below), it actually reinforces low rates of responding. This is because longer IRTs (the time between responses) inevitably produce lower rates of responding.

Differential Reinforcement of Other Behavior

The final differential reinforcement procedure we will discuss is **Differential Reinforcement of Other Behavior (DRO)**. In a DRO program, we reinforce any behavior(s) that occur during a specified period of time, provided that the target behavior is not one of them (Reynolds, 1961).

Another way to look at this type of program is that reinforcement is provided if the learner does *not* engage in the target behavior. For example, if swearing is targeted for reduction, reinforcement is delivered following a specified period of time in which swearing does not occur. If swearing is the only target behavior, the learner is reinforced if she talks, sleeps, kicks, cries, does her work, etc.

DRO procedures can be effective when addressing a constellation of target behaviors, where it is difficult to address replacement behaviors for each of the targets. In addition, DROs can be relatively easy to explain to the learner. Because it is based on reinforcement, DRO is considered a positive technique, and any intervals in which the target behaviors occur are followed by extinction. Finally, DRO programs can easily be incorporated into token economy systems.

Implementing DRO

When a DRO system is implemented, the starting point is to determine the length of the interval that must pass before reinforcement is delivered. One of the best ways to accomplish this is through careful collection and analysis of frequency data across intervals.

To accomplish this, establish a session length for observation, and divide it into equal intervals (one minute, for example). Then, track the frequency of the behavior during the session. After the observation, total the number of occurrences and divide it by the total session length to determine a per-minute rate. The per-minute rate is then divided by 60 seconds to establish an IRT. If the behavior occurs 60 times in a six-minute session, the rate is 10 per minute. This is used to calculate an IRT of six seconds.

When selecting an interval length to use with DRO, pick one that is slightly below the IRT to stack the odds in favor of the child's success in earning reinforcement. Then gradually begin to increase the interval length as the behavior decreases in rate over time.

One limitation of the DRO procedure is that it does not directly teach an alternate behavior to the child. Because of this, combining DRO with additional teaching or behavior-acquisition programs is highly recommended.

To summarize, reinforcement programs that both increase and decrease behaviors should be at the core of any effective behavior analyst's arsenal of behavior change tools. They lend themselves well to endurance, they are relatively easy to fade into more natural contingencies, and they produce little risk of side effects. They also are easier to tie into the function of the behavior.

Section D – The Use of Extinction to Reduce Problem Behaviors

As discussed in Chapter 6, extinction is the withholding of any consequence that previously served as reinforcement for a member of a functional response class. Extinction renders a behavior ineffective, as shown through the following example:

Carlos has a history of engaging in head slapping as a means of avoiding unfavorable environments like shopping malls. When he is driven near a road that leads to a mall, he frequently head slaps, which causes the driver to drive in a different direction. In this case, the head-slapping behavior has resulted in avoidance of the undesired environment.

A functional analysis has shown that the behavior is definitely maintained by avoidance. Specifically, it showed that the ambient noise of cavernous complexes like shopping malls is aversive to Carlos. The team decides that the most appropriate course of action is a DRA program that teaches Carlos to ask for avoidance of such places. However, his tendency to head slap before anyone can prompt him to ask sets up the potential for bogus reinforcement (in which the prompt is made after the behavior occurs).

Because the head slapping is rather low in intensity (no tissue damage occurs, even superficially), and because Carlos is only three years old, the team decides that they will employ extinction to reduce the head-slapping behavior. Carlos is driven to the mall, and head slapping is ignored. If it occurs, the car continues to turn into the mall and repeatedly approaches it. Should the behavior continue, Carlos is taken into the mall and required to remain there until the slapping stops.

This approach removes both the effectiveness and the efficiency of the behavior. There are certainly other types of programs that could have made it more effective, but extinction alone will have a reductive effect, if given enough time.

Ultimately, the method of extinction used depends on the function of the behavior:

- Extinction for attention-maintained behaviors indicates that attention is withheld (not necessarily removed – more on this later when we discuss time-out).
- Extinction for escape-maintained behaviors involves the prevention of escape from demands or other non-preferred experiences.
- Extinction for preferred item/activity-maintained behaviors includes the withholding of items or activities contingent on behavior.
- Sensory extinction can also be employed, in which sensory consequences of a behavior are somehow blocked, such as visual screening. In addition, foam implements such as helmets or gloves can be used to prevent the sensory consequences of head banging or finger biting – *but only if the FA shows that these behaviors are maintained by their sensory consequences.*

Extinction alone is sometimes a rather slow process, and is frequently accompanied by an extinction burst, in which the behaviors may temporarily increase in intensity, frequency, and duration. To mitigate some of these side effects, extinction programs are usually combined with reinforcement programs and other approaches.

Section E – The Use of Negative Punishment to Reduce Inappropriate Behaviors

Punishment may be a viable intervention option when other methods have been tried and failed. This is usually the case when we cannot gain sufficient control over the environmental variables that maintain behavior. Punishment comes with a plethora of caveats – it has potential risks and side effects, its effects are usually temporary, and it does little to teach a functional replacement. For more information, please refer to the detailed discussion in Chapter 6.

Negative Punishment

The least restrictive or intrusive way to implement punishment is through the use of **negative punishment,** or **Type II punishment**. Negative punishment involves the removal of a positive reinforcer contingent upon the problem behavior – for example, removing a preferred toy when a child hits a peer. In order for negative punishment to be effective, the learner must already have access to the reinforcer.

Specific negative reinforcement programs include **time-out from positive reinforcement**, in which the child's access to reinforcing events or items in the environment is terminated when target behaviors occur (Gast & Nelson, 1977). While there are many variations on this theme, the primary categories are **exclusion time-out** and **nonexclusion time-out**.

Nonexclusion Time-Out

Nonexclusion time-out occurs when a child is allowed continued access to the reinforcing environment, but not the reinforcing activities within the environment. One way in which this is implemented is the **removal of a specific reinforcer**.

An example is a child whose favorite cartoon is turned off for a specified period of time when she hits her brother. She does not have to leave the TV room, but a reinforcer was removed.

Another example can be found in the use of a **time-out ribbon** (Foxx & Shapiro, 1978). In this system, children are given a ribbon signifying that they can access positive reinforcement from the environment (particularly attention). If inappropriate behaviors occur, the ribbon is removed for a specified period of time, signaling to others that reinforcement should not be delivered. Note that this is nonexclusion time-out because the child is able to remain within the reinforcing environment.

Yet another example of nonexclusion time-out is the use of **contingent observation**. When contingent observation is used, the child is removed to another part of the reinforcing environment to see and hear others receive positive reinforcement while her access to that same positive reinforcement is terminated (Porterfield et al., 1976). **Planned ignoring** is the final way to implement nonexclusion time-out. With planned ignoring, the learner is allowed to be a part of the environment, but all attention is withdrawn for a specified period of time (Nelson & Rutherford, 1983).

Exclusion Time-Out

Exclusion time-out occurs when a child is removed from the reinforcing environment (to another room, to the hall, behind a full partition, etc.) for a specified period of time when target behaviors occur. In this situation, positive reinforcers are removed, in addition to the child's access to the environment itself. This type of time-out can prove extremely effective, because it minimizes the risk that other students or individuals in the environment will provide reinforcement that is not desired. It also can provide an element of extinction, because removal from the environment may limit the disruption caused by the inappropriate behavior.

Exclusion time-out does carry with it some special risks, though, including the possibility of bogus reinforcement for escape-maintained behaviors. Additionally, there may be resistance to being placed in an area outside of the reinforcing environment, which can lead to struggle and subsequent risk of physical harm. Finally, this struggle can also actually lead to a very intense level of positive reinforcement for the student seeking attention. Because of these factors, a functional analysis should be considered mandatory prior to implementing these techniques.

Regardless of the time-out method selected, research shows that the most effective length of time-out is no shorter than one minute, and no longer than 15 minutes (Nelson & Rutherford, 1983). Additionally, the effectiveness of time-out depends on the overall reinforcing nature of the conditions from which the child is removed. Therefore, every effort should be made to make sure the environment is rich with reinforcement when behaviors are appropriate.

Response Cost

Negative punishment can also occur in the form of a **response cost**, or removal of a specific amount of a positive reinforcer contingent upon the display of target behaviors (Foxx, 1982). Essentially, response cost is a fine, in that a reinforcer or a designated amount of a reinforcer is taken away, and not given back.

An analogy is a fine for speeding when driving. The ticket issued is a positive punisher that specifies the driver must relinquish a certain amount of money as a result of negative behavior (negative reinforcement/response cost). As a result, the frequency of speeding decreases, but the driver is never refunded the money forfeited for the fine.

Response costs can involve unconditioned reinforcers (food) conditioned reinforcers (items, toys, etc.), or conditioned generalized reinforcers (tokens, money, etc.). Generally, response cost is most effective if the items removed are powerful reinforcers. It is also usually necessary to ensure that a stockpile of reinforcers is available to avoid the "nothing left to lose" phenomena. In this case, all reinforcers have been taken away, so there is no reason for the learner to change his or her behavior. (Of course, there should be a contingency in place that allows the learner to earn reinforcement).

The Use of Positive Punishment

Perhaps the most controversial topic in behavior analysis is the therapeutic use of positive punishment. **Positive punishment**, or **Type I punishment**, involves the presentation of something aversive to the learner. Examples include requiring exercise, introducing pain, introducing restraint, or presenting undesired stimuli (such as disliked sights, sounds, smells, or tastes). Positive punishment tops the hierarchy of restrictive techniques, and is a place where the behavior analyst, teacher, or parent should tread with caution. It can also be one of the most formidable tools for reducing behaviors that have significant consequences, but for which other interventions have been unsuccessful.

Overcorrection

In terms of studied techniques, positive punishment takes several forms. First is the technique known as **overcorrection**, in which the person who misbehaves has to exert effort or exercise that is somehow related to the behavior itself (Foxx & Bechtel, 1983). Overcorrection takes two forms: **restitutional overcorrection** and **positive practice overcorrection**. Restitutional overcorrection requires the learner to restore the environment to a state that is vastly better than its state prior to the behavior. For example, a child who throws paper on the floor is required to pick up and dispose of all paper in every room of the school. The aversive stimulus is the physical effort that the child must expend, and the action is very much related to the target behavior.

Positive practice overcorrection requires that the learner engage repeatedly in the behavior that *should* have occurred. Using the scenario above, the learner would be required to repeatedly walk to the garbage can to throw away paper for a specified period of time.

Contingent Effort

Punishment can also come in the form of **contingent effort**, in which learners are required to exert themselves by performing unrelated exercise contingent upon problem behavior (Luce et al., 1980). In the case of the boy who threw paper on the floor, his teacher would be using contingent effort if she required him to do 100 push ups every time paper was thrown.

Contingent Restraint

With **contingent restraint**, a pre-determined form of physical or mechanical restraint is implemented for a specified period of time when target behaviors are exhibited. Usually, this type of punishment is not considered unless the behavior is one that can impose serious threats to the health and safety of the individual and/or those around him or her (such as severe aggression or self-injurious behaviors).

Application of Painful or Noxious Stimuli

Finally, positive punishment can involve the **application of painful or noxious stimuli**. This category includes corporal (bodily) punishment such as electric shock, spanking, etc. It also includes the introduction of unpleasant substances such as lemon juice, hot sauce, thymol, ammonia smelling salts, water mists, etc. Fortunately, these techniques are found only in highly regulated clinical settings, and are supervised by qualified personnel. If used, they are part of a closely monitored and comprehensive treatment protocol.

Note that these techniques are last-resort interventions that are usually reserved for cases in which the withholding of this type of treatment creates or maintains a significant risk to life and limb.

Hierarchy of Reductive Techniques:

Level I:
Antecedent/MO Manipulation
Differential Reinforcment
- DRO
- DRI
- DRL

Level II:
- Extinction

Level III:
Type II (negative) Punishment
- Time-out
- Response cost
- Removal of Specific Sr+/R+
- Planned ignoring

Level IV:
Type I (positive) Punishment
- Overcorrection
- Contingent effort
- Contingent restraint
- Presentation of noxious stimuli
- Presentation of painful stimuli

Basic Guidelines for Positive Punishment

If a positive punishment program is deemed necessary, there are several basic guidelines for the clinician to keep in mind:

1) The form of punishment selected should be the least restrictive, yet effective.

2) The adults administering the punishing stimulus should experience it themselves before the program is initiated.

3) Data should be recorded and used to determine whether or not the procedure is effective.

4) The clinician should be observant for the side effects of punishment, and for habituation to the aversive stimulus.

5) Punishment should be monitored frequently to ensure the integrity of treatment and to prevent abuse.

Discussion

This chapter is not intended to serve as a comprehensive treatment of reductive techniques, but is an overview only, with specific examples provided when appropriate. Reductive techniques are implemented all the time by parents who spank their children, by teachers who use them effectively and ethically, and by those who are in way over their heads. Because of this cross-section, it is clear that reductive techniques can be botched as easily as they can be implemented effectively. There are many sources of additional information on this topic, including Chapter 6 of this manual. We cannot stress enough that these sources should be studied carefully before proceeding with any implementation of reductive techniques, particularly punishment.

Our advice is to follow the rules we set out at the beginning of the chapter: to make data-based decisions as a team, and to consult professionals when necessary. We also advise that an ethical "safety net" be in place, in the form of written informed consent, human rights committees, and behavioral review boards.

References:

Carr, J.E., Coriaty, S., Wilder, D.A., Gaunt, B.T., Dozier, C.L., Britton, L.N., Avina, C., & Reed, C.L. (2000). A review of "noncontingent" reinforcement as treatment for aberrant behavior of individuals with developmental disabilities. *Research in Developmental Disabilities, 21*, 377-391.

Deitz, D.E.D., & Repp, A.C. (1983). Reducing behavior through reinforcement. *Exceptional Education Quarterly, 3*, 34-46.

Deitz, S.M. (1977). An analysis of programming DRL schedules in educational settings. *Behaviour Research and Therapy, 15*, 103-111.

Dunlap, G. (1984). The influence of task variation and maintenance tasks on the learning and affect of autistic children. *Journal of Experimental Child Psychology, 37*, 41-64.

Dunlap, G., Kern-Dunlap, L., Clarke, S., & Robbins, F.R. (1991). Functional assessment, curricular revision, and severe behavior problems. *Journal of Applied Behavior Analysis, 24*, 387-397.

Foxx, R.M. (1982). *Decreasing behaviors of severely retarded and autistic persons.* Champaign, IL: Research Press.

Foxx, R.M., & Bechtel, D.R. (1983). Overcorrection: A review and analysis. In S. Axelrod & J. Apsche (Eds.), *The effects of punishment on human behavior* (pp. 133-220). New York: Academic Press.

Foxx, R.M., & Shapiro, S.T. (1978). The timeout ribbon: A non-exclusionary timeout procedure. *Journal of Applied Behavior Analysis, 11*, 125-143.

Gast, D.L., & Nelson, C.M. (1977). Timeout in the classroom: Implications for special education. *Exceptional Children, 43*, 461-464.

Green, C.W., Reid, D.H., Rollyson, J.H., & Passante, S.C. (2005). An enriched teaching program for reducing resistance and indices of unhappiness among individuals with profound multiple disabilities. *Journal of Applied Behavior Analysis, 38*, 221-233.

Horner, R.H., Day, H.M., Sprague, J.R., OBrien, M., & Heathfield, L.T. (1991). Interspersed requests: a nonaversive procedure for reducing aggression and self-injury during instruction. *Journal of Applied Behavior Analysis, 24*, 265-278.

Lannie, A.L., & Martens, B.K. (2004). Effects of task difficulty and type of contingency on students' allocation of responding to math worksheets. *Journal of Applied Behavior Analysis, 37*, 53-65.

Luce, S.C., Delquadri, J., & Hall, R.V. (1980). Contingent exercise: A mild but powerful procedure for suppressing inappropriate verbal and aggressive behavior. *Journal of Applied Behavior Analysis, 13*, 583-594.

Mace, F.C., Hock, M.L., Lalli, J.S., West, S., Belfiore, P., Pinter, E., & Brown, D.F. (1988). Behavioral momentum in the treatment of noncompliance. *Journal of Applied Behavior Analysis, 21*, 123-141.

Nelson, C.M., & Rutherford, R.B. (1983). Timeout revisited: Guidelines for its use in Special Education. *Exceptional Education Quarterly, 3*, 56-67.

Pace, G.M., Iwata, B.A., Cowdery, G.E., Andree, P.J., & McIntyre, T. (1993). Stimulus (instructional) fading during extinction of self-injurious escape behavior. *Journal of Applied Behavior Analysis, 26*, 205-212.

Porterfield, J.K., Herbert-Jackson, E., & Risley, T.R. (1976). Contingent observation: An effective and acceptable procedure for reducing disruptive behavior of young children in a group setting. *Journal of Applied Behavior Analysis, 9*, 55-64.

Reynolds, G.S. (1968). Behavioral contrast. *Journal of Experimental Analysis of Behavior, 4*, 57-71.

Winterling, V., Dunlap, G., & ONeill, R. (1987). The influence of task variation on the aberrant behavior of autistic students. *Education and Treatment of Children, 10*, 105-119.

Zarcone, J.R., Iwata, B.A., Smith, R.G., Mazeleski, J.L., & Lerman, D.C. (1994). Reemergence and extinction of self-injurious escape behavior during stimulus (instructional) fading. *Journal of Applied Behavior Analysis, 27*, 307-316.

Chapter 13 Assessment—Your Guide to Effective Decision-Making At a Glance

Chapter Points

- Reinforcer assessment is used to identify meaningful reinforcers for a child. This plays a critical role in the success of any analogue functional analysis and subsequent treatment.

- The Assessment of Basic Language and Learning Skills (ABLLS) is a skills assessment tool based on Skinner's analysis of verbal behavior. It is an assessment, curriculum guide, and an ongoing skills-tracking system that allows for periodic updates.

- Curriculum-Based Assessment (CBA) or Curriculum-Based Measurement (CBM) protocols are assessment procedures that gain their information directly from a student's performance on skills that comprise his or her current instructional program.

- Assessment should be a thorough process that is integrated into instruction and ultimately drives instruction.

Key Terms

Preference Assessments

Personal Nomination

Reinforcer Surveys

Single Stimulus Presentation

Paired-Stimulus Presentation

Multiple Stimulus Preference Assessments

ABLLS

Curriculum-Based Assessment

Curriculum-Based Measurement

Norm-Referenced Tests

Chapter 13

Assessment

Your Guide to Effective Decision-Making

Chapters 10 through 12 were concerned with how to teach young children with autism. The focus of the two remaining chapters is on *what* to teach – and, possibly more importantly, on *what to teach first.*

When a child with autism is first presented to a behavior analyst, a functional assessment interview takes place. During this initial interaction, the behavior analyst probes to discover both deficits and excesses in behavior. A clear picture must be obtained so that he or she can identify behaviors targeted for acquisition, reduction, or eventual elimination.

By way of review, the opening portion of this chapter briefly summarizes the process of functional analysis of problem behavior, as well as the related topic of reinforcer assessment. This is followed by a more extensive discussion of skills assessment instruments used to identify behaviors targeted for improvement or acquisition.

What this chapter will *not* do is present a summary of every type of assessment available for children with autism. There are countless commercially available assessments that measure skill acquisition from a developmental and sensory deficit perspective; however, we have found that children with autism have specific needs that are not addressed by most of them. Further, it has been our experience that very few "off-the-shelf" standardized assessments are sensitive enough to provide information that can be incorporated into daily instructional sessions. Therefore, we are limiting our discussion to assessment methods and instruments we believe help fill the void.

It may also appear that we are presenting a bias toward behavioral assessments, as well as assessment of verbal behavior. To keep this in perspective, it is important to consider the core deficits associated with autism spectrum disorders as defined by the DSM-IV-TR. They include impairments in communication, social interaction, and patterns of behavior.

In the authors' opinions, most communicative issues can be addressed by an assessment of the learner's verbal behavior repertoire, albeit in conjunction with the standardized assessments favored by most speech-language pathologists. In addition, a well-developed assessment of a verbal behavior repertoire can account for many of the skills we typically consider under the "social" domain. Finally, we believe that the field of behavior analysis has offered several viable ways of assessing functions of problem behaviors, as well as reinforcer preference.

A note regarding other types of assessments: reading or math assessments that are appropriate for typical children are also appropriate for children with autism. Also, assessments of physical abilities, such as motor assessments associated with occupational and physical therapy, are not and do not need to be autism-specific. Finally, we are not presenting information on assessment of sensory integration or auditory integration, because there is not yet strong enough research-based evidence to support that these approaches benefit children with autism.

For readers in search of academic or sensory skills assessments, information can be found in the general assessment literature. We recommend Salvia and

Ysseldyke's *Assessment* (tenth edition) for its comprehensive treatment of general considerations and issues, as well as plenty of specific examples of assessments across domains.

Finally, we want to stress that assessment is most powerful when it is viewed as a process, not as a specific activity. There is a tendency for instructors to focus almost single-mindedly on purchased assessments that are conducted on an annual or semi- annual basis. These assessments may be a great starting point, but **the most powerful form of assessment that can be employed is ongoing, day-to-day assessment within the skill programs that are implemented**. This will be part of our later discussion of Curriculum Based Assessment.

Functional Analysis

Following the initial functional assessment interview, a behavior analyst typically conducts some form of baseline data collection to obtain an accurate frequency count of target behavior(s) over a period of time. Baseline data are collected for as long as it takes to establish stability. Once a stable baseline is in hand, the behavior analyst can confidently move ahead and begin planning and eventually implementing the analogue functional analysis.

Note: obtaining stable baseline data can sometimes be problematic in non-clinical settings, such as private homes and classrooms. Often, this variability is due to inconsistent observation and documentation on the part of parents, caregivers, or school personnel. Close monitoring and enhanced training provided by a behavior analyst can often rectify this problem over the course of a brief, one- or two-week baseline phase.

During the planning stages of analogue functional analysis, the behavior analyst uses information obtained from the initial interview to identify potential reinforcers that might be controlled and manipulated during experimental analysis. Favorite tangibles, such as food items or toys, can be removed for several days prior to the functional analysis session. This will increase the motivational operation for those items, as well as the possibility of a successful "tangible" analogue. In the same way, caregivers can refrain from engaging the child in preferred social activities such as tickling, rough play, singing, or dancing prior to the session, increasing the MO for social attention. Additionally, non-preferred tasks or activities that were identified in the interview process can be selected for use during the "demand" condition.

Following completion of the analogues, the behavior analyst will typically have a clear indication as to the function of the child's problem behavior. Development of an effective deceleration plan based on this experimentally derived function can then take place.

Section A – Reinforcer Assessment

Remember that the success of any experimental manipulation of behavior is based first on identifying meaningful reinforcement for the child. For this reason, we spend a good deal of time and effort before and during analogue functional analysis identifying potent reinforcers. This allows us to set up and test the greatest number of reinforcing contingencies to get the clearest results.

When going through this process, it is best not to rely solely on the opinions of parents or caregivers. The information they provide is often second-hand and subjective in nature, which can lead to reinforcer misidentification.

Preference Assessments

Over the past 35 years, considerable applied research has been conducted on **preference assessments**.

Preference assessments are helpful at the onset of instructional sessions, because what is reinforcing at one time may not necessarily be reinforcing at another time.[1] Additionally, a preference assessment should be conducted prior to any type of intervention that is based on reinforcement.

These assessments can be as simple as arranging the environment so that many potential reinforcers are available, and observing the child's interaction with each. A variety of other, more specific methods have been developed and tested, including *personal nomination* (Clements & McKee, 1968; Daley, 1969); *reinforcer surveys* (Fox & DeShaw, 1993; Rotatori et al., 1979); *single-stimulus* (SS) *presentation* (Green et al., 1988; Pace et al., 1985); *paired-stimulus* (PS) *presentation* (Dattilo, 1986; Fisher et al., 1992); and *multiple-stimulus* (MS) *preference assessments* (DeLeon & Iwata, 1996; Windsor, Piche, & Locke, 1994). Each of these is briefly discussed below.

Personal nomination involves directly questioning a child to ascertain his or her preferences. An example of this would be to ask, "What do you like?" in a general sense. To gain more detailed information regarding the child's pool of potent reinforcers, more specific questions, like, "Do you like M&M's?" or "Do you like tickles?" can be employed

Clearly, the greatest drawback of this method has to do with the population we are treating. The typical three-year-old child with autism may not be able to accurately answer such questions, which severely limits our ability to identify meaningful reinforcing stimuli.

Reinforcer surveys are indirect methods in which a caregiver or other adult who is well acquainted with the child completes a written survey designed to identify the child's most potent reinforcers. The survey gives the respondent a variety of example reinforcers that can be rated and later prioritized into a preference hierarchy for the child.

As with most indirect methods of assessment, the reinforcer survey is limited in its ability to empirically test respondent predictions. Subjectivity, opinion, and intuition tend to guide the completion of the reinforcer survey, and, as such, leave it wanting.

Unlike personal nomination and reinforcer surveys, the remaining three tools are considered direct methods, because they involve the systematic presentation of potentially reinforcing stimuli to the child.

With the **single-stimulus (SS) presentation** method, the child is presented with one potentially reinforcing stimulus at a time. The assessor records whether the child approaches/interacts with individual items, as well as the duration of each interaction. Comparisons are then made between the child's interactions with a wide variety of stimuli that were each singly presented. Preference is determined based on the length of the time spent with each item – the longer the interaction, the higher the preference.

While this method is superior to indirect assessment tools, it does have limitations with some children who tend to approach and interact with just about anything that

---

[1] See our discussion of motivational operations for a better explanation of why certain stimuli may be reinforcing at times and not reinforcing at other times.

is placed in front of them. The SS presentation method does not provide the assessor with the opportunity to observe the child making a choice between stimuli.

Paired-stimulus presentation resolves the choice-making limitations of the single-presentation method. In this approach, the child is presented with randomly paired stimuli from which to choose. This enables the assessor to rate the preference of each stimulus as it is compared with all other stimuli in the assessment.

These paired methods have also been criticized, however, because the presentation of a wide variety of stimuli in randomized pairs can take considerable time. This makes the entire assessment process logistically impractical in some settings.

Finally, **multiple-stimulus (MS) preference assessments** provide the scientific rigor of paired-stimulus presentations with a far more streamlined procedure. Rather than presenting potentially reinforcing stimuli either singly or in randomized pairs, the MS method presents large arrays of stimuli simultaneously to the child.

Repeated exposures to the same array, with the physical arrangement of the stimuli rotated to control for position preference, are conducted in brief, five-minute sessions. In order to remove any observer effect, the MS approach can also be accomplished in a *free operant* manner by allowing the child to approach the array alone, with the assessor located in an observation room using a one-way mirror or video recording equipment. And because the sessions are only five minutes in duration, the entire process can be completed within an hour.

In summary, we believe that, at the very least, some type of systematic manipulation and data collection should be involved when assessing preferences for children who are typically difficult to reinforce.

It is also important to note that the field has not yet developed a valid way to assess preference for activities and items that cannot be physically presented during the assessment.

Section B – Skills Assessment

As we've discussed, children with autism typically are deficient in behavioral repertoires related to language, cognition, and social skills. When addressing behaviors that may be lacking or in need of improvement, the behavior analyst must enlist the help of a systematic, organized means of assessing the child's present skill level.

While a myriad of instruments exist for evaluating language, cognitive, and social skills, one very popular assessment tool designed by behavior analysts provides an excellent starting point.

Assessment of Basic Language and Learning Skills (ABLLS)

Developed by James Partington and Mark Sundberg, the **Assessment of Basic Language and Learning Skills (ABLLS)** is unique, primarily because it is based on B.F. Skinner's analysis of verbal behavior.

As a quick review, Skinner's analysis viewed language as behavior, and in doing so, functionally analyzed how humans use language differently given different environmental contexts. This led Skinner to develop different types of expressive language, such as mands, tacts, and intraverbals. Utilizing this unique view of language can often yield a finer analysis of a child's deficits than standard language assessments, which consider many of these verbal operants merely as expressive language.

The ABLLS is designed as an ongoing skills-tracking system that allows for periodic reviews and updates. The initial assessment is usually conducted informally over a period of a few weeks (an abbreviated version that can be completed in a few hours is also available). Scores are tracked on a graphic system of grids that provides a visual analysis of the child's skill profile. Deficits are clearly identifiable on the graphic display, and updates allow for a visual tracking of the child's progress over time as intervention programs are implemented.

According to Partington and Sundberg, the ABLLS is an assessment, curriculum guide, and skills-tracking system for children with language delays (Partington & Sundberg, 1998, p.1). It is divided into 25 domains that assess four general categories of skills. The first category includes basic learner skills and is concerned primarily with language, social, play, and classroom behavior. It is within this category that a child's functional use of Skinner's verbal operants (mand, echoic, tact, receptive, and intraverbal) is evaluated.

The remaining three categories of skill assessment include:

- Academic skills (reading, math, writing, and spelling)
- Self-help skills (dressing, eating, grooming, and toileting)
- Motor skills (gross motor and fine motor)

The ABLLS is designed to take into account the motivational conditions (MOs) that are in effect when a child demonstrates a particular behavior. It assesses skills in both naturally occurring and contrived motivational situations, which creates a better picture of a child's performance across a variety of motivational contexts.

In addition, the ABLLS addresses the tendency for children with autism to display learning difficulties when presented with stimuli in a variety of sensory modalities (auditory versus visual). Task items are designed to evaluate the child's response when instructional stimuli are presented in solely auditory or visual modes, as well as in complex combinations of auditory and visual stimuli that more realistically portray how language is perceived in natural settings.

Generalization and spontaneity of language are also evaluated throughout the ABLLS, with complete sections of Basic Learner Skills devoted to *spontaneous vocalizations* and *generalized responding*. Assessment of generalization is built into each domain, including how skills are described relative to when they are displayed, with whom they are displayed, where they are displayed, and with what materials they are displayed. Spontaneity of language skills is also assessed for each of the specific verbal operants.

Because children with autism typically have the greatest deficits in language, cognition,[2] and social skills, most of the focus of our ABLLS discussion is on the first category of Basic Learner Skills. Deficits in these rudimentary areas seriously hinder any child's progress in academic, self-help, and motor skill acquisition. In fact, the prerequisite nature of these basic learning skills led Partington and Sundberg to describe them as "critical skills that are in need of intervention in order for a child

[2] Cognitive impairments are not a core impairment, but rather a co-occurring condition in the majority of children with autism.

to become more capable of learning from his everyday experiences" (Partington & Sundberg, 1998, p. 2).

Scoring the ABLLS

The ABLLS is designed simply as a task analysis instrument, with the complex behaviors that comprise human language and social interaction broken down into measurable steps that can be easily evaluated in a systematic manner.

Its user-friendly nature allows it to be completed by parents, teachers, behavior analysts, psychologists, speech and language therapists, or other professionals. The information gathered typically comes from three sources:

- Parents, teachers, or others who are well acquainted with the child, and who can offer information about specific task items to their best recollection.
- Direct observation of the child in particular situations, which yields information pertaining to specific task items.
- Direct, formal presentation of task items, which provides specific performance information.

The ABLLS scoring system is consistent across all domains. The following section presents some instructions and example graphics regarding scoring. However, these instructions will make the most sense if the reader reviews them alongside an actual ABLLS, so that the examples are viewed within the context of the assessment.

Each task item is presented as a row on a table that includes:

- A task number
- A range of scores
- Task name
- Task objective
- A question to ask about the child's skill
- Examples of responses
- Scoring criteria
- A notes section

The **task number** is a code that is always comprised of a capital letter and a number. The letter corresponds to the domain (e.g., Cooperation and Reinforcement Effectiveness is domain "A," Visual Performance is domain "B," etc.), while the number indicates where the particular task item falls within the task analysis of the domain. For example, "A1" refers to the first skill in the Cooperation and Reinforcement Effectiveness domain, while "A10" refers to the tenth skill in the same domain.

The scoring column for each of the task items involves four rows of numbers. The numbers in the "Score" column correspond with the possible scores in the "Criteria" column, which range from zero to the highest score (either 1, 2, or 4). A score of zero indicates that the child does not meet the lowest criterion specified for that task item as defined in the "Criteria" column. The number on the far right of the "Score" column represents the highest score possible for that task item.

Depending on the task, the scoring column will have four rows with the numbers 0 1; 0 1 2; or 0 1 2 3 4. The top row of scores for each item represents the initial assessment scores while the remaining three rows are reserved for updates of the ABLLS. The following is a depiction of the scoring column for a four-criteria task:

Task	Score	
A1	0 1 2 ③ 4	← Initial scoring
	0 1 2 3 4	← 1st update
	0 1 2 3 4	← 2nd update
	0 1 2 3 4	← 3rd update

The ABLLS is scored by reviewing and assigning a number for each task item within each domain. The score is assigned by circling the number that best represents the child's skill level at the time of the assessment.

Tasks that the child is unable to do, or for which the child is unable to meet the lowest criterion (score of 1), should be scored "zero." Also, if the child's deficits are so severe that they prevent him or her from participating in particular levels of activity (e.g., group instruction), a score of "zero" should also be given.

The information used to determine the score for a task item should come from one of the three sources described earlier. If the information is derived from parents or caregivers, care should be exercised to ensure that the respondent is very familiar with the child. Guessing should be avoided at all costs. If the parent or caregiver is unsure of the child's skill level, arrangements should be made to either observe performance of the skill in the natural environment or in a contrived, instructional situation.

Follow instructions to select one of two common objects. Upon request, the student will be able to select an object named by the instructor from an array of two common objects held or placed in any position in front of him. Can the student select a specified object from a selection of two common objects?

When a cup and a shoe are held in front of the student, the student will select "shoe" upon request.

It is also important for ABLLS respondents to consider the child's skill level *at the time of the assessment.* An emerging skill, or a skill that has been observed in the past (but is not presently being reliably demonstrated in the child's natural environment) should not be rated as meeting the criterion for mastery.

Sundberg and Partington suggest that generally, "It is better to underestimate a child's skill levels than to overestimate the level of performance because scores which do not meet the highest criterion level will be more likely to be reviewed for consideration of intervention" (Partington & Sundberg, 1998, p. 9).

Failure to intervene on these relative deficits can cause them to remain as weak spots in the child's language repertoire, and can cause problems in the future when more complex skills are being taught.

The following is an example of one task item from the ABLLS:

Task	Score	Task Name	Task Objective	Question	Examples	Criteria	Notes
C14	0 1 2 3 4 0 1 2 3 4 0 1 2 3 4 0 1 2 3 4	Follow instructions to select one of two common objects.	Upon request, the student will be able to select an object named by the instructor from an array of two common objects held or placed in any position in front of him.	Can the student select a specified object from a selection of two common objects?	When a cup and a shoe are held in front of the student, the student will select "shoe" upon request.	4 = receptively identifies 50 or more objects and can identify several different examples of most of those objects, 3 = identifies at least one example of 25 objects, 2 = 10 objects, 1 = identifies at least 2 objects	See Appendix 2: Receptive and Label List

In the preceding example, the assessor first asks the respondent if the child is capable of selecting a common item when requested from a field of two common items. If the respondent is confident that the child can make the selections unprompted, the assessor must determine the extent (quantitatively) to which the child can make them. If, in this manner, the child can select for 50 or more common objects, he or she receives a score of 4 (assessor circles 4). If the child's receptive selection is limited to less than 50 objects but more than 24, a 3 is circled. A score of 2 is earned if the child can select between 10 and 24 objects, and a score of 1 is earned if between 2 and 10 objects can be selected.

Skills Tracking System

Once the scores for the initial assessment have been completed, they are transferred to the graphic display located near the front of the ABLLS booklet.

The boxes on the grid are filled in to correspond to the score received for each task item. A colored pencil or marker is preferred, so that successive updates can be graphed in different colors to provide a clear visual representation of the child's progress. Scores of zero for any task item are left blank.

The examples to the right depict the transfer from ABLLS scores to the Skills Tracking System:

L1	0 1 2 3 ④ 0 1 2 3 4 0 1 2 3 4 0 1 2 3 4
L2	0 ① 2 0 1 2 0 1 2 0 1 2
L3	⓪ 1 2 0 1 2 0 1 2 0 1 2

Sample ABLLS Scores

L3 ○
L2 ○
L1 ○

Corresponding filled-in grids on the Skills Tracking System

Note: the small circle to the left of the task number on the grid should be filled in for any task item scored zero. This will indicate that the entry was scored zero, and not merely missed in the assessment process.

Developing Goals from the ABLLS

Once the ABLLS has been completed and the Skills Tracking System has been filled in, a visual inspection of the child's skills within and across domains will help prioritize needs. In most cases, skills are arranged in a prerequisite hierarchy from bottom to top on the Skills Tracking grids. By moving from the bottom to the top of the grid, one can easily identify target skills in the order they should be addressed, and can devise intervention programs to teach each target skill.

The Basic Learner Skills that encompass the first 15 domains of the ABLLS are fundamental to developing a child's skill as a learner. For this reason, we will briefly examine several of these domains, and will also discuss the child with autism's typical deficits and programmatic needs in these areas. By describing the domains in general terms, the reader can see the types of skills that should be assessed when developing programming for a child with autism.

While the ABLLS is first and foremost an assessment tool, it also serves double-duty as a tool that drives curriculum. So, while much of this discussion can also be applied to curriculum development (which is covered in Chapter 14), we include it here so that the reader will understand the integral link between the two processes. Assessment and curriculum development exist in a symbiotic relationship, in that they are dependent upon one another. While we present the skill domains here, specific details of the skill-building programs associated with them are presented at greater length in the next chapter.

Cooperation and Reinforcer Effectiveness

Our children usually come to us with very little experience sitting still and tolerating long periods of instruction. As a result, we spend a good portion of our initial interaction with them establishing ourselves as secondary reinforcers, so that compliance and cooperation are not such hard-won objectives. Making the work area and time spent with the therapist seem like "fun" to the child and engineering the work environment to successfully compete with existing reinforcement in the home or classroom are critical first steps in this process.

Visual Performance

We have found that skills requiring visual discrimination such as matching, sorting, or block imitation generally come quite easily to most of our children with autism. Even so, we do not neglect this domain during early programming. Visual performance tasks can provide a respite from the remainder of a child's curriculum, which might be heavily weighted with receptive and expressive language tasks. Moreover, we can build on the child's strengths and bring more complex visual skills under instructional control.

Receptive Language

Receptive language, which relies heavily on the ability to attend and respond to auditory stimuli, is generally one of the more difficult areas for children with autism. Receptive language is also a pivotal skill that governs how a child will progress with more complex instruction, because most conventional teaching of more advanced skills relies on verbal direction as the primary means of guiding the student.

In this domain, we begin by teaching both receptive labels (selecting an object based on a verbal request to do so) and receptive commands (performing an action based on a verbal request to do so). Quite often, it is necessary to build from motor imitation skills that must be taught first (see next domain).

Motor Imitation

As discussed in Chapter 7 on stimulus control, a child's ability to imitate is a necessary prerequisite for the use of modeling prompts to teach new skills. Our children are usually started out on an Action/Object Imitation drill that teaches them to imitate simple actions with common objects. This activity is usually successful due to the presence of the objects, which eventually serve as visual prompts for the action. From Action/Object Imitation, we typically move to Nonverbal Imitation (imitating motor movements without objects) and Oral Motor Imitation (imitating mouth movements and eventually pairing them with sounds).

Vocal Imitation

The natural progression from motor imitation to oral motor imitation leads to language programs designed to teach echoic responding. In the same way that motor imitation skills are prerequisites to using modeling prompts for future instruction, vocal imitation skills are required if we are to use echoic prompts to teach a child to "say" more complex intraverbal and tact responses.

Mands

One of the most powerful methods of teaching early language is to tie the child's responding to a strong MO by teaching mands. Teaching mands as functionally equivalent behavior can also significantly reduce reliance on a repertoire of aggressive, self-injurious, or tantrum behavior.

Tacts

A tact program is often enhanced by an existing echoic and receptive repertoire. For this reason, combining the development of echoic response with early receptive language skills can result in a solid tact repertoire. However, because many of our children embrace tacts, care must be exercised early on to move these beyond the scope of the "walking dictionary" and into functional conversational use.

Intraverbals

How a child responds to our language with his or her own is often difficult to establish without correct preparation. Instructional control, however, can be transferred relatively easily from established receptive language and tact responses to simple fill-in-the-blank intraverbal responses.

These early conversational building blocks are critical for our children, and shouldn't be neglected or passed over too quickly. A firm foundation of fill-ins will make future work on more complex reciprocal conversation much easier for the child.

Other Domains

Programs in the remaining Basic Learner Skills domains address syntax and grammar, play/leisure skills, social interaction skills, group instruction, classroom routines, spontaneous vocalizations, and generalized responding. These programs are developed as needed once the basics of cooperation and the rudimentary verbal operants are under way.

Skills Assessment Beyond the ABLLS

It is the authors' strong opinion that the most useful out-of-the-box assessment tool for anyone working with young children with autism is the ABLLS. This is also true for older children with limited communication skills who are not considered to be at the highest end of the autism spectrum. In terms of tracking vital skills for success in social and learning environments for this population, the ABLLS is second to none.

However, as useful it may be, the ABLLS cannot be the only approach to skills assessment for children with autism. Effective instruction is characterized by, in addition to other things, a process of *ongoing* assessment, strategizing, and modification. Once the ABLLS has identified a starting point for skills that must be taught, instruction can commence. However, as an assessment tool, the ABLLS is not utilized more often than every six months, and usually only once a year. In the interim, there must be a way to gauge how well or efficiently our children are moving along in their instruction. This is where ongoing systems of assessment come into play.

Instructional decision-making allows the instructor to determine the answers to the following questions:

- Am I teaching the right things?
- Am I teaching these things well within the current program?
- Does the student know what I have been trying to teach?
- How well does the student know what I have been trying to teach?
- Should I make a change in the way I present instruction?
- If so, what kind of change should I make?
- Was my change effective?

Ultimately, data must be collected that will allow us to answer these questions with precision, efficiency, and confidence.

Section C – Social Skills Assessment

One of the core deficits associated with autism spectrum disorders is impairment in social interaction. Despite this, many behaviorally based programs don't address social skills well enough. One of the reasons for this could be that there is not a great selection of practical and sound assessment tools available in this area. There are certainly many assessments that are targeted toward social skills, but few actually focus on observable, measurable behaviors that are associated with social interaction. We have found one such assessment tool that we would like to share with you.

The tool is called "The Social Skills Checklist," developed by Janis Krempa and Kelly McKinnon (Krempa & McKinnon, 2005). As part of their book, *Social Skills Solutions*, it is developed not as a standardized assessment, but as a criterion-referenced assessment that presents a series of skills that its developers feel are important steps in the development of adequate social skills. The tasks are written behaviorally, and the person completing the assessment must determine whether or not the child being assessed demonstrates the listed behavior. The assessment is broken into three levels of 10 "modules," each of which addresses a different area of social functioning.

Modules in Level 1 are as follows:

- **Module 1:** Joint Attention/ Attending
- **Module 2:** Greetings
- **Module 3:** Social Play
- **Module 4:** Self-Awareness
- **Module 5:** Conversations
- **Module 6:** Perspective Taking
- **Module 7:** Critical Thinking Skills
- **Module 8:** Advanced Language
- **Module 9:** Developing Friendships
- **Module 10:** Community/Home Life

Each module then lists several component skills. For example, Module 1 ("Joint Attention/Attending") includes items such as "follows eye gaze, point or gesture by others," and "turns and orients toward person when making requests." Module 6 addresses perspective taking, and includes items such as "labels/imitates emotions in pictures" and "looks for/find hidden objects and hides them."

As stated, the assessment is divided into three levels. Skills become more complex as the levels increase, and the names of some of the modules change from one level to the next. Regardless of level, each behavior is assessed in three contexts: 1:1 interaction/instruction, within a group, and in natural settings. This incorporates the idea of skill generalization, and allows those who develop skill programming to know the contexts in which the greatest effort should be focused. For example, if a student is able to ask for things using pronouns when working with his individual instructor, but not able to use pronouns in a natural setting (such as on the playground), then pronoun use is clearly not mastered.

Much like the ABLLS, The Social Skills Checklist seems to be of greatest value when used as a curriculum-driving tool. It is not scientifically developed, nor is it standardized, and therefore it cannot be used beyond the purposes of describing the existence or nonexistence of certain skills within a learner's repertoire. But by telling us whether or not these very important skills are intact, it gives us a direction for programming. We do not have to waste valuable time presenting instruction in contexts where skills are already being performed, and we can instead shift our focus to skills and environments that really need our attention.

Section D – Curriculum-Based Assessment

Once instruction has begun, the objective is to establish procedures that monitor a child's progress within his or her curriculum. This is best accomplished through the use of **curriculum-based assessment** protocols **(CBA)**, or **curriculum-based measurement (CBM)** protocols, which can be applied regardless of the child's skill ability, the nature of instruction, or the location of the instructional environment. While these are not necessarily interchangeable terms, CBA and CBM do share a defining feature: both assessment procedures gain their information directly from the student's performance on skills that comprise his or her current instructional program.

They differ in that CBA implies that the data collected will also help suggest specific interventions. On the other hand, CBM identifies the need for and effectiveness of interventions (Marston & Magnusson, 1988), but does not suggest any specific course of action.

Basically, curriculum-based means of assessment are any types of methods that aim to collect information on the learner's performance on skills that are part of curricular programming that is already in place. This can be as simple as a math test to assess student performance on current concepts, or a timed reading passage to determine whether or not the learner is decoding the material being presented in reading class. It can also be an oral demonstration of skills. There are as many ways to accomplish these assessments as there are to present instruction. How the actual procedures look depend on the type of skill being assessed, the methodology used to teach it, and the curricular materials themselves. Curriculum-based methods provide the instructor with objective data that will drive instructional decision-making.

Take, for example, the skill of labeling items from an array. An assessment such as the ABLLS can show us that a child is extremely limited in his or her ability to label objects. Because of this, we know that we should begin instruction in this area. However, the ABLLS will not help us determine whether or not we are going about this instruction in the right way. To make this determination, we utilize a form of CBA.

In this particular example, we can develop a measurement system that assesses accuracy alone (i.e., percentage correct vs. percentage incorrect), or one that addresses fluency (accuracy and speed). Given what we know about fluency and its ramifications on skill retention, endurance, application, performance, and stability, the authors lean toward CBM methods that measure fluency whenever possible.

In this case, a fluency assessment involves using materials in the presentation of instruction and conducting timings of 30 or 60 seconds, in which the child performs the targeted skill. Correct and incorrect responses are recorded during the timings. Afterward, the number of correct and incorrect responses are totaled and converted into a per-minute rate, and the resulting data are then graphed and compared to a frequency aim.

The frequency aim is essentially a performance standard to which the student's response frequency is compared. This comparison allows us to know whether or not progress is being made within the program, and at what rate. Frequency aims can be completely individualized, based upon the learning and performance characteristics displayed by the learner, or they can be based in some way on the average performance of a group of learners who also completed the task.

Curriculum-Based Assessment/ Curriculum-Based Measurement

- Assessment is conducted using materials and tasks from the students' instructional program
- Can be fluency-based
- Can be accuracy-based
- Can compare student to past performance
- Can compare student to performance of others
- CBM determines if intervention is necessary/effective
- CBA does the same, but also helps determine what intervention is necessary

This type of approach can be applied to a great many skills or target behaviors. There are times, however, when accuracy alone will suffice as a measure of performance. In these cases (such as when the goal is compliant responding over development of new skills, or accurate production of targeted speech sounds), cold probes can be conducted in which responses to a set number of trials are recorded and then graphed according to percentage correct. Similar to fluency data, these data are graphed and compared to both baseline and aims. Student progress toward the aim, or lack thereof, is an indicator of the effectiveness of the way in which the skill is being taught.

A Behavioral Model for Making Instructional Decisions

Progress measurements or assessments are only useful if they serve a purpose. For this reason, any curriculum-based assessment or measurement system must include a framework for using the information to drive decision-making.

Going back to the example of teaching multiple labels from an array, suppose that a fluency probe has been selected as the preferred assessment protocol. The daily fluency assessment is producing data that show no progress on the part of the learner. The assessment has done the first part of its job – it has identified the need for intervention or a change in intervention strategy. However, in order to be effective, this information must be used to determine the next step.

At this point, we would like to propose a model for instructional decision-making that takes into account the behavioral perspective. Antecedent conditions (conditions present *before* a behavior occurs), the behavior itself, and consequences to the behavior all play large roles in the establishment of new behavioral repertoires. Therefore, any attempt to deliver effective instruction should address all three.

The logical first step is to define the target behavior or skill itself, and it is important to do this with precision (a topic that will be addressed yet again in the following chapter). If our assessment data are showing no improvement, we can look to this component (the "B" – behavior) of the A-B-C sequence as a focal point of strategy change. Have we clearly defined the behavior or skill in question? If not, this could account for the poor assessment results. If one assessor has a set of criteria for correct or incorrect responding that differs from another's, the data will be skewed.

Another way in which the behavior itself can play a role in decision-making is by changing the nature of the response requirement to hasten success. Referring back to the concept of successive approximations, shaping a response with a lower response requirement can allow us to reach our terminal goal with greater efficiency. In other words, the target skill may be too difficult, and an intermediate step or steps may need to be acquired first.

In the same way, we may find that the behavior we are assessing is inappropriate given the student's mastery of prerequisite skills. In this case, we may change the target behavior and resulting program of instruction entirely to teach skills that are necessary prerequisites.

Decision-making should also take into account the antecedents to behavior. These are stimuli that are present prior to the exhibition of the behavior. In the case of skill instruction, antecedent stimuli can include the verbal S^D, the instructional materials used, the manner in which these materials are presented, or the ambient conditions of the environment itself.

Interventions based on the antecedent to skill performance can include changing the materials used, altering the pace at which instruction is provided, providing stimulus or redundancy prompts, or changing the location in which instruction is provided, to name but a few.

Finally, the consequences that follow a behavior play the largest role in determining whether the future frequency of that or similar behaviors will increase or decrease. Because of this, our strategy for making instructional decisions should also include options for making changes in the delivery of consequences to behavior.

In the case of skill instruction, consequences include error correction procedures, delivery of reinforcement, punishment, extinction, and consequence-based prompts. There are a number of possibilities for changing our approach based on the consequences we provide within instruction.

An example of a practical document that helps take into account each of these factors is the "Program Change Form" in Figure 13.1. This form is based largely on a similar form developed by Vincent J. Carbone, Ed.D., of the Carbone Clinic in Valley Cottage, New York.

Norm-Referenced Tests

An adequate approach to assessing a child with autism is multi-faceted. The ABLLS is the first assessment of its kind that provides its level of detail and curriculum-driving guidance for the practitioner or parent. However, as comprehensive as it may be, its results are completely individualized. Similarly, curriculum-based methods of assessment and measurement tend to focus on an individual's contact with particular curricular content. This is not a bad thing – if there is one consistent theme throughout this manual, it is that an individualized approach is the best way to solve any behavioral or educational problem.

In the field of education, however, there is a strong tendency for schools and professionals to provide some measures that compare student performance to standardized reference points. In the case of curriculum-based assessment, it is possible to make comparisons to a normative group, such as the performance of

Program Change Form

Learner:______________________ Skill program: ______________________

______________________ Date:______________________

Staff completing form: ______________________

Complete this form when the learner has (check one):

☐ Not achieved his or her fluency/accuracy aim after six consecutive data points

☐ Achieved or surpassed fluency/accuracy aim for three consecutive data points

Check the change that will be implemented. Draw a phase line and indicate change on performance graph.

Area One: Changes in stimulus presentation

	✓
Review S^D - it is appropriate and all staff are consistent in presentation. If not, achieve consensus and train. Change: ______	
Provide or alter stimulus prompting (inflection, visuals, proximity, position, etc.). Change: ______	
Alter instructional pace. Circle: increase reduce	
Alter field size. Circle: increase reduce	
Alter ratio of target to mastered items. Change: ______	
Alter materials. Change: ______	

Area Two: Changes in consequence delivery

Provide or alter response prompting (physical, gestural, modeling, etc.). Change: ______	
Alter reinforcement schedule. Change: ______	
Alter reinforcement type. Change: ______	
Check for true differentiation of reinforcement. Remediate if necessary.	
Error correction has become lax for skills that have been demonstrated independently. Tighten up procedures.	
Provide errorless instruction (continuous prompting) until skill is stronger.	

Area Three: General considerations

Skill is not attainable until prerequisites are taught. Change: ______	
Instructional control is not established. (Pairing issue, mand training, etc.) Change: ______	
Aim is too high or too low. Change: ______	
Circle: Remove program Introduce new set or S^D Move program to maintenance Change: ______	
Other:	

Fluency aim not met, but progress is being made. No changes necessary at this time.	

Adapted from the work of Vincent Carbone, Ed.D., BCBA

Figure 13.1

other students in a classroom, to establish frequency aims. However, these norms are not usually standardized.

Most educational systems solve this by relying on norm-referenced tests to provide part of the assessment picture. In a **norm-referenced test**, student performance is translated into a series of scores via statistical analysis, and then compared with others who also took the test.

Norm-referenced tests are controversial because they are usually written so that a small group of students does very poorly and a small group of students does very well. Consequently, most learners taking the test achieve an average score, and the resulting graphic display of performance data of the norm group creates a "bell curve."

Examples of these kinds of achievement tests include the California Achievement Test (CAT); Comprehensive Test of Basic Skills (CTBS), which includes the "Terra Nova"; Iowa Test of Basic Skills (ITBS) and Tests of Academic Proficiency (TAP); Metropolitan Achievement Test (MAT); and the Stanford Achievement Test. Tests developed in the same manner are also used within the assessment protocols of speech-language pathologists (such as the Peabody Picture Vocabulary Test – R), school psychologists (a myriad of "IQ" tests), and physical/occupational therapists.

In a norm-referenced test, scores are usually reported in terms of percentile ranks, by which one student's score is compared to those of the norm group. The norm group is selected to represent all of the people taking the test – so the test-maker's scoring system estimates how well the learner performed in comparison to all of the students who took the test. For example, a percentile rank of 67 on a norm-reference test indicates (estimates) that the student performed better than 67 percent of similar students who took the same test.

Some people find numerous problems with these kinds of assessment devices – many of which are valid. (A quick web search on the topic will produce a great amount of further reading.) Because of these concerns, most publishers of norm-referenced tests are quick to point out explicitly that these measures should not be used alone to make educational decisions. This seems to fly in the face of current policy-driven trends in education, where schools are held accountable for meeting standards based on norm-referenced testing alone.

Regardless of the controversy, these tools can be an important part of any assessment package, because they tell us how our work on isolated skills translates into improvement in skill development as compared to peers.

This can be especially valuable for people new to designing and managing instructional programs for children with autism, who often spend a great deal of time and effort teaching isolated skills that never translate into functional repertoires. Isolation of component skills is an absolute necessity, but progress within these skill domains is sometimes misleading. Improvement in scores on norm-referenced measures will likely not be seen if instruction is not geared toward generalization, if variations in stimulus conditions are not introduced appropriately, and if ongoing curriculum-based assessment is not well conceived or thorough.

Creating a Complete Assessment Package

A final consideration that should be addressed is the need to seek out assessment information from providers of related services. As we know, autism is often accompanied by issues with motor planning and development, speech production, and cognitive deficits. Calling upon professionals who have the specialized expertise to assess performance in all of these areas is necessary for a complete assessment package.

Procedures that they follow are likely to be similar to one or many of the procedures we have discussed, including observational, curriculum-based, and norm-referenced methods. However, these professionals have received a great deal of training to develop a keen eye for problems within their areas of expertise, and the information they provide can enhance an instructional program. Always remember, though, that everything we do is behavior, and that behavior is subject to influence by our contact with the environment. Try to filter assessment information through this premise to use it in the soundest way possible.

In Summary

Before moving on to curriculum development, we must summarize some key considerations that pertain to assessment.

First, assessment is a process that is integrated into instruction. It has ramifications that will determine what skills to teach, how to teach them, and how to plan for changes in strategy when necessary. Assessment should never end, for it allows us to make the right decisions when it is time to take the next step, and there is *always* a next step.

Second, assessment should be thorough, and it should take advantage of the many resources that are available. Children with autism have an extraordinary amount of instructional needs, so no one assessment or method of assessment will fit the bill. In this and previous chapters, we have presented ways of assessing reinforcer preference and skill performance, as well as problem behaviors and their functions. Our ability to perform precise assessments in all of these areas will undoubtedly have a significant impact on the efficiency of interventions. In short, assessment that is done well prevents us from wasting our children's time.

Third, and most importantly, assessment alone is almost useless. It only serves a functional purpose if it provides information we can use to drive the instructional process.

In the case of functional assessment, our behavioral interventions are tailored around assessment results. Assessment of skill performance should serve the same purpose. The only reason we want to know how well a learner is doing within a particular skill domain is to determine what, if any, changes need to be made to our instructional strategy.

References:

Clements, C., & McKee, J. (1968). Programmed instruction for institutionalized offenders: Contingency management and performance contracts. *Psychological Reports*, *22*, 957-964.

Daley, M.F. (1969). The "reinforcement menu": Finding effective reinforcers. In J.D. Krumboltz & C.E. Thorsen (Eds.), *Behavioral counseling: Cases and techniques* (pp. 42-45). New York: Holt, Rinehart, & Winston.

Dattilo, J. (1986). Computerized assessment of preference for severely handicapped individuals. *Journal of Applied Behavior Analysis*, *19*, 445-448.

DeLeon, I.G., & Iwata, B.A. (1996). Evaluation of a multiple-stimulus presentation format for assessing reinforcer preferences. *Journal of Applied Behavior Analysis, 29*, 519-533.

Fisher, W., Piazza, C.C., Bowman, L.G., Hagopian, L.P., Owens, J.C., & Slevin, I. (1992). A comparison of two approaches for identifying reinforcers for persons with severe and profound disabilities. *Journal of Applied Behavior Analysis, 25*, 491-498.

Fox, R.A., & DeShaw, J.M. (1993). Milestone reinforcer survey. *Education and Training in Mental Retardation, 28*, 257-261.

Green, C.W., Reid, D.H., White, L.K., Halford, R.C., Brittain, D.P., & Gardner, S.M. (1988). Identifying reinforcers for persons with profound handicaps: Staff opinion versus systematic assessment of preferences. *Journal of Applied Behavior Analysis, 21*, 31-43.

Marston, D., & Magnusson, D. (1988). Curriculum-based measurement: District level implementation. In J.L. Graden, J.B. Zins, & M.J.Curtis (Eds.), *Alternative educational delivery systems: Enhancing instructional options for all students* (pp. 137-172). Washington, D.C.: National Association of School Psychologists.

McKinnon, K., & Krempa, J. (2005) *Social Skills Solutions: A Hands-on Manual for Teaching Social Skills to Children with Autism.* New York: DRL Books.

Pace, G.M., Ivancic, M.T., Edwards, G.L., Iwata, B.A., & Page, T.J. (1985). Assessment of stimulus preference and reinforcer value with profoundly retarded individuals. *Journal of Applied Behavior Analysis, 18*, 249-255.

Partington, J.W., & Sundberg, M.L., (1998). *The Assessment of Basic Language and Learning Skills: Scoring Instructions and IEP Development Guide.* Pleasant Hill, CA: Behavior Analysts, Inc.

Rotatori, A.F., Fox, B., & Switzky, H. (1979). An indirect technique for establishing preferences for categories of reinforcement for severely and profoundly retarded individuals. *Perceptual and Motor Skills, 48*, 1307-1313.

Salvia, J., & Ysseldyke, J.E., Bolt, S. (2007). Assessment (tenth edition). New York: Houghton Mifflin

Windsor, J., Piché, L.M., & Locke, P.A. (1994). Preference testing: A comparison of two presentation methods. *Research in Developmental Disabilities, 15*, 439-455.

Chapter 14

Curriculum Development
A Task Not to be Taken Lightly
At a Glance

Chapter Points

- Curriculum development should stress depth over breadth.
- A well-conceived curriculum is marked by a complex arrangement of interrelated semi-linear paths that are integrated into a "big picture."
- An effective curriculum is one that is individualized for each learner whenever appropriate.
- Communication is the most significant area of deficit for our children and must therefore be the focus of early curriculum.
- A well-designed curriculum should, to a great extent, be self-maintaining.
- A combination of mand training and compliance training has proven to be most effective with early learners.

Key Terms

Cybernetic System

Skill Program

Functional Protest

Training

Curriculum Development
A Task Not to be Taken Lightly

Everything in this manual has led to this point. We've explored autism, as well as behavior – what it is, how to measure it, how to track it, how to reduce or accelerate it, and why it is or is not occurring.

This knowledge creates the foundation for our next step: developing a strong sense of what to teach (what behaviors to shape), when to teach it, and how best to approach specific skills.

In the following pages, we will discuss some underlying concepts of curriculum development. Using these concepts, we will demonstrate how to establish a program for children who are either very young or who are significantly affected by autism.

We will then discuss curriculum development for learners who span the autism spectrum, from the very low-functioning child to the child who is quite capable of formal language use, but continues to struggle with autism's core deficits. The reader will notice the following recurring themes throughout the chapter:

- Curriculum development should stress depth over breadth.
- A well-conceived approach is marked by a complex arrangement of interrelated, semi-linear paths that are integrated into a "big picture."
- Any effective curriculum is individualized for each learner whenever appropriate.

Section A – Foundations

Because nearly every area of a child's academic life involves communication, our skill programming efforts – especially the early ones – must focus on this vital domain.

It is also critical, early on, to establish programs that encourage and foster a productive, efficient relationship between the learner and the instructor. Remember that most children with autism are not initially receptive to instructional contingencies, due to their inability to see things from the perspective of others. This makes it impossible for them to understand why anyone would want them to do things that aren't of their own initiative. However, because instruction relies on compliance to directives, this skill becomes an important part of early learning.

Cybernetic Systems

When planning a curriculum, it is wise to abide by some basic principles of instructional design. These can be found within the concepts of Instructional Systems, a field that combines education and psychology. In particular, we are referring to a type of instructional system called a **"cybernetic" system** (Vargas), in which the system "steers" itself toward a more refined or better system as it moves along. This is accomplished through a series of steps and feedback loops.

Essentially, the steps of a **cybernetic system** are as follows (Eshleman):

1) Design of the system
2) Development of the system
3) Deployment of the system
4) Evaluation of the system
5) Redesign of the system

Each step includes a set of inputs, as well as a set of outputs.

Design Phase

The design phase lays out the basic foundations of what will be taught. In larger systems of instruction, this can include:

- Naming the course of instruction.
- Specifying the resources available to provide the instruction.
- Identifying overall knowledge that must be taught.
- Conceiving and pinpointing behavioral objectives.
- Developing modules of instruction based upon the organization of these objectives into groups.

Once all of this is done, the instructional design phase allows us to move forward with a general idea, or "blueprint" for how the system will take shape (Eshleman). In the case of programming for children with autism, an all-encompassing set of skills must be taught. Because of this, it is usually better to look at each semi-linear "branch" of the larger constellation of skills to be taught as a basis for its own instructional system.

Take, for example, the "branch" of teaching an early tact repertoire. To carry out the design phase of this skill, we must identify:

- The materials that will be available.
- The prerequisite knowledge of the learner.
- What we are hoping to accomplish through a tacting program (what kinds of tacts are going to be expected, and under what conditions).
- Who will present instruction.
- How we will separate the different objectives within this repertoire.
- How our plans within this programming will work together to accomplish goals or objectives.

Development Phase

The next step is to produce a completed, functional package or course of instruction based on the work accomplished in the design phase. By the end of this phase, the instructor or designer has a product for instructional purposes, such as texts, syllabi, materials, etc.

Note: when developing curricula for children with autism, we can take some liberties with this step to develop lesson plans or sequences of instruction for targeted skill repertoires. We will discuss the development of this kind of instructional plan, such as an "S^D" sheet, later in the next section.

Deployment Phase

The next step is to deploy the system that was produced as a result of the development phase. Again, this is related to the actual implementation of instruction as it appears in the working product or system. In our work with children with autism, this is the instruction that occurs according to our plan.

Evaluation Phase

Next, the system is evaluated using data gathered during deployment. They tell us how the instructor has performed throughout implementation of the system, how the learner has progressed, etc. These data are then used to identify system problems and strengths, as well as proposed changes.

Redesign Phase

The evaluation phase provides us with the information we need to redesign the system. If changes are necessary, we modify the system to provide remediation for the weak points, and we capitalize on and emphasize the strengths. After this has been completed, the entire process begins anew.

It is important to understand these concepts, because they illustrate the need to use data to continually assess and rethink our approach to skill development. They can also help to prevent the single most common problem when most new practitioners tackle curriculum development: taking a "cookbook" approach of utilizing tried-and-true ways to teach specific skills.

Practitioners who utilize this approach must be wary of techniques that fail to show progress in individual learners. Developing a curriculum for a child with autism is a new process *every* time – even if the course of action remains very similar from one case to the next. A cybernetic approach allows the instructional designer to constantly evaluate and redesign when needed.

In this way, curriculum development is an ever-changing process. Be very careful of practitioners who recommend approaching it in a very linear fashion – there should be an informed reason behind each decision.

Other Considerations

When a practitioner is laying the groundwork for effective curriculum design, two other issues should be kept in mind. First, a well-designed curriculum should be self-maintaining to the greatest extent possible. An important part of this is giving careful consideration to a skill's significance before deciding whether to teach it. How will it be applied in a functional way? What would generalized application of the skill look like? Once these questions are answered, we can begin to map the curriculum out a few steps at a time.

Each skill taught should dictate the short-term direction of the line of programming – in other words, the next step should incorporate the learned skill in some way. This continuous practice and application within the next step makes it less necessary to create special programming for skill maintenance. If a separate program must be developed to maintain the skill, it may be time to consider how functional the skill is in the first place.

Second, children with autism frequently possess "splinter skills," or isolated skills that are developed to a high degree, while other, more functional skills remain marked by significant deficits. For less-experienced practitioners, this can lead to a focus on areas where skill development comes about quickly, while work in true problem areas is neglected or under-emphasized.

This often happens because it is more reinforcing to teach skills that make the instructor feel more effective. If Sarah learns the name of every letter, number, or shape that is presented to her – but still cannot maintain eye contact for a three-second response, despite efforts to do so – many practitioners would be tempted to continue pushing for labeling skills. Eye contact would likely be non-emphasized.

The authors have seen similar cases in public schools. For example, in one fifth grade, math instruction for a student continued to push forward with computation at grade level, despite the learner's inability to use the skills to complete even first-grade level tasks. Any approach to curriculum development should include sensitivity to this problem.

Section B – Development of Skill Programs

Once assessment procedures have shown where skill instruction is necessary, and basic principles of effective curriculum design are understood, it's time to develop a plan of instruction. A number of different names are used to describe the instruction of particular skills, including "drills," "skill acquisition programs," or "lessons." For our purposes, we will refer to a skill-teaching program as a **skill program**.

Step One: Identify the Skill

The first step in developing a skill program is to identify the skill to be shaped through instruction. This requires a precise definition of the desired movement cycle as an indication of skill performance. To do this, we answer a number of questions, including:

- What is the topography of the behavior we are looking for?
- Do we have any other expectations, such as a specified endurance, or a latency time that is too high or too low?
- How many times must the movement cycle be completed to count as a successful performance of the behavior?

Once we have identified these criteria, we should define the target behavior in writing.

Step Two: Identify the Stimulus

Second, we determine what will serve as a stimulus for the response, as well as what we will do as instructors to occasion the response. (To review this step, please refer to the discussion of Discrete Trial Instruction in Chapter 10.) Once we have determined our stimulus, it should be defined in writing.

Step Three: Identify Prompting

Next, to ensure that the response occurs, we identify the types of prompting that will serve as secondary stimuli. When these are identified, they are put in writing, along with a procedure for fading prompts.

Step Four: Establish a Reinforcement Procedure

The next step is to determine how the target skill will be reinforced when it occurs. How will reinforcement be differentiated as the skill progresses? How will reinforcement be thinned as part of this process? A simple procedure that describes each of these steps should be written.

Step Five: Develop an Error Correction Procedure

What does the instructor do if the skill is not performed? In the event of an incorrect response, an error correction procedure must be determined, developed, and described in writing.

Step Six: Determine a Data Collection Method

There are many methods for data collection – the only option that doesn't exist is *not* collecting it. Whatever method is used, it is important to find a way to represent data visually via a line graph. All data collection procedures and materials should be documented.

Step Seven: Define Mastery Criteria

Next, mastery criteria must be specified in writing to let the instructor know when skill instruction for a particular target has been accomplished.

Step Eight: Create a Lesson Plan

Once all of these considerations are in writing, the final step is relatively easy: compile everything into a single document that serves as a lesson plan for skill instruction. This plan, known as a "program sheet," or "S^D sheet," serves as a procedural guide for skill instruction.

If it is well developed, and includes all of the information we have discussed, the program sheet will allow anyone responsible for teaching the skill to remain consistent with anyone else who is teaching the skill. It also sets a consistent level of expectation for the child's performance. This ultimately helps the instructor to focus efforts in an efficient way, and to avoid the wasted time often associated with inconsistent instruction and reinforcement.

What Do We Have to Teach?

This topic is sometimes mired in controversy within the field. There are practitioners who feel very strongly that once services are made available to a child with autism, the first "era" of instruction should exclusively focus on the development of a mand (or request) repertoire. This is a common belief espoused by providers of AVB (Applied Verbal Behavior) intervention.

We have already discussed many of the tenets of a verbal behavior-based approach to autism intervention. It is worth noting here, however, that many AVB practitioners also believe this type of instruction is best accomplished in the natural environment.

Given enough time, and with skillful use of NET techniques, it is true that an instructor will be able to reasonably pair him or herself with reinforcement. This approach also capitalizes on the notion that the learner's MO will drive instruction and responding, establishing an early connection between verbal behavior and reinforcement.

However, there is also a camp within the field that believes the first keystone of learning is early establishment of compliance to adult directives – in particular, the ability to receptively respond to instruction. Most of these programs begin with an emphasis on skill programs, such as coming to sit in a chair when called, responding with imitation to a model, or cooperating with simple receptive motor commands (such as clap, stand, etc.).

The point of initiating these skill programs very early on is to establish instructional control, so that the child will be tolerant of remaining within the instructional context as skills are taught.

The authors have managed to find a middle ground in the debate. First, we recognize that the most efficient way to establish a communicative repertoire with our children is through systematic mand training, in which the child's interests are capitalized upon in order to prompt some kind of communicative exchange. While this can and should be accomplished in the natural environment, we believe that it should also be done in a more highly structured and contrived one.

Second, instructional control is a huge issue with young children with autism. It can mean the difference between fast and efficient progression through skill programs, and slow and laborious progression. When a child's learning behaviors are not brought under instructional control, it becomes next to impossible to tell if performance during data collection is truly reflective of skill acquisition, or if it is indicative of a behavior problem. Gaining instructional control early on allows us to move beyond this issue, so that the question rarely arises.

Children with autism typically don't have many overt contingencies placed upon them prior to instruction. For this reason, even previously reinforcing items or activities can lose their value once they become contingent upon compliance to any kind of demand. Compliance training is essentially a process of differential reinforcement: an instructional request is made, and compliance is reinforced while non-compliant behaviors are placed on extinction. If instructional control does not exist, the ability to be very effective in mand fluency training efforts is often limited.

Our professional experience has shown us that the best outcomes are usually achieved when initial instruction takes a two-pronged approach. On one hand, request training and pairing with reinforcement is in place almost all of the time. On the other, compliance with simple requests is established through a process of differential reinforcement. We have implemented each approach exclusively, and we have combined them both at the very onset. When the focus has been split from the onset, our universal experience is that extinction bursts diminish, general compliance increases, and progression through skill acquisition programs is most rapid.

Guiding Principles

Regardless of where we place our focus, instructors should be guided by a few rather basic principles. The first is to ensure that the "master plan" hits major areas of skill development all along the way. Quite a bit of forethought is required, so that we know why we are teaching certain skills, and where we eventually hope to go with them. In this way, we constantly engage in a forward-thinking process. At the same time, if there is an idea of ultimate outcomes, information related to the "destination" can be used for a sort of reverse engineering that will determine the component skills necessary to take us to the final stop.

Second, it has been the authors' experience that many programs for children with autism focus on communication training to such a degree that all other areas of typical functioning are neglected. This is often because strength and fluency in a learner's communicative skill repertoire frequently pay huge dividends across all domains that are targeted for improvement.

However, a solid approach to curriculum planning for children with autism must also take into account the need to teach skills across *many* areas, including social skills, leisure, play, and academics. When we attempt to establish new skills in these areas, many children with autism must be taught them explicitly and directly.

How, exactly, does one go about including these skills? A great first step is to acknowledge that the same instructional strategies that are effective in shaping communicative or academic behaviors are effective in shaping *any* types of behaviors. Additionally, the instructor must define the skills to be taught, as well as identify the contexts in which the skills will be taught. Finally, a sense of the "big picture" is required, so that the instructor can realize where a skill may be headed, as well as any component skills that may be missing from the learner's repertoire.

Section C – Play and Leisure Skills

Typical children and adults spend a great deal of time engaged in play and leisure activities. The ways in which we spend our leisure time allow us to develop our interests and give us reasons to apply skills (like reading or motor abilities) in ways that are self-motivating. They help us form social bonds with people who share similar interests, and provide us with ways to escape stress. In short, leisure activities are the epitome of things we do entirely by choice, and are the source of much happiness.

Unfortunately, many individuals with autism seem to have an underdeveloped repertoire of leisure or play skills. This can be addressed by a well-balanced curricular approach designed specifically to help children with autism establish foundational skills. With these in hand, our children are able to take advantage of the benefits and opportunities that play and leisure activities offer us all.

Step One: Determine Your Learner's Interests

When teaching this group of skills, the first step is to decide which type of activity will be taught. Even in programs that make efforts to teach leisure activities, experience has shown us that the range of activities presented and taught directly is usually somewhat narrow. It doesn't have to be that way – think, for example, about some of the ways in which typically developing people choose to spend their leisure time:

We play board games, card games, or turn-taking games. Some of us spend time involved with sports, either as participants or fans. Some people enjoy learning about science in their free time, establishing bug collections or building dinosaur models. Collecting objects, like stamps, art, coins, or even stuffed animals can occupy free time.

Some people pursue acting, which may start as simple dramatic play among children, while others pass the time producing art. Computer activities are a pastime for many, as are building toys, video games, cooking, reading, writing, or simply relaxing with not a thing to do!

The bottom line of this discussion is that the ways in which people choose to spend their leisure time are as varied as the personalities of the people themselves. We must take this into account when we try to support a person with autism in developing leisure or play skills.

Once the instructor understands the range of possibilities available in this area, he or she can begin to narrow the focus to a few potential candidates (activities) for instruction. The most obvious place to start this process is by identifying the learner's interests.

This is accomplished by observing the types of activities that he or she gravitates toward, even as a spectator. What types of items seem to pique curiosity? Any reinforcer assessments that have been conducted will help guide the way. Naturally, if the individual is able to communicate well, he or she should be asked. As much as possible, use this information to identify a group of potential activities that will be the most meaningful for the learner, the most potentially reinforcing, and the closest to his or her current set of skills.

Step Two: Consider the Core Deficits (and Strengths) of Autism

When identifying potentially successful leisure activities for our group of learners, it may also be helpful to consider some of the core deficits (as well as characteristic strengths) associated with autism spectrum disorders. We know that many children with autism learn simple rules quite readily, so activities that are accompanied by specific and clear rules might lend themselves to success.

In some cases, social difficulties may preclude early success in team-oriented activities. It may be difficult for the learner with autism to understand the importance of selflessness when engaged in a fully cooperative team sport, such as football, soccer, or basketball. Additionally, the appearance of aloofness and struggles with team concepts may create undue pressures and even mistreatment at the hands of teammates who lack empathy. Obviously, these are all broad generalizations; however, the potential exists that team sports can pose unique challenges.

Having said that, children with autism can sometimes benefit from activities that encourage an individual-within-a-team mindset, such as swimming, golf, track-and-field competition, distance running, etc. These activities ultimately require performance that improves upon set standards, such as time or past performance, but can also offer the social benefits of team camaraderie.

The authors suggest looking into and trying any type of activity that looks like it would be a good fit for each individual learner. The parent or instructor should be mindful of the suggestions found in this section, but make decisions based on the unique circumstances of each learner.

Don't forget about the impact made across the United States in February of 2006, when Jason McElwain, a high school senior with autism, scored 20 points in three minutes for his school's basketball team. Jason was the team's manager for four years, and didn't ever get a chance to play, presumably because either his interests were more in line with working as a manager or because his coach and team didn't feel he could participate as a playing member of the team. Regardless, Jason showed, in a moment, that he was indeed up to the task, and amazed the nation with his feat.

Step Three: Examine the Leisure Activities of Families and Friends

After identifying the interests of the learner, take a close look at the interests of the learner's family and social group. Leisure activities are one way that friends and families bond with one another – on more than one occasion, parents have told us that they wish their child could enjoy the same types of activities as the rest of the family.

Ask families how they like to spend their time together. Do they like to go to amusement parks? Do they play games together? Are the child's siblings involved in a particular sport? The focus of the discussion should be on identifying activities that may be important to those closest to the learner. It is also important to pay close attention to the financial, time-related, and other resources available to the family. These will determine whether or not selected activities will be feasible options for the child.

Step Four: Assess Community Resources

Once the interests of the learner and those closest to him or her have been identified, the next reasonable step is to assess the resources that the community has to offer. For example, children who are interested in animals may benefit from programs offered at the local zoo. On the other hand, some activities of great interest may not be available in the learner's community. For example, the child and family may be extremely interested in alpine skiing, but live in a warm, arid climate where skiing isn't possible.

Step Five: Identify Targets for Instruction

At this point, the instructor should be able to identify some potential leisure skills that are appropriate targets for instruction. We recommend taking on no more than two or three of the strongest contenders as potential targets, for a couple of reasons.

First, the instructor has to make sure that more than one option exists. Throughout their lives, most people attempt a number of leisure or play activities that don't ever "stick" to become something that they enjoy over time. Our learners with autism are no different in this regard. There are many activities that look fun and enjoyable, only to lose their appeal once they are attempted. It is true that some activities might be thoroughly enjoyed once a basic set of skills are taught, so it is important to offer several exposures to an activity before giving up and moving on. However, a few alternatives should be "on deck" as backups in case the initial selection is not a success.

Second, we have to be sure that we don't spread ourselves too thinly. The instructor should keep in mind the mantra of "depth over breadth" – even though we are teaching leisure and play skills, we are still teaching skills. These skills will be most fluent and functional if they can be taught to a depth that will allow the learner to use them across settings and in the face of distraction. This requires that skills be targeted with sufficient intensity, something that simply cannot happen if the focus is too broad. By limiting the number of potential target skills to a few, we make it more likely that we will be able to provide more opportunities for instruction, prompting, practice, and reinforcement in each of them.

Step Six: Teach the Skill

As with any skill, the play or leisure skill is shaped into the learner's repertoire. The instructor should use differential reinforcement and effective prompting, and should set up reinforcing contingencies. If the learner does what is required or expected, then his or her performance should be reinforced in a meaningful way.

Special Considerations

When the instructor is engineering effective contingencies to shape play and leisure skills, there are two vital considerations:

- First, a response requirement must be identified and defined. What, exactly, must the learner do before he or she can access reinforcement?
- Second, a reinforcer that will be powerful enough to maintain the behaviors associated with the activity must be identified.

The following section examines these two considerations in a little more detail.

When identifying a response requirement, the instructor should look at several different levels of response. He or she must be able to identify the level of response the learner is capable of at this very moment. Then, the instructor must look at the level of response that will be necessary for independent engagement in the play or leisure activity. This will serve as the destination – and any level of performance between the skills the learner brings to the table and that destination is the journey that must be orchestrated.

To begin, a response requirement that is well within the learner's reach should be established. For example, if we are looking at puzzle completion, the learner may only be required to place one missing piece in a puzzle with all other pieces present and placed. In this case, the task is more representative of a visual-motor task, as opposed to one that requires high levels of discrimination. Discrimination, however, becomes a large player in independent puzzle completion.

One of the reasons that instruction is begun at a point where the learner is capable of emitting the desired response independently is to avoid making the activity aversive. If the instructor is trying to establish a leisure or play activity, he or she should always keep in mind that this is, by definition, an activity that is enjoyed and sought out voluntarily when free time is available.

Reinforcer identification may be a somewhat complex issue when dealing with these types of activities. Most of us engage in leisure or recreational activities because they provide their own reinforcement. In other words, we have grown to enjoy something about them. However, this does not always hold true when we are first acquiring the necessary skills. Many musicians will attest to the fact that they were forced to practice when they were first learning how to play their instruments, because practice of tedious scales or exercises is not usually fun. Also, for many, the lessons themselves would be terminated if the practice schedule wasn't kept up.

To counter this reluctance, many teachers of young music students use things such as stickers or special musical rewards (tickets to shows, free drumsticks, etc.) to motivate their young pupils to continue to practice. All the while, though, the children practice because they envision the day in which they will be able to play their instrument well enough to entertain themselves and others.

When applying this example to our learners with autism, though, we can't forget that we are dealing with individuals who have issues with executive functioning and other impairments. Most typical learners are amenable to reasoning about how hard work now will pay dividends later. Our learners, however, are much more literal and much more focused on the present.

This may require us to be more reliant upon unrelated reinforcers – at least at first – to shape up behaviors related to the targeted activity. For this reason, it will be very helpful to approach the instruction of these skills just like the instruction of *any* skill – with meaningful reinforcement provided following acceptable or desired responses.

Another consideration that will affect the ability to target and teach specific leisure activity skills is whether the targeted activity is open-ended or closed-ended. This will have an impact on the response requirement, which will in turn have an impact on determining when and how often reinforcement will be delivered.

Open-ended activities, such as dramatic play, may make it necessary to use some type of temporally-based (time-based) dimension within the definition of the response requirement. In other words, because there is no clear beginning or end to some activities, successful completion should be defined in terms of the amount of time in which the learner is engaged in the activity. Returning to the activity of dramatic play, the instructor can measure the length of time a child spends playing appropriately with a garage and car set, and require increasing amounts of time engaged in this activity.

Closed-ended activities, such as board games, building activities, and rule-governed sports frequently have a built-in signal that the activity has come to an end. For example, a puzzle or building activity is completed when the pieces are all utilized. Games like golf can end when a specified number of holes have been completed, and reciprocal activities, such as catch, can be based on the number of turns taken by the learner.

After sufficient thought has been given to the desired response requirement and how it will be defined, it is time to think about instructional methodology. Effective methods of presentation, prompting, and reinforcement hold true for instruction in leisure and play activities as much as they do for instruction in any other skill. Any of the effective teaching methodologies described in this manual will work, including Discrete Trial Instruction, video modeling and video self-modeling, basic shaping techniques, visual supports, and Forward and Reverse Chaining.[1] Whichever method is used, it is important to teach the skills in an effective manner, to gather data, and to use analytical skills to determine when and if a change in course is appropriate.

Section D – Selecting Skill Programs

Throughout the remainder of this chapter, the authors will explain an approach to curriculum development based on priorities that shift as the learner's skill repertoire advances. By no means are we attempting to provide an all-encompassing curricular

[1] While we did not cover chaining in this text, we highly recommend Timothy Heron's chapter on the matter in *Applied Behavior Analysis* (Cooper, et al., 1987)

path – the very complex nature of curriculum design for this group of learners makes it next to impossible to map out, with any degree of specificity, a course that will be the same for all learners.

What we *can* do is offer some examples of programming that reflect the changing instructional priorities that should be taken into account. We will also attempt to generalize some basic steps and considerations that must be made for all learners.

The remaining content of this chapter is organized in the following way:

- First, we will discuss the considerations that should drive the instructor's approach for most new learners. These learners include both the very young, as well as those who have significant developmental disabilities and have not yet received much intensive programming.
- Next, we will describe functional combinations with other early skill programs.
- Finally, we will discuss some concepts that are essential to teach to learners who are beginning to move into the world of advanced language comprehension, production, and use.

Section E – Beginning Programs

Young children with autism between the ages of two and three years typically have not been required to sit and attend to adult-directed instruction for extended periods of time. These same children typically display significant language and social skills deficits, as manifested by a severely limited mand repertoire.

Presented with a child who has a limited mand repertoire and little or no experience with performing skills under any form of instructional control, the teacher should design a language curriculum so that it initially focuses attention on these two fundamental skills.

Attending Skills

In order to conduct instruction of the intensity required in an EIBI program, the child must first be able to come to the instructional area when called, sit in a chair, and remain seated for the duration of the session.

"Come Sit" – Phase One

Teaching a child to come to the instructional area and sit in a chair on request is the first skill program within the domain of attending or "getting ready to learn" skills. The first phase of the "Come Sit" program involves establishing stimulus control of the response (coming and sitting when called) in the presence of the verbal command to "come sit."[2]

Before any instruction is given to the child, the instructor should, at the very least, spend several days getting to know the child and conducting an informal preference assessment. This process usually involves a good deal of observation to identify the types of activities the child finds pleasurable. Watching the child interact with his mother or father will usually yield some very good ideas as to what might be employed as reinforcement.

[2] While early instruction with this program may involve a consistent verbal S^D such as "come sit", we will want to rather quickly introduce other natural S^D's such as "come here", "come sit with me", or "come see me."

Direct testing of a wide variety of tickling, rough play, funny faces, noises, or songs should also be attempted during this assessment phase. We strongly recommend, however, that the teacher seek out social reinforcement right from the start and avoid reliance on "things" or "gadgets" as reinforcing stimuli for the young child with autism whenever possible.

As noted earlier in our discussion of discrete trial methodology, providing isolated play with a highly preferred tangible can erode any social connection that the instructor might be trying to establish with the child. The child often chooses to slip into his or her "own world" while interacting with the object, and awareness of the instructor quickly dissipates. If a tangible reinforcer is used, it is best to pair it with some form of obvious, direct, social reinforcement; for example, using the object to tickle, tease, or play along with the child.

Once the instructor has established a solid list of reinforcing stimuli to use during instruction, the "Come Sit" program can begin. All initial sessions of this program should be preceded immediately by a few minutes of vigorous play with the child, and the identified potent reinforcing activities paired with the instructor. In this way, a "bond" or "social connection" between the instructor and the child is established in close temporal proximity to the work that will be presented at the table.

Transition from the play situation to the table is accomplished when the instructor arranges the play activity so that it occurs near or next to the table. Once the instructor has the child clearly engaged in play, he or she merely moves to the table and gives the first S^D, "come sit," in a normal tone of voice. Prompting is provided simultaneously with the S^D to create an errorless learning situation for the child. If pairing with reinforcement has been done well, the child usually requires a minimal level of gestural or physical prompting to approach the chair and sit down.

Once the child is seated in the chair, the instructor provides potent social reinforcement like that provided during the play activity. For these first few trials, the child need only sit as long as it takes to reinforce the response of coming and sitting. Once the child meets that requirement, he or she is allowed to return to the play activity for approximately 30 seconds before the next trial begins.

At this point in the description, it is important to mention the operational definition of the target response (coming to sit when called). Effective prompt fading and the shaping of independent responding will require that this target response be clearly defined.

Generally speaking, this basic skill response is defined as a movement cycle that involves "uninterrupted movement (walking) toward the chair that is initiated within three seconds of the delivery of the S^D and is terminated when the child's buttocks contact the seat of the chair."

With each successive trial, prompting is faded and the delivery of reinforcement is differentially provided for more and more independent responding – in effect, transferring stimulus control from the prompts to the verbal S^D of "come sit." This can be accomplished nicely by using graduated guidance and shadowing. That is, when physical prompting is being used, the instructor starts by physically backing off from the prompt but keeping her hand near the child in the event that he or she stops moving toward the chair. That way, if movement ceases, the physical prompt can be quickly reinstituted. The proximity of the shadowing hand is then faded until neither physical prompting nor shadowing is required.

Up to this point in the training, the aversive nature of sitting in the chair should be negligible. The child should be receiving potent social reinforcement for coming/

sitting responses and the response requirement for these early trials (sitting for a few seconds) should be minimal.

The instructor should be aware, however, that the relative reinforcing quality of the play area can change from moment to moment, particularly when implementing this kind of program in a home setting. A carefully controlled instructional session can be quickly upended by the unannounced arrival of another family member, or by turning on the television in the next room. The child will eventually have to tolerate postponement of competing reinforcement, but during these early sessions it is best to try to control distractions and ensure that the instructor is the "best show in town."

If significant problem behavior is experienced in Phase One, chances are that either insufficient pairing of the instructor with reinforcement has occurred, or extinction needs to be re-visited. Even with the best pairing procedures, there may be times when neutral manual guidance is required.

"Come Sit" – Phase 2

Once the child has repeatedly demonstrated the ability to come and sit without prompting, the instructor can begin to consider increasing the response requirement once the child is seated at the table.

Presentation of an imitation task, such as placing a block in a bucket, can be a simple, low-effort task that the instructor can add to the first learning trial of Phase Two. Instead of merely being required to come and sit in the chair, the child now must come, sit down, and perform a simple imitation task before being allowed to leave the table. With subsequent trials, the instructor can add either additional trials of this same imitation task or other, similarly easy tasks.

As the work requirement increases, so does the aversive nature of the learning session. For this reason, positive reinforcers must be of significant potency to keep the child motivated to remain and complete the increasing number of trials. Our typical goal with young children experiencing instruction for the first time is to increase the number of trials to 15 or 20 per sitting.

This is typically where tantrum or other misbehaviors are first seen during instruction – particularly with children who have a learning history of negative reinforcement of misbehavior. Often, the increased response requirement acts as an MO that:

- Causes our positive reinforcers to lose potency.
- Causes negative reinforcement (escape) to gain value.
- Causes behaviors that have been negatively reinforced in the past (tantrum, aggression, SIB) to be more readily evoked.

The instructor can proactively address this issue by teaching the child to use a "Break" card during the early stages of the demand-fading process. A Break card is a simple visual device that is used in the fashion of PECS. Teaching a child to use a Break card involves a DNRA procedure, where the transfer of the Break card is negatively reinforced by providing the child with a brief break from the work situation. In this way, the Break card transfer becomes the functional equivalent (or alternate) skill to the child's misbehavior.

In order for this differential reinforcement procedure to work, the inappropriate members of the same functional response class (tantrum, aggression, SIB) must be placed on extinction. As explained in the previous discussion on extinction and negative reinforcement, this process involves not removing the task or the demand upon display of the inappropriate behavior. In other words, the child is kept at the table and required to complete the task regardless of tantrum, aggression, or SIB. When the instructor is training the Break card procedure, he or she also removes the Break card from the table when target problem behavior is displayed. In this way, the child is provided with a visual cue that escape is not available while they are engaging in inappropriate behavior.

In order for this process to be effective, and to not result in acute spikes in problem behavior during instructional sessions, the slow fading in of demands is usually conducted simultaneously with the training of the Break card use. This approach prevents the response requirement from being too quickly accelerated without the child having a well-established functional protest response in his or her repertoire. In fact, this process is often referred to as **Functional Protest Training**, which is a form of Functional Communication Training.[3]

Note: in order to teach the functional protest response (the Break card transfer), the child must come in contact with the extinction component of the differential negative reinforcement procedure. We have found that trying to avoid evoking problem behavior by dragging out the demand-fading process into a protracted series of minute steps only delays the inevitable incident of tantrum or aggressive behavior that will have to be placed on extinction.

Break cards can also be nicely incorporated into a token economy system. The authors have had great success in cutting a Break card into several pieces that can be earned (for varying levels of accurate/compliant responding) and reassembled like a puzzle. The actual break is not earned until the child earns all of the pieces and assembles the entire word "break." This is typically taught by cutting the card first into two, and then, over time and success, three, four, and finally five pieces (one piece for each letter of the word "break").

"Hands Down"

An early problem that we encounter with many of our children is their tendency to touch or handle the learning materials on the table before being provided with instruction to do so. This can prove very distracting to the instructor, and has detrimental effects on the child's learning – particularly when teaching discrimination skills, where the placement of learning materials is critical. A child who is constantly moving the objects around on the table will have a much more difficult time making complex discriminations between them when asked.

The procedure for teaching "hands down" or "hands quiet" is quite simple. First and foremost, all instructors working with the child must agree on an operational definition of "hands down." This can vary from child to child, but usually involves some placement of the child's hands in a neutral position (either on the table or on his or her lap) and keeping them there until instruction for the current program is given.

[3] V. Mark Durand's *Severe Behavior Problems: A Functional Communication Training Approach* (1991) is a resource devoted entirely to the topic of functional communication training.

The skill is taught by placing several objects of interest to the child on the table in front of him or her. The instructor then waits for the child to try and touch one of the objects. At that point, the S^D of "hands down" is spoken simultaneously with a physical prompt to move the child's hands into the neutral position. As with "Come Sit," early trials of "Hands Down" are presented in an errorless fashion. Prompts are then faded, using graduated guidance, until the instructor's verbal direction of "hands down" comes to control the child's response.

Part of our goal with this program is to begin to teach waiting and tolerance behaviors to the child. In the presence of a powerful reinforcer, the child is learning to wait for a reasonable amount of time before being told that it is okay for him or her to touch/play with the object. We do this by slowly fading in more time between the moment when the child's hands contact the neutral position and the reinforcer is delivered.

When this skill is generalized back into existing language programs, it can pose some problems. In most language programs that involve materials, we need to ensure that the child waits for the instruction to be fully given before they begin to respond by manipulating the learning materials.

The authors sometimes find that an instructor will rush the delivery of the S^D in an effort to prevent the child from jumping the gun and beginning to respond to the instruction before its completion. This can be highly problematic when the child begins anticipating the instruction and not attending to the verbal directions provided by the instructor. By purposely slowing down (sometimes to a rate of speech that is exaggeratedly slow), the instructor can build attending, compliance, and tolerance skills that will have far-reaching benefits in future programs.

"Look At Me"

Children with autism are often impaired in their abilities to establish and maintain eye contact during social interactions. For this reason, eye contact is one of the skills most commonly mentioned when parents are asked to identify areas in need of improvement with their child.

While it is readily agreed by parents and practitioners alike that eye contact is a serious skill deficit, there is not much of a consensus among autism experts as to how or when it should be taught.

Some DTI practitioners insist that formal programs be adopted to directly teach eye contact at a very early point in the child's curriculum. These usually amount to a shaping procedure that utilizes a verbal S^D, such as "look at me," paired with gestural or physical prompts that guide the child's head to orient his or her eyes toward the instructor. Prompt fading then ensues, with transfer of control to the verbal instruction.

Anyone who has ever tried this approach is aware of the persistence that children with autism can display in averting their eyes – no matter how their heads or the instructor's is positioned.

One alternative tactic is for the instructor to hold a preferred tangible near their eyes as they simultaneously give the "look at me" S^D. If the tangible item is a potent reinforcer, there may be sufficient motivation on the part of the child to track the preferred item. In doing so, his or her eye movement is shaped toward the terminal behavior of looking at the instructor's eyes. The tracking object can then be faded out over subsequent trials.

Some behavior analysts hold another opinion regarding teaching eye contact via a formal program. They contend that this behavior can be shaped simply by conducting imitation programs that focus on facial movements, or by touching facial features. These programs require the child to momentarily look at the instructor's face in order to discriminate the action to be imitated. The use of the No-No-Prompt feedback loop is quite often sufficient to consequate errors and shape up appropriate eye contact without the necessity of conducting a formal eye contact program.

Tolerance to Interruption & Transitions

Another common concern expressed by parents of young children with autism is that their children have great difficulty managing transitions between activities. An adult request that one activity end so that another can begin often results in significant tantrum, aggression, or SIB. This is seriously problematic for a family, because it impedes their ability to perform normal functions in the community when their child is present, including shopping, recreation, dining in restaurants, etc. The fear of having to deal with severe tantrum while in the community quite literally causes these families to isolate themselves.

Dr. Vincent Carbone has developed a very effective program for teaching young children with autism to tolerate interruptions of preferred activities and transitions between preferred and non-preferred activities. The authors' interpretation of this program, which is described here, varies in certain aspects from Dr. Carbone's. The program is comprised of two separate training procedures – one in the discrete trial format, and one that utilizes Natural Environment Training.

In the natural environment, the procedure is as follows:

1) The child is approached (within three-to-five feet) and is asked to leave a preferred activity and comply with a demand to do something else, such as putting away the toys and coming to the dinner table.

2) If the child complies and does not engage in any problem behavior, reinforce with praise, social contact, or tangibles. Deliver other reinforcers as needed to maintain the child in the activity to which successful transition has taken place.

3) If the child engages in problem behavior as soon as the transition is requested, the demand must not be removed and access to the preferred item or activity the child is being asked to give up must not be allowed.

4) In addition, no other reinforcers (attention, promises of future rewards, etc.) should be delivered. Instead, the demand should be kept in place and physical guidance used to obtain compliance with the demand.

5) In some cases, an additional consequence, such as a contingent effort procedure or other reductive interventions may be necessary.

6) Appropriate reinforcers in the new activity should be delivered once the child is complying without guidance and without problem behavior.

   A more contrived, mass-practiced version of this procedure is utilized via discrete trial training. The procedure is as follows:

1) The child is placed in a preferred activity and allowed some time for the reinforcing value of the activity to build.

2) The demand that will soon be placed on the child for transitioning to a less-reinforcing activity is determined.

3) At first, demands during practice are easy and relatively effortless, within sight of the reinforcing activity just removed, and for only a brief period of time (e.g., a count of 10 once engaged in the less-preferred activity). An example might be to ask the child to put down a toy and sit in a chair just three feet from the activity for the count of 10, with the offer of a promised reinforcer.

4) The reinforcer for complying with transition is the delivery of the promised reinforcer and the opportunity to immediately return to the preferred activity following the count of 10.

5) If the child engages in problem behavior as soon as the transition is requested, the demand must not be removed and access to the preferred item or activity the child is being asked to give up must not be allowed. In addition, the promised reinforcer should be removed. Instead, the demand is kept in place and physical guidance is used to obtain compliance with the demand. In some cases, an additional consequence (e.g. contingent effort) may be necessary as well.

6) When the child has mastered transitioning/complying with a few demands, the number of demands is increased, along with the distance from the reinforcing activity and the length of time in the non-preferred activity. How this is done will vary, depending on the child and the data obtained once the program is implemented.

7) The decision-making process on increasing the parameters of the demand will ultimately be guided by the data.

8) The counting procedure and any other stimuli used to make the transitions initially easier are faded.

9) Many trials of this program should be conducted every day, with the child's responses recorded on the Interruption/Transition Data Sheet. Entries should describe the demand/task for each trial, if problem behavior occurred (noting specific behaviors), the level of prompting that the child required to complete the demand, the duration of the demand, and whether or not contingent effort was utilized.

As with the Break card program described earlier, Dr. Carbone's transition procedure does not shy away from presenting demands to the child, or cushioning the child's environment to avoid situations that might evoke tantrum or other problem behavior. The extinction component will most likely evoke problem behavior, and the program requires that to happen in order for the learning to take place. The slow fading in of duration, distance, and task difficulty is designed to ameliorate the general aversive nature of the transition – but they will not absolutely prevent tantrum or other problem behavior from occurring. The escape extinction component must be included to ensure that these behaviors are not reinforced.

Section F – Mand Training

The second part of our two-pronged approach to beginning curriculum is devoted to mand training.

While functional protest training and the interruption and transition strategy are used to address problem behaviors maintained by negative reinforcement, mand training is used to address problem behaviors that have been strengthened by the provision of positive reinforcers.

Very early in programming, our children need to learn how to use vocal speech, sign language, or some form of picture exchange to communicate their wants and needs. Then, they need to use this new mand repertoire to replace the established, faulty mand repertoire that is comprised of problematic behaviors. (The relationship between problem behavior and appropriate verbal requesting behavior (basic mands) was made clear in the Differential Reinforcement section of Chapter 10).

While many subtle variations exist in mand training (usually having to do with the communication modality of vocal speech, sign language, or picture exchange), the basic process remains relatively the same for all children. The following is a standard mand fluency training procedure:

1) A variety of toys, food items, and activities of interest are placed within the child's immediate reach/visual field. These reinforcers are scattered about the room to encourage the child to move about and sample from what is available.

2) Demands are reduced to a minimum (or zero if possible) while this training session is conducted.

3) Throughout the training session, a *blocking stimulus* is used to evoke an appropriate mand. For example, if the child chooses to play with a ball, his access to the ball is physically blocked and the verbal mand "ball" is *very quickly* prompted (the speed of the prompt is critical).

4) The verbal mand is followed with praise and access to the item.

5) As trials progress, the instructor should begin to use a time delay prompt to fade out the verbal (echoic) prompt.

Examples of mand trials include:

- Blocking initial access to a food or drink item (**mand**: "[food item].").
- Blocking continued access to a food or drink item (**mand**: "[food item].").
- Blocking access to a toy item by placing a hand over it (**mand**: "[toy item]").
- Giving the child a tightly closed container with a reinforcer inside that he or she can see – or a food container that is still sealed. (**mand**: "open.").
- Standing in the doorway when the child wants out of a room/house (**mand**: "out.").
- Tickling the child and then abruptly stopping (**mand**: "tickle.").
- Mom abruptly putting the child down (**mand**: "up.").
- Mom abruptly picking the child up from an enjoyable activity (**mand**: "down.").
- Physically interrupting jumping behavior (**mand**: "jump.").
- Withholding one shoe or coat when getting ready to go outside (**mand**: "shoe." "coat.")

Between mand training sessions and natural mand situations throughout the day, we recommend learners receive at least **400-500** mand trials **every day**.

To quickly and firmly establish a spoken mand, the new behavior must be reinforced on a CRF schedule. This is sometimes difficult for parents and teachers to come to grips with, because it appears that we are spoiling the child by "giving her everything she wants." On the contrary, this is a necessary, temporary component of mand training. Once proficient mands are established, the schedule of reinforcement is thinned and the child is taught about "waiting."

Learning to wait has a great deal to do with first teaching the child that "wait" does not mean the same thing as "no." For many of our children, the word "wait" has been equated with "no," and, as such, has taken on aversive value as a secondary punisher.

Teaching waiting, then, requires a stimulus fading procedure and (usually) some form of visual stimulus prompt – either a gesture (raised index finger) or a "Wait" card (similar to the Break card). The following is the standard training with a "Wait" card developed by Andrew Bondy of Pyramid Educational Consultants (Bondy, 1996):

1) When the child mands, the "wait" card is presented as the instructor simultaneously says, "wait."
2) Following one second of waiting (defined as quiet sitting without grabbing at the reinforcer), the exchange of the "wait" card is prompted.
3) The instructor reinforces with the item as he or she says, "Good waiting!"
4) Any premature attempts to transfer the "wait" card are physically redirect as the instructor says, "Remember, you are waiting."
5) The instructor begins with one second of waiting and increases in one-second increments for the next several trials (for a total wait interval of five seconds reached at the final trial).
6) Waiting during subsequent trials can be increased in five-second increments.
7) Once 30 seconds of waiting has been reached, "while-you-wait" activities for the child are introduced. These activities should be of slightly lesser reinforcing value than the original item.
8) Data are usually taken on the last trial of the mand session – noting the duration of the wait interval for only the last trial. The following session (the next day) begins with the child waiting for that same duration and then moving on in five-second increments.

As with all effective behavior analytic teaching procedures, mand and waiting training employ well-researched techniques such as MO manipulation, time delay prompting, and stimulus fading. They strive to make learning as errorless as possible, and provide the student with repeated opportunities for practice and success.

Positive reinforcement-based training programs (manding and waiting) must also incorporate an extinction component in their procedures.

If the child engages in tantrum during a mand trial, the reinforcing item is removed from sight – or, if an activity is being requested, the activity is either denied or terminated. The child is also typically timed-out from attention or other alternative positive reinforcers while the tantrum persists. Prompts to "use your words" are not presented once tantrum is exhibited, because this allows the display of tantrum to occasion a prompt or the addition of assistance to the child.

During mand or waiting procedures, the display of tantrum usually results in ignoring until the problem behavior ceases. Interjecting a compliance task following calming also aids in distancing the tantrum from any prompts to mand appropriately. The compliance task also provides the child with a positive, functional response that can be reinforced, rather than directly reinforcing the "tantrum-calming down" behavior chain. Once the child complies without tantrum, the instructor moves back to the mand or waiting training trial.

Accepting "No"

One final beginning program is the "Accepting No" procedure. Sometimes, conditions exist when a child must receive a flat-out denial to an appropriately voiced request. As we noted earlier, the word "no" carries with it considerable aversive connotations for most of our young children with autism. It is quite often one of the few words that parents report their child understands. Unfortunately for most of these children, this "understanding" is manifested as severe emotional reactions, tantrum, aggression, or SIB.

Teaching a child to handle hearing the word "no" without resorting to any of these problematic behaviors is something that most parents are obviously eager to hear about. The following is an adaptation of a program developed by Dr. Vincent Carbone for teaching a child to accept "no." As with his Interruption and Transition program, it is split into a DTI and a NET version. Please note that these procedures should not be attempted with children who do not possess a strongly established, appropriate mand repertoire in either vocal speech, sign language, or picture exchange.

In the natural environment, the procedure is as follows:

1) When the child mands for an item, he or she is told "no." As "no" is said, a reinforcer is brought up or another activity is offered by saying, "But you can have or do this [reinforcer] instead."
2) If no problem behavior occurs, the alternate reinforcer is delivered.
3) If problem behavior occurs, it is not attended and the alternate reinforcer is removed.
4) If implementing this procedure in public, guided compliance to an alternate task as discussed during manding and waiting training is used.

In the more-contrived discrete trial setting, the procedure is as follows:

1) The child is enticed with an object of interest.
2) The child's mand is followed with the "no, but you can…" statement.
3) The consequence is the same as NET.
4) A couple of trials of "no" are followed by a request with "yes," and access to the requested item or activity is allowed.
5) Trials of "yes" and "no" responses are repeated in random rotation.

Section G – The "Next Step"

Once critical readiness and compliance skills have been assessed, discrimination training begins. Discrimination training is essentially the programming that shapes selective responding when a child is presented with several response options. In other words, discrimination training allows the learner to emit the "correct" response when faced with a specific stimulus. Discrimination is at the heart of academics, including numeracy and literacy.

The Importance of Functional Responses

In order to be a proficient communicator, the symbolic and relational nature of language systems must be understood. Simply put, words only acquire meaning through their functional relationships to the objects, events, activities, or other stimuli that they represent. For most of us, these relations are derived rather naturally.

This is not the case for children with autism. In fact, many studies are now being conducted to show the connection between language impairment, intellectual ability, and other cognitive domains, and a person's ability to produce derived relational responses. Basically, we have to find a way to teach the relationships between environmental stimuli and their corresponding linguistic, functional, and operational implications.

For example, when teaching a child to receptively discriminate objects, we teach him or her to select a specific object (e.g. a ball) when instructed to *give me* that object ("Give me the ball") from a field of several different objects. Initially, the learning that goes on involves very tight stimulus control – the child selects only the one ball used in the training and is provided with reinforcement. The behavior is taught directly, and is obviously contingency-shaped.

Further teaching will be required for the child to generalize this ball-giving response to other balls that might not look so much like the original ball. If this instruction does not occur, our child with autism is likely to recognize only that first ball as a ball. This obviously limits the functionality of the child's language.

When we teach the child to select multiple examples of balls, he or she begins to learn the relation between the spoken word *ball* and a variety of objects found in his or her environment.

At this point in the instruction, the child is relating the word *ball* to various environmental objects based on formal similarities of the objects; that is, on how the objects look alike. For example, a golf ball, a tennis ball, and a basketball are all spherical objects and therefore easily recognizable as balls.

Movement beyond this *understanding* of the word *ball* may involve teaching the functions of balls (throwing, kicking, hitting with a bat or racquet, catching, etc.), which will help further discriminate balls from other formally similar objects, like globes, balloons, cantaloupes, etc.

If each of these extensions of our teaching is successful, we might say that the child now *knows* the meaning of the word *ball*. We would also hope that the child could now recognize novel objects that fit the definition of *ball* without having to be directly taught all of them individually. This type of derived relational responding is more in line with how typically developing children learn language.

Finally, we would depart from formal relations to more arbitrary relations as we teach our child how balls are related to other objects in our environment – such as through their inclusion in the category of *toys*. In this way, the child learns the relation between an object known as a *ball* and a larger group of vastly different looking objects known as *toys*.

A comprehensive discrimination-based curriculum teaches the conditions under which certain responses result in reinforcement. It also teaches a range of functional responses that become part of a larger constellation of social and academic behaviors.

If our advice has been read and followed to this point, the groundwork for discrimination training has probably been laid. Our focus here will be on building a receptive and expressive vocabulary. For this, we will rely heavily upon the basic receptive skills taught through the "learning to learn" activities already presented.

Modeling Prompts

In our discussion of prompting strategies, we mentioned the need for certain prerequisites to be established before a particular type of prompt is implemented. We also recommended versatility and flexibility in implementation of prompting strategies. Therefore, early instruction should focus on teaching skills that will allow different types of prompts to be used.

One of the most helpful prompts involves modeling a task that will be performed by the learner. This is especially useful when the task involves vocal production, because we cannot physically prompt the movement of vocal chords and internal oral-motor configuration.

We begin by teaching the prerequisite skills involved in responding to modeling prompts. These skills all involve generalized imitation.

To teach imitation, we usually start with gross motor actions involving tangible objects (such as placing a block in a bucket). As opposed to simply modeling a gross motor action such as clapping, using an object provides a secondary S^D in the form of a static object that is utilized in the response. (If we were to try to teach our first imitative responses with actions such as clapping, all remnants of our model would disappear once we delivered the "do this" instruction while clapping. With an object, the item remains in view even after the instruction has been delivered.)

Physical prompting should be used to attain the desired response, and then faded until the response is under the stimulus control of the instruction alone.

Once some independence has been achieved with a few types of actions, some selection-making skills within the action/object imitation should begin. The instructor should use novel actions with objects to teach some generalization of core imitation skills very early on.

Performing the same actions with particular objects should be avoided. For example, once some independent responding has been shaped with a block in a bucket, the action should be varied. The bucket should be tapped with the block, moved back and forth on the table, or used to knock on the table. Doing this serves a few purposes:

- It teaches the learner to attend to the entire instruction and avoid mechanical responses.
- It teaches the notion of "You do what I do."
- It makes it possible to move more quickly through imitation-based programs.

Soon, the learner is able to move to gross motor, fine motor, and oral motor imitation. All of these will help the instructor shape up communicative skills in the form of vocal speech or sign language.

The Skill of Imitation

When is an imitation program considered completed? Our advice is to think about what the program is designed to accomplish. While many interventionists move on from a basic imitation program as soon as a large number of motor movements can be imitated, we advise against this. Instead, we believe it is important to look at the skill of imitation itself.

Imitation programs are not used to teach specific actions. They are used to teach a learner the "ability" to imitate. Therefore, we believe that imitation programming should be continued until the instructor is confident that the learner is able to imitate models of *novel* actions performed by the instruction.

Every now and then, it makes sense to test how the learner responds to the "do this" instruction when it is paired with an action that the learner has never seen in an instructional context. This will prevent "scrolling" through responses, and will teach the learner that the true desired response topography to "do this" is attention to the instructor, followed by an attempt to complete the modeled action. **It is important to continue imitation instruction until this type of generalized imitation begins to take shape.**

Receptive and Expressive Vocabularies

Another focal point at this time is the development of a receptive and expressive vocabulary. One of the first places to begin building this vocabulary is through the implementation of a receptive labeling program. With these programs, the learner is asked to identify a specified object or picture, and does so via pointing, giving the item to the instructor, or otherwise indicating a firm response.

Ideally, the first items targeted are those with the most meaning for the child. While the instructor should not hesitate to use highly preferred objects, they should be avoided very early on in this programming, as the child's desire for the object may interfere with his or her ability to select alternate objects when asked. As proficiency in this program improves, these highly motivating objects can be incorporated into the instructional sessions, which will increase the functionality of the skill.

The instructor should make sure that the items are placed in random locations, and that they are frequently moved away from the table. This is done to prevent other factors from eventually gaining stimulus control over responses. For example, in some cases, children may respond to "give me cup" at the table, but have no idea what to do when the cup is not directly in front of them on the table. If the items are placed on the floor next to the learner, on a shelf next to the table, or somewhere in plain view across the room, the child learns that a cup is a cup, no matter where it is located. Approaching this program in this way also begins to shape the skill of scanning, which will be important down the road.

Once the learner has demonstrated that receptive labels are being acquired somewhat consistently, we typically introduce targets within a field of three at a time. It is important for the instructor to make changes in field size, number of targets, placement, etc., based on what the data are showing. If something is working, it should be continued. If not, the teaching program should be revised.

Note: we have found that many children with autism struggle with early receptive programs. In most cases, this can be avoided by focusing on teaching scanning and simple discrimination with a single item at the beginning of training.

Depending on the instructor's success in teaching vocal behavior to the learner, receptive labels ("Give/show me") naturally progress to expressive labeling ("What is it?"). With both expressive and receptive labeling, the objective should be to move as quickly as possible to create a large bank of knowledge and labels that the learner can call upon when the context demands it. The instructor should teach as many labels as the learner's success will allow, and always look for multiple exemplars (different pictures/representations of the same item) once basic responding is established.

At this early point, we continue to build upon the receptive instruction-following skills that have already been established. Here, we begin to teach other types of receptive instructions, such as actions like clapping, waving, jumping, running, etc. In addition to building general knowledge, these skills continue to build compliance and develop auditory discrimination.

Basic Sequencing Skills

When basic skills are learned in all of the areas previously discussed, the instructor can begin to utilize these programs to teach basic sequencing skills. These are precursors to language comprehension and eventual reading. Imitation can develop into multiple-step imitation, receptive labels can be given for all items in an array ("Give me the shoe, the cup, and the ball,") that also includes distracter items, and the learner can begin to expressively label more than one item at a time. This is where seriation is taught at its most basic levels.

Matching to sample can begin at this point, as well. At first, the instructor teaches the learner to place objects with identical objects, but can quickly move to objects that are similar, such as three-dimensional objects to two-dimensional pictures of the same object, or one type of cup with another type of cup. This builds scanning abilities, and also serves as a foundational skill for many other areas.

At the same time, the instructor should begin to require more specificity within mands, and require that the learner continue to develop sentence-formation skills.

Early Programs Beyond the Basics

Once basic responding has been developed (such as coming when called, responding to receptive commands, basic tacting, etc.), the instructor can begin to teach more abstract skills like categorization and more advanced sequencing.

Function, Feature and Class

At this point, the concepts of function, feature, and class (FFC) are introduced. These become important precursors to topical conversation; for example, if someone is talking about their favorite color, it is inappropriate to respond with information about what you did with your parents the night before. In other words, our ability to participate fluently and appropriately within conversations is somewhat related to our ability to classify and sort the information we receive.

The authors teach functions receptively by first asking the learner to show us things that are used for specified purposes. For example, we instruct: "Give me something you drink from," and the learner identifies a cup from an array. Likewise, we teach the same thing expressively. At this point, we also teach the relational "flip side." If we can ask the learner to intraverbally name something used for drinking, we should also be able to ask the learner to intraverbally name what is a cup for.

We begin category instruction as another type of receptive labeling. Instead of identifying single objects, the label becomes a name for a *group* of objects. To do this, we may place several distinct groups of pictures on the table: a group of animals, a group of foods, etc. We then ask the learner to point to the specified group. This program can then move in many different directions receptively and expressively (examples can be found in the "Sample Skill Programs" area of the CD-ROM that accompanies this manual).

"Features" include component parts, such as wheels, windows, and doors of a car; physical attributes, including color, shape, and size; and other topographically related information pertaining to the object of discussion. Each of these areas is targeted individually.

Information regarding FFC can be incorporated across skill programs. It can be tied into matching programs, category programs, receptive and expressive language programs, and can be used within reciprocal conversation programs. We suggest that FFC skills be taught individually before combining them with one another or with additional programs.

Intraverbals

As soon as any expressive language skills surface, it is time to begin work on intraverbals. This is usually easily started within fill-in programs, where the learner fills in a missing word that is left out of a sentence spoken by the instructor. With early learners, this is usually best accomplished by omitting words from songs. It is important to make sure that the place where the "blank" is inserted in the statement or song is changed from time to time, so that the song itself does not acquire stimulus control over the response. If this happens, the learner will avoid listening to the song from the beginning to end, and the response may be accurate for the wrong reasons.

For example, many people use the song "Twinkle, Twinkle, Little Star" for work on fill-ins. They establish a pattern where they always sing, "Twinkle, twinkle, little ____," and have the learner fill in "star." However, when they try to place the space as follows: "Twinkle, twinkle, _____," the learner may still say "star," as opposed to "little." For this reason, it is always important to make sure that instructions actually cause the learner to go through the desired processes to formulate a response, as opposed to simply allowing the presentation to allow generic responding for the wrong reasons.

Summing Up

At this point, a learner should be able to:

- Follow basic instructions.
- Make simple requests for items or activities that are reinforcing.
- Begin to expand both expressive and receptive vocabularies.
- Understand concepts associated with functions of objects, various features, and categories.
- Develop imitative and match-to-sample repertoires.

At the same time, a relatively high level of instructional control should exist, so that while the learner is able to ask for breaks, he or she would rather work with the instructor.

Numerous skill programs can be tackled at this early stage. The instructor should consult with the samples included with the CD-ROM, and can also rely on examples provided in works published by Lovaas (2003), Maurice, Green et al (1996, 2001), Leaf and McEachin (1999), Romancyzk (1996), etc.

All of these offer many suggestions and complete skill programs that can be implemented with learners with autism. Our hope, however, is that this manual will provide a guide to implementing skill programs like these, and will develop an understanding of why they are important within the larger scheme of language development and social interaction.

Section H – Intermediate Programs

Where does the instructor go once basic skills have been established? At the "intermediate" level, the process of "weaving" together various component skills into more complex, functional skills begins. As the authors have said, it is important to think about curriculum development for learners with autism as a non-linear path, which we have likened to a set of tree branches. A leaf cannot exist if the trunk is not first established, followed by large branches, smaller branches, and finally the fingers to which the leaf is attached. Many other branches coexist, and some of them can be traced back to common foundations.

Tact Refining

At the intermediate level, the focus should be on refining the learner's tact repertoire. Tacts should be learned for letters, colors, shapes, numbers, emotions, and physical activities.

At this point, the instructor should only accept full-sentence responses. This is a good habit to get into as soon as the learner is ready, because encouraging sentence production through differential reinforcement also shapes up sequencing skills. In turn, this will help to avoid the auditory sequencing issues that are manifested as syntax problems in many children with autism. By encouraging full sentences as part of the response requirement, we are shaping skills that will be helpful throughout programming.

"Tightening" Stimulus Control

At this level, the instructor should also begin to tighten up stimulus control over response formats. If sentences are produced, he or she should make sure that the response's format matches that of the instruction. For example, if the learner is asked, "What do you play with?" and the learner responds with "It's a ball," there is a bit of a disconnect between the formats of the stimulus and response.

It may seem overly critical to shape such fine points of response production. However, we have found that not doing so may enable the learner to receive reinforcement for responses without really having to attend to the entire S^D. Then, when more advanced programs like refined "Wh-question" programs are implemented, the learner is unable to accurately answer the questions that are presented.

The "tighter" the stimulus control at the early and intermediate stages of programming, the more likely the learner will be attentive and will be able to engage in the subtle discriminations necessary for successful conversation. It also allows the instructor to avoid problems such as scrolling through possible responses, stimulus over-selectivity, and poor generalization. Over time, stimulus control must be loosened, so that responses can be delivered across varying (more natural) stimulus conditions. This will also create a level of versatility in the learner's response patterns.

At this level, the learner also begins to use sentence-formation skills to describe objects in his or her natural environment. The skills learned in FFC programs enable the learner to answer questions like, "Tell me about a bicycle."

Identification of Objects Described

There is a flip side to the previously described program, known as identification of objects described. In this case, the instructor lists the attributes, function, features, or class of a particular item and the learner must identify the item based on the information given. There can easily be a transfer from a tact/intraverabal mixed operant to a pure intraverbal response for these types of programs.

Pronoun Instruction

Pronouns are one of the most difficult language skills for learners with autism to master, and many of these learners struggle with them for years, even when other types of language are well established. The reason for these acquisition problems could be centered on the complexity of the skill from a perspective and relational standpoint. This is illustrated in the following example.

Tom tells Holly to place her hand on his nose ("Put your hand on my nose"), and then asks her who is touching his nose ("Whose hand is on my nose?"). At first, Holly has to respond to "your" as a pronoun representing the hand that belongs to her. When asked, however, she responds to the same hand by labeling it "my" hand. The appropriate pronoun (surrogate label) changes, depending on whether one is the listener, the speaker, or an observer.

Perhaps because of issues of executive functioning, perspective taking, and relational responding, children with autism need very intensive and explicit instruction in this area. If a learner is going to be successful with conversation, the instructor should continue to work on pronoun combinations until they are as advanced as possible. He or she should also incorporate switching between the perspectives of listener, speaker, and observer.

Sequencing Skills

Sequencing skills play many important roles in subsequent programming. They enable us to recount events that transpire throughout our days, follow instructions, and understand cause and effect in many cases. From a totally functional level, sequencing skills allow a learner to be more accepting of schedules, and knowing the sequence of the day aids in transitions.

Sequencing can involve auditory sequencing (such as completing multiple-step instructions in the order in which they were delivered), visual sequencing (patterning, placing pictures that tell stories in order, and replicating arrays of items after a delay), and motor sequencing (being able to navigate through complex activities).

A natural companion skill to this early sequencing work involves verb tense. This is a good time to start shaping verb tenses, including past, present, future, and past/present progressive tenses. This can be combined with a locations/actions program, in which the learner is given an instruction to go to a specific location and perform a specific action, and then report on his or her activities upon return.

For example, the learner is instructed: "Go to the door and clap." When he or she returns, the instructor asks, "Where did you go?" or "What did you do?" It is important, for the sake of language comprehension, that both actions and locations are varied, as well as the order in which questions are asked. This type of skill also provides more work on sequencing skills, as well as an eventual framework for reporting past events, which is a staple in topical conversation.

Reciprocity

At the early learner level, the instructor can approach basic reciprocity by playing simple turn-taking games, such as rolling a ball or a truck back and forth, placing objects in containers, or picking objects up. At the intermediate level, these efforts are stepped up, and we incorporate previously acquired expressive programming.

For example, the learner and instructor can take turns picking up cards from a pile. The instructor says, "My turn," and picks up a card. Then, he or she directs the learner to do the same. The instructor holds the card so that the learner can see him or her, stating, "I have a (cow)." The learner then follows suit by saying, "I have a (car)." The instructor should make sure that the learner is required to show the object, as a way to develop an appreciation for the perspective of the audience/listener, and also to make sure that the learner holds the item at eye level when showing it.

This program can delve into many areas, such as categories, functions, and features. For example, the instructor can state that a cow is an animal (category) that says "Mooo" (function), and the learner may report that his or her car is a vehicle (category) that goes "vroom" (function). The instructor should make sure that the reciprocal statement corresponds to the statement used as a model – which is another basis for topical conversation.

"I Don't Know"

At this point, when the expressive label or tact repertoire is fairly strong, it is a good idea to introduce the concept of "I don't know." This program is set up like a typical expressive labeling program, where the learner is asked to name what he or she sees. An unknown object is placed in the array, and the learner is prompted to say, "I don't know." This program naturally progresses to one in which the learner is taught to mand for information, such as, "What is that?"

Gender Identification

We start gender identification at this stage of the learner's development. The instructor should make the distinction between boy, girl, man, and woman. When selecting materials for initial instruction in gender identification, the instructor should try to find pictures that are "classically" masculine or feminine, because obvious pictures of male versus female help to avoid confusion.

Ultimately, the goal is for the learner to be able to receptively and expressively identify the gender of all of those that he or she deals with on a regular basis. This includes family members, friends, and teachers. At this point, gender pronouns should be incorporated into the pronoun program as well.

Social Information

By now, the learner should be working on learning (and intraverbally demonstrating) important social information, including his or her name, parent's names, address, and things he or she likes to do. This is important for both safety and conversational reasons.

At first, this information is presented via question-based instruction, but can quickly be moved into presentation via reciprocal communication. The instructor can require simple point-by-point reciprocal exchanges, or can move forward into reciprocal exchanges that more closely resemble topical conversation, such as a Statement-Statement-Question program.

In this program, the instructor issues a statement, such as, "I like to eat pizza." The learner reciprocates with a statement ("I like to eat applesauce."), followed by a question ("Do you like to eat applesauce?"). The instructor should focus, of course, on the ways in which the information is used, not just the type of information used. The more versatile a learner is with general knowledge, the more versatile he or she will be with the information within functional contexts.

Categories

By now, the learner should be able to label items according to their categories, identify a member of a specific category, and be able to engage in some reciprocal communication using category as a critical attribute for response selection. After this has been established, the instructor should work on generative responding, or "freeing up" the operant.

Free operant behaviors are those which, given an initial cue, do not require a separate S^D for each individual response. In the case of addition, a restricted operant is in place if the learner responds with the correct answer each time a flash card is presented containing an addition problem. A free operant is in place if a page with many problems is presented with an initial cue to add. The number of responses is not limited in any way by the behavior of the person providing the instruction.

In the case of categories, this is accomplished by asking the learner to name as many members of a particular category as possible. The cue would be something like this:

"Tell me a bunch of animals – as many as you can." This requires that the learner engage in some generative responding. At first, it may be helpful to use some visual prompts, such as a page that contains pictures of representative members of the category, together visually in one place. Then, the pictures can be faded out, either by actually covering increasing parts of them with a piece of paper, or by allowing the learner to look at the sheet for decreasing periods of time prior to asking him or her to name the items in the category.

Identifying Falsehoods

Going deeper, the instructor may start to look at programs that involve identifying falsehoods. The early learner should be working on some basic Yes/No responding, such as responses to object labels. At this intermediate level, however, the instructor can begin to incorporate FFC into this type of programming to instruct the learner to identify falsehoods. For example, he or she can ask questions, like "A fork is for brushing your teeth, right?" The learner should be able to respond, "No."

This can begin very simply and acquire more complexity as the learner's skill level grows. As soon as possible, the instructor should require full sentence responses with accurate syntax to provide needed practice for developing auditory sequencing skills. An appropriate answer would now be, "No, a fork is not for brushing teeth." Eventually, this programming should be taken even further, so that part of the response requirement is a correction of the false information: "No, a fork is not for brushing teeth. A fork is for eating."

Symbolic Skills

Much of what we talk about in everyday conversation, as well as nearly every form of literary or theatrical entertainment, involves symbolism of some kind. Because individuals with autism tend to have very literal comprehension of language and images, they must be instructed in areas that build on symbolic skills. This will enable them to make more sense of complex social and play interactions with others. It will also give them the ability to be more flexible and versatile within their own play repertoires, and will enhance their abilities to entertain themselves when leisure time is available.

Finally, symbolic skills are at the heart of reading comprehension. Letters are symbolic representations of sounds, and words are symbolic representations of events, objects, or concepts.

It is the authors' opinion that early work on these skills may be happening all along, by modeling play skills with toys. However, modeling alone is typically not an effective way to teach skills to our group of learners. Like any skills, pretend or symbolic skills should be taught explicitly, directly, and with plenty of prompting, as well as plenty of opportunities for reinforcement of desired responses.

With that in mind, the instructor should start a formal "pretend" program. At first, things like animals or favorite toys can be used, and the child asked to pretend that he or she is these things. For example, the instructor can instruct: "Pretend you are an elephant," and then model for the child a way to make a "trunk" and ways to walk and sound like an elephant.

Very early on in this program, it is fine to reinforce any attempts to engage in appropriate responses. However, to avoid robotic and rote responses (which will prove meaningless in any kind of functional context), the instructor should start to shape up responses that require the learner to really "get into it," and take on the characteristics of the thing he or she is pretending to be. This program does not have to limit targets to animals – learners can pretend they are objects (such as helicopters and trains) as well.

Basic pretend skills lay the foundation for symbolic play, which moves into new areas that require use of pretend objects in functional ways. Here, tasks are introduced, such as: "Pretend you are brushing your teeth," or "Pretend it is time for the bears to have breakfast." A dramatic play repertoire is gradually built, while at the same time a platform is shaped up that can be used to practice language (within play routines) while the learner is having fun.

Receptive Blocks

One of the early forms of imitation targeted for beginners is block imitation, where a simple block structure is placed in front of the learner, and he or she is given blocks to construct an identical structure. Gradually, more blocks are added to increase the size and complexity of the structure, distracter blocks are introduced, and the model is moved from a three-dimensional structure to a nearly identical two-dimensional picture, to maybe even a photograph.

At the intermediate level, and going hand-in-hand with work on developing symbolic skills, work can begin on the program known as "Receptive Blocks." In this program, the learner is instructed to build particular objects (i.e. a car, a house, a boat, ice cream, etc.) and then shown a model of how these things can be represented by blocks. Many of these targets are taught through a shaping process. The instructor will know if he or she is effective with instruction and getting closer to the desired outcome of this program if the learner can be asked to build something for which the structure of the blocks has not been shown.

An illustration of this can be found in the experience of one of the authors, who worked with a young learner in this program. Typically, we come to instruction with a pretty sizable collection of items for which we have figured out and taught block representations. This particular boy was taught approximately six of them, including a house, a train, and a bulldozer. While we were preparing to probe a design that wasn't taught (an airplane, for example), the child said, "Look! Ice cream!" He was pointing to a design he conceptualized and constructed using a narrow triangular block for the cone and a semi-circle block for the scoop of ice cream. At this moment, it was apparent that he had made the leap from imitative and receptive block construction to truly symbolic block construction.

Section I – Programs For the Advanced Learner

To this point, the authors have merely scratched the surface of potential programs for beginning and intermediate learners. Once a learner has gotten to the point where the instructor is considering more advanced programming, there are simply far too many directions in which to go to describe in this (or any) manual.

This becomes even more pronounced as the complexity level of target skills increases. At the advanced level, almost every skill calls on combinations of previously mastered prerequisites. Responses should begin to be more diverse, so that the level of stimulus control that was so necessary during very early programming can be loosened up a bit. Responses at this level can also be much more complex – so the learner should be provided with a little more "room" within his or her response format, and the instructor can be a little less direct with prompting.

Trials can also become less discrete, because questions can be used as prompts. Finally, the learner is coming closer to natural conversational and interactive skills at this stage, so instruction should be provided in ways that resemble having conversations with the learner, as opposed to simply issuing very clear S^D's that evoke very rigid responses.

Moving forward, we will provide examples of skill programs the instructor should consider for a learner at the advanced level.

Problem-Solving Skills

At the intermediate level, skills were taught regarding basic identification and rectification of false information. Those skills can now be applied toward identifying less obvious absurdities. For example:

- Can the learner look at a picture of something that is amiss (a missing part, an impossibility like a duck rowing a boat, or a wrong use of an object, such as a person using a banana as a telephone) and be able to explain what is wrong with the picture?
- Can they elaborate why this is wrong?
- Do they have the generative skills to know how to propose a solution that would make the picture more plausible?

These are all extremely important problem-solving skills – we often encounter situations in life that are not quite right, and we have to identify the problem, its cause, and possible solution(s). Learning how to recognize absurdity also paves the way toward developing a more sophisticated sense of humor in our learners. Numerous gags and jokes are built on the notion of absurdity!

Storytelling

Established sequencing and describing skills can be used as a springboard toward storytelling. An advanced level of sequencing is required for the learner to retell stories that are represented in pictures, and is also helpful when the learner is asked to recount his or her day.

A typical conversational interaction involves relaying one's past experiences to another person in response to a cue that renders it appropriate to do so. The instructor can begin this programming by having the learner retell a story from pictures he or she just placed in order from a sequencing set. Shortly after, instruction moves into telling stories about single pictures depicting events, and then moves on to telling stories about favorite activities.

Eventually, the learner should be given a "story starter," such as, "There was a lion walking in the jungle…" and be expected to generate an original story based on that information. Over time, stories should increase in length and contain specified parts (such as specific plot or setting elements, or a particular number of characters).

Sequencing

At this level, sequencing can move beyond the basics, with the introduction of programs that require the learner to sequence objects by size, time, and other attributes. Sequencing by size involves giving the learner objects to put in order from smallest to largest, or vice versa. This can then move entirely into the intraverbal domain, where objects are listed and the learner is required to verbally place them in the specified order. An example of sequencing by time is as follows: "Put these things in order from what you do first to what you do last: eat dinner, make dinner, eat breakfast." Practically any attribute that lends itself to comparison can be used to set up a sequencing activity.

Exclusion

Knowledge of what a concept is does not necessarily translate to knowledge about what it is *not*. Because of this, the idea of "not" must be taught, and more alert listening skills must be developed on the part of the learner. The instructor should incorporate all previous instruction into this programming, which can be fun and challenging for the learner.

An example of exclusion programming can include an S^D similar to the following: "Tell me all of the foods you can think of that are not hot." To be successful, the learner must be able to keep a few pieces of information in his or her working memory, while calling on conceptual skills to generate an accurate response. The process can be quite complex, and many of our learners lack these skills unless they are directly taught. Exclusion can be taught receptively ("Give me something that isn't…") and intraverbally, and instructional targets should be spread across function, feature, and class.

Perspective Taking

Our success within social interactions depends on our abilities to "read" other people and situations. For this reason, the instructor should begin to teach important skills regarding perspective taking.

How behavior is modulated within conversation is directly related to understanding the other person's perspective. We rephrase statements if it appears that our audience does not understand what we have said. We soften our comments if we see our listener becoming defensive. All of this takes into account, first and foremost, that the listener has his or her own perspective, and formulates thoughts and opinions that are different from our own.

It is important to teach the learner with autism (whose symptoms include depicting a sense of self-centeredness) that others may see things from a different point of view, literally and figuratively. Many believe that these skills cannot be taught through direct instruction, but this is simply not true. At least at a very basic level, a learner with autism can be taught to track the eye movements of another, and to describe what that person sees.

Simple, early programming to develop perspective taking can consist of overemphasizing the instructor's gaze at a particular object in a well-defined array. Large stuffed animals or dolls can also be used as the model by turning the eyes and head of the doll or animal toward an object from an array. This keeps the instructor's eyes free to see if the learner is tracking the eye and head movements of the model.

From here, it is easy to shift to the natural environment, asking the learner to tell the instructor what he or she is looking at. This can move into other areas of more abstract perspective taking, which require that the learner not only see what the instructor sees, but also have the ability to use the information. For example, the learner can be asked if he or she thinks that the instructor can see something, while a visual obstruction is placed between the instructor's line of sight and the object, but not between the learner's line of sight and the object. This leads the learner to develop an appreciation for his or her audience, which can result in the learner being able to adjust and rephrase if messages are not clear.

Pictures can also be used with perspective-taking activities. Many fun interactions can be centered on identifying what certain characters portrayed in a picture might be seeing, hearing, or feeling. This also helps develop inference-making skills, which are invaluable when deriving meaning from written information later on.

Advanced Skills, Academics, and Materials

The advanced learner with autism is also very likely to be working on academic skills. For reading and math, the authors recommend utilizing the Direct Instruction materials available from providers such as SRA Direct Instruction, Saxon Math, and the like. What the instructor should look for is a system based on the principles of direct instruction, which are behaviorally based and scientifically validated through decades of research. These programs generally provide scripted instruction as a way to ensure accurate and efficient stimulus presentation, indication of responses that should be reinforced, and error correction strategies that should be implemented when anything other than correct responding occurs.

In addition, most of these systems rely on a very well designed pedagogy, in which concept development is hastened by the systematic provision of examples vs. non-examples of target concepts. These are accompanied by selection of instructional stimuli that utilize critical attributes to ensure that stimulus control is acquired in the most effective manner.

To be effective in providing direct instruction, it is extremely important that the instructor does not stray from the script provided. Often, teachers feel the need to augment the prescribed instruction with further explanation, more "creative" activities, and different error correction. It is true that many of the lessons, when conducted as scripted, lack certain elements of creativity. However, they have been developed and adjusted over a long period of time to provide instruction that is clear, concise, efficient, and effective.

Introducing instructional components that are not part of the designed package can have detrimental effects on the pace of the program, as well as on the overall effectiveness of the designed instruction. It is true that some children may require additional instructional strategies, but the instructor should be sure to separate these from the direct instruction curriculum.

Visual Supports

Academic skills can also be strengthened by the use of visual supports. These can include concept/attribution maps, story maps, the utilization of "Power Thinking" strategies, and visual schedules that serve as a static cue after instruction has been delivered. Any of these approaches can be researched further by simply entering them into an Internet search engine. They have been associated with effective instruction for many years, and there are far too many of them to describe in this chapter.

The Mand Repertoire

The instructor should develop a more sophisticated and solution-oriented mand repertoire for the advanced learner with autism. At this level, the learner should be asked to respond to vague information with mands for further information. An example of this skill is modeled in typical conversation, where one person says to another, "I am really hungry," and the second person typically responds with a mand for information, such as, "What would you like to eat?" Our learners do not automatically know how to process information such as vague statements and generate requests for information, and must be taught to do so.

Like any skill, this can be shaped through instruction, prompting, and differential reinforcement. The instructor can generate a list of vague statements, such as "I went somewhere yesterday," "I like to play with some toys," or "I have something for you." The learner can then be taught to respond with questions that naturally follow from the statement.

Obviously, it is not possible to generate a list of every possible vague statement that can evoke a question. Therefore, the instructor should continue to work on this program until the learner is able to generate a mand from novel, randomly presented statements. The program is not truly mastered until the learner is able to ask questions given information she or he has never heard before.

Advanced Language Processing

Advanced language activities, such as those found in the book *Teach Me Language* by Lorelei Dake and Sabrina Freeman (1996), are extremely useful when teaching sophisticated verbal behavior to the learner with autism. Challenging activities that require some relational responses include word association programs, where the instructor presents a set of words and the learner has to explain why they go together. In the "contingent words" program, the learner is presented with a word and has to *generate* a word to accompany it, followed by an explanation.

There are many types of programs that target advanced language repertoires, and *Teach Me Language* is a great place to begin. Additionally, vendors such as Linguisystems and Great Ideas for Teaching provide a terrific selection of original materials geared toward strengthening language at all levels of development. There are also many very helpful activity books, such as *Talking in Sentences* by Marilyn Toomey (Toomey, 1997), that are available through vendors who cater to autism specialists and speech/language pathologists.

Because we have begun to discuss specific curricular materials that will help implement programming for learners with autism, it is necessary to say a few words about materials selection. Regardless of the learner's skill level, great care must be given to the properties of the materials selected to ensure that they gain stimulus control for the right reasons. Photo cards for vocabulary development should be as clear and uncluttered as possible, and non-photographic cards should be as realistic as possible.

Small manipulatives are very helpful for many programs, as long as the instructor takes care that the materials do not gain bogus control over desired responses. The materials utilized as examples and non-examples should be the same and different with regard to the critical attributes targeted for discrimination. For example, it is better to use green and red cars that are exactly identical in all other ways than color, as opposed to using a block of one color and a crayon of another color).

When it comes to materials, the authors recommend a number of vendors, including:

- **Linguisystems**, which produces a terrific series called "No Glamour" that lends itself particularly well to behaviorally driven instruction. This is just one part of the company's wide selection of helpful materials.
- **Great Ideas for Teaching**, which offers a wonderful selection of activity books geared toward listening and sequencing skills.
- **Different Roads to Learning**, which is another excellent source for teaching materials, including photographic card sets, software, and instructional management supplies (timers, token systems, etc.).
- **Frank Shaffer**, which produces excellent sequencing card sets.
- **LDA** and **ColorCards**, which produce cards for instruction.
- **Stages Learning**, which produces "Language Builder" cards.
- **Webber**, which produces many sets of the instructional materials available from the above vendors.

In addition, instructors can find small manipulative items in almost any teacher supply catalog. As with any type of product, there will be differences in price and quality – the most important decision to make when selecting materials is whether or not they will allow the instructor to effectively and efficiently meet the needs of the learner. It is always best, too, to have several types of materials on hand when teaching concepts, so that generalization is more easily acquired.

The authors would like to share several other considerations that may be helpful for instructors:

- To get the most out of instructional time, manage and organize curricular materials.
- Keep similar materials organized in plastic containers.
- Keep materials from current programs handy for each student. (In the authors' program, for example, each student has a set of cubbies within his or her work area that houses reinforcers, materials related to current targets, and anything necessary to provide instruction and record data.)
- Prior to instruction, make copies of all reproducible materials ready.
- Laminate reproducible pages for use with dry erase markers to save time and paper. Some products, such as the Workbook Window, perform extremely well for these kinds of tasks.

Before concluding this chapter, the authors would like to reiterate several critical concepts that play key roles in effectiveness with a learner.

We encourage readers to remember that depth (the level to which a learner is fluent and functional with a skill, as well as the degree of generalization within the skill) is far more important than breadth (the number of programs in which the learner has received instruction).

We strongly advise against "cookbook" approaches. One of the reasons that the skill program samples found on the DVD that accompanies this manual are placed in alphabetical as opposed to chronological order is to avoid the notion that all of the possible skills missing from a learner's repertoire must be taught in a very rigid and specific manner.

Rather than looking for an approach that tells the instructor exactly what to teach and in what order, we recommend an approach that "cooks from scratch." In other words, assess, select appropriate skills, teach (with effective approaches to instruction, error correction, prompting, reinforcement, and fluency), reassess, and begin the process anew. Preliminary and ongoing assessment protocols should provide plenty of accurate and valid information to light the way – and by collecting data at every step of the process, the reader will know if he or she is headed in the right direction.

Finally, there are skills that must be taught, and there is certainly a general hierarchy of priorities. This chapter was developed to point out some of the considerations and representative skills that should be targeted at each step of the learner's development.

Recommended Vendors

- Great Ideas for Teaching (www. Greatideasforteaching.com)
- Different Roads to Learning www. Difflearn.com
- Linguisystems www. Linguisystems.com
- Mayer-Johnson
- Frank Schaffer Publications
- Super Duper Publications
- LDA
- ColorCards
- Webber Language Materials
- Stages Learning (Language Builder cards)

In addition to the plethora of currently published manuals and guides that advise on curricular issues for learners with autism, there are approximately 200 sample skill programs to look at and utilize as part of this package. However, there are *thousands* of skills that can be taught to learners. Readers should feel confident enough to generate their own skill programs if an assessment indicates that a skill is missing.

Section J – Final Recommendations

While there are no empirically-validated data describing the level of intensity that a program must adhere to in order to achieve maximum impact, the authors' experience has shown that the children who benefit most are those who receive between 30-40 hours of intensive instruction per week. However, we have also seen cases where, given around-the-clock support in terms of follow though with incidental teaching and behavioral consistency, as little as 12 hours of intensive instruction per week has made a tremendous impact. Keep in mind that "instruction" means any kind of structured interaction that aims to shape specific skills or behaviors. This means that parents can (and should) be responsible for providing much of this interaction.

What we stress is that the quality of the instruction, combined with an "always-on" approach to looking for instructional opportunities in the natural environment, should be the first considerations made when developing an intensive program.

After these considerations have been made, we recommend planning as much intensive instruction into the learner's schedule as is feasible, given familial, financial, and social constraints.

Effective instruction can be carried out in a number of formats, as long as the instruction is sound. Therefore, components of both DTI and NET may be carried out in both 1:1 or small group formats. Keep in mind, however, that 1:1 formats will allow a certain level of instructional control for either the very young or very disruptive learner. As the learner advances, though, small group (and even, eventually, large group) instruction should enter into the picture.

Generally speaking, the earlier the onset of instruction, the better the outcome will be. Naturally, the ways in which instructions are presented may be different for an extremely young child. In the case of a child under two, instruction should resemble play, be very brief, of rather low intensity, and very child-directed.

On a personal note, the authors hope that this manual is useful, and that it provides enough information to begin making well-informed decisions regarding effective instruction for the learner with autism. Given proper instruction, it is far more likely that an individual with autism will encounter more opportunities for independence, will be more able to express his or her wants and needs, and will be able to reach his or her fullest potential.

Be steadfast, though, and realize that nothing worth having comes without an investment. Countless hours and a great deal of talent and energy must be invested if you, the reader, are to realize your greatest potential as a person capable of making lives better. The families of children with autism will likely invest their trust in you to advise them well. Most importantly, the learner with autism will make the greatest investment of all – the time learning new skills, the effort required to become fluent with them, and the trust that you will make this learning process as enjoyable as it can be.

The learner shares every part of your instruction – including triumphs and failures. However, the learner also is the recipient of the greatest dividends. A child with autism who learns to communicate at any level, and who can become a more capable advocate for him or herself than was possible before intervention is the biggest winner of all.

Good luck to you and your learner as you embark on your journey.

References:

Bondy, A.S. (1996). *The Pyramid Approach to Education: An Integrative Approach to Teaching C hildren and Adults With Autism.* Newark, DE: Pyramid Educational Consultants, Inc.

Eshleman, J.W. Instructional Systems. http://members.aol.com/johneshleman/ins// s.html

Freeman, S. & Dake, L. (1996). *Teach Me Language: A Language Manual for Children With Autism, Asperger's Syndrome and Related Developmental Disorders.* Langley, BC: SKF Books.

Koegel LK, Koegel RL, Jarrower JK, Carter CM. Pivotal response intervention I: Overview of approach. *Journal of the Association for the Severely Handicapped,* 1999; 24: 174-85.

Lovaas, O.I. (2003). *Teaching Individuals with Developmental Delays: Basic Intervention Techniques.* Austin, TX: Pro-Ed.

Leaf, R. & McEachin, J. (1999). *A Work in Progress: Behavior Management Strategies and a Curriculum for Intensive Behavioral Treatment of Autism.* New York: DRL Books.

Maurice, C., Green, G., & Luce, S. (1996). *Behavioral Interventions for Young Children With Autism.* Austin, TX: Pro-Ed.

Maurice, C., Green, G., & Foxx, R.M. (2001). *Making a Difference: Behavioral Intervention for Autism.* Austin, TX: Pro-Ed.

Romanczyck, R., Lockshin, S., & Matey, L. (1996). *Individualized Goal Selection Curriculum.* Apalachin, NY: Clinical Behavior Therapy Associates.

Toomey, M. (1997). *Talking in Sentences.* Marblehead, MA: Circuit Publications.

Index

T

U

V

W-Z